Trinity and Transformation

Trinity and Transformation

J. B. Torrance's Vision of Worship, Mission, and Society

edited by
Todd Speidell

WIPF & STOCK · Eugene, Oregon

TRINITY AND TRANSFORMATION
J. B. Torrance's Vision of Worship, Mission, and Society

Copyright © 2016 Todd Speidell. All rights reserved. Except for brief quotations in critical publications or reviews, no part of this book may be reproduced in any manner without prior written permission from the publisher. Write: Permissions, Wipf and Stock Publishers, 199 W. 8th Ave., Suite 3, Eugene, OR 97401.

Wipf & Stock
An Imprint of Wipf and Stock Publishers
199 W. 8th Ave., Suite 3
Eugene, OR 97401

www.wipfandstock.com

paperback isbn: 978-1-4982-8937-5
hardcover isbn: 978-1-4982-8939-9

Manufactured in the U.S.A.

J.B. Torrance on the Dornoch Firth
combining his two favourite activities
– reading theology and fishing!

Contributors

Alan J. Torrance, Ph.D., Professor of Systematic Theology, St Mary's College, University of St Andrews; *torrance@st-andrews.ac.uk*

Jeremy Begbie, Ph.D., Thomas A. Langford Research Professor of Theology, Duke Divinity School, Duke University; *jeremy.begbie@duke.edu*

Murray Rae, Ph.D., Professor of Theology, University of Otago; *murray.rae@otago.ac.nz*

Alasdair Heron, M.B.E., D. Theol, late Emeritus Professor of Theology, University of Erlangen

Michael Jinkins, Ph.D., President and Professor of Theology, Louisville Presbyterian Theological Seminary; *mjinkins@lpts.edu*

Kerry Dearborn, Ph.D., Professor of Theology, Seattle Pacific University and Seattle Pacific Seminary; *kdearborn@spu.edu*

Tim Dearborn, Ph.D., Director, Lloyd John Ogilvie Institute for Preaching, Fuller Theological Seminary; *timdearborn@fuller.edu*

Graham Redding, Ph.D., Master of Knox College, Dunedin, New Zealand; *master@knoxcollege.ac.nz*

R. Scott Rodin, Ph.D., President, Kingdom Life Publishing; *publisher@kingdomlifepublishing.com*

Alexandra Radcliff, Ph.D.; *alexandra.radcliff@stonybrookschool.org*

C. Baxter Kruger, Ph.D., Director of Perichoresis Ministries; *cbkruger@bellsouth.net*

Robert C. Doyle, Ph.D., Visiting Lecturer, Moore Theological College, Sydney and George Whitefield College, Cape Town; *rcdoyle@me.com*

Andrew B. Torrance, Ph.D., Programme Leader for Scientists in Congregations, Scotland, University of St Andrews; *abt3@st-andrews.ac.uk*

Roger Newell, Ph.D., Professor of Religious Studies, George Fox University; *rnewell@georgefox.edu*

Jeffrey Y. McSwain, Ph.D., Founder, Reality Ministries, Inc., Durham, NC; teaching faculty Grace Communion Seminary, Grace Communion International; *jeff.mcswain@gci.org*

Douglas A. Campbell, Ph.D., Professor of New Testament, The Divinity School, Duke University; *dcampbell@div.duke.edu*

Jeannine Michele Graham, Ph.D., Associate Professor of Religious Studies, George Fox University; *jgraham@georgefox.edu*

Gary W. Deddo, Ph.D., President and Professor of Theology, Grace Communion Seminary, Grace Communion International; President, Thomas F. Torrance Theological Fellowship; *gdeddo@tftorrance.org*

Stephen May, Ph.D.; *smaysfiction@hotmail.com*

Jock Stein, Editor, Handsel Press; *jstein@handselpress.org.uk*

Contents

Preface	iii
Part I Tributes	
1. Introduction, *Alan Torrance*	1
2. Eulogy at the Service of Thanksgiving, *Jeremy Begbie*	17
3. Sermon from Romans 8, *Murray Rae*	23
4. An Appreciation, *Alasdair Heron*	25
Part II Essays	
5. A Pedagogy of Grace, *Michael Jinkins*	32
6. Learning from Teaching, *Jeremy Begbie*	43
7. Fifteen Years of Teaching *Worship, Community and the Triune God of Grace*, *Kerry Dearborn*	53
8. From Pragmatism to Participation: the Impact of Trinitarian Faith on Missiology, *Tim Dearborn*	62
9. Prayer and the Priesthood of Christ, *Graham Redding*	68
10. Epistemology, Freedom and the Faithful Steward, *Scott Rodin*	77
11. James B. Torrance and the Doctrine of Sanctification, *Alexandra Radcliff*	85
12. God in the Hands of Angry Sinners, *C. Baxter Kruger*	92
13. Lifting of the Curse: Athanasius on Making Sense of the Divine "Wrath" and "Propitiation" in the Doctrine of Reconciliation, *Robert C. Doyle*	109
14. John Calvin and James Torrance's Evangelical Vision of Repentance, *Andrew Torrance*	134
15. The Stuttgart Declaration of 1945: a Case Study of Guilt, Forgiveness and Foreign Policy, *Roger Newell*	157
16. Sheep or Persons? What Luke 15 Has to Say about Agency and Persons with Intellectual Disabilities, *Jeff McSwain*	*175*

17. Covenant or Contract in the Interpretation of Paul, *Douglas A. Campbell*	193
18. "The One for the Many" Theme in James Torrance's Theology, *Jeannine Michele Graham*	213
19. "Thrown Back on Ourselves": James Torrance's Critique of Pelagianism in Christian Life and Worship, *Stephen May*	233
20. James B. Torrance on The All-Inclusive Humanity Of Jesus Christ, *Gary Deddo*	258

Part III Primary Source Essay

The Unconditional Freeness of Grace, *James B. Torrance*	276

Part IV Poems and Memorabilia

Touching Point *and* The Director's Cut, *Jock Stein*	288
I Know not How to Pray, *James B. Torrance*	290
Post Card From Karl Barth	291
Photographs	292
J.B.'s Teaching Diagram: Trinitarian, Incarnational Model	293

Indexes

People and Subjects	294
Scripture References	303

Editor's Preface

As the essays in the present volume suggest, James B. Torrance's theology spoke to many aspects of Christian life and vocation. JB (as many students affectionately called him, just as they referred to T. F. Torrance as TF), proclaimed a gospel of grace based on the triune God. For our Father makes himself known to us through the gift of his Son and Spirit, giving to us what he demands of us. The ministry, service, and mission of the Church attest to the triune God of grace and his transforming work in the world. The topics in this book reflect the fruitfulness of JB's trinitarian-incarnational theology for a wide range of theological, pastoral, and social concerns, all of which were vital concerns of J. B. Torrance.

The first word of gratitude goes to Jim Tedrick, Managing Editor of Wipf and Stock Publishers, because he approved and welcomed this book of constructive essays built upon the theology of James B. Torrance. Next, we thank the following editorial staff of *Participatio: The Journal of the Thomas F. Torrance Theological Fellowship* for their time in preparing this book for publication: Jeannine Michelle Graham, Asst. Editor, Albert L. Shepherd V, Copy Editor, and Jock Stein, Production Editor. They helped revise and ready our 2014 *Participatio* journal volume to be available now as a book.

Alan Torrance, son of JB, and Andrew Torrance, son of Alan and grandson of JB, deserve our final word of thanks in their roles as invaluable advisers to this book's aim to further J. B. Torrance's theology. We're grateful for Alan's introductory essay on the significance and legacy of JB's theology and for Andrew's essay on evangelical repentance, which was a key theme for JB. We also acknowledge their permission to include JB's essay "The Unconditional Freeness of Grace," which is now available for the first time in a book.

Todd H. Speidell

Part I

Tributes

Chapter 1

Introduction
Alan J. Torrance

My father thought about Christian theology continually – almost obsessively. It could be exhausting! After a lecture tour with him around South Africa during the apartheid years, Alan Lewis commented that my father was so preoccupied with the theological fallacies underpinning apartheid, that he failed to notice signage or follow map directions. Had Alan not taken vicarious responsibility for this they would have become completely lost. Even in the midst of having his documents checked by airport security, he turned to Alan to make a theological point. Phone calls and visits from my father invariably involved sustained discussions of theology and points of biblical interpretation. The only times when my father was able to switch out of theological mode was when he was body-surfing in the ocean or fly-fishing on his beloved Scottish lochs – when his quest for a *Horizontverschmelzung* switched from the biblical authors to the fish.

So what was the key to this all-consuming passion? It was considerably more than intellectual fascination with a system of thought or ideas. Although he was excited by the unparalleled explanatory power of Christian theism, it was no abstract religious commitment that motivated this passion. Rather, he was driven by an all-absorbing commitment to serving the living Jesus Christ and an unwavering conviction that there is and, indeed, could be no more significant Reality than the One who is the risen, ascended Lord over every facet of created reality. The incarnation of the eternal Son *as* (and not merely *in*) the human Jesus constituted the all-transforming Reality in the light of which every area of life (individual, social, and political) required to be conceived, reconceived, and, indeed, "reschematised."

But the incarnate Word was no mere static or formulaic "reference point" because for JB the Christian life meant that we are oriented by a dynamic Reality that is irreducibly *personal* in nature. Although this relationship commands our intellect, it is emphatically not one of mere intellectual acknowledgement. He saw it as constituting an event of communion. For this reason, he was no less passionate in his commitment to the Body of Christ in all its concrete forms. The perception of God's radically inclusive love for humanity found expression in a radically inclusive and, as anyone who knew him will confirm, utterly genuine love for other people – whatever their background, status, ethnicity, abilities or inabilities, mistakes or struggles. Again, what grounded this was neither a liberal inclusivism nor an abstract personalism. As he continually emphasised, to know who Jesus Christ *is* is to see everyone, not least our enemies, as embraced and forgiven *en Christo*! This inclusive orientation toward others explains the oft-made comment that he never ceased to be a pastor at heart. What must be recognised is that his commitment to the church stemmed from his faith in the one who is the cornerstone of its existence.

JB was and remained an evangelical. His passion for theology stemmed not from a passion for its intellectual coherence and unparalleled explanatory power but from his perception of who God is toward us as the person of Jesus Christ – a perception that, as he saw it, was given in and through the transforming and creative presence of the Holy Spirit. Generations of students heard him emphasise the priority of the "who question" over the "how question" in Christian theology. His whole approach to the task of theology, as also his engagement with political issues (be it civil rights, the tragedy of the apartheid regime, the struggles in Northern Ireland, or the problem of deprivation in the two-thirds world), was motivated, informed, and moulded by his concern with the "who question" – *who* God is and, therefore, *whose* we are!

His passion was neither fearful nor driven. He continually reminded me personally that we need not "tremble for the ark." He was refreshingly free of any driven or Pelagian sense of commitment to communicating the gospel. His theological engagement combined passion with a sense of *shalom*. What captivated him was the perception of unconditionally good news – the all-inclusive affirmation of our dignity and humanity that stemmed from the person of Jesus Christ and this, as he would often stress, sets us free, free to trust. "Take no anxious thought for the morrow!" was a favourite quote. The effect of his manner was to generate enthusiasm in his students. Despite facing heavy criticism from liberal and conservative alike and despite frustration with church politics and casual attitudes to the gospel, he never doubted that his calling to serve the church was the highest possible vocation.

JB placed a surprising amount of weight on the relevance of Christian "experience." Although he did not see himself as a "charismatic" (though he was more positively disposed toward it than his elder brother), he attached a great deal of significance to "evangelical experience." There was clearly, for JB, a significant "knowledge by acquaintance" that was mediated by the Holy Spirit and through which one was presented with the reality of God's grace in the person of Jesus Christ. If people had not come to faith, for whatever reason, or were casually "liberal" in their views, he put it down to the fact that they simply had *not yet* been privileged to have had that "evangelical experience." Far from making him judgemental, it generated a compassionate attitude to those who had not yet been addressed and set free in this way. Significantly, there was nobody for whom he did not desire that experience – and, far more importantly, he believed that there was nobody for whom *God* did not desire this transformative event of recognition.

Clearly, this evangelical experience does not take place in a vacuum. For JB, although God's work was not contingent upon the effectiveness of the church, the Spirit actively transformed people by the witness, proclamation and outreach that characterised the life of the Body of Christ. For JB, the agent was categorically not the church *per se as an institution*, but God's triune mission to the world in which the church was given to share. It was imperative, therefore, that the life of the church was true to the inclusive love and forgiveness that characterised the triune mission of God to humanity in which the church participated. For this reason it was also imperative that the church be true to what it is in Christ – one, holy, catholic, and apostolic. For JB, to be an evangelical is to be radically ecumenical. It is both to recognise and to witness to the fact that this oneness is *ontological* – and certainly not simply "federal." The divisions of the covenant community whereby our acceptance of others was conditional (contractual) upon their acceptance of "our" formulations of the truth tragically undermined the witness of the church, in JB's view.

It was in and through an evangelical witness that was united, inclusive, affirmative, and liberating for the hearer that the Spirit transformed those who heard the gospel. This transformation was motivated neither by fear (fear of Hell) nor self-interest (hope of Heaven or earthly benefits), but by perceiving the concrete love of God in Jesus Christ addressed concretely and specifically to every individual hearer as a "thou" – "Thou art the person . . . !" The whole orientation of the hearer both to God and to their neighbour, the world, was reschematised in and through their being presented with the fact that their humanity had been assumed, redeemed objectively *en Christo*, and was now being handed back to them by pure grace as a new/renewed humanity. All that is required is for them to recognise that fact, say "Amen!" to it, and, thereby, be set free to live out of the reality of their objective sanctification in Christ.

Significant Factors in JB's Upbringing and Theological Development

It is neither my task nor intention to provide a biographical account of JB's development. Any attempt to couch a person's theology in the circumstances of his life can all too easily serve to relativise a person's faith by providing an explanation of it with reference to the circumstances of their life. I have already attempted to provide what I believe would be his perception of the impetus, warrant and grounds of his passion for theology. Its source lies, quite simply, in his perception of the inconceivably gracious embrace of humanity by the "triune God of grace" – a perception that was grounded in his deep devotion to the scriptural witness.

Several features of his life shed light on his appreciation of the nature and character of this embrace – as also of its implications. First, he was born in China and lived there with his parents and five siblings until he was six years old. When life became too dangerous for the family, his mother brought her six children home to Scotland sailing down the Yangtze River in extremely dangerous circumstances. My father vividly remembered the family watching bandits playing cards as he hid with his mother and siblings in a small boat in a reed bed having said farewell to his father. He also remembered crouching on the deck of a gunboat they boarded further down the river hearing bullets hit the low sides of the decking. What was to have the greatest impact of all, however, was leaving his father. Such was his father's commitment to the gospel that he stayed behind in China and my father and siblings didn't see him again for seven years. The impact of this on the family was unquantifiable. The degree of commitment they had witnessed in their parents and the cost that the family had had to pay generated a profound sense of how much we should be willing to sacrifice for the gospel. It is important to see the commitments of JB and also TF in that context. Their disillusionment and impatience with casual theological liberalism and with theological approaches driven more by a desire for academic recognition than faithfulness to the gospel require to be seen against that background. Moreover, the extent of their parents' love for their enemies and longing for the conversion of the Chinese they sought to reach testified to their conviction as to how much all these people meant to the Lord. To question the extent or to imply limits to God's love for them was anathema – it could only undermine every facet of their outreach.

Second, the poverty they faced as a family also had an impact. Not only did it serve as a reminder of what discipleship entails, it meant that JB and his siblings had to remain among the top three students in their year in order to have their fees covered. JB excelled at school but even more so at university. He took a four year honours degree in philosophy under two of the greatest Scottish philosophers of the twentieth century – Norman Kemp Smith and John Macmurray. Both considered JB the brightest student they had ever taught. After a spell in the air force, he was no less successful in theology receiving an unprecedented one hundred percent in two different essays from two different professors.

Third, there was his "black day." JB was profoundly involved in evangelical circles and he never ceased to regard himself as an evangelical. He was president of the IVF while studying philosophy in Edinburgh and went on to lead the largest mission ever organised by the Christian Union in Scotland. While in London, he worked alongside Martin Lloyd Jones as his youth pastor. All of this culminated in what he described as possibly the most influential (and distressing) experience of his theological development. He was invited to be a keynote speaker at a Tyndale Fellowship conference in London alongside James Packer and Martin Lloyd Jones, in July 1953.[1] At this event, the subject of limited atonement came up – a topic that had been little discussed in post-war evangelical circles. My father found himself outnumbered on the platform when he offered an emphatic rejection of limited atonement, insisting that the God who became human loved and forgave his enemies just as he told us to love and forgive our enemies – seventy times seven, that is, unconditionally. God was in Christ reconciling the world to himself and those who deny Christ "reject the Lord who bought them."

What distressed him most was the fact that Martin Lloyd Jones supported limited atonement. As he once explained to me, it was this event that led him to devote most of the rest of his career to analysing the elements that had led to the emergence of a doctrine that he, like his missionary father, regarded as a heresy – one that tragically misrepresented the character of God, the integrity of the incarnation and the nature of God's mission to the world in Jesus Christ. It meant that we could no longer tell people that God loved them or that Christ died for them. Indeed, ultimately, on this understanding, no-one could ever be sure, this side of the *eschaton*, that they were loved by God or that Christ died for them.

The extensive notes in JB's substantial, personal library of Scottish and Puritan theology (now to be established in his name in the John Richard Allison Library, Regent College, Vancouver) is testimony to the care with which he read the substantial corpus of Scottish theology and, indeed, Puritan works. Throughout, he was driven by a desire to understand the dynamics and emphases that could generate what he perceived to be such doctrinal confusion – a confusion that had led such a high proportion of the Scottish population to walk away from their reformed heritage.

Fourth, it was not only in Scotland, however, that he witnessed the devastating effects of what he saw to be the misappropriation of Calvin and the nature-grace model. JB's perception of the all-inclusive humanity of Christ, that is, the one in whom people of all races and colours found their humanity assumed, redeemed, and sanctified, meant that he was radically opposed to all forms of racism. To see one's neighbour *en Christo* was to see that person loved and their dignity affirmed. It was a further cause of profound distress to see his fellow

---

1 For details of this conference, see Tom Noble, *Tyndale House and Fellowship: The First Sixty Years* (Leicester: IVP, 2006).

reformed theologians in South Africa either endorsing racism or suggesting the church should not allow its christological affirmations to shape its interpretation of nature, the orders of creation, and the role of the state. In that tragic context, the "nature-grace model" (which he also saw as driving the Calvinist doctrine of limited atonement) served to underpin the endorsement of separate ethnic development by certain Christian leaders. It also served to challenge any attempt to critique a political endorsement of apartheid on theological grounds by appealing to a creation-redemption and related state-church dichotomy. The perception of God's purposes in Christ should not influence political decisions because Christ's work had to do with salvation and not creation and related exclusively, therefore, to the life of the Church. It concerned the spiritual realm and not to the political realm. JB insisted, however, that Jesus Christ is Lord not just of the church. He is Lord and Head of the whole human race. He is, moreover, the one through whom and for whom all things were *created*. It is by looking to him that we perceive God's inclusive purposes for creation, for humanity *per se* and not just for the church. Moreover, to see a person as loved and died for by Jesus Christ is to be committed to recognising and affirming their humanity.

JB vehemently opposed the apartheid regime on theological grounds. He lectured extensively in the universities and seminaries in South Africa arguing that the only valid appropriation of John Calvin's theology in the context would commit the theologian to recognise the Lordship of Christ over every sphere of life – and he was the one in whom there was neither Jew nor Gentile, black nor white, and in whom all people found their dignity affirmed. To recognise the headship of this Christ over all creation could only involve unambiguous opposition to apartheid. Indeed, he argued precisely this with De Klerk during the apartheid years prior to his leading South Africa in its radical change of course. JB's concern was not to try to meddle in politics or tell the South Africans how to run their country. Rather, he saw it as his duty to speak *as a Christian theologian* for whom God's purposes for creation were to be interpreted in the light of Jesus Christ the creative Logos made flesh.

Similar concerns drove his involvement in debates in Northern Ireland. There he found himself addressing two forms of civil religion. As in the case of Afrikaner nationalism, the "troubles" in Northern Ireland were the consequence of two parallel forms of romantic nationalism that led to diametrically opposite conclusions. Both parties fused a political agenda, a romantic and highly selective interpretation of history and religious affiliation. The tragic outworkings of this were, yet again, there for the world to see. His response was to plead for the Catholic and Protestant churches to recognise the sole headship of Christ and to rethink their affiliations from that centre. Again, he challenged the use of the nature-grace model and a state-church dichotomy. To be a Christian of any denomination was to be committed to confessing that "Jesus Christ, as he is attested for us in Holy Scripture, is the one Word of God which we have to hear and which we have to trust and obey in life and in death" (*Barmen Declaration*). To confess the Lordship of Christ was for Catholic and Protestants to seek, together, to cease to allow their loyalties and enmities to be "schematised by the secular order" but to be reconceived and transformed in joint recognition of the headship of Christ *in whom* we are reconciled both to God and to each other.

During this period he established close ties with the Roman Catholic Bishop of Down and Connor, Cahal Daly, who was later to become Primate of all Ireland and then a Cardinal. JB urged Bishop Daly to call for an ecumenical "Belfast Confession" to reiterate the affirmations of the Barmen Declaration formulated in the context of nationalism and civil religion in Germany and the Belhar Confession which emerged in the context of civil religion and romantic nationalism in South Africa. As a result of their relationship and his commitment to working for reconciliation, JB was invited to participate in highly secret conversations (lives would have been lost had news of this been leaked) with Jerry Adams of the IRA and key Protestant leaders.

Fifth, at home in his native Scotland, JB was concerned by the failure of the church to communicate the gospel to its young people. He believed the failure of Calvinism to communicate the love of God and the extent of God's all-inclusive commitment to humanity had profoundly undermined the outreach of the church in Scotland. The God of hyper-Calvinism was an object of fear, not of love. The exclusive fencing of the tables that continued to shape the mind-set of the parishioners in Croick Church in Strathcarron was still evident in the 1970s. Even then only one member of the deeply devout, local community went forward to receive the sacraments in the annual Church of Scotland communion service. The rest of the community were insufficiently confident that they discerned within themselves evidences of election.

Consequently, when he was appointed convenor of the Panel on Doctrine of the Church of Scotland he set out, successfully, to challenge the church's practice of refusing to allow believing children to participate in the Lord's Supper. Again, what motivated him was his inclusive, christocentric vision – that children belonged to Christ by right of creation and redemption and that it was a primary function of the church to witness to children that they did indeed belong. The practice of excluding children from the Lord's Supper until they reached their mid to late teens communicated the opposite message – that they did not belong and could not receive the bread and wine until they met the relevant conditions. The effect was to present the church as an exclusive religious club rather than the family of the one Father, the Body of Christ – of which our children were members by virtue of their baptism. This he challenged fearlessly! His passionate vision of the all-inclusive humanity of Christ and the unconditional nature of God's covenant commitment to humanity led him to confront the contractualism that haunted the life of the church and distorted and undermined its witness.

More fundamental than any of the above, however, was JB's love of Scripture. He read and devoured it – always with a pencil with which he scribbled in the margins. During what would turn out to be my final phone conversation with him the evening before he died (suddenly and unexpectedly), he and my mother were on different phones in different parts of the house. While my mother chatted I became aware that there was an ominous silence at Dad's end. "Dad, are you watching the news?" I asked, in a somewhat censorious tone. "No!" he replied. "So what *are* you doing?" There was a pause and then he confessed, rather sheepishly, "I'm reading my Bible!"

Key Emphases in JB's Theology

Elsewhere, I have provided an extended account of the key emphases integral to his approach.[2] I shall summarise these briefly.

First, for JB, the heart of the faith was the doctrine of the Trinity which he saw as impacting on every facet of the Christian life. The New Testament witnesses to a communion of love that defines the very being of God. To say that "God is love" is not to suggest that God only became loving with the emergence of the contingent order as an object of his love.

---

2   Alan J. Torrance, "The Bible as Testimony to our Belonging: the Theological Vision of James B. Torrance," in *An Introduction to Torrance Theology: Discovering the Incarnate Saviour*, ed. Gerrit Scott Dawson (London: T&T Clark, 2007), 121-134.

God is love because there is mutual loving in his innermost being from all eternity, quite independently of the existence of creation. JB never claimed the term "social trinitarian" for good reasons. To the extent that trinitarian theology affirms the mutual love between the Father and the Son in the Spirit, he was simply seeking to be true to the biblical witness – references to the relationship between the Father and the Son "before the world existed" and "before the foundation of the world" (Jn. 17:5 and 17:24). Such an emphasis should not be construed as an attempt to fit trinitarian theology into some Procrustean "social" bed. Nor is it simply based in John's gospel. The intra-trinitarian relations opened up to humanity through the incarnation of the Son as Jesus Christ underpin the entire witness and message of the New Testament.

Second, to affirm the doctrine of the Trinity is irreducibly bound up with affirming the incarnation. Without the hypostatic union, the Trinity becomes irrelevant and the whole grammar of "abiding" as John would have it, of sharing, as Hebrews' doctrine of the priesthood of Christ has it, and of participation (*koinonein/metechein*) which lies at the heart of Paul would be meaningless. The very suggestion that God should be so radically present to us and identify so radically with us is, of course, foolishness to the philosopher. But the ways of God are not the ways of women and men. For JB, as also for TF, the grammar of grace is to be conceived in terms of the unable-to-be-anticipated reality of the participation by alienated, hostile creatures through the Spirit in the incarnate Son's communion with the Father. To appreciate this we need to appreciate the two-fold movement represented in and through the hypostatic union, namely, that God comes to humanity *as God* (anhypostatic movement) and God comes to humanity *as man* and presents humanity redeemed and sanctified in himself to the Father (the enhypostatic, human-Godward movement). For JB, the incarnation embodies both movements and, without both, the incarnation is lost and the New Testament witness ceases to make sense. The weakness of the history of Western thought has been its emphasis on the former without perceiving the need to hold both together.

Third, this leads to JB's emphasis on the vicarious humanity of Christ – he is the one who has come on behalf of the many, to be our representative, our priest-king. In him the many find their humanity cleansed, renewed, and now presented to the Father. What is presented is not simply some generic humanity and, as he insisted, Pauline participation has nothing to do with Platonic participation.

In Jesus Christ each and every one of us finds our worship, prayers, and intercessions lifted up, sanctified and presented by the one who is the sole Priest and Representative of each of us. The very nature of our ongoing life of worship and, indeed, ethics (worth-ship) is to be conceived, therefore, in terms of this very concrete participation, by the Spirit, in our sole priest, intercessor and *leitourgos*. In worship we are not "turned back upon ourselves" to try and generate what God requires of us. Worship and, indeed, every facet of our response (all that is required of us by the *torah*) is to be conceived as participation, by grace, in Christ's fulfilment of these *dikaiomata*, in his Amen, in his "Yes" to the Father, and in his worship. In the Eucharist and in prayer and, indeed, in every facet of the Christian life the Spirit seeks to lift us up to share in his perfect response and ongoing worship offered on our behalf.

Fourth, in order to grasp this radically inclusive gospel we are required to grasp the theological nature of God's covenant commitment to humanity. JB was, indeed remains, famous (notorious?) for insisting that God's relationship to humanity was to be interpreted in covenantal terms and emphatically *not* in contractual terms. "The God of the Bible is a covenant God and not a contract God!" And this covenant is unconditional and unconditioned by considerations of human worth. For precisely these reasons, however, it is also places us under unconditional obligations – something, of course, which a contract cannot do! Now JB certainly did not deny that there are "ifs" in the Bible – indeed, he had a Bible (what was referred to as his "if Bible") in which there was a carefully researched analysis of every single occurrence of that (massive) little word that has such massive theological significance. For JB, there were descriptive "ifs" and prescriptive "ifs" and both were entirely appropriate in the context of covenant relationship.

This is something that everyone recognises in the Christian understanding of the "covenant of marriage" which is a covenant commitment based on love and which is unconditional – one promises to love "for better or for worse, for richer, for poorer, in sickness and in health . . . ," that is, *unconditionally*. Prescriptive "ifs" would take the form, "If you wish to have a happy, fulfilling marriage, do not beat your wife, do not commit adultery . . ." Descriptive "ifs" articulate the consequences of the way you behave in your marriage. If you are faithful, forgiving, selfless in your relation to your spouse, this is likely to engender mutual trust and *shalom*. If you are unfaithful, if you deceive, if you get your priorities wrong, this will lead to a loss of trust, insecurity, loneliness and an undermining of the *shalom* that God intends married couples to know. Not only is grasping the difference between a covenant and a contract vital for understanding the nature of marriage, if we fail to grasp this, we can only fail to appreciate the force of the obligations within a marriage. A contractual relationship means that obligations are no longer apodictic, they become conditional: if you are unfaithful, then I am free within the conditions of the contract to reciprocate. If the deal is contractual, then either party is effectively free to depart from the contract at any point and accept the contractual consequences. This is no more the Christian understanding of God's (unilateral) covenant with humanity than the Christian understanding of the (bilateral) covenant of marriage. A covenant places us under *unconditional* obligations.

For JB, it misconstrues every facet of biblical theology to suggest that God comes to us and proposes a bilateral contract where we are free to choose one of two or more options on the understanding that each has a different set of rewards. Such a "contract God" is the projection of the crudest models of human interaction displacing the God of Christian worship for a pauper! For JB, disillusionment with such a tawdry "god" has disillusioned and demoralised Christian congregations, undermined any real assurance of God's love and commitment, and, as a result, emptied the churches. Preaching is reduced to exhortations and condemnations pressuring people to meet the conditions of the contractual deal, effectually "turning people back upon themselves" such that they look away from Christ – and in its Calvinist form leading people to search desperately within themselves for "evidences of election," that is, evidences that they are loved and have not been elected from all eternity to be the objects of reprobation and that, therefore, Jesus' satisfaction of the contractual conditions of their being forgiven apply to them and save them from being the objects of God's wrath.

In radical contrast, God comes to us in an act of love that transcends anything that humanity could imagine and makes a unilateral, covenant commitment to us in all our sin and alienation. But grace does not stop there. The eternal Son then fulfils, on our behalf and in our place, the obligations that stem from this unilateral covenant. It is the indicatives of this inconceivable work of grace that sustain the imperatives of law. The latter flow from the former. To reverse that order is, of course, to turn the gospel on its head by making a covenant into a contract. And that, as JB argued, is the universal temptation of the human heart!

Filial not Legal

For JB, the witness of Scripture is thus to a God who created us to be daughters and sons. God's primary purposes for all humanity are filial and not legal. The *torah* spells out the obligations of the God who, in love, has delivered us from the land of Egypt to be his sons and daughters. It is when we discern that God's purposes are from beginning to end "filial" that we are liberated to look away from ourselves (*excurvatus ex se*) in joy and confidence to live in the light of the love in which God addresses each one in Jesus Christ as his loved and forgiven children.

Evangelical versus Legal Repentance

JB's emphasis on the filial goes hand in glove with a further key emphasis. In order to appreciate the nature of God's transformative work in our hearts, it is imperative that we are clear about the distinction between "evangelical" and "legal" *metanoia*. Arguably, the central weakness of the Western *ordo salutis* is its endorsement of the fact that repentance is to be conceived primarily in terms of the imperatives of law (*lex* as opposed to *torah*) and the condemnation implicit in the presentation of law to sinners. For JB, God transforms sinners by presenting them with the gospel – the good news that the Son has taken what is ours in an act of love, healed and transformed it, and now presents us with our humanity cleansed and sanctified as a gift of pure grace. It is in and through the recognition, therefore, of the length and depth and breadth of God's love and the extent of God's forgiveness that the Spirit gives us the eyes to see that we belong to him by right of creation and by right of redemption and in and through this recognition brings about our transformation. For JB, the parable of the "Prodigal Son" and the account of Jesus' encounter with Zacchaeus illustrate the transforming impact of the unconditioned and unconditional affirmation of our dignity by the one whom we recognise as having first loved us.

The substance of this good news is actualised in the vicarious humanity of Christ as this denotes "the one on behalf of the many" and the "many in the one." As we have seen, for JB, Athanasius' dictum that the eternal Son took what is ours and gives us what is his does not refer simply to the work of Christ prior to his death or resurrection. Rather, it refers to his whole life and thus his ongoing ascended life as the sole priest of our confession, as our *leitourgos*. He takes our worship and our intercessions and makes them his so that we might participate, by the Spirit, in *his* ongoing worship and repose in the fact that whereas "we do not know how to pray or worship as we ought" our frail and compromised prayers and worship are taken up by the sole mediator of our prayer and worship and presented to the Father in him. JB's essay for Barth's *Festschrift* was indicative of his perception that Karl Barth ought to have taken fuller account of John Calvin's emphasis on the ongoing priesthood of Christ.

Conclusion

JB did not publish a great deal despite the fact that he read voraciously. He preferred to communicate his theological vision to his students to whom he was devoted by teaching. What he did write, however, exhibits analytic skills that find expression in a rare clarity and lucidity. This has been misconstrued in an age which too easily confuses obfuscation with theological depth. Particularly frustrating is the extent to which his detractors fail to engage his analyses with equal analytic care. It is fashionable, for example, to dismiss (even ridicule) his emphasis on the significance of distinguishing a covenant from a contract when it comes to interpreting God's relationship with humanity. I have yet to come across a scholar who has had the courage to argue against JB that it is not a unilateral covenant but a bilateral contract or that it is not relevant to make a theological distinction between these! This is, in part, a reflection of the re-emergence of "federal theology" and the doctrines of the double decree and limited atonement. (Recently, the advocates of the latter have opted for the more upbeat expression "definite atonement" though it is not entirely clear that "definite non-atonement" would not be more accurate.) It is at this point, however, one recognises a weakness in JB, as also in TF. A strong argument can be made to show that their approach was in harmony with a central (arguably, *the* central) trajectory in Calvin's thought. However, they were too slow to admit that there is also a double predestinarian trajectory in Calvin which they should have acknowledged and critiqued! There are points when Calvin appears to go beyond scriptural warrant in his references to the decisions made in God's secret counsels (Cf. *Institutio* 3:21). At the same time, the vast body of his *Institutio* has a very different theological flavour to that of his more scholastic successors.

Were JB alive today, his philosophical skills would doubtless be deployed in defending the significance of the Trinity and the hypostatic union against contemporary tendencies that threaten them. He would question those who wish to insist on attributing metaphysical simplicity to God in ways that lead not only to modal collapse but also to property collapse of a kind that ultimately leads to agnosticism. He would also question the growing tendency to affirm apophatic approaches to God, *a priori* endorsements of divine ineffability, and, indeed, arguments that there is no *real* relationship between the creature and the Father. However, he would be unlikely to argue against these with reference to *a priori* philosophical assumptions (although he could). He would be more likely to engage in what might be termed "analytic, biblical dogmatics" that seeks to ask whether these teachings really do represent faithful, rigorous engagement with God's self-disclosure in the incarnate Word – the mutual love between the Son and the Father from before all worlds, the fact that the Word became flesh and thus that God speaks, that we have an apodictic duty to proclaim who God is and to affirm that God's being can be articulated. He would ask whether an emphasis on the unreality of the relationship of human creatures to God can make any sense of Jesus' relationship to the Father. Is that to be regarded as "unreal"? JB (and TF) would be likely to see such contemporary tendencies as examples of the cyclical attempt to reintroduce the Arian *chorismos*, the gulf between God and the creation that has been overcome in Immanuel, the presence with us once and for all of the one through whom and for whom all things were created. For both brothers, the incarnate Son is both fully God and fully human. And this union of God and humanity in the person of Jesus Christ is the reality that stands at the heart of human existence and that requires us to interpret every facet of our communion with God in heart and mind and the life not only of the church but of the world from that centre.

In the small town of Roslin, a few miles south of Edinburgh, there are two pieces of granite. The first is located in the garden of the Community of the Transfiguration and was discussed in my father's book. It is a sculpture carved by an artist who was banished by his family and his church when he confessed that he was gay. In the community in Roslyn where he had turned up broken and homeless he discovered a sense of belonging that he had never known in the church circles in which he had grown up. On leaving the community he gifted the community a sculpture that portrayed two men locked in an embrace. The only difference between them was the holes in the palms of one. When asked what the sculpture portrayed, he explained that it was the second Adam embracing the first Adam.

A few hundred yards away, in the grounds of Roslin Chapel, stands another piece of granite, which is JB's headstone. Inscribed on it are words chosen by my mother: "He died as he lived, filled with gratitude for the unconditional love and forgiveness of the triune God of grace."

Every facet of JB's theology sought to articulate the implications of that belonging the ground of which is the communion of the Trinity and the Son's union and identification with humanity in Jesus Christ. To recognise that we belong, despite our alienation and confusion, serves to transform every facet of our understanding and all our allegiances both in relation to God but also in relation to God's world. To know the gospel of grace is to be set free. JB's theology endorsed that and his life reflected it.

Chapter 2

Eulogy Delivered at the Service of Thanksgiving, Greenbank Parish Church, Edinburgh, 28th November 2003

Jeremy Begbie

On a murky morning in the autumn of 1976, I nervously entered a lecture room somewhere in the labyrinth of New College, Edinburgh, not knowing quite what to expect. I'd been persuaded to do a theology course to fill a gap in an arts degree. And the first lecturer was James Torrance. Bespectacled, in a tweed jacket, he was soon pacing the floor, New English Bible at his side, the blackboard awash with diagrams. I confess that much of what he said was lost on me – after all, I'd never really opened a Bible up to that point. But I was completely captivated. By two things. First, he seemed to be having the time of his life (which is more than I could say for a lot of the lecturers I'd encountered up until then). There seemed to be a steady heartbeat of joy. He had about him the aroma of a Feast that I knew I'd never been to, a great Banquet I'd not yet enjoyed. And the second thing that captivated me? The God he talked about seemed to be very hospitable and welcoming – a God of "grace" (he kept calling him), a God who longed for our friendship, a God who had done something momentous to make that friendship possible ("once and for all," he kept saying, puzzlingly).

Towards the end of the lecture, I couldn't help wondering: maybe these two things were connected. Maybe he had this joy because he actually *knew* this hospitable, welcoming God. He certainly seemed to be on pretty good terms with him. In fact he opened the lecture with a prayer. (What an odd thing to do in a University, I thought.)

I could never be the same again. Stepping out of that lecture room was the first step on my journey to a living faith.

And *joyful hospitality* was in so many ways the hallmark of his life. It was Alan, his son, who'd persuaded me to go and hear him. (I came to the Father through the Son, in more ways than one.) And through Alan, invitations to Greenbank Crescent came thick and fast. But even without an invitation, I found a ready welcome there. Whatever the time of day, the door seemed permanently open. James and Mary embodied a kind of hospitality that I had simply never known before, eased along by endless cups of tea and carefully blended hot chocolate, served in front of a blazing gas fire and a rather overheated poodle called Louise. Whether in that warm-hearted house, or when bird-watching with him on the sands of Tyninghame, or strolling with him on his beloved Pentland Hills, he treated you with an utterly disarming generosity. As I struggled for faith, I assailed him with crass and clumsy questions; never once did he make me feel stupid or ignorant (even though I radiated both qualities in great measure). He gave me room to ask anything I wanted – because he had met a hospitable God who had made room for him.

An anecdote from those days says it all. One frosty day at Greenbank, the family were just about to give thanks before an enormous Christmas dinner when a tramp turned up on the doorstep asking if they could spare a sandwich. James immediately welcomed him in, sat him at his place at the table, presented him with his turkey dinner, then discreetly slipped out to the kitchen and cooked himself bacon and eggs. Why? Because he knew a hospitable God, who invites us to feast at his Table.

At that time he was Senior Lecturer in Christian Dogmatics at Edinburgh University. On the day he left, after sixteen years there, a packed Rainy Hall honoured him with tumultuous applause and a standing ovation. I joined him later as a divinity student in Aberdeen, where he was appointed a professor. There was little doubt in our minds that the vibrancy of that place in the late 70s and 80s owed more to him than perhaps anyone else. You couldn't help but notice how students flocked to him from all over the world; how no one dared miss his lectures; how when he was Dean of the Faculty, he shunned all political posturing and secret, behind-the-scenes scheming, because all that mattered to him was the *open* secret of the gospel. Again at the heart of all this was a ministry of hospitality: the unforgettable generosity he and Mary showed in the granite grandeur of Don House, his legendary patience with stressed undergraduates, and with scores of postgraduates – theological travellers who had caught the Torrance magic from his lecture tours all over the USA, Canada and South Africa, and now had to be with the man himself.

To all of us he opened his heart, because he knew a hospitable God whose very nature was to open his heart.

His hospitality was also ecumenical. There was no doubt about his passionate commitment to the Church of Scotland – he was a member of this Church for over 30 years, for a number of years Chair of the Church's Panel on Doctrine, and unswerving in his dedication to the Kirk in countless other ways. But that didn't stop him overseeing official conversations between the C. of S. and the Scottish Roman Catholic Church – in Belfast, he was as welcome in Catholic Seminaries as he was in Presbyterian Manses. Nor did it stop him representing his Church in intensive conversations with the Lutherans, and indeed the Anglicans – my own denomination. (Quite honestly, it feels very strange for me, a died-in-the-wool Anglican, to be giving this address in a setting so saturated with Scottish Presbyterianism. But then again, perhaps it's not quite so strange, when we recall James' passion for Church unity.) And why the ecumenical zeal? Because he believed that as the hospitable God welcomes us through the cross, so we must welcome each other.

Having said all this, there was nothing sentimental about James' hospitality. If he felt that the Good News was being compromised in any way, he would say so, and say so boldly. Who can forget that wide-eyed gaze of horror when he sensed that some vital piece of Christian truth had been mocked or sidelined – when he felt that the richness of trinitarian worship had been turned into a bland unitarianism, for example, or when he felt the political demands of God's grace were ignored? In visits to South Africa, he was fearless in highlighting just why apartheid was such an affront to God, with theologians and politicians alike. Once at a function in Edinburgh, he bumped into Alex Salmond, then leader of the SNP, and bluntly warned him the dangers of certain kinds of (what he called) "romantic nationalism." (He never did tell me Salmond's response.) And, of course, he was tireless in trying to disentangle Calvin from some brands of Calvinism, so concerned was he that the glorious covenant love of God would be turned into a deadening contract, so concerned was he that the Reformed tradition would be wrongly caricatured as legalistic, melancholic and fatalistic. Not everyone shared his views, of course. Sparks could fly. Many times he found himself attacked, often unjustly and often by people with half his erudition. And that would often hurt him deeply. But never once did I see him treat his opponents with anything other than grace, gentleness, forgiveness, patience. Why? Because he believed that's the way the hospitable God had treated him.

There was also nothing intellectually weak about his generosity. Here at Edinburgh, he gained a First in Philosophy, including a Senior Medal in Moral Philosophy, Logic and Metaphysics. Among his teachers was the eminent moral philosopher, Professor John Macmurray, who towards the end of his academic teaching life remarked to a colleague that James had been the most brilliant student he'd ever taught. (One of the last things Macmurray did was dictate a reference for James, when he applied for the chair at Aberdeen – a tribute indeed.) A First in theology from New College followed, and then studies in Marburg, and later in Basel with Karl Barth, and further research in Oxford.

With this kind of training it was hardly surprising that he pioneered critical work in the history of theology, not least Scottish theology, and hardly surprising that he could argue a case with astonishing power. But never once did he use his mind to hurt, or put down, or to show off – only to make God's hospitality more accessible. At Invergowrie, where he was a parish minister for seven years, a church member once found out about his distinguished academic background. She famously remarked: "I never knew our minister was such a clever man . . . When you talk to him, you wouldn't think he had a brain in his head!"

He did of course have a brain, a formidable one, but he was a pastor first and foremost, and a pastor never uses his intelligence to dazzle, but only to turn the spotlight on the God who welcomes us unconditionally, whatever our intelligence. So at Aberdeen, to those who were terrified of entering the frightening mansion of systematic theology, he would, in effect, greet you at the door and delight in taking you into all its rooms, calming your fears. He'd introduce you to all his friends in that spacious residence: McLeod Campbell, Athanasius, Calvin, Duns Scotus, Andrew Murray. And if you didn't understand something, almost instantly he'd make it crystal clear. With so many other teachers, you'd go into a class confused, and you'd come out realising your confusion had been much deeper than you first thought. With James, you'd go in confused, you'd come out inspired. Needless anxieties were dissolved by a memorable story from parish life, a lucid diagram, or a simple phrase you could take away and chew over (simple, but never simplistic). Of course, that cost him a lot of intellectual work behind the scenes. But you didn't know that. As that woman at Invergowrie found out, he didn't want you to know he was clever, he wanted you to know the welcoming, hospitable God whom he knew, the trinitarian God of grace. In short, *here was a man who lived and breathed what he believed.*

As a father, he embodied the unconditional love of the triune God he knew in his heart. As his daughter Marion told me the other day, when he forgave you, he not only forgave, he forgot as well.

As a grandfather to seven boys (no less!), he embodied a kind of relaxed playfulness that comes easily when you know you really are forgiven, and you can "let go."

As a teacher, he gave us a vision of what theology could be – not something to be stored away in some dusty attic of the intellect, but something to be lived out in everything you do and are. Head and heart, mind and will, together. *He lived and breathed what he believed.*

And because of that, he inspired literally thousands. Many, of course, hoped that he would write more. Yes, thankfully, there are many articles. And a few years ago a book appeared, *Worship, Community and the Triune God of Grace*, a book which encapsulates so much of what made James tick. And then there are the Warfield Lectures, still to come in print. Even so, many longed for a larger legacy of writing. Fair enough. But surely his greatest legacy are the people he inspired, and that's a legacy you can never put between the pages of a book, a legacy that will reverberate down the generations long after we've gone. In one place, Paul writes to the Corinthians: "we don't need letters of recommendation . . . *you are* my letters of recommendation." If you want to see James' letters of recommendation, you don't need to go to words on a page. Go and meet the teachers all over the world who found their vocation through his example, many of them in prestigious academic and Church posts – his own son Alan, inspiring scores of students at St Andrews; and so many others, in Cambridge, Seattle, Vancouver, Montreal, South Carolina, Georgia, Texas, Mississippi, California, Cape Town, New Zealand, Australia – and, yes, I could go on. Go and meet the woman I bumped into in Atlanta earlier this week who told me: "James made me believe that I did have a brain and I could teach the gospel, when everyone else told me I didn't stand a chance" – she's now teaching in a major Christian University. Go to the hundreds of ministers who found through him that they did have something to preach after all. And, not least, go to the likes of that man James bumped into on Newport Beach, California (so memorably evoked in his book); the man who'd drifted away from the Church, and whose wife lay terminally ill at home, but who heard through this open-hearted Scottish minister in swimming trunks that God did not condemn him, but that Christ was praying for him in his agony and desolation and could offer an enduring hope. He insisted James came and prayed with her at her bedside, and later wrote to James to say he and his wife had spent their last days abiding in the love of God, and that she was now – in *his* words – "safe in the arms of Jesus." Go and meet the likes of people like that and you will see James' greatest legacy, a legacy beyond price.

And on the day he died, he was still at it – inspiring. Only hours before he passed into glory, he spent an hour with his grandson, Andrew, sharing with him the best news in earth or heaven, news of the Father's welcome, news of the Son's dying and rising, news of the Spirit's empowering, news of divine generous hospitality. What an hour that must have been.

And it was, of course, James' radical, huge-hearted generosity that made his memorable habits all the more endearing. The way in which so often after lunch, his digestive system would overwhelm his ability to stay awake. The frantic grasping at the various pockets of his blue jacket to locate that ever-elusive pair of glasses. His fascination with alarm clocks (multiple alarm clocks), fed by his anxiety about getting to places on time. All wonderfully unself-conscious habits – but then, someone so mastered by the grace of God doesn't really have time to be that self-conscious.

Of course, I know that nothing that I've said this morning is going to remove the ache of loss that so many of us feel. And none will feel it more than Mary, with whom James enjoyed almost fifty years of marriage. James used to insist over and over again that we find out who we really are in relation to others, as we are loved and as we love in return. I wonder if there is any married couple for whom that could be more true.

Also we know that for Alan, Heather and Marion and their families, and for Tom, Grace, Margaret and David, and their families, these will be very poignant days, when gratitude for this extraordinary man is going to be pierced many times by a sense of absence, a sense of a great light having gone out.

But we also know that if James could speak to us now, he would want to assure us

– that the God whom he knew, is not "a God out there somewhere" (as he used to say), but a God who comes to meet us in the human High Priest, Jesus Christ;

– that in him the darkness we now know has already been vanquished and daybreak is assured;

– that the heavy sorrow we carry has already been felt and borne by him, and will one day give way to singing, when the hospitable God will finally welcome us, as he has welcomed James, to his eternal Feast.

Chapter 3

Sermon

Murray Rae

READING: Romans 8: 1-4, 12-17, 31-39

There is a meditation often read at funerals that begins with the line, "Death is nothing at all." That is not true. Death is real. It wrenches from us those whom we love and tears at our hearts, for death means that we will not see or touch or hear them anymore. Death is not nothing. It brings grief and tears and rearranges our lives in ways that are not easy to endure.

In the face of death, therefore, we are not unaffected but stand before it as people in need – in need of God, in need of one who has passed through death and can intercede for us in our loss, in our grief and in our uncertainties about how to go on without the one upon whose love we have relied.

It was one of the great themes of James Torrance's life – that he never grew weary of proclaiming – that intercession is offered for us. There is one who intercedes, who takes our grief, our uncertainties, our inadequate praise, who helps us in our weakness and takes us to the Father's heart. Romans 8 from which we have read this morning testifies to that. "He who did not withhold his own Son, but gave him up for all of us, will he not with him also give us everything else? . . . It is Christ Jesus, who died, yes, who was raised, who is at the right hand of God, who indeed intercedes for us." And earlier: "The Spirit helps us in our weakness for we do not know how to pray as we ought, but that very Spirit intercedes with sighs too deep for words."

There are times in our lives when the inadequacy of our own prayer and the limits of our own resources become starkly apparent. Bereavement can be one of those times. But precisely at such times God in his grace can make us profoundly aware that we are upheld – upheld by the prayers of others, upheld by his church, upheld above all by his Word and Spirit. So when in our sorrow we can only utter the words "my Lord" and hope, that hope is well founded. He who did not withhold his Son, will he not also give us everything else?

Paul concludes his great chapter in Romans with the well known words, "For I am convinced that neither death nor life, nor angels, nor rulers, nor things present nor things to come, nor powers, nor height nor depth, nor anything else in all creation, will be able to separate us from the love of God in Christ Jesus our Lord." Not death! Not even death can separate us from the love of God. For all the apparent finality of death, for all that it leaves us stricken with grief, it is not the last word. There is yet the Word of God: "I am the resurrection and the life. I am the Alpha and the Omega, the beginning and the end. See, I am making all things new." With that promise we may look forward to the day when every tear will be wiped from our eyes, when death will be no more, when mourning and crying and pain will be no more, and we will receive in all its fullness the gift of participation through the Spirit in the Son's communion with the Father.

For I am convinced, says Paul, that death will not separate us from the love of God in Jesus our Lord. In that confidence and in that faith, let us today know not only sorrow, but also thanksgiving and hope. Amen.

Chapter 4

James Torrance: an Appreciation

Alasdair Heron[1]

Some twenty years ago a Divinity student in New College, Edinburgh, was driven close to distraction by the complexities of Christian Dogmatics. Another student brought her to James Torrance. He calmed her fears, answered her questions and showed her how to cope with the demands of the Dogmatics syllabus. That may appear nothing out of the ordinary – but I know what it meant for that student, for she is my wife and still today remembers with gratitude the trouble James Torrance was prepared to take to listen to her difficulties and to help her find a way through them. In our family James counts even today as something close to a saint for this reason alone!

These days are long past. My wife is no longer terrified of Dogmatics, has indeed learned from our daughters to treat the pretensions of theological professors with affectionate disrespect. The said daughters had a head-start not vouchsafed to their mother: they grew up in the home of a theological teacher and learned from infancy not to regard theologians as repositories of all wisdom and knowledge. Here too James played a part in the days when he and I were colleagues in New College in the seventies, not least by his willingness to take time off from serious academic work to entertain them, notably by drawing pictures of rabbits in patched trousers and chewing carrots in order to distract the rising generation from such creative pursuits as dismantling their father's bookcases, tearing up his papers or scribbling with crayons on the walls of his office.

---

1   Alasdair Heron had planned to write an essay for this special tribute volume to James Torrance, his professor, colleague and friend, but he died on May 7th 2014. We thank Jim Tedrick, managing editor of Wipf and Stock Publishers, for permission to reprint Heron's tribute in the James Torrance *Festschrift* (*Christ in our Place: The Humanity of God in Christ for the Reconciliation of the World*, eds. Trevor Hart & Daniel Thimell, Pickwick Publications, 1-8).

Have such personal, even trivial reminiscences any place in an academic *Festschrift?* Not, perhaps, according to the normal pattern of this literary *genre*. That pattern would demand strict concentration on the properly academic – e.g. on the scientific character of James' work, the logic of his theological method, his contributions to the advancement of the logical thinking. Just such a concentration would, however, risk missing the real heart and core of his character and widespread influence. James Torrance is not and never was a cloistered academic, but a pastor, a guide for the perplexed, a man of faith whose goal and interest was above all the nurturing and guiding of others in the way of that same faith. Theological reflection, theological writing and theological teaching was for him firmly anchored in (and related to) the community of faith, a community far wider and broader than the purely academic. Theology as he understands and practices it is both existential and ecclesiastical. It is not merely a matter of dusty books or rarified ideas or brilliant theories; it is a personal quest and responsibility in the service of the church, and as such involves not only the mind but also the heart of the theological teacher. It requires and demands *integrity* of the sort portrayed in the metrical version of Psalm 15:

> The man that walketh uprightly,
> And worketh righteousness,
> And as he thinketh in his heart,
> So doth he truth express.

James Torrance is a highly qualified and experienced academic theologian, but he is more than that. He is an honest man, an honourable man, and a Christian man. These are not merely academic qualities; they are of even greater worth. "A king can mak' a belted knight ... An honest man's abune his might" (Burns). We do not need the warnings of McDiarmid's drunkard regarding the thistle to appreciate beyond all couthy Scots sentimentality, the value of an honest man in a Chair of Theology. That is what King's College in Aberdeen has been privileged to have in these last years – not a time-server, not a self-advertiser, not a crafty manipulator of university or ecclesiastical politics, but an honest, honourable Christian man who cares for the Church and for the students who flocked to him from all over the world, and whose academic work is pursued in order to take up and deal with the issues presenting themselves in that setting as requiring attention.

Where, then, do the roots of James Torrance's theology lie? What has made him such a valued, appreciated and beloved colleague and teacher?

The answer lies first of all in the man himself. He is a man so mastered by the Gospel of Jesus Christ that he lives from the evangelical message of forgiveness and reconciliation. That is his daily bread, the air he breathes, the substance and tenor of his teaching. He has not, so far as I am aware, written any hymns;[2] but had he done so, they would have been similar to George Matheson's or George Herbert's:

> Teach me, my God and King
> In all things thee to see,
> And what I do in anything,
> To do it as for thee.

> O love that wilt not let me go,
> I rest my weary soul in thee;
> I give thee back the life I owe,
> That in thine ocean depths its flow
> May richer, fuller be.

James Torrance has the rare gift of enabling the simplest parishioners, the most perplexed theological students to sense that they are fledglings destined and called to fly in the atmosphere of the eternal grace of God. The warm humanity of his personality is not only a natural gift; it is the radiation of conviction, the conviction of one who knows himself to be constrained by the love of Christ and can therefore do none other than express and convey this witness to others as both claim and liberation.

Had James Torrance done nothing more than impressed this message on successive generations of theological students, he would have made an abiding contribution. But he has done more. He has fostered and encouraged pioneering research in the history of Scottish theology, not least with the aim of uncovering and disposing of the clouds of melancholic fatalism, of resignation and determinism, which even today shadow our Scottish Reformed heritage. A whole series of doctoral dissertations undertaken under his supervision witness to his activity in this field, as do his own published writings, which are very largely concerned with reviewing and correcting aspects of the traditional Scottish Reformed theology and showing the difference between the teaching of Calvin and what later developed as "Calvinism." That he has more than once been publicly attacked by would-be "Calvinists" of a conservative sort is an indication of what sensitive nerves he has struck – though his aim in

---

2   *Editor's Note:* James Torrance did indeed write a hymn, *I know not how to pray*, which is printed on p. 279.

striking them was never to wound but to heal; to allow the power of the Gospel to shatter the fetters of rigorism and legalism which the deeply religious are particularly inclined to fasten on themselves and on others.

The nerve of his teaching is perhaps best caught in a series of antitheses which he has constantly reiterated and impressed on his students through nigh on thirty years: *gospel* rather than *law*; *evangelical* rather than *legal* repentance; the *indicative* of grace as prior to the *imperative* of obedience; the primacy of the question "*Who* is Jesus Christ?" over the question "*What* has Jesus Christ done for us?" The combined impact of these antitheses was accurately grasped by a group of students in New College, Edinburgh, in the mid-seventies in a mildly satirical "Prayer for JBT" which ended: "Through Jesus Christ our Lord, who is in column one as well as column three." The hidden reference for the initiate is to James' well-known diagram – a diagram which he not only laid out on the blackboard in many a class, but was also ever-ready to sketch out afresh ("have you seen my diagram?") on the back of an envelope drawn from his filing-cabinet in the inside breast-pocket of his jacket. The point of this diagram, reduced to its simplest essential terms, is that the primary and all-determining reality with which we have to reckon is God's good favour towards us, signed and sealed in Jesus Christ as the love with which we are loved from before the foundation of the world (column one). The imperative of God Law, God's demands upon us – column two – depends on the primary indicative; and the message of reconciliation – column three – does not introduce Jesus Christ for the *first* time simply as the answer to our failure to fulfill the Law, but returns to him as the Alpha and Omega on whom indicative and imperative alike depend, for in his incarnation, crucifixion and resurrection all the purposes and promises of God are once and for all gathered up and put into effect, "for us and our salvation."

In this emphasis and this shaping of the horizons of rising generations of theological students, James Torrance made no claim to be "original" or to break fresh ground in academic theology. He was concerned far more to bear witness to the abiding foundation of all Christian faith as the promise leading us forward to the Kingdom of God. In this, he belongs firmly in the main-line tradition of Scottish academic theology – a tradition which has by and large concentrated more on the paedagogical responsibility of university teacher than on demanding academic originality from him, much less making original research achievements the primary criterion for university appointments. This tradition can be and has been criticized as failing to encourage in Scotland the kind of untrammeled interest in pure thought which has been the glory of modern German theology. The criticism may not be entirely unjustified, but the warning of H. R. Mackintosh in a famous and much quoted remark more than a half century ago also deserves to be heeded: "Theology is created in Germany, corrupted in America and corrected in Scotland." The remark of the Czech theologian Josef Hromadka also comes to mind: after he had studied in more than one German faculty of theology, it was when he came to study in Aberdeen with the elder Professor David Cairns that he "found the solid ground of the Church under his feet." Theological work needs its outriders and pioneers; it will in any case find numerous misinterpreters and distorters, in America and elsewhere; Scotland's contribution may well still be that of a solid common-sense, of a reorientation towards what really matters. It is no disgrace if Scottish theology is primarily concerned with the *corrective* and *stabilizing* task, with helping students to find the solid ground of the Gospel and the Church under their feet.

To draw this out a little further; there are at least three distinct tasks which present themselves to a teacher of Systematic Theology today. The first is that of *edification,* the straight-forward education of students who need to be informed, challenged and strengthened in their Christian theological commitment. This demands a high degree of personal engagement on the part of their teachers, of contact and exchange between teachers and students. It involves an intensive *pastoral* responsibility of the teacher. Our Scottish tradition of theological education has rightly placed this as the first priority on the agenda of our Divinity Faculties. The Divinity Faculty is first and foremost a "school of faith," not merely a talking-shop for the batting-around of ideas good, bad or indifferent. The tenant of a Chair of Systematic Theology in a Scottish Divinity Faculty has a special opportunity and responsibility to influence the ideas, the self-understanding and the professional goals of his students. This pastoral and paedagogical task has its own special evangelical and missionary importance, not least because of its essentially *personal* nature.

I have been privileged to see at first hand and from various sides how splendidly James Torrance has filled this role over a good quarter of a century, first in Edinburgh, then in Aberdeen. First as a student, later as a colleague in Edinburgh, later still as an external examiner in Aberdeen I could never fail to notice his genuine care for his students and his paedagogical concern that they grasp the fundamentals of the matter. In teaching he is visibly concerned to *communicate* – which is by no means always the case with University teachers who sometimes can seem to be conducting a private dialogue with their material, a dialogue for which the presence of hearers is quite incidental. But then – and there is a direct connection – James Torrance was a preacher before he became a lecturer or professor, and he approaches his teaching with the same seriousness with which he approaches his sermons. It can often enough happen that theological students in the course of their classes suddenly begin to wonder what the material they are studying really has to do with their future vocation as ministers; in James Torrance's classes the question generally does not need to be asked because the connections and implications are apparent. Those who do not recognize them for themselves will have them pointed out anyway!

The second task is that of encouraging *theological research* in the form of independent study, especially at honours and postgraduate level. This research is by its nature generally historical in character, inquiring into the shaping and articulation of theological themes in the more or less recent past on the principle that cutting one's teeth on such history is the appropriate continuation of what has been learned at undergraduate level and the best preparation for theological work in the future. At this level, the teacher is less an *edifier* than a *supervisor*, responsible for guiding the work by advice and criticism whose intention is to bring the student to the point where he can engage independently in his own constructive work, where indeed he can discern for himself what questions arise out of the material and find ways of resolving them. The special character of such research work, properly undertaken, lies in the fact that it cannot simply be programmed in advance; the methods and results have to emerge through genuine first-hand engagement with the material on the part of the student. The supervisor has the role of *critical enabler* who accompanies the work without seeking to dominate it or to determine in advance what conclusions ought to be reached.

A glance at the statistics of the Aberdeen Divinity Faculty over the last decade can show how popular it has become as a centre for postgraduate study, not least for students from overseas. These postgraduate students, so important for the life of a faculty, are not all working in Systematic Theology – but a goodly number of them are. Nor can there be any doubt that James Torrance's own travels and contacts through the years have been responsible for many of those students coming to Aberdeen.

The third task is that of *critical and constructive theological rethinking*. James Torrance's main concern and interest here has been in the history of Scottish theology, especially in the strengths and weaknesses of the tradition of Federal Calvinism. While he has published less than many of us would wish – and hope that he yet will do – his articles in this field deserve to be required reading in any course on the history of Scottish theology, covering as they do such central themes as the teaching of the *Westminster Confession*, the controversy around 1720 concerning *The Marrow of Modern Divinity*, the notion of the Covenant and the work of John McLeod Campbell. Not that this is his only field of interest – he has, if I see aright, published on those topics because of his awareness of the issues arising are of direct contemporary relevance as well, especially in the Scottish context – for his teaching ranges much more widely with special emphasis on the lessons of the development of modern theology since the Enlightenment for fundamental principles of theological method, and on the interface between theology on the one hand and philosophy, ethics and politics on the other.

Yet another aspect of James towards work deserves to be highlighted: he is not merely a theological teacher but also an active and committed Churchman contributing at many levels to the theological work of the Church as well as the University. The Church of Scotland's Panel on Doctrine, the Scottish Church Society and the Church Service Society have all drawn on his time and talents, as have the World Alliance of Reformed Churches and the British Council of Churches. The value and demands of such contributions are often not widely known or recognized; all the more reason to emphasize them here.

But to return to the point where we began: in James Torrance we do not seek to honour simply the professor or the member of Church committees or the far-travelled ambassador for his faculty in Aberdeen. We honour the man who in such fair fashion integrates all these capacities and qualities, activities and achievements. For myself, I wish to pay tribute to a respected teacher to whom I myself owe so much, a colleague with whom it has always been a delight to work, and a friend. It is hard to believe that one so youthful and energetic is now approaching retirement age; I am certainly not alone in hoping that a certain increase of leisure will give him occasion and opportunity to distill the fruits of his experience and studies in future publications.

Part II

Essays

Chapter 5

A Pedagogy of Grace
Michael Jinkins

Professor James B. Torrance entered the classroom like a vision from another age. His black master's gown billowing behind him as he passed through the oaken door, chilled winds off the North Sea whipped in gusts and swirls across the quadrangle of King's College following him right into the drafty ground-floor classroom. By halfway through his lecture, what with his own whirlwind of frenzied scribbling on the ancient rotating chalkboard, Professor Torrance's gown would be dusted with chalk to compete with the snow on the college lawn. The whole classroom scene, played out in the shadow of the centuries' old chapel tower of King's College, was like something out of another time.

What was most impressive, however, and what has stayed with me, was not the picturesque vision our professor presented, but his embodiment of a potentially life-transforming pedagogy, a pedagogy grounded in a rich hermeneutical method and a theology of grace. The course which best exemplified this pedagogy was on the foundations of modern theology. Beginning with leading figures of the European Enlightenment and culminating with (then) contemporary theologians, Professor Torrance surveyed major developments in philosophy and theology from the late eighteenth century onward. The structure of his lectures was particularly crucial to his approach. He presented each major figure in two movements, to borrow a musical metaphor.

In the first movement, Professor Torrance would do his best to crawl into the skin of the theologian or philosopher whose ideas he wanted to present that week. He gave us an opportunity to glimpse reality from the perspective of that figure and to sense that person's sensibilities. Rejecting any temptation to caricature or stereotype figures with whom he might disagree (indeed, at this stage in his pedagogical cycle, we generally did not know how he regarded each thinker), he went deep into the historical context that gave rise to the thinker's ideas, exploring the inspirations, concerns, and motivations behind them and the *Weltanschauung* that shaped them. He sought to understand each figure from the inside out, and he communicated this desire to understand with remarkable sympathy. His aim was to allow us to glimpse the unique genius of that person's insights.

Whether exploring Friedrich Schleiermacher or Wilhelm Dilthey, G. F. W. Hegel, Albert Schweitzer, H. R. Macintosh, or Karl Barth, Professor Torrance embodied a kind of intellectual empathy, a generosity of thought, that inspired many of us — as soon as a morning's lecture had finished — to race across campus to the Queen Mother Library to read these philosophers and theologians for ourselves. Time and again I was reminded by these lectures that there was no philosopher or theologian on our syllabus whose thought was *not* worthy of our serious study, and I often keenly felt a judgment on my own casual, sophomoric criticism and dismissal of intellectual giants. These lectures invited me to enlarge my spirit of generosity as a scholar and caused me ever after to pause before offering a critical rebuttal to the ideas of another. But, while the first movement was more than just a prelude, it was far from the end of the symphony.

The second movement (generally played out in a class two days later) built on the first, but critically. With the dogged-determination and subtle probing of a skilled barrister cross-examining a reluctant or hostile witness, Professor Torrance analyzed every aspect of the thought of the figure before us. He would enter again into the assumptions that had shaped the thinker's ideas, laying bare hidden fallacies. He would trace out the implications of a thinker's logic, demonstrating where the arguments had broken down. He would reflect on the attitude and sentiments that gave rise to the figure's worldview. And in all he did, he accomplished his critical task without exhibiting the least rancor or contempt toward the figure before us. He treated each person with respect, as anyone would wish to be treated. Never did one sense that he had built a mere "straw man" for purely rhetorical or polemical purposes.

Many of those who sat in his classroom have remarked subsequently that James Torrance's greatest legacy to his students was not so much the astonishing scholarship he contributed to a fresh understanding of "the covenant of grace" or his championing of theological figures like John McLeod Campbell, important as such contributions undoubtedly were and indebted as we are to his research and lucid writings. Rather, his greatest legacy to his students was the quality of character he communicated to us in and through his teaching. This has variously been described as "pastoral," "gracious," or simply "humane." And these descriptors ring true. But there was also a methodological sophistication to his intellectual empathy and a theological commitment that gave rise to it.

The Hermeneutics of Empathy

Perhaps the place in James Torrance's literary corpus that provides the best understanding of his pedagogy is his essay "Interpretation and Understanding in Schleiermacher's Theology: Some Critical Questions" published in the *Scottish Journal of Theology* (1968). In this essay, in the process of presenting his arguments, Torrance follows the pedagogical rhythm with which his students became familiar: he moved from something like a sympathetic, even empathetic, identification with a thinker in service to a careful, descriptive explication of his thought to a critical engagement with *and* examination of that thought; all of which occurs within a framework in which grace prevails. In the substance of the argument in this perceptive essay, Torrance shows where he follows and precisely how he departs from Schleiermacher's hermeneutical model and along the way demonstrates those qualities we saw in his pedagogy.

Beginning with an affirmation of Schleiermacher's decisive role in establishing the idea that it is impossible to separate "theological inquiry from the task of hermeneutics," Torrance observes that, for Schleiermacher, "the task of theology" is to scrutinize "the relation between the language in which we articulate our faith, and the 'faith', 'piety', 'feeling', 'self-consciousness' which find outward expression in such language." As he explains memorably: "The genetic task of tracing religious language to its source in feeling, Schleiermacher saw to be fundamental to hermeneutics."[1]

---

1 James B. Torrance, "Interpretation and Understanding in Schleiermacher's

Schleiermacher's hermeneutical approach emerged from his experience as a seasoned translator and interpreter of various literary texts, as Torrance notes:

> From his studies of the Pauline letters and the Platonic dialogues which he translated into German, Schleiermacher saw that to understand a text we must see it as the outward literary creation of a living mind. Therefore the interpreter must penetrate through the outward text, by an act of empathy and imagination, and enter into the mind of the author to understand both the author and his work in their wholeness. Consequently what is needed is a twofold understanding, what Schleiermacher called a grammatical and a psychological or technical understanding.[2]

Friedrich Schleiermacher (and, of course, Wilhelm Dilthey, also, following Schleiermacher) stands in a stream of Continental thinkers who were exploring how one can read and understand the literary products of that "foreign country" we call "the past."[3] Schleiermacher's hermeneutical approach, at least at its empathic and imaginative roots, is similar to that of Giambattista Vico, Johann George Hamann (who was influential for Søren Kierkegaard) and Johann Gottfried Herder[4]

Theology: Some Critical Questions," *Scottish Journal of Theology*, Vol. 21 (Sept. 1968), No. 3, 268.

2   Ibid., 269.

3   E. P. Hartley's famous opening passage from his novel, *The Go-Between* (1953): "The past is a foreign country: they do things differently there."

4   As Sir Isaiah Berlin has chronicled, Giambattista, Johann Georg Hamann, and Johann Gottfried Herder also, with their own distinctive emphases, argue for a hermeneutic of empathy. Berlin says of Vico: "His deepest belief was that what men have made, other men can understand. It may take an immense amount of painful effort to decipher the meaning of conduct or language different from our own. Nevertheless, according to Vico, if anything is meant by the term 'human', there must be enough that is common to all such beings for it to be possible, by sufficient effort of imagination, to grasp what the world must have looked like to creatures, remote in time or space, who practiced such rites, and used such words, and created such works of art as the natural means of self-expression involved in the attempt to understand and interpret their worlds to themselves." (Isaiah Berlin, "Giambattista Vico and Cultural History" in The Crooked Timber of Humanity: Chapters in the History of Ideas, Henry Hardy, editor (London: John Murray, 1990), 60.) Berlin profiles Vico, Hamann and Herder as key representatives of a "counter-Enlightenment." Berlin describes Vico's optimistic epistemology over-against strict relativists like Spengler and Westermarck who believed humanity to be "encapsulated in a box without windows and consequently incapable of understanding other societies and periods" of history (60). For Vico, as Berlin

(the significance of whom is noted in chapter eight of Barth's *Protestant Theology in the Nineteenth Century*[5]), as we see in Torrance's description of Schleiermacher's *interpreter who penetrates through the outward text* "by an act of empathy and imagination." Schleiermacher further described this hermeneutical approach as "an act of divination," as much or more an art than a science. Although the interpreter must "scrutinize the texts," attentive to grammar, literary structure and syntax, equipped with the best scholarly knowledge available to philology and cultural history; and while the interpreter needs "psychological or technical understanding" in order "to discern behind the outward appearance of the text the creative individuality of the author's mind, his ideas, his apperception of reality, the inner structure of his thought," ultimately Schleiermacher's hermeneutics requires a "sympathetic imaginative intuition" to "divine what is in the author's mind," perhaps even "to understand an author better than an author understands himself." Torrance writes, reflecting the Romantic soul of Schleiermacher's perspective, "it may take a genius to interpret a genius."[6]

As with Vico, Hamann, Herder and Dilthey, Schleiermacher's hermeneutic is indeed grounded in the spirit of Romanticism, rejecting a purely mechanistic approach to the text's yielding of meaning. "The greatness of Schleiermacher," writes Torrance, "was that he saw that hermeneutics is not simply a literary technique, but raises the whole question of the nature of understanding and is therefore basically a philosophical or theological discipline."[7]

---

explains in his earlier essay, "The Counter-Enlightenment," "it is possible to reconstruct the life of others societies, even those remote in time and place and utterly primitive, by asking oneself what kind of framework of human ideas, feelings, acts could have generated the poetry, the monuments, the mythology which were their natural expressions." One particularly feels the kinship between Schleiermacher and others laboring in the hermeneutical vineyard of the period in Berlin's description of Herder who believed that we can bridge the hermeneutical gap by engaging our capacity for what he called "Einfühlung (feeling into)," an effort that includes both an empathetic imagination and careful, disciplined scholarship to understand the expressions of another culture. (Isaiah Berlin, "The Counter-Enlightenment," in *Against the Current:* published 1979, 10.)

5   Karl Barth, *Protestant Theology in the Nineteenth Century,* Brian Cozens and John Bowden, tr., Colin E. Gunton, intro. (New Edition, Grand Rapids: Eerdmans Press, 2002), 299-326.

6   Torrance, "Interpretation and Understanding," 270.

7   Ibid., 271.

Torrance's pedagogy reflects at this point a measure of respect for Schleiermacher's hermeneutics (and the strain of romanticism in which Schleiermacher stands), recognizing that everyone has a "susceptibility (*Empfänglichkeit*) for the experience of other people and therefore the possibility of understanding what other people have said."[8] The respect Torrance reflects for the humanity of the figures he attempts to interpret assumes the human capacity to recognize ourselves in others. But it is precisely at this point that we must also be attentive to the second movement in the rhythm of Torrance's pedagogy that takes it beyond even the most enlightened cultural relativism demonstrated in Schleiermacher's hermeneutic.

Hermeneutics and the Question of Truth

Torrance observes that "any attempt to evaluate Schleiermacher's contribution both to hermeneutical study and to theology would demand an examination of his epistemology and his views on the nature of human consciousness in terms of which he interpreted faith."[9] First, Torrance writes, we must see that "our words are the external expression (*Ausdrücke, Lebensäusserungen*) of our innermost feelings and consciousness, and therefore the outward words and actions of an author (or a particular church) give to the interpreter the clue to the mind and purposes of the author (or worshipping community)."[10] Second, we must recognize that "language is the medium of communication between one subject and another and it is only in terms of our own self-understanding ... that we can understand the mind of another."[11] So far, so good, Torrance says, for Schleiermacher.

Torrance appreciates the fact that both Schleiermacher and Dilthey "brought out into the open a fundamental feature of human speech, that in large measure our statements are the overt expression of our inner subjectivity, and that this inner relation between language and speaker is of major importance in the quest of 'meaning.'"[12] We would affirm the fact that theological language is human language, that it is expressive

8 Ibid., 271.
9 Ibid., 271.
10 Ibid., 271-272.
11 Ibid., 272.
12 Ibid., 272.

of the faith of persons, and that the faith expressed is historically and culturally conditioned. We can, therefore, empathetically enter into some degree (perhaps even some large degree) of understanding of the meaning of another's expression of his or her faith, or that of a whole community, though temporally and spatially removed from them, because we recognize a common humanity between them and us, and because we sense in ourselves, through the exercise of imagination and sympathy, the possibility of similar feelings and actions. What a human mind has conceived, we may (through disciplined literary and historical methods, but also through imagination and sympathy) comprehend. "But," Torrance continues, "the question must be asked whether this preoccupation with the subjective reference of language and the accompanying view of faith do not preclude Schleiermacher from an adequate consideration of the 'objective' 'factual' reference of theological statements."[13]

Herein lies the critical distinction between Torrance and Schleiermacher with reference to the hermeneutical task. For Torrance, "Christian doctrines are not only expressions of inner faith. They are either true or false, and they derive their truth or falsity in large measure from those realities which are other than ourselves but to which we are objectively related in faith. Our statements about reality have a denotative semantic meaning as well as a subjective 'interpretic' meaning."[14] Indeed, Schleiermacher himself believes in the objective truth of the core matters with which our faith contends.

Torrance makes it quite clear that he sees Schleiermacher as a Christian theologian concerned with seeking the truth. He recognizes Schleiermacher as a theologian devoted to articulating Christian doctrines in a manner that bears witness to the person and redemptive work of Jesus Christ. For Schleiermacher, God is objectively real and Christianity cannot be understood in abstraction from the historical existence of Jesus of Nazareth whom we believe to be the Christ. But, Torrance asks, when "faith is defined non-cognitively as the feeling of absolute dependence, and carefully distinguished from any kind of subject-object relationship, how is it possible to do adequate justice to the truth content of Christian doctrine?"[15] Perhaps the most critical question Torrance raises in this

---

13 Ibid., 272.
14 Ibid., 272-273.
15 Ibid., 273.

essay is raised in this context: "Is it not the weakness of Schleiermacher, as of the romantic tradition in general, that his preoccupation with the relation of language to human self-consciousness, for epistemological and other reasons, commits him to a position where questions of truth and falsity are subordinated to the question of subjective meaning?"[16]

A hermeneutic that stops at the point of establishing a sense of empathy in understanding the meaning of a text, even a hermeneutic that stops at the point of imaginatively divining the mind of the author (if such a romantic goal really is possible) has misunderstood its task, at least if it is a hermeneutic concerned with theological matters. When it comes to theological realities, Torrance argues, we have a responsibility to look "beyond our formulations of the truth to the Truth which we encounter through them, and which gives our statements the truth or falsity they have."[17]

His critique of Schleiermacher's hermeneutic culminates in the description of the character of theological language which, Torrance believes, "has a threefold reference demanding a corresponding threefold understanding." Theological language, he argues, is concerned ultimately with the life and character of the God revealed in Jesus Christ. It is, in this sense, "objective, factual, denotative reference directing" to God. Theological language is human language, but it is not merely speculative language because theology (a word about God) is reflective of the act of the Word who is God. God's self-revelation opens the door to speak truthfully about who God is. "This must," Torrance writes, "be primary and control everything else if our language is to be in any way transparent of the Truth."[18] Theological language is also, of course, "a formal, coherent, connotative, syntactical reference, as in the systematic formulation of doctrines or the formal structures of worship." Finally, it is certainly "subjective, existential reference where our language expresses the faith of the heart and mind of the Church."[19] According to Torrance, Schleiermacher reflects the fallacy of Romanticism at large, "to subordinate" (or even, we might add, to abrogate) the first understanding in favor of the second or (even more likely) the third. But, this hermeneutical approach un-tethers Schleiermacher's engagement of

---

16   Ibid., 273.
17   Ibid., 275.
18   Ibid., 276.
19   Ibid., 276.

theological texts from a cognitive, objective claim to ontological truth about God as God is in Godself.[20]

The reason Schleiermacher's hermeneutical approach is delimited in this fashion, Torrance argues, relates directly to the epistemological solution he offers to the intellectual world inherited from Immanuel Kant. While he rejected Kant's attempts to "ground belief in God in the practical reason, the moral will," Schleiermacher "sought to identify faith with the affective side of human existence, assigning it to a moment in consciousness more inward and anterior to the deliverances of both the theoretical and practical reason and therefore beyond the subject-object relationship of cognition and conation."[21] But his attempt to ensure the autonomy and integrity of religious faith in this manner – understanding religious faith as the "feeling" or intuition "of absolute dependence (*schlechthiniges or allgemeines Abhängigkeitsgefühl*)" – has the unfortunate effect of meaning that "[o]ur statements about God are statements about the manner in which the feeling of absolute dependence is to be related to Him ... But we cannot speak of God as in any way given as an object of cognition, for this would be to identify faith with the sensibly determined self-consciousness."[22] Our statements of faith, consequently, are statements about ourselves. Torrance discerns in Schleiermacher a desire to preserve "the otherness of God" and to "recognize the absolute difference between the non-givenness of God and the givenness of the sensible world," but his attempt to do this "throws theology back upon the self and the deliverances of the self;" thus Schleiermacher "commits himself to that anthropological determination of the content of doctrine which has brought the charge of subjectivism."[23]

Beyond Empathy to a Pedagogy of Grace

As Torrance leans into his closing interrogation of Schleiermacher – and the questions he raises remain today some of the most perceptive ever posed, not only of Schleiermacher, but of modern (and, now, postmodern) theology as well – Torrance demonstrates the core of his own theological understanding that takes us beyond a hermeneutic of

---

20   Ibid., 277.
21   Ibid., 279.
22   Ibid., 280-281.
23   Ibid., 281.

empathy to a hermeneutic (and, therefore, a pedagogy) of grace. One can almost visualize the barrister leaning across the railings, thundering his questions in the face of a recalcitrant and hostile witness:

"Why identify perception with sense-perception and cognition with subject-object relation appropriate to sense-perception?" he asks Schleiermacher. "Why identify objectivity with sensory objectivity or the objective realities of faith with the objective world of a myth-making consciousness? Where such identifications are made, what alternative has theology but to resort to some programme of demythologizing or regarding doctrines anthropologically as accounts of the religious affections set forth in speech?"[24]

Then, unexpectedly, our interrogator relaxes his features. The barrister mops the sweat from his brow, and perhaps glances at the judge for a moment. He turns to the court and unexpectedly speaks *for* the defendant in the dock. He begins to defend the man he has just peppered with questions. Torrance says, "It is clear, as we have seen, that Schleiermacher's *practical intention* is not to reduce all statements about God to mere statements about the self, but rather to say nothing about God which could not be derived from our religious self-consciousness." In doing this, he is attempting to reinterpret Christian doctrine in his own time, in terms that can be understood by his audience, including also (we are left to assume) "the cultured despisers" of Christian faith. What Schleiermacher has done has had the unfortunate consequence of undermining our best attempts to bear witness to Jesus Christ as the incarnate Son of God the Father. This we are duty-bound to recognize. However, Torrance seems to say, Schleiermacher's failure must be understood in the context of what he attempted to accomplish.[25]

It is at this point that an understanding, a *specifically theological* understanding, seems most evident in Torrance's approach. And it is this understanding which, I believe, provides the impetus to his pedagogy. In order to understand someone, we must love them. This is not simply a statement of devotional sentiment, but an expression of enormous theological consequence. This insight runs through Torrance's covenantal thought, through his appreciation of John McLeod Campbell and forms the core of his critique of the contractual conditionality of Federal Calvinism. One never comprehends that which one holds in contempt,

---

24 Ibid., 281-282.
25 Ibid., 282.

but grace provides the framework in which understanding can flourish. The sympathy and empathy Torrance demonstrates for those with whom he critically engages was not ultimately the product of a hermeneutical method, humanistic or romantic, though it was not unrelated to this. Rather his hermeneutic as a whole seems to argue a theological point, that if we wish to understand others (and this includes even our most ferocious and antagonist interlocutors), we must know them as they are known by God, and God is love. And so it was that every thinker James Torrance examined seemed to his students larger and more worthy of our study at the end of his examination, and the theological work in which we were engaged was enlarged as well by grace.[26]

---

26 Torrance's interest in hermeneutics dovetailed with his teaching also when he served as an external examiner for Anthony C. Thiselton. Thiselton's book, *The Two Horizons: New Testament Hermeneutics and Philosophical Description with special reference to Heidegger, Bultmann, Gadamer and Wittgenstein* (Exeter: The Paternoster Press, 1980), represents an edited version of the Ph.D. thesis which Professor Torrance examined. He also wrote the "foreword" to the published text.

Chapter 6

Learning from Teaching: Theological Education in the Light of James Torrance

Jeremy Begbie

Those of us who were fortunate enough to encounter James Torrance as a teacher will never forget the experience. By the time I sat at his feet in the late 1970s, he had developed a distinctive style of lecturing. His tweed jacket bulging at the pockets under a chalk-brushed academic gown, a battered green copy of the New English Bible at his side, he paced energetically between blackboard and handwritten notes, regularly removing his glasses to look you directly in the eye and press a point home. This was a teacher utterly immersed in his subject, and utterly determined that we were similarly immersed. He was, quite simply, captivating.

Countless teachers (including this writer) owe not only their discovery or re-discovery of the gospel to him, but their belief that teaching this gospel could be an exhilarating and fruitful vocation. There was a kind of irresistible momentum surrounding him, an unstoppable succession of teaching and learning, learning and teaching which continues to this day.

As far as his teaching method was concerned, in many respects he was out of keeping with the dominant trends of his time. Certainly in today's academy he would come across as distinctly outmoded. There was no visual material (apart from some pivotal diagrams), relatively few handouts (again, apart from the diagrams), no explanation of learning goals or outcomes. Most noticeably, the dominant mode was the lecture – a communicative tool under sustained attack today by educational theorists. Copious research is cited to demonstrate both the supposed ineffectiveness of solo lecturing and its many dangers – in particular, the way it encourages a belief that teaching chiefly consists of the "downloading" of data, the communication of information, and the way it can foster a "top-down" authoritarianism, a lack of attention to the integrity of the learner. For James, lectures were always lectures, not open discussions or group exercises – quite literally "chalk and talk." Seminars tended to consist largely of him speaking. And he generally taught on his own. Even in more relaxed one-to-one conversation, though immensely gracious and patient, he could not resist enthusing about what he had just been discovering or reading, always eager to explain, elucidate, persuade. He was a lecturer to his core.

And yet I want to suggest – admittedly against most contemporary fashion – that a refreshing wisdom was being exemplified in James' practice as a teacher, a wisdom which ought to give us pause in the current educational milieu, and from which all aspiring theological teachers today would do well to learn. At the heart of this wisdom lies an extraordinarily basic yet crucial truth: that the *way* in which something is communicated is inseparable from its material content, that the process of teaching is to be determined at every point and in every way by the subject-matter in hand. This does not mean for a moment that insights from modern educational theory are to be shunned *a priori*, but it does mean insisting that whatever is being taught cannot be conveyed in ways that are alien to its nature. "The nature of the object prescribes the mode of knowing" – James used to quote John Macmurray's aphorism frequently, in order to press home his conviction that epistemological access to the gospel was shaped from beginning to end by the content of that gospel. Just the same, surely, applies to pedagogy. The nature of the gospel prescribes the mode of teaching. That James embodied a kind of teaching thoroughly in keeping with the shape and momentum of the gospel is, I think, undeniable. It is by no means the *only* practice that could do so, but it is nonetheless one worthy of sustained attention from those today who are called to teach the "faith once delivered to the saints." I offer reflections on four characteristics of his practice.

The Truth Within?

I recall vividly once asking James about his "philosophy of education." It was a pretentious question from a raw undergraduate, but as always he answered graciously. He pointed me to the first pages of

Søren Kierkegaard's *Philosophical Fragments*, a text which he later went on to teach in a series of remarkable seminars. Here the question from Plato's dialogue *Meno* comes to the fore: "can the Truth be learned?" If we already possess the truth, we cannot properly be said to seek it. If we do not possess it, then we do not know what it is that we seek.[1] The Socratic (and idealist) response to the dilemma is to insist that we already know what we pursue; nothing irreducibly new is or can be learned. All knowledge and thus all learning is finally a form of recollection (*anamnesis*), an unearthing or bringing to light of what is already immanent in our minds. All teaching reduces to a form of midwifery – the teacher brings to birth what lies within. Thus, as Murray Rae summarises it, "the teacher is merely incidental, and bears no essential relationship to the truth learned ... [and] just as the teacher is accidental, so too is the historical occasion in which the truth is recollected."[2] For what matters eternally is the idea or truth gained, not the person who conveyed it nor the event of its delivery.

As we might expect, James led us through Kierkegaard's withering exposure of the theological bankruptcy of this outlook, its drive towards an atemporal, ahistorical christology and its reduction of human learning to self-discovery. But no less important, he also embodied in practice the implications of Kierkegaard's rebuttal. If it belongs to the very character of the gospel that its truth does not reside within us as an endowment waiting to be actualised – it both is, and *needs to be* given, through a divine initiative of unconditioned, unconstrained grace – then those who attempt to teach it can never see themselves as mere midwives, mere elicitors of what is already "there" in the depths of some supposedly primordial human nature. In Kierkegaard's words, "if the learner is to acquire the Truth, the Teacher must bring it to him."[3] To be sure, this is not to be used as a justification for any and every form of lecturing, and certainly not of the type that is, in effect, monological and manipulative – unconcerned with the particularities of the context and condition of the learner. But it is to recognise that theological teaching will have at its heart the dynamic of a disclosure of something intrinsically novel, something whose origin is quite extrinsic

---

1   Søren Kierkegaard, *Philosophical Fragments* (Princeton, N.J.: Princeton University Press, 1969), 11.
2   Murray Rae, *Kierkegaard's Vision of the Incarnation: By Faith Transformed* (Oxford: Clarendon Press, 1997), 7.
3   Kierkegaard, *Philosophical Fragments*, 17.

to the world's possibilities, a *kerygma*, a declaration whose material content is discoverable only by being oriented to an action we did not and could not generate: the self-communication of God in Jesus Christ. It is hardly surprising that many spoke of the boundary between preaching and teaching being blurred in James's classes: that is as it should be.

More than this, and even more disturbing, Kierkegaard continues: "[the teacher] must also give [the learner] the condition necessary for understanding [the Truth]."[4] This will inevitably grate in the contemporary educational climate. The view that God's action in us threatens our dignity, diminishes our freedom, is a myth that dies hard. My colleague at Duke Divinity School, Stanley Hauerwas – another hugely influential teacher – addresses the matter with characteristic punch:

> As a way to challenge such a [liberal] view of freedom, I start my classes by telling my students that I do not teach in a manner that is meant to help them make up their own minds. Instead, I tell them that I do not believe they have minds worth making up until they have been trained by me. I realize such a statement is deeply offensive to students since it exhibits a complete lack of pedagogic sensitivities. Yet I cannot imagine any teacher who is serious who would allow students to make up their own minds.

"Learner-centred education" has become something of a mantra in recent times. There is something enormously important about the sentiment it represents, not least the danger of ignoring the skills and capacities of the learner, and thus indulging in a kind of oppression. However, this proper concern must not be confused with the assumption that a learner is immune to sin, intellectual or otherwise, or that apprenticeship to a teacher – someone who inhabits tradition and is radically re-shaped by it – is unnecessary.

In order to respect the learner, after all, we need to have some conception of what kind of animal this learner actually is, what is in his or her best interests. It is notable that James never did anything to imply that his students were wholly sanctified, or that "grace" was merely to be added to a spiritually intact, pre-existing "nature," or that we already possessed the requisite conceptual equipment to "make up our own minds." For him, the criteria for the recognition of revelation *as such* were assumed to be built into the event of revelation itself. God's self-gift in Jesus Christ is designed to enable the transformation, the *metanoia* that is required

---

4   Kierkegaard, *Philosophical Fragments*, 17.

to learn the gospel. Bluntly put: it took a crucifixion to make theological education possible, and it takes the Spirit to make it actual within us. Theological teaching which attempts to side-step all this can hardly be described as being "sensitive to the learner" – just the opposite. To care for the learner is to care that their humanity flourishes, and if we believe that in the last resort we are learning through the action of the One who alone has made our flourishing possible, then learning by its very nature will be a process whereby we will be re-centred outwards – turned "inside out" by the Spirit to share in the humanity of Christ. We will not be left to ourselves at any stage – intellectually or in any other respect. We will be re-made – not only *once* we *have* learned something, but in order *that* we can learn anything in the first place.

Less is More

It is something of an irony that for many years James was a professor of Systematic Theology but that in several important senses his teaching was anything but systematic. For example, if "systematic" is taken to imply the strict deduction of truth from a logical axiom or principle, then the term is quite inappropriate. He was famously opposed to what he saw as the revived Aristotelianism in some Calvinist schemes of salvation, in which a strict, symmetrical arrangement of light and darkness flows inexorably from a divine and inscrutable decree. He was all too aware of the danger of some Procrustean imposition of pre-existing rational forms on the substance of faith, an appeal to a supposedly neutral, ideologically pure "reason" to which even the gospel is to conform. Or again, if "systematic" is interpreted as connoting an all-embracing comprehensiveness, then we are working with the wrong category. James certainly believed in the limitless application and scope of what he taught – nothing was "out of bounds" if Christ was indeed Head not only of redemption but of the whole creation. His style differed markedly from what some might see as a more English way of doing theology, where the short essay becomes the favoured genre, and truth is, so to speak, "inched towards" rather than conveyed in large, all-embracing sweeps. James could paint in bold colours and with very broad brushstrokes. Nonetheless, there were large areas of theology about which he said surprisingly little – creation and eschatology, for example. He was not in any sense a "totalising" thinker.

On the other hand, for him theology and theological teaching were anything but disordered, haphazard or arbitrary enterprises. Consistency and coherence mattered. It was a consistency and coherence, however, that arose not from an axiom or principle but from the impress of personal reality, together with all that was bound up with that reality: Jesus Christ, God-with-us, God as one of us, the very climax and *cantus firmus* of the Scriptural text. Christ is the one in whom all things find their coherence, the one in whom our humanity has been assumed and is, so to speak, "re-systematised" as we are united to him. I once heard Rowan Williams being asked what he wanted today's ministers-in-training to learn more than anything else. He replied "I want them to sense the pressure out of which Christianity burst." That is what James gave us: a sense of the explosive but glorious pressure of the gospel which erupted in the redeeming presence and activity of Jesus Christ. The coherence of his teaching flowed from the coherence of that pressure.

This gave his teaching an extraordinarily lucid appeal, not the appeal of a closed aesthetic system but the open-ended appeal of the logic of grace, the *ratio* of a divine hospitable movement enacted in a Person. Hence the gravitation in most of James' research and writing towards soteriological themes, energised by a christological core: the priority of grace over law, the distinction between an unconditional covenant and a conditional contract, the continuing vicarious humanity of Jesus, the giftedness of trinitarian worship. Hence also his distrust of the discrete stages of the traditional *ordo salutis*: "first justification, then regeneration, then sanctification" …etc. For him, as for Calvin, these were all inseparable and overlapping aspects of union with Christ, something which the tidiness of popular quasi-narratives of salvation could easily obscure.

This fairly radical focus released him (and his students) from that all too common anxiety of trying to cover everything. There were many questions and issues he simply never got around to addressing, and it never seemed to cost him any sleep – something I found immensely liberating as a student. Bound up with this was a refreshing freedom from the tyranny of trying to read everything. Though he possessed a large library, the books that accompanied him in teaching were relatively few, and although he kept up with major journals, he never gave the impression of frantically trying to keep track of every development, every article, every conference, every new fashion. There was a sort of quiet confidence that if the news of the triune God of grace was caught and celebrated in depth, the things that mattered would unfold in their own way and in their own time.

Inspiration

At the risk of gross generalisation, one of the differences I have discovered between academic teaching in North America and Britain is that the ability to carry instant appeal and magnetise an audience will tend to be regarded positively in the United States, to a far greater extent than on the other side of the Atlantic. In the UK those who generate large attendance at lectures or catch the attention of the media will tend to be distrusted, quickly suspected as being superficial, lacking the kind of weight that speaks of serious scholarship. There is also a significant stream of educational theory that is deeply wary of the individual teacher: indeed, I have often heard it argued that there is something intrinsically more Christian about team-teaching, for it models a collaborative dynamic, prevents the self-aggrandisement of the charismatic "star," encourages the virtues of modesty, co-operation and mutual support.

The concerns here doubtless need to be heard. The pernicious effects of being immersed in an ever-widening celebrity culture have been well rehearsed by many, not least in the Church. Christian educationalists rightly warn of personality cults, blinkered perspectives, inexperienced learners being manipulated by devious rhetorical moves. However, speaking to students over the years about their theological education has made me wonder if there is not something important to be learned from those places that readily encourage the distinctiveness of particular teachers and their gifts. I have often been told, for example, about the importance of a teacher being given "space" to expound and develop a partcular perspective, even if it might provoke vigorous disagreement.

In this light, I would suggest there is a place for rehabilitating the category of *inspiration* if we are to think about the role of the theological teacher today. It is almost impossible to think of James without using the language of "inspired" or "inspiring." I have no wish to recommend a recovery of what James used to call "rugged individualism" – something he rightly attacked frequently. But perhaps we need to recover a truth well grounded in the New Testament: that there will always be some who are particularly gifted to lead others in ways that we would naturally call "inspiring," and, moreover, that such a gift needs to be recognised, and given room to flourish.

This could well be developed in relation to a rich, trinitarian pneumatology, a doctrine of the divine Inspirer, the Holy Spirit. I can only sketch some of what this might involve. When we speak of a theological teacher as "inspired" or "inspiring," what is it we are trying to say, and what *ought* we be trying to say, theologically?

First, and perhaps most obviously, we are speaking of a momentum of *attraction*. It belongs to the Spirit's particular ministry to stimulate and generate in us a curiosity, a desire to learn, a keenness to "go with the flow" of the teacher. This attraction should not, of course, terminate on the teacher – this is just the danger of personality cults – but through the pull of the Spirit move us on to that endlessly attracting and attractive giving and receiving of Father and Son, opened out to us in the humanity of Christ. (There is much talk of "desire" in theology today, especially in relation to the Spirit; perhaps rather more needs to be said about the Spirit's appealing, attracting power, the other side of human desire, so to speak.)

In addition, second, we are probably speaking of a strong sense of the *wanting to be where the teacher is*. In the presence of those teachers we call inspiring, we are likely to want to inhabit their world, get caught up in what they are caught up in, excited by whatever is exciting them, even if we cannot grasp or understand it at the time. Jesus prays: "Father, *I want those you have given me to be with me where I am*, and to see my glory, the glory you have given me because you loved me before the creation of the world. (John 17:24). Christ himself is the "place" where, as Calvin expressed it, our salvation is "comprehended," contained; and he is the one who inhabits the trinitarian "space" into which we are invited. When we are inspired by a theological teacher, we are being "placed" by the Spirit to be where Jesus *is*: to be with the risen, human Son in the presence of his Father.

Third, in the presence of an inspiring teacher, there will be a sense of the *inexhaustibility* of the subject-matter in hand. The learner is left with a sense that there is always more to learn, more to discover, more to indwell, and – just as important – with a sense that this "more" is not paralyzing (like the sight of an impossible mountain to climb) but endlessly enriching and life-giving. This picks up on our earlier discussion of systems. I have learned much from teachers who have given me clear-headed schemes which, for example, enumerate all the biblical "data" on a particular topic, but I have gained rather more from those, like James, who make it very clear that any truth known now is but a minute fraction of the whole, a mere foretaste of what is to come, and that even in the eschaton there will always be "more than we can ask or imagine." Again, pneumatology emerges as crucial here: for it is the Spirit whose generative movement in us engenders a sense of the limitlessness and freedom of God's ways with us, of the gospel's breadth and infinite possibilities, and at the same time assures us that entering and exploring that limitlessness will be, although demanding, always life-enhancing, a taste of the eternal abundance to come.

Fourth, an inspiring teacher will likely leave us with the impression that *nothing can be quite the same again*. The term "life-changing" is no doubt over-used today (like "game-changing") but it is hard not to use some such phrases when thinking of James's teaching ministry. To the extent that a Christian teacher is caught up in the transformative momentum of the Spirit, and that person's capacities are indeed being re-constituted in the image of the Son, then to be "inspired" by such a teacher will mean that in principle there is no part of our lives that will not be changed.

This opens the way for a final reflection.

Language and Life

> Lord, how can man preach thy eternall word?
>   He is a brittle crazie glasse:
> Yet in thy temple thou dost him afford
>   This glorious and transcendent place,
>   To be a window, through thy grace.
> But when thou dost anneal in glasse thy storie,
>   Making thy life to shine within
> The holy Preachers; then the light and glorie
>   More rev'rend grows, and more doth win:
>   Which else shows watrish, bleak, and thin.
> Doctrine and life, colours and light, in one
>   When they combine and mingle, bring
> A strong regard and awe: but speech alone
>   Doth vanish like a flaring thing,
>   And in the eare, not conscience ring.[5]

Here George Herbert (1593–1633) bears witness to the sheer absurdity of preaching, but also to its wonder. Frail and transient language gains a holy and persuasive power when God's life radiates through the life of

---

5 George Herbert, "The Windows," in *The English Poems of George Herbert*, ed. Helen Wilcox (Cambridge: Cambridge University Press, 2007), 246–47.

the preacher. The old English prayer book turns this into a prayer: "Give grace, O heavenly Father, to all bishops, pastors and curates, that they may both by their life and doctrine set forth thy true and lively Word."

I recall vividly an evening when James was poring over a two-volume thesis of which he was the external examiner. This vast corpus of erudition was written by a young scholar named Anthony Thiselton, and was later to appear in print as *The Two Horizons,* one of the most influential books in theological hermeneutics of the last century.[6] Key to that dissertation was the work of the philosopher Ludwig Wittgenstein, whose insistence on the integration of language and "life-setting" was only just beginning to be felt in theological circles (especially in the evangelical arena). Wittgenstein made much of the embeddedness of all language in "forms of life," social patterns of thought and behaviour of which we may be only tacitly aware, but without which language could not function and without which it can never properly be understood: "to imagine a language is to imagine a form of life (*Lebensform*)."[7] The content, logic and force of language are inextricably bound up with conventions, traditions and habits into which we are born and which shape us at every turn.

It has often struck me that one of the things that made James so convincing as a teacher was the conspicuous consistency between what went on in the lecture room and the "forms of life" a visitor would find in his house. The language of dogmatics in the classroom was never (to pick up another Wittgenstinian term) a "private language" but rather one interwoven with a *Lebensform* he had learned through his devoutly Christian upbringing, many years of pastoral ministry, and decades of worship and prayer, and which he exemplified perhaps most obviously and strikingly when at home. Hospitality, patience, attentiveness, generosity, trust – these were the marks both of the covenant of grace he so lucidly expounded in words, and of the domestic life he embodied. "Doctrine and life" did indeed "combine and mingle" as the life of the triune God shone "within the Preacher." And even now, this brings "strong regard and awe."

---

6   Anthony C. Thiselton, *The Two Horizons: New Testament Hermeneutics and Philosophical Description with Special Reference to Heidegger, Bultmann, Gadamer, and Wittgenstein* (Exeter: Paternoster Press, 1980).

7   Ludwig Wittgenstein, *Philosophical Investigations* (Oxford: Blackwell Publishing, 1953), ¶19.

Chapter 7

Fifteen Years of Teaching *Worship, Community and the Triune God Of Grace*

Kerry Dearborn

"Whatever you do, avoid systematic theology," my husband (a pastor) advised. "It's a misguided attempt to try to fit God into dry human constructs and presuppositions," he warned. But Masters level requirements are not easily negotiated, so I registered for a Systematic Theology class with a Scottish theologian named, James Torrance. This decision would alter the entire direction of my life, along with the lives of my husband and our children.

I remember rather vividly my first encounter with James Torrance, the start of a two-week summer intensive course through Fuller Seminary's Seattle extension program. Leaving our three small children every evening for two weeks was rather a challenge, especially since my husband, Tim, was an intensely busy mission pastor at University Presbyterian Church.[1] As I entered into the classroom, James greeted us all in his lilting Scottish accent and warm, caring tone. When he launched into his lecture I can still remember the feeling of being caught up in worship.

This systematic theology did not seem like dry abstractions at all. Rather, throughout the course I felt the invitation to experience the living reality of God in Jesus Christ as revealed in the written word of God, and as present now by the Holy Spirit. Professor Torrance challenged us to let go of our unfounded presuppositions about God, and rather to embrace Christ as the true revelation of God, the one in whom "all the fullness of God was pleased to dwell and through whom God has chosen to reconcile all things" (Col. 1:19).

---

1   See Tim Dearborn, "From Pragmatism to Participation: The Impact of Trinitarian Faith on Missiology," in this volume.

He encouraged us with the wonder of Christ's ongoing mediation, quoting Hebrews 7:25 and reassuring us that, "Jesus ever lives to intercede for us." He drew us into the grace of the triune God, reminding us of Paul's encouragement from Romans 8:26, that when we don't know how to pray, "the Spirit of God intercedes for us with groanings too deep for words." God had not merely come down in Jesus Christ to give us a good example of how to live, which we by our own efforts somehow had to work hard to emulate.

Rather, Professor Torrance described a "double movement of grace."[2] God had come to us in Jesus by the Holy Spirit, had taken on our flesh and blood and been tempted in every way as we are, yet had lived our covenanted human response to God perfectly. Jesus' offering had become our offering, his life our life, his death our death, and his resurrection and new life, our resurrection and new life. The Spirit is with us to draw us into this perfect life of Christ, to share in his intimate relationship with the Father. This was the breathtaking news that God had joined his life to ours in Christ, and had lifted us into God's own triune life to be with God forever.

Through Professor Torrance's teaching I was introduced to the wonder of the gospel that included, but was so much more than, the forgiveness of our sins. This good news centered on God's desire to come and dwell with us and to lift us up into the communion of the triune Persons. This was not God at a distance, but rather God who had loved us from all eternity, and who in Christ had adopted us as sons and daughters into God's own family. This was no escapist and individualist doctrine of how to get to heaven when we die, but rather a message of such radical political and social implications that it had inspired Professor Torrance to go repeatedly to South Africa to challenge theological constructs that supported apartheid and to Northern Ireland to challenge theological rationales for sectarianism.

It was as if scales fell off, and all the fragmented bits of my theology that didn't quite fit together were rearranged and integrated around God's self-revelation in Christ, present now as the one Mediator between God and humans through the Holy Spirit. The realization that I was embraced by the two hands of God, the Son and the Spirit, with Jesus interceding for us from on high (Heb. 7:25), and the Spirit praying for us from within us, was both liberating and deeply consoling.[3]

---

2   James Torrance, *Worship, Community and the Triune God of Grace* (Downers Grove, IL: InterVarsity, 1996), 65.

3   Torrance described this Irenaean view of God in *Worship, Community and the*

I was so inspired by these classes with Professor Torrance that I asked if I could bring my skeptical husband to listen in on the class scheduled for the evening of our anniversary. Professor Torrance graciously agreed, and life was never the same. During an evening when we hosted him for dinner, he invited us both to pray about pursuing Ph.D. studies with him at King's College, Aberdeen. He turned to me and said, "Kerry, we really need women who are centered in Christ and who are solid theologians to teach theology. Please consider this and pray about this, won't you?" I was rather astonished by this invitaion, affirmation and vision. Having had only one woman professor throughout my time in university and graduate school, it never occurred to me that this was something I could pursue, especially in the field of theology. And since my husband and I were both activists and parents of young children, we thought the idea of pursuing PhD's was fascinating but rather unrealistic. Little did we know . . .

By the time I began my own theological teaching career, Professor Torrance had published the heart of his Systematic Theology courses in *Worship, Community and the Triune God of Grace*. I have used this book in almost every introduction to theology class I have taught, as well as in my graduate level, "Doctrine of God" course. The liberating impact on my students has generally been threefold.

1. Scales Falling Off

Like me, for my students the first experience in exposure to Torrance's theology is one of scales falling off, those encrusted layers of false presuppositions about God that have little to do with God's revelation in Christ. In his book, Torrance offers a striking contrast between a human-centered approach to worship, which he calls, "unitarian worship," and a trinitarian approach to worship that is consistent with the biblical revelation of God in Jesus Christ and Christians' profession of faith in the Apostles' and Nicene Creeds.[4] Students connect deeply with his description of a rather common approach to worship in which worship is associated with what happens on Sunday morning, and is largely about what we the worshippers are doing and experiencing.

As one student wrote recently,

Triune God of Grace, 65-67.
4   Ibid., 19-24.

> Unitarian worship is (1) human-centered worship. It focuses on what (2) we can do to worship God – on *our* faith & *our* worship & *our* prayer & *our* offering to God. (3) We become our own priesthood instead of Jesus . . . In unitarian worship a constant fear may be that we are not 'good enough' or that our efforts are not 'good enough.' But in trinitarian worship, it's not about us . . . Worship is no longer me trying to reach across a gap but rather rejoicing in God's presence and provision for me in Christ.

Another student summarized unitarian worship as follows,

> This unitarian style worship takes the focus of worship off of God and puts it onto ourselves instead. It is more concerned with what is visible, such as the pastor and worship leaders than the triune God. In this style of worship God is viewed at a distance and there is no personal or intimate connection with God. The unitarian style is very human-centered compared to trinitarian worship.

Many students become aware that they have for the most part adopted a deistic view of God, a remote God who is hard to reach, and who is uninvolved in their daily lives. They have believed that God has given them a ticket to heaven through the death of Jesus on the cross, but in the meantime, that it is up to them to try to muddle through. They can request God's help from time to time, but mostly the Christian life has been about their efforts and their struggles to measure up.

For many of them the trinity they have known is "the Father, the Son, and the Bible." They believe that the Father's wrath has been appeased by the death of his Son, and Jesus has completed his job of covering over our sin. They tend to respond in one of two ways to these beliefs. Some have felt the weight of trying to live out Jesus' command and to work hard to figure out what would Jesus do (WWJD), *if* he were here. Others have dismissed obedience as legalism, and tried to sooth themselves that Jesus' death paid the price so they are justified by grace through faith whatever they do. Most realize that they have been so steeped in radical individualism and the need for self-reliance that they have been largely closed off to the reality of God's presence with them by the Holy Spirit. One student wrote that without a sense of the intimate relationship we can have with God in Christ through the Holy Spirit, God has been "just the vending machine God, who is distant and up in the sky."

Reading and discussing Torrance's book, students also awaken to the reality that they have reduced "worship" to just a brief period each week during a worship service, and to primarily mean when they are singing. Worship for them was related to going to church, which "can be a drag since it is all about us performing. It can be tiresome to know we have to perform every Sunday."

2. New Vision

Four significant paradigm shifts for students hopefully occur through the baptism of their theology in the Christ-centeredness and trinitarian richness of James Torrance's book and theology. The first is that worship is so much more than what they do when they are singing each week in a church service. "This is a revolutionary concept," wrote one student. "It means that our *entire* lives are for the glory of God. Worship becomes not an event, but a style of life. Even outside of the service, the triune love of God is still active. This has the power to change the world."

Other students comment on the freedom of knowing that worship does not begin when a church service starts nor does it center on them. Rather, "I get the privilege of participating in the ongoing worship of heaven, and the communion of the Trinity by the Spirit in the Son."

Second, understanding the ontological transformation that occurs through the life, death and resurrection of Christ is profoundly eye opening for students. It is a radical departure from the extrinsic christology most have known. The blinding scales of equating the entire gospel with "Jesus came to die for my sins so I can go to heaven when I die" seem to adhere tightly. Thus it takes much prayer, discussion and study before it becomes evident that atonement begins when Jesus is born and joins his life with ours. When they begin to consider that as Torrance taught, reconciliation is the heart of the gospel, there is a sense of wonder that God wants at-one-ment with them. They begin to realize that here is a God they can trust, a God who is for them, rather than against them. Here is a God who desires our cleansing, healing and restoration, rather than a God whose wrath needs to be appeased.

The vicarious nature of Christ, whose birth is "the birthday of the whole human race,"[5] who lives my life, offers his obedience for me, and has completed the covenant for me, is like an entirely new language for many of my students. Students read with awe from Torrance's book:

---

5   St. Basil, *On the Nativity of Christ* (*Patrologia Graeca* 31: 1473A) (attributed though with uncertain authorship).

> The good news is that God comes to us in Jesus to stand in for us and bring to fulfillment his purposes of worship and communion. Jesus comes to be the priest of creation to do for us, men and women, what we failed to do, to offer to the Father the worship and the praise we failed to offer, to glorify God by a life of perfect love and obedience, to be the one true servant of the Lord. In him and through him we are renewed by the Spirit in the image of God and in the worship of God in a life of shared communion. Jesus comes as our brother to be our great high priest, to carry on his loving heart the joy, the sorrows, the prayers, the conflicts of all his creatures, to reconcile all things to God, and to intercede for all nations as our eternal mediator and advocate. He comes to stand in for us in the presence of the Father, when in our failure and bewilderment we do not know how to pray as we ought to, or forget to pray altogether. By his Spirit he helps us in our infirmities.[6]

Third, students resonate deeply with the idea that Christ is present with us by the Spirit to empower us to participate in his life and ministry, particularly caring for and advocating on behalf of those who have been marginalized and disadvantaged. This generation of university students has a heightened awareness of the need for Christian engagement in social justice. Yet, taking the world's problems on their shoulders can feel overwhelming, depressing and daunting. To realize that they are not alone, that it is not their ministry, but God's, and they are invited and empowered by the Holy Spirit to share in it is both exciting and empowering. As one student wrote, "Because I know the triune God of love, I have no reason to fear and I have no reason not to get my hands dirty" participating in the Spirit's work of bringing heaven to earth.

Fourth, students discover their views of others and of creation changing. They grasp how a human-centered approach can turn God, others, and creation into something to be exploited. Torrance alludes to the pragmatism of our culture through a story in which a man overlooking waterfalls and Yosemite Valley's stunning beauty from the Sierra Nevada mountains saw it merely in terms of the water that could be accessed through building a dam there.[7] In class we talk about their Bible Study groups that tend to be focused on needs, how to solve problems and how to get God and others to meet their needs. Students reflect on their language about trying to "fit God into their lives" and

---

6   Torrance, *Worship, Community and the Triune God of Grace*, 14.

7   Ibid., 70.

realize that idea is as absurd as trying to fit the ocean into a recently dug hole in the sand.⁸ They begin to grasp why "Who is God?" is the central theological question, rather than the many "how to" questions that, as Bonhoeffer wrote, can be our way of trying to make ourselves the center and to classify and box God into our mental categories.⁹

When they operationalize this new Christ-centered, "Who is God?" framing of their theology, they realize it doesn't make sense to ask, "What would Jesus do?" As Torrance writes, "The Christ whom we remember is not an absent Christ."¹⁰ He is the resurrected and living one who abides with us and in whom we are invited to abide. Rather they begin to ask, "What is Jesus doing now, through his Spirit, and what would it look like for us to participate in Christ's work by the power of the Holy Spirit?"

Understanding that God in Christ has joined his life with theirs opens their eyes to the reality that God has joined his life in Christ with all people, and with even the created order. A student responded, "I am able to look at all things beautifully created through the Father, Spirit and Son, rather than looking at how everything can best benefit me. I am able to focus on communion with others, knowing that the triune God created us and our world through God's triune love."

3. New Identity

Finally, having their vision cleansed to see God more fully in light of the revelation of Jesus Christ raises some deep questions about their own identity. Initially they ask, "If everything is done for me in Christ, if he fulfilled the covenant for me and on my behalf, what is left then for me to do?" They feel the wonder of God's love and embrace of them, and their connection with others and with creation, all loved and reconciled by God (Col. 1:20). Yet, they wonder what it means for their lives and vocation that they have been "incorporated into Christ."¹¹

---

8   We connect this idea with the legend about Augustine's encounter with the boy on the beach who says his attempts to fit the ocean into his little hole, were like Augustine trying to fit the Trinity into his mind.
9   Dietrich Bonhoeffer, *Christ the Center*, tr. Christian Kaiser Verlag (New York, NY: Harper & Row, 1960), 30.
10 Torrance, *Worship, Community and the Triune God of Grace*, 87.
11 Ibid., 79.

In order to deal with this, students spend a fair amount of time in small groups studying passages like John 15:1-17, and the more than forty Pauline passages that refer to our life "in Christ."[12] We cover the board with brief summaries of these passages, "justified in Christ," "redeemed in Christ," "beloved in Christ," "sanctified in Christ," "new creations in Christ" . . .

As students peruse the board, they gain a sense of awe at the implications of seeing their lives now "hidden in Christ" (Col. 3:3). They realize more deeply that they have been drawn into the loving communion of God and begin to see themselves cleansed, recreated, filled, and empowered to share in God's purposes for the world. Rather than having to strain to create their identity, they see that it is a gift from God in Christ, some thing for which they can be thankful, joyful, and trusting in terms of its daily implications. In the words of one student,

> We may approach worship and living as thankfulness towards God's beautiful perichoretic communion and by doing that I think we will learn to love one another better, because we are able to take off the shackles of performance and instead recognize we all are invited to join in God's loving communion.

Torrance expressed it this way:

> What is the Christian answer? . . . to return to "the forgotten Trinity" – to an understanding of the Holy Spirit, who delivers us from a narcissistic preoccupation with the self to find our true being in loving communion with God and one another – to hear God's call to us, in our day, to participate through the Spirit in Christ's communion with the Father and his mission from the Father to the world – to create in our day a new humanity of persons who find true fulfilment in other-centered communion and service in the kingdom of God.[13]

Conclusion

Like many of my students, my husband and I felt a desire to go deeper in our understanding of these profound truths and their implications for our

---

12 Cf. Smedes' comments that "Being in Christ is not only the fundamental fact of the individual Christian's existence, it is the whole new reality. It is not a side issue of Christian life. It is the new life." Lewis Smedes, *Union with Christ: A Biblical View of New Life in Jesus Christ* (Grand Rapids: Eerdmans, 1983), 59.

13 Torrance, *Worship, Community and the Triune God of Grace*, 41

lives. In less than two years after taking the class with James Torrance, we sold our house, Tim quit his job, and as a family of five, we moved to Banchory, Scotland to begin our work with Professor Torrance at the University of Aberdeen. Neither of us had a clear sense of where it would lead or how it would work. We felt a gracious invitation to leave our more human-centered and pragmatic approach to life and to steep ourselves more fully in the wonder of God's triune communion. We entered into a community rich in prayer and relationships and the gift of having James Torrance as our guide into life lived more fully in communion with the Father, Son and Holy Spirit.

Torrance's insights have been integral to my teaching ever since.

Chapter 8

From Pragmatism to Participation: the Impact of Trinitarian Faith on Missiology

Tim Dearborn

James Torrance must have sighed with incredulity after his first conversation with me as his newly arrived Ph.D. student. How could someone so experienced be so theologically illiterate? I fulfilled the British stereotype of an American evangelical – pragmatic, solution and task oriented, with minimal theological training. I may have had a couple of Masters degrees, and completed the one-semester course in Systematic Theology that was requisite for ordination in the Presbyterian Church (USA), but otherwise I was not only illiterate, I was disdainful of systematic theology.

I justified my disinterest by naïvely disparaging systematic theology as an human effort to box up God in logical categories. How could the microscope of mental analysis guide our understanding of the living reality of the infinite God? I maintained that more important than endless disputes about doctrinal minutiae was our engagement in mission in the world. After all, wasn't the primary instrument for knowing God relational encounter rather than abstract logic? Our relationship with and service of God were surely more important than our doctrines.

However, that conviction had led me, via my wife Kerry, to Professor Torrance's office as a burned-out, human-centered, pastoral mission activist. (See the previous chapter for further account of this journey.) My focus for a decade had been on the attempt to do great things for God (or were they for my own "sanctified" ambitions?), modeled after the life of Christ, with occasional, in moments of desperation, pursuit of guidance from the Spirit. That was the extent of my trinitarian theology. My preaching and sermons had been exhortations to "do more, love more, serve more, obey more" so that we cared for this world that God so loves.

Like many mission fanatics, my ministry was driven by deficits – all the unmet needs in the world and all the unsatisfied quest for significance in my own life – rather than by trusting confidence in the sovereign goodness of God. God's people are often eager to obey, and the congregation I served engaged in many remarkable acts of service in our city and around the world. But this carried the weight of an exhausting human-centered enterprise, rather than the joyful confidence that we've been "rescued from the power of darkness and transferred into the kingdom of the beloved Son", in whom all things are summed up and reconciled (Col. 1:13-19). The fullness of God might well dwell in the beloved Son, but my life was focused on the emptiness and poverty of the world – and my own need to make a difference in it. I was determined that for once in history there would be a church more concerned about the needs of the world around it than the furnishings of the building within. I repeated with enthusiasm Emil Brunner's stirring claim, "The Church exists by mission just as fire exists by burning."[1]

Rather than commenting on my functional idolatry, or raising the question, might I be worshipping God to get God's guidance and provision for the success of *my* mission and the fulfillment of *my* ambitions rather than worshipping God for God's own sake – Professor Torrance simply said, "Why don't you begin by reading the Cappadocian Fathers? Come back and see me after you're done." I was too embarrassed to admit that I'd never even heard of them.

Three months later I returned to his office after feasting on their rich trinitarian faith and the wonder of our life being "in" Christ and not just "like" or "for" him. Theosis, perichoresis, and participation by the Spirit through the Son in the life of the triune God opened up for me transformative, utterly new dimensions of Christian life. The following nine months were a banquet of remedial theological education under Professor Torrance's tutelage, following the same broad guidance as he gave with the early Patristic Fathers. "Read Augustine's *Theological Treatises*." "Read the entire *Summa*." "Read all of the *Institutes*." "Now read all of *Church Dogmatics* and then we can start talking about your dissertation topic." I met with him one on one less than a dozen times over my two years in Aberdeen, but these guided encounters with trinitarian faith restored my soul and reshaped my engagement in mission.[2]

---

1   H. Emil Brunner, *The Word and the World* (London: SCM Press, 1931), 108.

2   For the author's brief analysis of the implications of perichoresis for soteriology and missiology see T. Dearborn, "God, Grace and Salvation," in *Christ in Our Place*, ed. Trevor Hart and Daniel Thimell (Exeter: Paternoster Press, 1989), 265-293.

Following Aberdeen, I taught missiology for two years at a small evangelical seminary in Europe. Students came from throughout the world and were stunned to hear of grace not simply as "God's unmerited favor" but as God's life and action for us. Is it really true that God's love is not simply an act of God's will but is the overflowing of God's triune being – that God exists in a communion of loving relationships? Why have we not heard before that salvation isn't simply our justification by faith but is our participation together in the life of God? And could it be true that mission and evangelism aren't our human-centered efforts to serve God and bring others into the Kingdom, but are our Spirit-empowered participation in God's work to set the world right?

"Is this really the gospel?" they would ask. "Is it ok to believe this? It seems too good to be true." Students who had been taught that one could never preach or say to someone that God loved them, because we couldn't be sure they were part of the elect, were stunned by the assertion that when John 3:16 says "for God so loved the world," John really meant "the world." We needn't engage in an exegetical dance to limit "world" in that verse to merely the elect.[3]

My theological approach to mission shifted from asking "What is God's will, what are the world's needs, and to what response is God calling us?" to "What is God doing in the world and how is God inviting us to participate in it?" I say "theological approach" to mission because my "functional approach" has involved continual succumbing to, confession of, and repentance from the idolatry of my own effort. The Spirit has persistently called me to focus on God, and on God's actions in and for creation rather than on the world's deficits or my ambitions and obedience. Discerning God's powerful and redeeming presence is more important than devising our own solutions to people's problems. As James Torrance would often say, "We must first look long and hard at 'Who Christ is', before we can adequately answer 'What he has done' and 'How he has done it.'"[4] If this is true of our knowledge of God, how much more is it true of our knowledge of what God is doing in the world and of our role in God's mission? Rather than the wearisome effort to address a bottomless pit of unmet needs, with guilt and sacrificial giving driving

---

3   "We deny that all mankind are the objects of that love of God." John Owen, *The Death of Death in the Death of Christ*, reprint of original edition, 1647 (London, Banner of Truth: 1958), p. 115.

4   James Torrance, "The Vicarious Humanity of Christ," in *The Incarnation*, ed. T. F. Torrance (Edinburgh: The Handsel Press, 1981), 144.

our response – our involvement in mission is more like a treasure hunt to discern signs of God's presence and kingdom in our midst, and then live out our Spirit-empowered response in holiness, grace and gratitude.

Admittedly, I became so enchanted by the truth of perichoresis that I probably overused it, applying it to everything. Making tea became a perichoretic act of mutual indwelling and participation. Over the decades since then, I've frequently succumbed to the human-centered idolatry of my own effort, sanctifying my own ambitious need for impact and success by sprinkling a little perichoretic holy water over "my" ministry. At those moments I recall James' question, "Have you seen my diagrams?" and been reminded that our life is hidden in Christ, and that Christ offers the perfect response of faith, obedience, worship and service on our behalf, as we are united by the Spirit into his life and action. I'm reminded that we engage in mission with humble confidence and dependent gratitude, rather than strain and manipulation.

As a recovering narcissistic pragmatist, I've had many opportunities to witness the power of God at work well beyond our human agency. While serving for ten years as Director of Faith and Development for World Vision International, I had the privilege of seeing the acts of God in complex humanitarian crises. During the height of the recovery effort to the 2004 tsunami in Aceh, Indonesia that killed 170,000 people, I engaged with our Director of Interfaith Relations in conversation with the director of Islamic shariah law in the area. Shariah police were established after the tsunami, and constantly patrolled the streets looking for and punishing every offense. Public canings in the city square were commonplace. As the largest Christian relief organization serving there, with hundreds of Muslim staff working for us, there were many questions about our motives and activities. The tensions were high and it was uncertain that World Vision would be permitted to remain in Aceh.

Our meeting occurred during the same week in October 2006 as the West Nickel Mines massacre of Amish school children in Pennsylvania. The Bande Aceh newspaper first announced it with headlines highlighting how dangerous infidel America is, where children weren't even safe at school. However the tone changed the next day as accounts of the Amish response to the massacre emerged. Acehnese society was stunned by the ways the Amish extended extravagant grace and mercy toward the perpetrator and his family.

The Director of Shariah Law, a well-educated scholar with a Ph.D. in Islamics from a University in Cairo was more interested in talking about the Amish than about World Vision. "Tell me," he asked, "do the Amish respond this way because of their culture, or is it because of their Christian faith?" I replied that their culture was shaped by their faith and by their daily reading of the Sermon on the Mount.[5] They lived the gospel commitment to always practice forgiveness because that is the way of God. He sat silently. Without expecting a reply, and almost as a form of personal reflection, he mused, "I wonder what our world would look like today if America had responded to 9/11 that way?" He went on not only to support World Vision's work in Aceh but also to encourage the Christian staff of World Vision to engage more regularly with one another in worship, prayer and Bible study.

I wonder what would it mean for our personal lives, our witness and even for human history if we actually did live by the Spirit in the Son as "participants in the divine nature" (2 Pet. 1:4)? Theology is anything but an esoteric academic human-centered pursuit. Good theology, when lived in the harsh realities of life, can change not just individuals but societies.

On another occasion I was in Gaza, meeting with Abuna Manuel, the Roman Catholic priest for Gaza. He had given World Vision a request for playground equipment. This was perplexing since Gaza needed so many, seemingly more urgent things, such as health care, clean water, jobs, security, justice and freedom. When I asked him about this priority, he responded with an indirect answer. He recounted how a few days earlier, on one of the days of Ramadan, he was in the midst of raising the host during Mass when he heard a small commotion at the door of the church. One of the staff was urging some people to leave. Troubled, he finished the Mass and ran to the door to see what had been the problem. To his dismay, he saw a contingent of all the Muslim clerics of Gaza City walking downcast away from the church. Running to them he asked, "Brothers, what is wrong?" They replied, "We wanted to come to the church to extend to you a Ramadan blessing but were turned away. We are so grateful for the ministry of your church in Gaza."

The church didn't merely serve the few Christians of Gaza. Its school, ministries of compassion and advocacy for justice had impact throughout the troubled community. Abuna Manuel then went on to say words that have remained with me ever since. "The children of Gaza are losing their capacity to play," and especially to play together as Muslims and Christians. "Play is the pathway to laughter, laughter opens up the

---

5   For an excellent account of this see Donald Kraybill, et al. *Amish Grace: How Forgiveness Transcended Tragedy* (San Francisco: Jossey-Bass, 2007).

door to joy, and joy leads us to hope. Without hope people are willing to do desperate things. We need to help the children of Gaza learn how to play again." The Catholic Church and the children of Gaza received their playground equipment.

Mission is our joy-filled participation in this extravagant, divine dance of love. The triune God is at work in our world interceding for all creation's groans, drawing all of life back into the harmony for which it was created and for which it is redeemed in Christ. I can't echo Brunner's stirring call any more. The Church doesn't exist by mission. The Church exists by God's grace, as the Spirit in the Son pours out the fiery life and love of God into us. Nor can I proclaim any more that the Church of God has a mission in the world. We don't. Rather, the God of mission has the Church in the world. God's world, God's mission, God's work, God's victory – and our joyful participation in it. That change of subject and object changes everything. P. T. Forsyth proclaims this with clarity by saying, "The weakness of much current mission work and much current preaching is that they betray the sense that what is yet to be done is greater than what has already been done ... The world's gravest need is less than Christ's great victory."[6]

While seldom even using the word "mission," James Torrance led me on a journey that has impacted my approach to life in the world.[7] We don't build or bring the kingdom of God. That's not our work. Rather, as Paul says in the passage cited earlier in Colossians, we are "transferred" to the Kingdom. To be transferred is to be carried across, transported, literally "ferried across" to the Kingdom. In God's extravagant grace, the Spirit ferries us in Christ from the domain of darkness to the kingdom of light. Our role is to give consent to this change, to agree with the work of God and then to bear witness to it with courage and kindness through lives transformed to bear the fruit of the Spirit. The Kingdom of God is not built by our strenuous service but comes to us in "righteousness and peace and joy in the Holy Spirit" (Rom. 14:17). And so we pray for the Church, "May the God of hope fill you with all joy and peace in believing, so that you may abound in hope by the power of the Holy Spirit" (Rom. 15:13). Abounding hope in the utter reliability of the triune God of love is one of the legacies of James B. Torrance.

---

6   P. T. Forsyth, *Mission in State and Church* (London: Hodder and Stoughton, 1908), 10, 16-18.

7   For further development of the author's understanding of this see T. Dearborn, *Beyond Duty: A Passion for Christ, a Heart for Mission,* Revised edition (Seattle: Dynamis Resources, 2013).

Chapter 9

Prayer and the Priesthood of Christ

Graham Redding

I know not how to pray, O Lord,
so weak and frail am I.
Lord Jesus to Your outstretched arms
in love I daily fly:
For you have prayed for me.

Although I know not how to pray,
Your Spirit intercedes,
convincing me of pardoned sin;
for me in love He pleads
and teaches me to pray.[1]

Included in JB's legacy of published material is a hymn he penned around 1981 on a topic and activity that lay close to his heart: prayer. "I Know Not How To Pray" gives voice to an aspect of prayer that JB stressed repeatedly, based on his reading of the New Testament, namely that prayer, properly understood, is a trinitarian event involving the mediation of Christ our High Priest and the activity of the Holy Spirit. As such, prayer is a learnt activity. Jesus taught his disciples to pray; and through the Holy Spirit he continues to teach his church how to pray.

Over the course of his teaching career, JB wrote and spoke repeatedly on the subject of prayer and the priesthood of Christ. The purpose of this brief article is not to rehearse his arguments, which can be found in many publications, but rather to explore the liturgical implications of viewing prayer as a learnt activity. In a sense, this article represents the continuation of a conversation I had with JB in 1998 when I visited him in Edinburgh to talk about certain aspects of my own research on the subject of prayer and the priesthood of Christ.

---

1   Verses 1 and 4 of "I Know Not How To Pray," reproduced in full on p. 279.

Prayer as a Learned Activity

JB's hymn stresses a fundamental truth about prayer, drawn from scripture, namely that we need to be taught how to pray, for we do not know how to pray as we ought. "Lord, teach us to pray," was a need voiced by Jesus' disciples,[2] and it has been a need of his church ever since. Making this the starting point of prayer counters a strong tendency in religious life for prayer to be regarded as just another form of self-expression, whereby *we* come before God in prayer to give *our* adoration, to express *our* needs and to voice *our* concerns. Whilst such prayers might be utterly sincere, reflect heartfelt devotion, and even be uttered in Jesus' name, they tend to lack any real sense of the mediatorial role of Christ and the enabling role of the Holy Spirit. As JB often pointed out, they constitute a unitarian model of prayer, not a trinitarian one. They are Pelagian rather than participatory. Such prayers are prone to being unnecessarily wordy and long-winded, especially when delivered extemporaneously. In such circumstances we would do well to heed the warning that Jesus gave to his disciples against heaping up empty phrases as the Gentiles of his day were prone to do.[3] Rambling stream-of-consciousness prayers have no place in public worship.

By way of contrast, it seems to me that a church which takes to heart the need to be taught how to pray is likely to do at least two things: adopt a contemplative posture and seek the mind of Christ.

Adopting a Contemplative Posture

"Be still and know that I am God," the Lord declares in Psalm 46.[4] Being still in the presence of the Lord necessarily involves slowing down and entering the sort of existential space wherein we might hear the same "still, small voice" that Elijah heard,[5] and take Mary's prayer of submission as our own: "Here am I, the servant of the Lord; let it be with me according to your word."[6] Being still and receptive in this manner involves an embrace of holy silence, holy because it represents not the

---

2   Luke 11:1.
3   Matt. 6:7.
4   Ps. 46:10.
5   1 Kings 19:12.
6   Luke 1:38.

absence of noise but rather the presence of the Spirit. Such silence, Thomas Merton once declared, is the mother of speech:

> Life and death, words and silence, are given us because of Christ. In Christ we die to the flesh and live to the spirit. In Him we die to illusion and live to truth. We speak to confess Him, and we are silent in order to meditate on Him and enter deeper into His silence, which is at once the silence of death and eternal life – the silence of Good Friday night and the peace of Easter morning.[7]

Directed silence is a time honoured liturgical tool in the church's endeavour to adopt a suitably contemplative posture in order to hear what the Spirit is saying to the church and to acknowledge that, in the church's weakness, the Spirit "intercedes with sighs too deep for words."[8]

Silence is not the only tool of course. Other things help instil in us a contemplative posture and a receptive spirit. They contribute to what we might call the aesthetics of worship, and include such things as architectural design, the physical layout and adornment of the worship space, and the liturgical use of ritual, music, gesture, movement, art, and symbol. Some of these forms will involve words, but many of them will engage us in non-verbal ways. These will vary from tradition to tradition, but one thing they will have in common is the ability to help us contemplate the holy, to convey a sense of mystery, to make deeper connections for us, to open up fresh lines of inquiry, and to somehow encourage us to consider things as they truly are in the sight of God, not simply as they appear to be to us.

Seeking the Mind of Christ

"Let the same mind be in you that was in Christ Jesus," Paul exhorted the church in Philippi.[9] Praying in the name of Christ necessarily involves discerning, as much as we are able, the mind of Christ, our brother in prayer, and to pray as he prompts us to pray. How will the church do this? I would suggest by prioritising four things:

---

7   Thomas Merton, *No Man is an Island* (New York: Shambhala Publications, 1955), 274.
8   Rom. 8:26.
9   Phil. 2:5.

(1) Abiding in him whose prayer life the church shares by the power of the Spirit.

(2) Keeping the prayer that Jesus gave his disciples at the centre of the church's prayer life.

(3) Allowing the scriptures to mould and inform the church's prayers.

(4) Drawing upon the church's own rich heritage of prayer.

Let us now reflect briefly on each of those aspects.

Abiding in Christ

The language of abiding in Christ is a striking feature of John's gospel. As the Son abides in the Father so those whom the Son calls abide in him. How do they do this? By feeding upon him who is the very bread of life, for as Jesus declares: "I am the living bread which came down from heaven; if anyone eats of this bread, he will live forever; and the bread which I shall give for the life of the world is my flesh."[10] The eucharistic connotations of this declaration are clear and go a long way toward explaining why the "breaking of the bread" or the Lord's Supper was so quickly established as a defining characteristic of early Christian worship.[11]

Many years later, in his *Short Treatise on the Holy Supper of our Lord Jesus Christ*, John Calvin used the language of "nourishment" and "participation" to describe the core purpose of the Lord's Supper: It is *nourishment* for the soul, preserving and strengthening, confirming and fortifying us in the promises of salvation and the benefits of Christ's death on the cross and, at the same time, delivering us from condemnation. And it is an essential means of *participation* in Christ's humanity and eternal life. Calvin brought together these notions of nourishment and participation in a simple declaration that "in order to have our life in Christ our souls must feed on his body and blood as their proper food."[12]

For many churches today, a rediscovery of the importance of abiding in Christ (and not merely following his example) will be bound up with a recovery of a robust sacramental theology and practice, especially in

---

10 John 6:51.

11 Cf. Acts 2:42.

12 Calvin, *Short Treatise on the Holy Supper of our Lord Jesus Christ* (1540), section 13.

relation to the Lord's Supper. Such a recovery will be concerned not just for asking, "How often should the sacrament be celebrated?" but more importantly, "How do we see ourselves in relation to the sacrament?" Moving towards a more regular celebration of communion might be a good thing for many churches to do, but it will not in itself address the second question, which goes to the heart of our ecclesiology. What do we believe actually takes place around the Lord's Table? Is the Lord, through his Spirit, truly present? Do we believe, along with Calvin, that a real spiritual union with Christ occurs at his Table? And, do we see Word and Sacrament, pulpit and table, as being integrally related to one another in Christian life and worship?

Keeping the Lord's Prayer at the Centre of the Church's Prayer Life

When Jesus responded to his disciples' request to be taught how to pray, he didn't just give them a lesson on prayer; he gave them an actual prayer. Although the Matthean and Lukan versions of that prayer vary somewhat, there is a high degree of consistency between the two, and it is clear that the prayer formed the basis for subsequent catechetical instruction and liturgical recitation in the early church. It still has much to teach us, not least of which in relation to its form of address, its succinctness, and the nature of its petitions. Hallowing the Father's name, yearning for his Kingdom, relying on him for life's basic necessities, knowing we are forgiven and cultivating an ability to forgive others, confessing our vulnerability before the forces of trial and temptation – these are all core aspects of living the Kingdom-life and of understanding the mind of Christ. We pray according to his instruction, confident that this prayer has not only been given by him; it is fulfilled in him.

Allowing the Scriptures to Mould and Inform the Church's Prayers

In Luke's account of the Emmaus journey (Luke 24), the risen Christ comes alongside two disciples, engages them in conversation about what they have heard but do not yet understand and, beginning with Moses and the prophets, proceeds to interpret himself to them through the scriptures. The church has long held up this story as a model for the ministry of the Word, but it can be applied equally to the task of liturgical preparation. Preachers and liturgists alike are called to approach scripture not for the purpose of analysing, mastering, applying, and appropriating a given text, but rather to indwell it and to listen for, and to convey, the voice of Christ through it. The ancient monastic practice of *Lectio Divina* encapsulates this approach. It consists of four phases of engagement (reading, meditating, praying, and contemplating), each of which is conducted in, with, and through Christ, the one to whom the scriptures bear ultimate witness and from whom they derive their deepest meaning.

Approached in this way, scripture becomes a fertile ground for prayer. It not only offers us a rich store of prayers, including of course the Psalms, but also many of its texts lend themselves to being given fresh liturgical expression through song, chant and prayer. The widespread appeal of the kind of meditative singing that is characteristic of the likes of the Taizé Community is indicative of the effectiveness of this form of liturgical engagement with scripture. Harold Best helpfully argues that "the prayers of Scripture should be studied and assimilated as our prayers, and we should learn to craft parallel prayers, using these as templates and using our best thought and best language."[13] And perhaps we should add, our best music.

Drawing upon the Church's rich Heritage of Prayer

A church that takes seriously the need to be taught how to pray will look not just to the scriptures but also to the legacy of prayer bequeathed to it by the communion of saints, including mystics and theologians, pastors and poets, liturgists and intercessors. It will mine a range of liturgical traditions and compile a suitable repertoire of prayers, ancient and modern. It will thus draw upon the wisdom of the saints as it seeks the mind of Christ for its own time and place.

Behind this great heritage of prayer, of course, lie countless godly lives, from which we can learn much. Some of these folk will be celebrated heroes of faith, but others will be much closer to home, including parents and grandparents. Knowing this to be the case, churches have much to gain by encouraging and cultivating the habit of family devotions, for it is in the home that so many things are modelled for children by their

---

13 Harold Best, *Unceasing Worship: Biblical Perspectives on Worship and the Arts* (Downers Grove: InterVarsity Press, 2003), 102.

primary caregivers and imparted to them, including the discipline and joy of prayer. Indeed, this was precisely the childhood experience of JB and his brothers Tom and David. As David once described it: "Our love for the Scriptures and our theological education started from a very early age with our parents' teaching . . . Our parents had a steadfast faith in God, a love for the Word of God and a firm belief in the power of prayer. Every day we met for family worship which was led by one of our parents. This continued from our earliest days of infancy until one by one we left home."[14]

To Whom do we Pray?

When prayer is understood in terms of a trinitarian activity, it is clear that although prayers may be addressed to any person of the Trinity, for all three persons are fully divine, our primary form of address must be to the Father, for it is to him alone that the Son and the Spirit direct our worship, and it is to him alone that the Lord's Prayer is addressed. That said, a question arises concerning the many other ways of describing and addressing God in Scripture and in the life of the church: Are they rendered obsolete in light of the Trinity?

In the final chapter and appendix of his book, *Worship, Community and the Triune God of Grace*, JB helpfully addressed the issue of God-language and worship. He correctly pointed out the distinction between referring to God by the name that God has decreed and the use of biblical similes and other metaphors to convey certain characteristics of the one whom we have been instructed to address as Father. Thus understood, trinitarian language does not prohibit the continued use of similes and other metaphors, but it does provide a normative reference point and interpretive framework for them. A PCUSA paper, "The Trinity: God's Love Overflowing", puts it this way:

The language of Father, Son, and Holy Spirit, rooted in scripture and creed, remains an indispensable anchor for our efforts to speak faithfully of God. When secured, an anchor provides both necessary stability and adequate freedom of movement. If our lifeline to the anchor is frayed or severed, the historic faith of the one holy catholic and apostolic church risks being set adrift. With this anchor in place, however, we are

---

14 *An Introduction to Torrance Theology*, ed. Gerrit Scott Dawson (Edinburgh: T&T Clark, 2007), 2.

liberated to interpret, amplify, and expand upon the ways of speaking of the triune God familiar to most church members. We are freed to speak faithfully and amply of the mystery of the Trinity. We may cultivate a responsible trinitarian imagination and vocabulary that bears witness in different ways to the one triune God known to us from scripture and creed as Father, Son, and Holy Spirit. Faithfulness to the gospel frees us to honour and continue to use this faithful way of speaking of the triune God even as it frees us to adopt other faithful images. Rather than simply repeating the word "God" in prayer and liturgy, we are free to broaden our vocabulary for speaking of the triune God, emboldened by the rich reservoir of biblical and traditional terms, images, and metaphors.[15]

The provisional nature of prayer and the language it draws upon is expressed very well in this footnote to all prayers, penned by C.S. Lewis:

> He whom I bow to only knows to whom I bow
> When I attempt the ineffable Name, murmuring *Thou*,
> And dream of Pheidian fancies and embrace in heart
> Symbols (I know) which cannot be the thing Thou art.
> Thus always, taken at their word, all prayers blaspheme
> Worshipping with frail images a folk-lore dream,
> And all men in their own unquiet thoughts, unless
> Thou in magnetic mercy to Thyself divert
> Our arrows, aimed unskilfully, beyond desert;
> And all men are idolaters, crying unheard
> To a deaf idol, if Thou take them at their word.
> Take not, O Lord, our literal sense. Lord, in thy great,
> Unbroken speech our limping metaphor translate.[16]

Conclusion

Acknowledging a need to be taught how to pray, and adopting liturgical practices that facilitate this process, are critically important for the church if it is to avoid the twin dangers of self-expression and activism in relation to the act of public worship. These dangers are acute,

---

15 "The Trinity: God's Love Overflowing," Office of Theology and Worship, PCUSA, 2004, lines 330-342, www.pcusa.org/media/uploads/theologyandworship/pdfs/trinityfinal.pdf.

16 *The Oxford Book of Prayer*, edited by George Appleton (Oxford University Press, 1985), 70.

due partly to the prevalence of western culture, which in many respects is alarmingly frantic, pragmatic and self-focused, and due partly to the realities of institutional decline and the resultant pressure to try harder and to do more. So much public worship today suffers from verbiage and from being reduced to just one more activity among many. In many ways it has become, as JB observed, unitarian, insofar as it "has no doctrine of the mediator or sole priesthood of Christ, is human-centred, has no proper doctrine of the Holy Spirit, is too often non-sacramental, and can engender weariness. We sit in the pew watching the minister 'doing his thing,' exhorting us 'to do our thing,' until we go home thinking we have done our duty for another week! This kind of do-it-yourself-with-the-help-of-the-minister worship is what our forefathers would have called 'legal worship' and not 'evangelical worship' – what the ancient church would have called Arian or Pelagian and not truly catholic. It is not trinitarian."[17]

How might we respond to this dilemma? What I have sought to argue in this article is that at least one critical aspect of our response will be found in that ancient prayer request of the disciples, which JB faithfully and persistently kept before the church, "Lord, teach us to pray!" followed perhaps by a simple prayer of confession: "Almighty God: you have no patience with solemn assemblies, or heaped-up prayers to be heard by men. Forgive those who have written prayers for congregations. Remind them that their foolish words will pass away, but that your word will last and be fulfilled, in Jesus Christ our Lord. Amen."[18]

---

17 Torrance, J. B., *Worship, Community and the Triune God of Grace* (Downers Grove: InterVarsity Press, 1996), 20.

18 *The Worshipbook* (Philadelphia: The Westminster Press, 1970), 202.

Chapter 10

Epistemology, Freedom and the Faithful Steward

R. Scott Rodin

In 1988 I sat in my first Systematic Theology I course, unsure of what to expect from the visiting professor from the northeast of Scotland. Professor James Torrance began our class by drawing a diagram on the board that looked like a cross between an electrical circuit board and an American football pass play. Lines connected the words Yahweh and Israel, Father and Jesus, Church and We. Other lines were labeled R1 and R2, covenant and Spirit. An array of lines ran between the word "one" and "all nations," "one" and "Jews," "Gentiles," "male and female," and others.

We would soon learn that this was what Professor Torrance called the *trinitarian Incarnational Model of Theology*. As he unpacked this model over the weeks that followed, he introduced me to a world of theological thought I had never known. Thinking back now over the past 25 years, that model continues to give shape and depth to my writing, teaching and personal faith journey. This has been most pronounced in my work on the theology of the faithful steward, which I developed in *Stewards in the Kingdom, The Sower,* and *the Third Conversion,* and the theology of the steward leader, which I presented in *The Steward Leader*. This body of work is built on five pillars, all of which rest on the bedrock of Torrance's trinitarian incarnational model.

1. The Centrality of the "Who Question"

Perhaps the greatest gift I received sitting under the teaching from James Torrance was the discovery of how a Christo-centric epistemology was central to all theological thought. What was commonly referred to as the "who question" became the lens through which theology, and its ethical implications were to be viewed. This focus provided my theology not only its center, but also its direction. Theological inquiry became what Anselm called *fides quaerens intellectum*, faith seeking after understanding.

The first major implication for my work on a theology of the steward was to propose that we stop talking about stewardship and focus instead on the journey of the faithful steward. In the Christian not-for-profit world in North America we are obsessed with techniques, tactics, and checklists. We like to be told how to accomplish complex tasks in simple steps. The church and the para-church world have obliged by preaching and teaching about what it means to practice faithful stewardship, with precious little discussion about who we are in Christ and what that means for the work of the Holy Spirit in us, transforming us into faithful stewards. This error can be traced back to similar missteps where the church has talked about discipleship apart from the transformed heart of a disciple, the works of Christ apart from the person of Christ, the attributes of God apart from the nature of God, and so on. Torrance refers to this in his *Existential, Present-day Experience Model* of worship:

> He [Bonhoeffer] pleaded for following the biblical pattern of giving priority to the question of *who* over *what* and *how* – that we interpret the atonement and personal faith in terms of the incarnation (the triune God of grace) and not the other way round. The pragmatic, problem centered preoccupation with the question of *how* in our Western culture can so readily reduce the gospel to the category of means and ends.[1]

Nowhere does Torrance state this more succinctly and powerfully than in his oft-quoted phrase, "more important than our experience of Christ is the Christ of our experience."[2]

By reclaiming our Christo-centric epistemology, and the rich trinitarian theology that follows, we are invited to rediscover the heart of God, his intentions toward us and, as a result, our own nature, purpose, and vocation.

---

1   James B. Torrance, *Worship, Community and the Triune God of Grace* (Downer's Grove: IVP Academic, 1996), 28-29.

2   Ibid., 34.

The basis of the theology of the faithful steward is found in knowing who God is through his self-revelation to us in Jesus Christ, the triune movement of God toward us. If we are God's stewards, called according to his command and empowered for his service, then we must seek knowledge of God only through a participation in the life of the Son's revelation of the Father in the power of the Holy Spirit. This is the foundational methodology from which the rest of the theology of the faithful steward was developed.

2. Rediscovering a Doctrine of Creation

The second component of the theology of the faithful steward comes from a rediscovery of a doctrine of creation that now emerges with greater clarity from Torrance's trinitarian incarnational model. At the heart of this doctrine are the concepts of certainty and freedom. In my book, *Stewards in the Kingdom* the essence of James' theology comes through clearly:

> What we know in Jesus Christ and what we believe in the power of the Holy Spirit is that this God is a God of grace our God who is for us! We know and believe that Christ came to establish his kingdom and that through the spirit we have been called as people of that kingdom therefore we also know and believe that our God has a purpose for us and a future for us. All this we know for certain because the word was made flesh and dwelt among us. All this we believe with confidence because the sun has revealed to the heart of God to us and that revelation is revealed and confirmed to us by the spirit.[3]

Knowing our Creator with such great certainty allows us to know ourselves with equal certainty; who we are, why we were created, our vocation and our future. Jesus Christ revealed God's gracious and loving intent in our creation. He created us as an act of his love, and he did it in complete freedom:

> In his love he commits himself to be our God, to be for us, to become subject to limitation, to suffer and to bear our sin. Yet he

---

3   R. Scott Rodin, *Stewards in the Kingdom* (Downer's Grove: InterVarsity Press, 2000), 59.

chose this freely in accordance with his divine nature. He is the
God who loves in freedom and who is free to love.[4]

From this certainty of God's nature and this understanding of creation as the outpouring of both the freedom and love of God we can better understand his creative intent. The theology of the faithful steward is built on the understanding that God created us for whole, rich and meaningful relationship in four spheres of our created reality. These spheres represent the full picture of how we bear the image of a triune God. We were "relationally wired" from the beginning. We were created for relationship with God, our self, our neighbor and the creation itself. In each of these spheres God creates us in freedom for our free and joyous response. We bear God's image as caretakers of our relationships in all four spheres. They were given to us as gifts that we might tend and nurture each to God's glory. This gives shape and direction to our vocation. Everything we do in this life takes place in and through these four spheres of relationship. When we view them as gifts we can embrace our calling as stewards.

3. The Pervasiveness of the Fall

From this relational understanding of our creation we gain a proper perspective of the all-encompassing effect of sin. The fall brought brokenness at all four spheres – our relationship with God, with our self, with our neighbor, and with creation.

Evil had its three moments in the history of humankind: rebellion against God, and enmity toward neighbor (and creation), and sin against self. Both that which defined our essence and that gave meaning to our existence were destroyed in our great act of unfaithfulness.[5]

If we do not understand this pervasive view of the effect of sin, we will miss entirely the great story of redemption and its impact on us in our calling as faithful stewards. An incomplete doctrine of creation has led to a meager doctrine of the fall, which has robbed the cross of its full significance. Here again Torrance's trinitarian incarnational model serves us well by reminding us that in the incarnation Christ bore vicariously the fullness of our humanity. That included our brokenness at all four relational levels. His atoning sacrifice was not just a cure

4   Ibid., 61.
5   Ibid., 93.

for our loss of relationship with God, but a victorious triumph over all brokenness, to which the entirety of the Old Testament bears clear witness. Thus Torrance loved to quote Gregory of Nazianzus, "the unassumed is the unredeemed."[6] Bearing our full humanity, Christ became the great high priest, providing once and for all the atoning sacrifice for our sin. Torrance's understanding of Christ as the "one on behalf of the many" was built on this understanding of the all-pervasive nature of the fall of humanity.

This is critical for our theology of the faithful steward. Until we embrace the magnitude of our sin and understand that every aspect of God's created intent was tarnished, twisted and broken by our sinful rebelliousness, we cannot embrace with joy the full implication of what was won for us on the cross. Further, unless we see in Christ the representative of the fullness of our sin, we will be left to try to practice good acts of stewardship instead of understanding our calling as a participation in the life and work of the one true Steward.

4. The Faithful Steward

I fear that in American evangelical theology we have lost the understanding that the life of a follower of Jesus Christ is a participation in the work of Christ himself. We seem to have bought in to a post-resurrection deism that separates our work for Christ from his work for us and in us. This is nowhere more apparent than in our teachings on stewardship. Once we have been "saved," that is, our relationship with God healed and restored because of the historic death and resurrection of Christ, we are now thrown back upon ourselves to figure out how to live differently as a result. When it comes to stewardship, that commonly devolves into discussions of tithing, volunteering for the church and making sure we have a will. The more it becomes "our work for God" the more bereft it is of passion, sacrifice and joy.

Instead we must come to see that all of life, our relationships in all four spheres, were lost in the fall, fully restored in Christ and given back to us as a precious gift. I use the chart on the next page to depict this movement from creation to fall, cross to restoration.

---

6   Gregory of Nazianzus *Epistles 101*. See T. F. Torrance, *Theology in Reconciliation* (London: Geoffrey Chapman, 1975), 112, 154, 167.

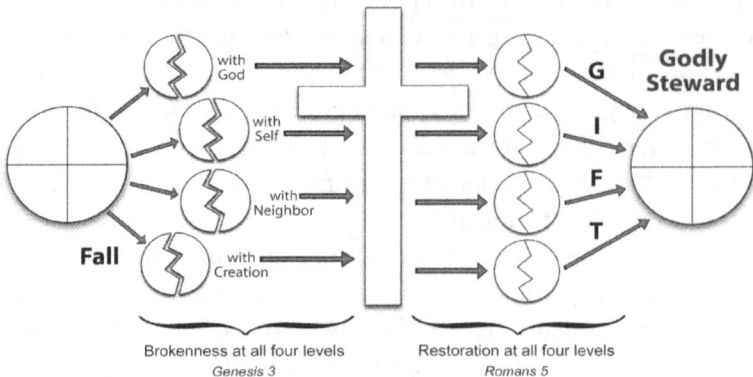

This chart represents a fundamental re-formation of our understanding of our call to be faithful stewards. If the cross brought restoration of our broken relationships at all four levels, then our vocation as followers of Jesus Christ is to be participants with Christ in his ongoing work of bringing healing and restoration in all four spheres. The key here is that all of life, lived out in every sphere of relationship is a gift made possible through the blood of Christ and given to us by the love of God through the power of the Holy Spirit.

5. Freedom and Worship

The fruit of this theology is absolute freedom. This life is not our own, but every part of it belongs to God. As his gracious gift to us we are now freed to invest ourselves fully in kingdom life. The marks of that life are our obedience to the true owner of all things, and deep joy in our participation with him in his work.

This diagram reminds us that there is no room in our life for the building of a second kingdom. Yet this is the enemy's agenda, to deceive us into believing that some parts of these relational spheres really do belong to us. This is nothing more than a reenactment of the sin of Eden, questioning the goodness of God and replacing our trust in him with the desire to grab for control and become the lords of our own little kingdoms. We fool ourselves into believing that we can live simultaneously in these two kingdoms, God's and ours. Yet experience tells us that everything we place in our own kingdom will become the source of our anxiety, fear, stress, and dissatisfaction. The theology of the faithful steward continually brings us back to the cross and helps us remember that, just as the incarnation was Christ's vicarious assumption of the fullness of our humanity, so the cross was his redemption of that same fullness. Any attempt to reclaim back for ourselves a counterfeit sense of ownership is a denial of what was assumed for us in Bethlehem, borne for us on Calvary, and redeemed for us on Easter Sunday.

We were created to be one-kingdom people, and in response to the devastating effect of the fall, the cross of Christ redeemed and restored us to that same status. Now we live out that calling as stewards through our participation in the life of the one Faithful Steward who lived the life we could not live, died in our place for sins he did not commit, rose again to declare victory that was beyond our grasp, and now ministers in us and through us to do the work we are powerless to do on our own. This ministry continues when we are called into positions of leadership. Again drawing from so much of James' theology I wrote:

> As we are being transformed into godly stewards, we are freed to fulfill our vocation as steward leaders. It is God's calling, Christ's redemption and the Holy Spirit's transformation that we rely on for our success. In this way, leadership is a work of our triune God in us and through us. And if that is God's work, and we are called to obediently respond, then we are

Finally, one of Torrance's greatest contributions to my theology was his view of worship. He helped me appreciate that the life of the faithful steward is a life lived as a sacrament, a holy offering to God. For that reason Torrance's view of worship gives us the fullest expression of his trinitarian, incarnational theology, and hearing his own words onfreed to lead courageously and humbly, and to trust God for the increase.[7] the subject is a fitting way to end this brief article.

The second view of worship is that it is the gift of participating through the Spirit in the incarnate Son's communion with the Father. It means participating in union with Christ, in what he has done for us once and for all, in his self-offering to the Father, in his life and death on the cross. It also means participating in what he is continuing to do for us in the presence of the Father and in his mission from the Father

---

7   R. Scott Rodin, *The Steward Leader* (Downers Grove: InterVarsity Press, 2010), 62-63.

to the world . . . This view is trinitarian and incarnational. It takes seriously the New Testament teaching about the soul priesthood and headship of Christ, his self offering for us to the Father and our life in union with Christ through the Spirit, with a vision of the church as the body of Christ. It is fundamentally sacramental, but in a way which enshrines the gospel of grace – that God our Father, in the gift of his Son and the gift of the Spirit, gives us what he demands – the worship of our hearts and minds. He lifts us up out of ourselves to participate in the very life and communion of the Godhead, that life of communion for which we were created.[8]

---

[8] Torrance, *Worship, Community and the Triune God of Grace*, 20-22.

Chapter 11

James B. Torrance and the Doctrine of Sanctification

Alexandra Radcliff

Introduction

James B. Torrance has a profound understanding of the vicarious humanity of Christ, which he explores most notably with regard to our understanding of worship.[1] This chapter examines the implications of the vicarious humanity of Christ for the outworking of our sanctification.[2] Torrance gives little attention to this subject, perhaps characteristic of his reformed tradition's sensitivity to works-righteousness which led to a focus on the objective work of God. However, the objectivity of Torrance's account of our salvation in Christ offers a valuable foundation for a liberating understanding of the outworking of sanctification.[3]

Torrance was acutely troubled in his time by preaching and teaching that placed its focus on works that the believer must do.[4] His presentation of salvation in intimate, ontological, and filial terms challenges any understanding of sanctification as a detached, legalistic, anthropocentric

---

1   See James B. Torrance, *Worship, Community and the Triune God of Grace* (Carlisle: Paternoster Press, 1996). Although Torrance only had this one monograph published, it continues to be reprinted and a considerable number of copies are being sold.

2   A broader exploration of this subject can be found in Alexandra Radcliff, *The Claim of Humanity in Christ: Salvation and Sanctification in the Theology of T. F. and J. B. Torrance* (Eugene, OR: Wipf & Stock, forthcoming 2016).

3   Use of the word "liberating" is not to be associated with a political theology; rather it expresses how we are set free from the burden of trying to earn what has already been definitely achieved for us in Christ so that we can freely grow into that reality.

4   James B. Torrance, "Strengths and Weaknesses of the Westminster Theology," in *The Westminster Confession in the Church Today*, ed. Alasdair Heron, (Edinburgh: The Saint Andrew Press, 1982), 44–45.

endeavour. Extending the implications of Torrance's soteriology to the doctrine of sanctification, human activity is affirmed in its proper place, that is, as the free and joyful participation by the Spirit in what Christ has already accomplished for us so that we might enjoy intimate communion with the triune God of grace.

The Vicarious Humanity of Christ

Torrance conceives of salvation and sanctification in terms of Christ vicariously assuming our humanity and ontologically transforming it in the depths of his very being. For Torrance, the incarnation is the beginning of the atonement. In the very act of the divine assuming fallen human flesh, it cannot but be transformed. He asserts, "We are not just healed 'through Christ' because of the work of Christ but 'in and through Christ.'"[5] Jesus' whole life is of atoning significance. As both God and man, Jesus fulfils both sides of the relationship between God and humanity. Jesus lives a life of perfect faithfulness to the Father, in our place, turning our humanity back to a right relationship with God: "In our name, on our behalf, in a human body, Jesus lived a life of prayer, a life in the Spirit in communion with the Father, to sanctify our humanity."[6]

Everything that Jesus does in his humanity affects all humanity. Torrance believes that this is expressed by Jesus' assertion, "For them I sanctify myself that they too may be truly sanctified" (Jn. 17:19).[7] Christ's death is the death of sinful humanity.[8] Torrance points to Paul's assertion, "One died for all and therefore all died" (2 Cor. 5:14).[9] Christ's resurrection is the raising of humanity as a whole new creation. His ascension raises humanity to the right hand of the Father.[10]

> The Son of God takes our humanity, sanctifies it by his vicarious life in the Spirit (John 17:17-18), carries it to the grave to be

---

5   James B. Torrance, "Christ in our Place," ed. Gerrit Scott Dawson and Jock Stein, *A Passion for Christ: The Vision that Ignites Ministry* (Edinburgh: Handsel Press, 1999), 47.

6   Ibid.

7   Ibid., 45.

8   Torrance, *Worship, Community and the Triune God of Grace*, 71.

9   James B. Torrance, "The Priesthood of Jesus: A Study in the Doctrine of Atonement," T.H.L. Parker ed., *Essays in christology for Karl Barth* (Plymouth: Latimer, Trend and Co., 1956), 172.

10   Torrance, "Prayer and the Priesthood of Christ," *A Passion for Christ*, ed. Dawson and Stein, 62.

crucified and buried in him, and in his resurrection and ascension carries it into the holy presence of God. "And by that will, we have been made holy through the sacrifice of the body of Jesus Christ once for all" (Heb. 10:10).[11]

Whilst there is a strong appreciation in Torrance's evangelical tradition of the God-humanward movement in Christ and his work of atonement on the cross, there can be a failure to recognise this human-Godward movement in Christ and the far-reaching nature of his substitution which encompasses his whole life. In focusing upon what God has done for us, without an account of Christ's vicarious humanity, the human response falls upon us and demands our own efforts. Torrance presents a radically objective account of salvation and sanctification whereby Jesus offers the perfect human response in our place and on our behalf. We are saved and made holy in Christ prior to any contribution that we could offer. Our sanctification is a definite reality in Christ. We are truly changed in the depths of our being, not simply forgiven and given a second chance to be good. Our own actions do not make us any more holy than we already are; rather, they are a manifestation of the holiness which we already definitively possess in Christ. To many today who believe that, having been justified by faith, it is now the Christian's task to work out his own sanctification, this is a vital message of life and liberation.

Drawn to Participate by the Holy Spirit

For Torrance, the far-reaching nature of Jesus' vicarious ministry continues today, as he intercedes for us as our ascended High Priest.[12]

> That life of worship and communion with the Father which Jesus fulfilled in our humanity, did not end in death. Having offered for us a life of perfect obedience to the Father, culminating in the one perfect self-offering for all people and all nations, Jesus rose from the dead and returned to the Father to intercede for us (Rom. 8:34) as our great High Priest (Heb. 4:14). As the eternal Mediator of an eternal covenant, he now appears on our behalf in the presence of God that we might be accepted as sons and daughters (Eph. 2:13ff., 1 Tim. 2:1-6, Heb. 4:14; 9:24; 7:25).[13]

---

11 Torrance, "Christ in our Place," 62.
12 Ibid., 45.
13 Torrance, *Worship, Community and the Triune God of Grace*, 72.

When Christ's ascension is only understood in terms of his withdrawal from humanity, we can be made dependent upon our own endeavours to work out our sanctification. The believer can feel under a tremendous burden to appropriate in his life the sanctification which Christ has definitely achieved. According to this perspective, God did his part in Christ; now we must do our part to apply the benefits of Christ with the aid of the Holy Spirit.

However, the Holy Spirit does not enable the autonomous believer to work out his own sanctification; the Holy Spirit enables the believer to participate in Christ's definitive sanctification. Sanctification is a reality in which we participate, rather than a potentiality to be actualized. Torrance's understanding of Christ's continuing ascended ministry means not only that Jesus has already definitely sanctified us, but that we are drawn up by the Spirit to freely share in that reality, and in the Son's intimate communion with the Father. Torrance writes:

> Therefore we have to hold two things together. First, he has *already* taken our humanity into the Holy of Holies, the presence of the Father in his own person. Second, he comes to us *today* by the Holy Spirit to take us with him into the Holiest of All, to present us "without stain or wrinkle or any other blemish" to the Father (Eph. 5:27).[14]

Communion with the Father

According to Torrance's understanding of salvation, the descent of Christ in the incarnation leads to the ascension of humanity to participate by the Spirit in the life of God. We are not only saved but given to share in the intimate communion of the triune life. At Pentecost, Jesus pours out his Spirit so that by the Spirit we might share in this communion.[15]

> It is as if the whole purpose of the incarnation, death, resurrection and ascension, is in order that we might receive the Holy Spirit, that the triune God of grace might bring to fulfilment the purposes of creation in sanctifying our humanity in Christ, that we might be brought into a life of holy communion, a life of prayer.[16]

---

14 Torrance, "Prayer and the Priesthood of Christ," 58.
15 Ibid.
16 Ibid., 59.

Torrance believes that a pastor's first and foremost mission is not to direct people with what is the right or wrong action to take, but to direct people to Christ so that we might share by the Spirit in his intimate relationship with the Father:

> It seems to me that in a pastoral situation, our first task is not to throw people back on themselves with exhortations and instructions as to what to do and how to do it, but to direct people to the gospel of grace – to Jesus Christ, that they might look to him to lead them, open their hearts in faith and in prayer, and draw them by the Spirit into his eternal life of communion with the Father.[17]

Torrance deeply regretted the way in which some preachers sought to inspire people to holiness through the law and fear of the consequences of disobedience.[18] He does not do away with the law; he believes that although God makes the covenant for us, it demands a response from us.[19] However, Torrance seeks to uphold our human activity in its proper place. He repeatedly insists that "the indicatives of grace are always prior to the obligations of law and human obedience."[20] If the imperative to lead a holy life is preached prior to, or in detachment from, the indicative truth that we are sanctified in Christ, we are thrown back upon ourselves to attempt to accomplish it for ourselves. However, Torrance perceives that the imperative is preceded by God's indicative act of grace in Christ's vicarious humanity whereby we have been made holy. Therefore, we are liberated to follow the imperative, not by relying upon our own resources, but by relying upon the vicarious humanity of Christ, in whom we may participate by the Spirit.

For Torrance, we fulfil the law not by adhering to static rules but dynamically through the presence of the Spirit in us and our participation in Christ.[21] When Torrance writes of God's filial purpose for humanity in the context of atonement, this might also be applied to the outworking of sanctification in the Christian life: "... God's primary purpose for humanity is 'filial,' not just 'judicial,' where we have been created in the image of God

---

17 Torrance, *Worship, Community and the Triune God of Grace*, 34.

18 Torrance, "Strengths and Weaknesses," 49.

19 James B. Torrance, "Covenant or Contract? A Study of the Theological Background of Worship in Seventeenth-century Scotland," *Scottish Journal of Theology* 23 (1970), 23; 55.

20 James B. Torrance, "The Covenant Concept in Scottish Theology and Politics and its Legacy," *Scottish Journal of Theology* 34 (1981), 230.

21 Torrance, "Prayer and the Priesthood of Christ," 61.

to find our true being-in-communion, in 'sonship,' in the mutual personal relations of love."[22] In the outworking of sanctification, God's primary purpose for humanity is not to adhere to external rules and regulations (judicial) but to participate by the Spirit in the Son's communion with the Father (filial). As we share by the Spirit in the Son's filial relationship with the Father, the outworking of sanctification is a natural consequence.

Conclusion: Claim and Liberation

John Webster has expressed the recurrent concern that this theology of Christ's vicarious humanity "may dissolve the human action in incarnational grace."[23] If Christ has accomplished everything for us in our place and on our behalf, there seems to be nothing for us to do. However, this is to wholly misunderstand the place of human action. Christ's vicarious humanity rightly diminishes any human response that is merit-based and therefore burdensome, and affirms human action in its proper place, that is, as a free and joyful response of sharing by the Spirit in what God has already accomplished in Christ. We are called to action, but this action comes from a contemporaneous place of rest and satisfaction in what has been definitively accomplished in Christ. Alasdair Heron wrote of Torrance:

> James Torrance has the rare gift of enabling the simplest parishioners, the most perplexed theological students to sense that they are fledglings destined and called to fly in the atmosphere of the eternal grace of God. The warm humanity of his personality is not only a natural gift; it is the radiation of conviction, the conviction of one who knows himself to be constrained by the love of Christ and can therefore do none other than express and convey this witness to others as both claim and liberation.[24]

---

22 James B. Torrance, "The Doctrine of the Trinity in our Contemporary Situation," in *The Forgotten Trinity: A Selection of Papers presented to the BCC Study Commission on Trinitarian Doctrine Today*, ed. Alasdair I. C. Heron (London: British Council of Churches, 1991), 15; Cf. Torrance, *Worship, Community and the Triune God of Grace*, 26–27; Torrance, "Prayer and the Priesthood of Christ," 60.

23 John Webster, "T.F. Torrance 1913–2007," *International Journal of Systematic Theology* 10:4 (2008), 371.

24 Alasdair Heron, "James Torrance: An Appreciation," *Christ in Our Place: The Humanity of God in Christ for the Reconciliation of the World: Essays Presented to James Torrance*, ed. Trevor Hart and Daniel Thimell (Exeter: Paternoster Press, 1989), 3. Cf. Alan Torrance: "His life and theology were characterized by a joy borne of

This chapter has sought to further explore what compelled Torrance by extending the liberating implications of his soteriology to the doctrine of sanctification. Humanity is wholly claimed in Christ prior to anything that we can contribute. An all-embracing claim is thereby placed upon humanity: the obligations of grace. However, sanctification is not a daunting, arduous endeavour. We are set free to grow into the ontological reality of who we are in Christ as we share by the Holy Spirit in the incarnate Son's intimate communion with the Father.

Torrance has a keen understanding of the prospective aspect of the atonement: we are not only retrospectively forgiven of our sins but also adopted as sons and daughters of God to share by the Spirit in the Son's communion with the Father.[25] Torrance has an insightful understanding of what Christ by the Spirit has done for us vicariously in human flesh but he does not offer much exposition on what a person's life in Christ by the Spirit might look like. Although Torrance does not spell out the shape of the Christian life, his life is a dynamic testament to the radical ethical and socio-political imperatives of his theology. Torrance boldly challenged apartheid in South Africa and the religious and political conflict in Northern Ireland.[26] However, the benefit of not statically spelling out the shape of the Christian life is that he evades the danger of moralistic interpretation. Moreover, whilst his theology might leave us with various questions regarding the Christian life, Torrance directs us to where we can find the ultimate answer: through participating by the Spirit in the Son's intimate communion with the Father.

---

knowing the welcoming hospitality of God in Christ and the overwhelming and liberating sense of belonging which that generated. His overwhelming desire in life was that all might know that it applied to them too." Alan J. Torrance, "The Bible as Testimony to Our Belonging: The Theological Vision of James B. Torrance," *An Introduction to Torrance Theology*, ed. Dawson, 119.

25 This language of "prospective" and "retrospective" comes from John McLeod Campbell, whose understanding of the atonement Torrance greatly admired and advanced. See John McLeod Campbell, *The Nature of the Atonement* (Edinburgh: Handsel, 1996).

26 See James B. Torrance, "Calvin and Puritanism in England and Scotland," Address to the Congress for the Advancement of Calvin Research, 12–14 August 1980, Pretoria, South Africa; James B. Torrance, "Southern Africa Today: The Kairos Debate: Listening to its Challenge," *Journal of Theology for Southern Africa* 55 (1986): 42–45.

Chapter 12

God in the Hands of Angry Sinners

C. Baxter Kruger

> The prime purpose of the incarnation, in the love of God, is to lift us up into a life of communion, of participation in the very triune life of God.[1]
>
> *James B. Torrance*

What was the Holy Spirit doing as Jesus was ridiculed, unjustly condemned, beaten and tortured, and then crucified on the cross? Jesus was conceived in the Spirit, baptized in the Spirit, lived his entire life in the Spirit, and offered himself up on the cross in the Spirit. How then do we understand the Holy Spirit in relation to those horrible hours of Good Friday? Captivated, as many of us have been by the penal theory of atonement, this question, as Moltmann notes,[2] rarely surfaces. There is little wonder. The theory contends that, as the Father placed the sin of the world upon Jesus, he then poured out his wrath upon Jesus instead of upon us who deserved it, hiding his face from Jesus, abandoning his own Son in utter rejection.

> The doctrine of penal substitution states that God gave himself in the person of his Son to suffer instead of us the death, punishment and curse due to fallen humanity as the penalty of sin ... That the Lord Jesus Christ died *for us* – a shameful death, bearing our curse, enduring our pain, suffering the wrath of his own Father in our place – has been the wellspring of the hope of countless Christians throughout the ages.[3]

---

1 James B. Torrance, *Worship, Community and the Triune God of Grace* (Carlisle: Paternoster Press, 1996), 21
2 See Jürgen Moltmann, *The Spirit of Life* (Minneapolis: Fortress Press, 1992), 62.
3 Steve Jeffery, Michael Ovey, Andrew Sach, *Pierced for Our Transgressions* (Wheaton: Crossway Books, 2007), 21.

One cannot but think of George MacDonald here: "Good souls many will one day be horrified at the things they now believe of God."[4]

In the context of the idea that the Father poured out his wrath on his own Son it is striking to ask about the Holy Spirit. What did the Holy Spirit do when the Father rejected his Son? What happened in the Holy Spirit's heart, if we may so speak, when the Father forsook his Son and cursed Jesus? If we accept this notion of the Father rejecting and damning his own Son on the cross then we are left with the Holy Spirit simply and profoundly torn between the two. Did the Holy Spirit have to choose a side? Which one? Or perhaps the Holy Spirit is like a mother caught between an angry husband and her only son. Perhaps here we see the reason there is so little discussion of the Holy Spirit in the context of Jesus' death. If what there is in us of a godly mind can manage to stomach the idea of an actual separation between the Father and Jesus, surely we are convicted of our folly to think of the Holy Spirit's heart being ripped apart as well.

But what if we reversed the theory? What if, instead of seeing the Father forsaking his own Son on the cross, we see the death of Jesus as the penetration of the oneness, the togetherness, the communion, the blessed life of the Father, Son and Holy Spirit into the gnarled abyss of our alienation? What if the death of Jesus is not about sinners in the hands of an angry God, but about the triune God in the hands of angry sinners? What if the crucifixion is not about abandonment, but its opposite, union? What if the purpose of Jesus' death is to find *us,* to establish his relationship with us in our sin and death and bondage, and to recreate us in the Holy Spirit?

> The prime purpose of the incarnation, in the love of God, is to lift *us* up into a life of communion, of participation in the very triune life of God.[5]

Or as St. Irenaeus said so beautifully, "our Lord Jesus Christ, who did, through his transcendent love, become what we are, that he might bring *us* to be even what he is himself."[6] The aim of Jesus' death was not to

---

4   George MacDonald, *Christ in Creation: Unspoken Sermons,* ed., by Rolland Hein (Vancouver: Regent College Publishing), 292.

5   James B. Torrance, *Worship, Community, and the Triune God of Grace* (Downers Grove: IVP), 21, emphasis added.

6   Irenaeus, *Against the Heresies,* in *The Ante-Nicene Fathers,* volume I (Grand Rapids: Eerdmans, 1987), V, preface, emphasis added.

suffer the wrath of his Father, but to make personal, healing, life-giving, forgiving contact with us sinners, at the root of our sin and alienation. He died to unite himself with us at our most sickening worst, and to make us sinners heirs with him of his *Father* and of the *Holy Spirit* (Rom. 8:17).

> For that was the very purpose and end of our Lord's Incarnation, that He should join what is man by nature to Him who is by nature God, that so man might enjoy His salvation and His union with God without any fear of its failing or decrease.[7]

Union

The purpose and the nature of atonement are found in the very identity of Jesus Christ, as are the work and heart of the Holy Spirit. As the early Church confessed in the Nicene Creed, Jesus Christ is the Father's eternal Son:

> Light from Light, true God from true God, begotten not made, of one substance with the Father (*homoousios to Patri*), through whom all things were made . . .

This confession was designed to call a halt to any notion that Jesus Christ was less than fully divine. He belongs to the circle of divine being, of the same being as the Father. What we meet in Jesus therefore is not a form that God assumed for a season in his relationship with us, but the living expression of God's eternal life. There was never a time, Athanasius argued against the Arians, when the Father was alone and simply God, not Father, without his Son and Spirit.[8] "The Holy Trinity is no created being."[9] The union of the Father, Son, and Spirit that we see so vividly lived out on the pages of the New Testament is not something that came into being two millennia ago. This is an eternal relationship, an eternal union predating creation.

As the Father's eternal Son, he is the one, as the apostles testify[10] and the Creed affirms, in and through and by and for whom all things were created and are sustained:

---

7   *The Orations of St. Athanasius Against the Arians* (London: Griffith, Farran, Okeden & Welsh), II.70; cf. III.34, and IV.6.

8   Ibid., I.11; 17-18. See also St. Hilary of Poitiers, *A Select Library of Nicene and Post-Nicene Fathers of the Christian Church*, second series (Grand Rapids: Wm. B. Eerdmans Publishing Company), *Exposition of the Orthodox Faith*, VIII.

9   Ibid., I.18.

10 See John 1:1-4; Col. 1:16-17; Heb. 1:1-3; 1 Cor. 8:6.

> In the beginning was the Word, and the Word was with God, and the Word was God. He was in the beginning with God. All things came into being by Him; and apart from Him nothing came into being that has come into being. In Him was life; and the life was the light of men (John 1:1-4).

Note these words from the cloud of witnesses.

> The simple meaning is that the Word of God was not only the fount of life to all creation, so that those which had not yet existed began to be, but that his life-giving power makes them remain in their state. For did not his continued inspiration quicken the world, whatsoever flourishes would without doubt immediately decay or be reduced to nothing.[11]

> All creatures, spiritual and material, are created in, through and by Christ . . . it is He Who sustains them in being. In Him they 'hold together.' Without Him they would fall apart.[12]

> There is already and always a relationship between the Son of God and the world and it now, uniquely, takes the form of personal presence.[13]

The critical point here, affirmed by Calvin, Merton, and Gunton, is that the eternal Son is the Creator and Sustainer of all things, and as such he is the source of our being, without whom we would simply

---

11   John Calvin, *The Gospel According to John*, translated by T. H. L. Parker (Grand Rapids: Eerdmans, 1988), 10-11. For more on Calvin's view of Christ as mediator of Creation, see Julie Canlis, *Calvin's Ladder* (Grand Rapids: Eerdmans, 2010), 55-61. Note also Calvin's comment on Acts 17:28: "Now, we see that all those who know not God know not themselves; because they have God present with them not only in the excellent gifts of the mind, but in their very essence; because it belongeth to God alone to be, all other things have their being in him. Also, we learn out of this place that God did not so create the world once that he did afterward depart from his work; but that it standeth by his power..." John Calvin, *Commentary from the Acts of the Apostles* (Grand Rapids: Baker Book House, reprinted 1981), 168-169.

12   Thomas Merton, *The New Man* (New York: Farrar, Straus and Giroux, 1961), 137.

13   Colin Gunton, *The Christian Faith* (Oxford: Blackwell Publishing, 2002), 98. Note here Thomas F. Torrance's comment: "Since he is the eternal Word of God by whom and through whom all things that are made are made, and in whom the whole universe of visible and invisible realities coheres and hangs together, and since in him divine and human natures are inseparably united, then the secret of every man, whether he believes or not, is bound up with Jesus, for it is in him that human contingent existence has been grounded and secured." Thomas F. Torrance, *The Trinitarian Faith* (Edinburgh: T&T Clark, 1988), 183.

disappear, or "lapse back into non-existence," to borrow again from Athanasius.[14] Before he became incarnate, the Son of the Father already had a relationship with the human race.

When this Son became a human being he was not therefore *creating* a relationship with the human race; he was establishing his existing relationship, his existing union with all things *inside his humanity*. On the one side, the incarnation was not an event of divine divorce. When the eternal Son became human, he did not leave the Holy Spirit behind or abandon his Father. It is the One who is *homoousios to Patri*, and the Son who is in the Holy Spirit who became flesh, establishing his union with his Father, and his anointing in the Holy Spirit in his humanity. On the other side, the One who became human is the "*arche* of the creation of God" (Rev. 3:14), the source and meaning of all creation. All things have their existence in him. St. John is emphatic, "apart from him nothing came into being." The very identity of Jesus Christ speaks volumes. Note here the beautiful summation of Thomas F. Torrance:

> With the Incarnation, God the eternal Son became Man, without ceasing to be God and without breaking the communion of the Holy Trinity within which God lives his own divine life. In the birth and life of Jesus on earth human nature and divine nature were inseparably united in the eternal Person of God the Son. Therefore in him the closed circle of the inner life of God was made to overlap with human life, and human nature was taken up to share in the eternal communion of the Father and the Son in the Holy Spirit.[15]

In Jesus Christ – the incarnate Son – the Father, the Holy Spirit, the human race, and all creation are not separated, but *together in relationship*. The incarnate Son, Jesus Christ himself, is the relationship. For in him, in his own person the blessed Trinity and broken humanity are united. His humanity is the union.

Standing before this Jesus we are poised to see the nature of the atonement as the union not only of the Son and our humanity, but the union of the incarnate Son (and his Father, and the Holy Spirit) and us sinners. "The Word became *flesh*" (John 1:14, *sarx*, not simply *anthropos*).

---

14   Athanasius, *On the Incarnation of the Word of God*, (London: A. R. Mowbray, 1963), §6.

15   Thomas F. Torrance, "Come, Creator Spirit, for the Renewal of Worship and Witness," in *Theology in Reconstruction* (Grand Rapids: Wm. B. Eerdmans Publishing Company, 1975 reprint), 241.

For what benefit would there be for us sinners – blind and broken, faithless and trapped in the alienation and bondage of the evil one – if Jesus assumed our humanity, yet did not reach our *flesh?*[16]

The incarnation, and the death of the incarnate Son are about union with us. Anything less than the true, real, personal union of Jesus Christ – the Father's eternal Son incarnate, and the One anointed in the Holy Spirit – with the fallen human race is unworthy of the word 'salvation.' Here the penal substitution theory, with its vicarious punishment and imputed righteousness, proves itself inadequate, and profoundly too impersonal. The legal tradition of the Latin West is haunted, if not outright embarrassed, by a single question from St. Gregory Nazianzen: "How does this touch me?"[17] What real benefit is it to us to be declared legally clean, and to be given a robe of external righteousness, when we are still broken, alien, sinful inside? Who, to remember MacDonald again,[18] will ever be comfortable in the presence of the Father, Son, and Holy Spirit in whom there is no darkness (1 John 1:5) or even a hint of shadows when all they have is an imputed righteousness covering the alienation residing within their hearts?

Did not Jesus himself pray that *we* would be *in* him, and with him where he was? "Father, I desire that they also whom thou hast given me, be with me where I am" (John 17:24). And where is Jesus but face to face with his Father, in his bosom? (John 1:1; 18). The broken, indeed evil

---

16   Note here St. Gregory's famous statement: "For that which He has not assumed He has not healed; but that which is united to His Godhead is also saved. If only half Adam fell, then that which Christ assumes and saves may be half also; but if the whole of his nature fell, it must be united to the whole nature of Him that was begotten, and so be saved as a whole," Gregory Nazianzen, *A Select Library of the Nicene and Post-Nicene Fathers of the Christian Church,* second series, vol. VII (Edinburgh: T&T Clark), Ep. CI. Note also St. Athanasius: "As, on the one hand, we could not have been redeemed from sin and the curse, unless the flesh and nature, which the Word took upon Him had been truly ours (for we should have had no interest by his assumption of any foreign nature); so also man could not have been united to the Divine nature, unless that Word, which was made flesh, had not been, in essence and nature, the Word and Son of God. For that was the very purpose and end of our Lord's Incarnation, that He should join what is man by nature to Him who is by nature God, that so man might enjoy His salvation and His union with God without any fear of its failing or decrease," *The Orations of St. Athanasius Against the Arians,* II.70; see also I.40; and Irenaeus, *Against the Heresies,* V.14.3.

17   Gregory Nazianzen, *A Select Library,* Ep CI.

18   Here see especially the sermons, "Justice," "The Last Penny," and "Righteousness," in George MacDonald, *Christ in Creation: Unspoken Sermons,* ed., by Rolland Hein (Vancouver: Regent College Publishing), 63-81, 167-176, 177-187, respectively.

conscience can never stand on external accounting in the presence of divine, shadowless light. What is needed is the mind, the heart, the soul of Jesus Christ himself, the love of Jesus in his union with his Father in the Holy Spirit, setting up shop, as it were, inside the very core of our alienation. Anything less leaves the broken and alienated us destitute of the trinitarian life – legally clean perhaps – but lost to the communion of the Father, Son and Holy Spirit. "I have made Thy name know to them, and *will* make it known; that the love wherewith Thou didst love Me may be in them, and I in them" (John 17:26). "And this is eternal life, that they may know Thee, the only true God, and Jesus Christ whom Thou hast sent" (John 17:3).

Submission

Yet how is Jesus to make contact with us in our fallen humanity? How is he to bring his union with us in his humanity into our alienation? How is he to unite sinners with the Holy Spirit, and lost sons and daughters with his Father? How does Jesus Christ *reach us,* and deliver *us* from evil? Not by suffering the wrath of his Father, but by *submitting to us* in our darkness. The crucifixion of Jesus Christ – the Father's eternal Son incarnate, the One anointed in the Holy Spirit – involves the shocking submission of the blessed Trinity in him to us as sinners in our greatest iniquity as it took shape in the murdering tutelage of the father of lies.

Note this beautiful vision of heaven penned by Jonathan Edwards:

> There, even in heaven, dwells the God from whom every stream of holy love, yea, every drop that is, or ever was, proceeds. There dwells God the Father, God the Son, and God the Spirit, united as one, in infinitely dear, and incomprehensible, and mutual, and eternal love. There dwells God the Father, who is the father of mercies, and so the father of love, who so loved the world as to give his only-begotten Son to die for it . . . There dwells Christ in both his natures, the human and the divine, sitting on the same throne with the Father. And there dwells the Holy Spirit – the Spirit of divine love, in whom the very essence of God, as it were, flows out, and is breathed forth in love, and by whose immediate influence all holy love is shed abroad in the hearts of all the saints on earth and in heaven. There, in heaven this

infinite fountain of love – this eternal Three in One – is set open without any obstacle to hinder access to it, as it flows for ever.[19]

Edwards is here at his theological and poetical best, painting this breathtaking picture of the cascading fountain of trinitarian life and love. If we but change the *location* of Edward's infinite fountain from 'heaven' to 'our hell' we will at once behold the astonishing meaning of Jesus Christ as atonement in himself, "the Lamb of God who takes away the sin of the world," and "the one who baptizes in the Holy Spirit" (John 1:29, 33). *There* – not removed from us – but *inside us,* inside our death and appalling blindness, inside the trauma of our sin and alienation, *in our hell,* "this infinite fountain of love – this eternal Three in One – is set open without any obstacle to hinder access to it." This is what Jesus Christ did on the cross; he reached us sinners in our greatest sin; he united all that he is with his Father in the Holy Spirit – the life, the communion, the fullness, the holiness, the righteousness and joy – with us in our unrighteous collusion with the wicked one, and its iniquity and death, and terrorizing guilt and shame.

Jesus loved us. Jesus found us, embraced us, accepted us as we had become in the dastardly schemes of evil. How did Jesus Christ reach us? How did he penetrate the terror of our souls? How did the Son of the highest unite himself with us at our lowest? How did the one who was rich become poor (2 Cor. 8:9), and he who knew no sin become sin on our behalf? (2 Cor. 5:21). Here, we can agree with the penal theory that that key was Jesus' submission to the will of his Father. Yet we refuse to accept the perverse notion that it was his Father's will to pour out his wrath upon his own Son.[20]

Scripture is clear. The insolence, the scorn, the mocking derision, the despising shame, the wrath poured out on Calvary's hill did not originate in

---

19 Jonathan Edwards, *Charity and Its Fruits* (Edinburgh: The Banner of Truth Trust, reprinted 1982), 327-328.

20 Note here St. Hilary's comment on his antagonist's misuse of *'The Eloi.'* "They construe this into the expression of a bitter complaint, that He was deserted and given over to weakness. But what a violent interpretation of an irreligious mind! How repugnant to the whole tenor of our Lord's words! He hastened to the death, which was to glorify Him, and after which He was to sit on the right hand of power; with all those blessed expectations could He fear death, and therefore complain that His God had betrayed Him to its necessity, when it was the entrance to eternal blessedness?" St. Hilary of Poitiers, *A Select Library of Nicene and Post-Nicene Fathers of the Christian Church,* second series (Grand Rapids: Wm. B. Eerdmans Publishing Company), *On the Trinity,* X.49.

the Father's heart, but in ours.[21] "Behold, we are going up to Jerusalem; and the Son of Man will be delivered up to the chief priests and scribes, and they will condemn him to death, and will deliver him up to the Gentiles to mock and scourge and crucify him."[22] It was not the Father or the Holy Spirit who beat Jesus, detested him, cursed him, and abandoned him; it was the human race. *We mocked him. We cursed him. We crucified him.* As Jesus himself suffered our rejection, as he endured our betrayal, and submitted himself to bear our hostility, he was personally entering into our iniquity. The Lord was causing the iniquity of us all to encounter or meet (*paga*) him, as Isaiah prophesied (Isa. 53:6, cf. Heb. 9:28; 1 Pet. 2:24).

Here is shocking, amazing grace, divine, humble, and astonishing love. He came to his own and his own received him not (John 1:11). Indeed his own damned him with a curse, siding with the enemy in blasphemy.

> Away with *him,* away with *him,* crucify him!
> Pilate said to them, "Shall I crucify your King?"
> The chief priests answered, "We have no king but Caesar"
> (John 19:15).

"He was despised and forsaken of men," as foreseen by the prophet (Isa. 53:3). "For consider him who has endured such hostility by sinners against himself" (Heb. 12:3). Down, down he went, into the twisted abyss of darkness, into the shame, into the perversion of our humanity, underneath the waves of evil's bitterness as it took form in our curses. "Cursed," St. Paul says, interpreting Moses, "is every one who hangs on a tree" (Gal. 3:13), and the apostle deliberately misquotes Moses, leaving "by God" out of his apostolic mind. For it was not the curse of his Father that the merciful Son endured, but ours. For how could the One who knows the Father meet us in our darkness where his Father is unknown except by allowing us to pour our enmity upon him until the waves of our misery overcame him and he at last had our eyes in the great darkness?

---

21 For more of my thoughts here, see *The Shack Revisited* (New York: Faith Words, 2012), 179-195; and *Across All Worlds* (Jackson: Perichoresis Press, 2007 and Vancouver: Regent College Publishing, 2007).

22 Matt. 20:18-19; see also 16:21; Mark 10:33-34; Luke 24:7; John 18:35; 19:16, 18, and Heb. 12:3.

"My God, my God, why have You forsaken me?" (Matt. 27:46; Mark 15:34 Ps. 22:1). This was a cry of true identification with us. Here Jesus made contact with the bottom of the abyss, with Adam in his treachery trembling in the bushes, with us and our broken eyes in blackest darkness, where fear has refused all light and hope, and the Father's face is tarred with the brush of evil's insanity. Here, in this place, in this prison of twisted lies, in this trauma of hopelessness where the Holy Spirit can scarcely be felt, Jesus comes to seek and to save that which is lost (Luke 19:10).

Of that moment none can know.[23] It had to be. His love drove him to meet us as we were, and to become what we are. No fragment of our broken, guilt-ridden humanity could be lost. For his joy, his Father's mission, the desire of his heart was to bring blind sinners to see, to hear, to *know* his Father, to "bring us to God" (1 Pet. 3:18), and "many sons to glory" (Heb. 2:10), to bathe in the fountain of the communion of the blessed Trinity. He had to submit himself to our blindness. He had to find the real us. But not for a moment did his Father or the Holy Spirit forsake him in his pain. This is not the story of divine abandonment, but of shocking grace, wherein the Son of the Father finds his way to the bottom of our sea. He submits himself to the destructive forces of our disaster, and as he does, as he identifies with us to the full he takes on our eyes, sees what we see, and feels what we feel, without ever losing his trust in his Father's presence and love. Never – not for the slightest moment, from all eternity – had he not seen his Father's face or felt the Spirit's presence. But now he comes to us. Now he meets us in the terror of evil's darkness. We damned him, and without a word he accepted our damnation – and he died in the horror of the great delusion.[24]

---

23   Note George MacDonald's insight: "It was a cry *in* desolation, but it came out of Faith. It is the last voice of Truth speaking when it can but cry. The divine horror of that moment is unfathomable by the human soul. It was blackness of darkness. And yet he would believe. Yet he would hold fast. God was his God yet. *My God* – and in the cry came forth the Victory, and all was over soon. Of the peace that followed that cry, the peace of a perfect soul, large as the universe, pure as light, ardent as life, victorious for God and his brethren, he himself alone can ever know the breadth and length, and depth and height." "The Eloi," in *Unspoken Sermons, Series 1-3 in One Volume* (Whitethorn, California: Johannesen, second printing, 1999), 112.

24   Note MacDonald again: "Never had it been so with Him before. Never before had He been unable to see God beside Him. Yet never was God nearer Him than now. For never was Jesus more divine. He could not see, could not feel Him near; and yet it is 'My God' that He cries," George MacDonald, *Christ in Creation*, 334.

The Psalm declares to us the hidden truth that in this moment of terror, when the incarnate Son's vision joined ours in the deep darkness, and he identified with us in our sin, when he cried out in the terrible pain of the cloud of unknowing, his Father's love stood fast as always. "For he has not despised nor abhorred the affliction of the afflicted; neither has he hidden his face from him; but when he cried to him for help, he heard" (Ps. 22:24).[25] Crying out, "It is finished!" (John 19:30), Jesus breathed his last breath in the trauma of our dungeon, "Father, into thy hands I commit My Spirit" (Luke 23:46).

It was not his Father who banished his own Son from life, but us. And our blessed Lord Jesus received our judgment, bowed before it, suffered its loathsome anger, and in doing so turned our rejection into the mercy seat, the place where the triune God personally endured the hostility of sinners in our bondage to evil. He died in the arms of our betrayal – *and he was not alone.* The Father and the Holy Spirit were in him. "God was in Christ," as St. Paul teaches (2 Cor. 5:19; see Heb. 9:14). "Behold an hour is coming, and has already come, for you to be scattered, each to his own home, and to leave me alone; yet I am not alone, because the Father is with me" (John 16:32). It is precisely this "withness" that constitutes the atonement, and the way of our salvation. Neither the Holy Spirit nor the Father were spectators to the pain of Jesus. This was not a moment when the Holy Spirit was torn between two loves; this was the moment of the astonishing humility of the triune God, wherein the Father was in his Son and the Holy Spirit refused to be absent, and together in Jesus himself the unspeakable communion of the blessed Trinity found its way inside our estrangement, establishing forever the fountain of overflowing life inside the broken cistern of our alienated humanity.

Can we not hear Jesus' heart? "Father, I desire that they also, whom thou hast given me, be with me where I am, in order that they may behold my glory" (John 17:24). He is saying, "Father, I desire that they may see my essential nature as your Son, the anointed One, the One in whom my brothers and sisters live and move and have their being, that they may be liberated to live in the freedom of my heart, that they may *know* that I am in you, and they are in me, and I am in them (John 14:20). Father, in the Holy Spirit, I will go into the belly of the beast to bring good

---

25 See John McLeod Campbell, *The Nature of the Atonement* (Edinburgh: Handsel Press, and Grand Rapids: Eerdmans, 1996), 202 ff. Note the striking progression of Psalms 22, 23, and 24, foreshadowing the death, resurrection, and ascension of Jesus Christ.

news to the afflicted, to heal the broken hearted, and to deliver my family from the evil one (Isa. 61:1; Luke 4:18). I will submit myself to the wrath and anger, the malice and injustice, the unholiness and bitter rage that originates in the father of lies, and yet has now formed in their minds and hearts and wills." "I have made Thy name known to them, and *will* make it known" (John 17:26). "I will enact your forgiveness. I will judge them, I will discern good from evil in them, divide evil from their hearts, and condemn sin in the flesh (Rom. 8:3; Heb. 4:12). I will take my brothers and sisters, and all creation, down in my death. As I allow myself to be damned by the human race in its collusion with evil's schemes, I will 'commit my spirit' to your care, to our oneness, to our communion, in everlasting agreement with your heart and with the Holy Spirit, in whom our oneness reigns. I will wait for you my Father, and for the Holy Spirit in the great darkness that our union and communion in the Holy Spirit may quicken me and all creation with life as I see your face."

And so Jesus turned toward Calvary, and the human race, both Jew and Gentile, joined as one man against the Father's Son. He submitted himself to us in our blindness. As we murdered the Father's Son incarnate, he established his existing union with us, and with creation, inside our sin, using our rejection of himself as his way of union with us as sinners. In the insanity of darkness we cut off the Father's Son incarnate, and he accepted our murder and transformed it into the way of our adoption, the reconstitution of our relationship with the triune God. In Jesus Christ, the Holy Spirit and the Father have descended into our hell, and used our betrayal of Jesus as the way to get there. Jesus is in himself the one mediator between God and fallen humanity (1 Tim. 2:5), the very place where the life of the blessed Trinity intersects our dying and death.

> Behold, the tabernacle of God is among men, and he shall dwell among them, and they shall be his people, and God himself shall be among them, and he shall wipe away every tear from their eyes; and there shall no longer be any death; there shall no longer be any mourning, or pain; the first things have passed away. And he who sits on the throne said, "Behold, I am making all things new." And he said, "Write, for these words are faithful and true." And he said to me, "It is done. I am the Alpha and the Omega, the beginning and the end. I will give to the one who thirsts from the spring of the water of life without cost" (Rev. 21:3-6).

The Father and the Holy Spirit

As we focus on the Father's presence in Jesus' suffering, or on the fact that far from rejecting Jesus and abandoning him at the crucial hour, "God was in Christ" (2 Cor. 5:19), we are given eyes to see the deep, inner meaning of our justification, reconciliation, and adoption in Christ. Justification is not a mere external verdict, but the "end of us as sinners"[26] in Jesus' death. In Jesus Christ, Adam and his fall, and we in Adam were taken to our end, delivered up to destruction, crucified, put to death, and buried.[27] Reconciliation is not a legal arrangement wherein we were forensically forgiven consequent upon Jesus' suffering our punishment. Reconciliation is our end and new beginning in Jesus himself as we were recreated in his resurrection in at-one-ment with the Father in Jesus.[28] Adoption is not an abstract doctrine; it is reality. In Jesus – as he accepted our beatings, our scorn, our despising betrayal unto death – the Father was finding us, the broken, rebellious, sinful us, and there he embraced us, and using our crucifixion of his Son *for* us (or, *against* us), he put us to death in him, and brought us to life in Jesus in his resurrection, and lifted us up in his ascension into his own life with his Son. Who cannot but marvel at the redemptive genius at work here? Our contribution to our justification, and reconciliation, and to our inclusion in the life of the blessed Trinity was to reject and kill the Father's eternal Son incarnate. And the Father transformed our treachery into our own death, resurrection and ascension in Christ, using our sin as the way of his forgiving embrace.

What was the Holy Spirit doing as Jesus became "the likeness of sinful flesh" (Rom. 8:3) and entered the domain of darkness? Refusing to abandon the beloved Son, the Holy Spirit was *in* Jesus submitting himself to angry sinners as "his *companion* in suffering."[29] "On Golgotha the Spirit suffers the suffering and death of the Son without dying with

---

26 Karl Barth, *Church Dogmatics*, (Edinburgh: T&T Clark), V/I, 253.

27 See Barth, *Church Dogmatics*, V/I, 250-256; 295-296; 93-96. For a collection of striking quotes from a diverse group of Christian writers on our death and resurrection in Jesus see "Appendix: A Few Quotations on Our Inclusion in Jesus' Death," in C. Baxter Kruger, *The Shack Revisited*, 253-259.

28 If we must speak of the wrath of God in the context of the death of Jesus, then Jesus himself is the wrath of God, the fiery, passionate, holy, unrelenting divine opposition to our destruction. This opposition, this wrath of the Father, Son and Holy Spirit is embodied in Jesus' vicarious death, and is 'satisfied' in our resurrection and recreation and ascension in Jesus.

29 Jurgen Moltmann, *The Spirit of Life*, 62.

him."[30] As Jesus endured our hostility, the Holy Spirit was finding his way inside our death and alienation.

> Hence in the union of divine and human natures in the Son the eternal Spirit of the living God has composed himself, as it were, to dwell with human nature, and human nature has been adapted and become accustomed to receive and bear that same Holy Spirit.[31]

In fellowship with Jesus, the Holy Spirit, according to Irenaeus, "accustomed" himself "to dwell in the human race, to rest with human beings, and to dwell in the workmanship of God."[32] And did so not as a watered down spirit, but as the Holy Spirit, "the Lord, and giver of life."[33]

On the one hand, the ongoing, unbroken relationship between the Holy Spirit and Jesus becomes the way of his resurrection and victory.

> It is precisely his suffering with the Son to the point of death on the cross which makes the rebirth of Christ from the Spirit inwardly possible. The Spirit participates in the dying of the Son in order to give him new "life from the dead." Because he accompanies Christ to his end, he can make this end the new beginning.[34]

Who can fathom the mystery here? The Holy Spirit cannot die, yet must enter death, and did, in Jesus. Moreover, if the Holy Spirit is "the eternal light in which the Father knows the Son and the Son the Father,"[35] and if eternal life is knowing the Father, as Jesus teaches (John 17:3), then the

---

30   Ibid., 64.

31   T. F. Torrance, "Come, Creator Spirit," in *Theology in Reconstruction*, 246; see also Thomas F. Torrance, *The Trinitarian Faith*, 189.

32   Irenaeus, *Against the Heresies*, III.17.1; see also III.20.2; III.18.7; III.19.1; and IV.20.4.

33   "He came as the Spirit who in Jesus has penetrated into a new intimacy with our human nature, for he came as the Spirit in whom Jesus lived through our human life from end to end, from birth to death, and beyond into the resurrection. And therefore he came not as isolated and naked Spirit, but as Spirit charged with all the experience of Jesus as he shared to the full our mortal nature and weakness, and endures its temptation and grief and suffering and death, and with the experience of Jesus as he struggled and prayed, and worshipped and obeyed, and poured out his life in compassion for mankind." Thomas F. Torrance, "Come, Creator Spirit, for the Renewal of Worship and Witness," in *Theology in Reconstruction*, 246-247.

34   Jürgen Moltmann, *The Spirit of Life* (Minneapolis: Fortress Press, 1992), 68.

35   Jürgen Moltmann, *The Trinity and the Kingdom of God* (London: SCM Press, 1981), 176.

resurrection of Jesus from the dead is integrated with the awakening of Jesus' communion with his Father in the Spirit. Accompanying Jesus on the cross the Holy Spirit becomes the eternal light shining in the darkness of Jesus' death revealing to him the Father's face in the grave. In the Spirit, the unspeakable communion of the Father and Son, "this infinite fountain of love" found its way inside the netherworld of our darkness and death and bondage leading into Jesus' resurrection, and triumph over the forces of darkness. Hereby he rendered "powerless him who had the power of death, that is, the devil" (Heb. 2:14), and he took "captive a host of captives" (Eph. 4:8).

On the other hand, the unbroken relationship between the Holy Spirit and Jesus becomes the way of our recreation in communion with the Father in Jesus – the answer to Jesus' prayer. The crucifixion and resurrection of the incarnate Son constitutes the recreation of all things in the Holy Spirit, in Jesus Christ himself, and the eternal reordering of divine-human relationship. Not only was the Father in Christ together with the Holy Spirit, but recall that in his incarnation Jesus established his existing relationship with us in his own humanity, and now in dying establishes his relationship with us, and with all creation, in our death. Jesus alone died, but he was not alone. As the apostles testify, when Jesus died, we died (2 Cor. 5:14). When he rose, we rose. "Blessed be the God and Father of our Lord Jesus Christ, who according to His great mercy has caused us to be born again to a living hope through the resurrection of Jesus Christ from the dead" (1 Pet. 1:3). There and then, in infinite, overflowing mercy, the triune God "made us alive together with Christ . . . and raised us up with him, and seated us with him in the heavenly places in Christ Jesus" (Eph. 2:4-6; cf. Col. 3:1-4).[36]

The outpouring of the Holy Spirit upon "all flesh" (*sarx*, Acts 2:17; Joel 2:28) at Pentecost is the natural fruit of the Holy Spirit accompanying Jesus into death in his union with us in our "flesh" (*sarx*, John 1:14). Pentecost is the manifestation of our inclusion in Jesus' own baptism in the Holy Spirit. In Jesus, and in his death, the Holy Spirit meets us, relates himself to us, knows us, and understands us in our plight. Having found his way inside our alienation in Jesus' suffering, the Holy Spirit (and

---

36 "We needed an Incarnate God, a God put to death, that we might live. We were put to death together with Him, that we might be cleansed; we rose again with Him because we were put to death with Him; we were glorified with Him, because we rose again with Him," Gregory Nazianzen, *A Select Library*, The Second Oration on Easter," XXVIII.

all his gifts) knows how to give us ears to hear Jesus' own cry, "Abba! Father!" (Gal. 4:6; Rom. 8:15). Having accustomed or attuned himself to us in our darkness, the Holy Spirit knows how to fulfill Jesus' prophecy: "In that day, you shall know that I am in my Father, and you in me, and I in you" (John 14:20). As the Holy Spirit 'composed' himself to dwell in us in Jesus, he is now at work inside our shattered souls 'recomposing' us from the inside out. This work of the Holy Spirit is not an abstract word from on high. This is an internal work, inside our inner worlds, involving an ongoing revelation not "to" our intellect of a distant Savior and an external salvation, but an unveiling "in" us of Jesus himself (Gal. 1:16), "Christ in you, the hope of glory" (Col. 1:27), an unveiling which manifests our union with Jesus in his death, resurrection and ascension into the Father's embrace.

In the Holy Spirit, the living Word (*logos*) speaks (*rhema*) to us in person, inside our own broken hearts, inside the bizarre world of lies that beset our wounded minds, inside the dastardly delusion. As Jesus addresses us in the Spirit, our alien and hostile minds (Col. 1:21), our afflicted conscience (Heb. 9:9-14), our ignorance, our darkened understanding, and alienation from the life of God (Eph. 4:18) are gradually discerned and revealed to us. In the Spirit, the healing light of the triune God searches and exposes, the Word pierces and divides (Heb. 4:12) and we are given the mind of Jesus himself (1 Cor. 2:16), and seeing through Jesus' own eyes we are liberated to reject darkness and evil, and to turn (*pros*) face to face with his Father in the Holy Spirit.[37]

Now, in the creative presence and witness of the Holy Spirit, "charged with all the experience of Jesus as he shared to the full our mortal nature and weakness,"[38] by the authority (*exousia*) of his own inner knowing, and his own unearthly assurance (*parrhesia*) which he shares with us, Jesus commands us to believe, to agree with him, to take sides with him against the way we see his Father, and ourselves, and others, to rise in his courage and faith and faithfulness, breaking all agreements with the wicked one, and to open our hearts to the Father himself, to receive his forgiveness, his love, his embrace, and to live in "the freedom of the glory of the children of God" (Rom. 8:21) in the Holy Spirit. There, inside of our own broken souls 'this infinite fountain of love – this eternal Three in One – is set open without any obstacle to

---

37 Note here John 1:1 (*pros ton Theon*) and 14:6 (*pros ton patera*).
38 See note 32.

hinder access to it, as it flows for ever' becoming a river of living water flowing out of our innermost beings (John 7:38).

A Prayer[39]

Lord Jesus Christ, beloved and eternal Son of the Father, *Homoousios to Patri,* anointed of the Holy Spirit, incarnate, crucified, resurrected and ascended Lord of all creation, I believe in you. With great joy, with the praise of my whole heart I acknowledge and agree that you have found me in my darkness and sin, laid hold of me and taken me down in your death, freed me from sin and evil, quickened me with new life in your resurrection, and lifted me up into your Father's arms in your ascension. All of me, and mine, every war-torn fragment, every fearful, unbelieving, broken part is in you, in your Father, in the Holy Spirit. I rest in you, Jesus, lover of my soul, my Savior, my Salvation, my Saving Act, my King, my Liberator, the author and finisher of my faith, healer of my wounded heart. You have included me in all that you are and have in your union and face-to-face communion with your Father, and you have included me in your own anointing in the Holy Spirit. You have included me in your victory over evil and wickedness, and in your session at the Father's right hand, above all rule and authority in heaven and on earth. Nothing can separate me from you, your Father, and the Holy Spirit.

Worthy are you Lord Jesus Christ, Father's Son, Anointed One, Lamb of God who takes away the sin of the world, the One who baptizes in the Holy Spirit, Victorious Warrior, worthy are you of all praise and adoration and worship, now and forever. Thank you for being my Savior, my Good Shepherd, my High Priest, my true and faithful witness, the Captain of my salvation, my Alpha and Omega, healer of my broken soul. I rest in you, and await your Word to me today. Amen.

C. Baxter Kruger (Ph.D., Aberdeen) is the author of 8 books, including *The Great Dance, Across All Worlds,* and the international bestseller, *The Shack Revisited.* He resides in Brandon, Mississippi with his wife Beth of 31 years. He is the Director of Perichoresis, an international ministry proclaiming the truth of our adoption in Jesus Christ to the world. Dr. Kruger's website is www.perichoresis.org.

---

39   This is part of a larger prayer originally posted as a blog on "Baxter's Ongoing Thoughts," October 7, 2013 (http://www.perichoresis.org/baxters-blog.html). Used by permission from Perichoresis, Inc.

Chapter 13

Lifting of the Curse: Athanasius on Making Sense of the Divine "Wrath" and "Propitiation" in the Doctrine of Reconciliation

Robert C. Doyle

Contemporary Difficulties

Several contemporary authors and song writers in the Evangelical tradition reflect the difficulties the Christian tradition has faced in giving an appropriate and lucid account of two recurring themes in the Bible's presentation of atonement – the wrath of God, and propitiation. On the one hand, we are invited to sing "He chose to send his precious only Son, to punish him for sins we've done,"[1] and on the other, to believe that "for Paul, wrath is not a divine property or essential attribute of God... (1 Thess. 1:9-10) Even in this context, divine anger or retributive justice are alien concepts, since these assume... that God's sense of holiness must be requited."[2] "Christ's work... is primarily directed toward human sin and not God's wrath."[3] Now, all these authors nuance their understandings in ways that both reflect the biblical material and moderate the seeming starkness of the statements cited above. Further, it is quite proper to note that, unlike love and holiness that eternally mark the relations between the persons of the Trinity,

---

1   "At the Cross", words by Bryson Smith, music by Philip Percival. 1996 Plainsong Version, © Words: 1996 Emu Music Australia, Inc. URL: http://www.harptabs.com/song.php?ID=10130.

2   Joel B Green & Mark D. Baker, *Recovering the Scandal of the Cross: Atonement in the New Testament & Contemporary Contexts* (Downers Grove: InterVarsity Press, 2000), 54.

3   Stanley J. Grenz, *Theology for the Community of God* (Grand Rapids: Eerdmans, 2000), 347.

wrath is a response of that love and holiness to the depths of human wickedness. But that is not the same as making wrath in some sense distant from who God is in himself and his saving acts in the world.

These contemporary formulations are, of course, far from the radical solution offered by C. H. Dodd, in which the wrath of God is a somewhat impersonal "inevitable process of cause and effect in a moral universe."[4] Indeed, wide-ranging biblical studies, while appreciative of the depth of C. H. Dodd's work, will affirm that in the Old and New Testaments "the *orgē* word-group serves to illustrate the character of God", and that John the Baptist, Jesus and Paul stress the reality of the future wrathful judgment of God whom Israel and the rest of Adam's race have deeply and personally offended.[5] With respect to "propitiation", the *kipper* group in the Hebrew Bible and *hilaskomai* group in the Greek Testaments are not reducible to just expiation or removal of sin. Colin Brown concludes that C. K. Barrett's comments on Paul's use in Romans can be applied to Old Testament passages too: "It would be wrong to neglect the fact that expiation has, as it were, the effect of propitiation; the sin that might have excited God's wrath is expiated (at God's will) and therefore no longer does so."[6] After canvassing the options for understanding *hilastērion* in Romans 3:25, C. E. B. Cranfield follows Chrysostom in affirming:

> On the whole it seems best to accept (iv) ("a propitiatory sacrifice"). . . . We take it that what Paul's statement that God purposed Christ as a propitiatory victim means is that God, because in his mercy he willed to forgive sinful men and, being truly merciful, willed to forgive them righteously, that is, without in any way condoning their sin, purposed to direct against his own very Self in the person of his Son the full weight of that righteous wrath which they deserved.[7]

---

4   *The Epistle of Paul to the Romans* (London: Hodder, 1932), 23.

5   H. C. Hahn, "Anger," in *The New International Dictionary of Evangelical Theology, volume 1: A-F*, ed. Colin Brown (Exeter: Paternoster Press, 1975), 111, and passim 105-13.

6   *The Epistle to the Romans* (London: Adams and Charles Black, 1957), 78. Cited from C. Brown "ἱλασκομαι," *The New International Dictionary of Evangelical Theology, volume 3: Pri-Z*, ed. Colin Brown (Exeter: Paternoster Press, 1978), 157, and passim 148-66. See also N. T. Wright's comments on Romans 3:25-26, with reference to the debate concerning propitiation versus expiation, in *Interpreter's Bible Commentary* volume 10, ed. P. J. Sampley et al. (Nashville: Abingdon, 1998), pp. 519-20.

7   *The Epistle to the Romans, volume 1* (Edinburgh: T. & T. Clark, 1975), 216-7, and footnote 1.

But there is a current pushback on viewing the propitiatory elements of atonement in this way. In a Mennonite tradition of affirming a "nonviolent God", drawing on contemporary scholarship that further develops C. H. Dodd's views,[8] J. Denny Weaver has argued for an acceptance of a divine wrath that is interpreted in his narrative Christus Victor model of atonement as representing one of the two stances from which we, the human race, view the salvation drama, love being the other. "Wrath" signifies "an act of judgment as long as we continue in bondage to the powers of evil that enslave us."[9] The Son carries out the Father's will not by in any sense being a propitiation of a personal divine wrath, but by making the nonviolent reign of God visible in the world. This is the Jesus we meet in the scriptural narrative. In him, as the "mercy seat", we have both stances from which to view the atonement. As the "mercy seat" (*hilastērion*), the crucified Christ is the "the throne of God's presence – where atonement is made."[10] Although nonviolent, Jesus' confrontation of the evil powers was an active resistance, not passive, and it cost him his life. The resurrection vindicates Jesus' revelation of the Father's nonviolent and liberating will for his creation, and is the defeat of the evil powers. It now enables a discipleship that itself resists evil and "upholds a message of liberation for both oppressed and oppressors."[11]

In this way, through our involvement in the divine drama, Weaver draws together atonement and discipleship into an indissoluble whole, unlike more abstract satisfaction theories which separate the believer from the cross event. In the context of Weaver's argument for a narrative Christus Victor model, "wrath", then, is reconfigured away from a personal outpouring of righteous anger by the holy and merciful God of Israel to a standpoint from which we can appropriately view our all-too-human bondage to evil. We see "wrath" not from God's perspective, for he is essentially nonviolent, but that of the narrative and our involvement in it as sinners in willing bondage to the evil powers.[12]

---

8   For example: Arland J. Hultgren, *Paul's Gospel and Mission* (Philadelphia: Fortress, 1985), 54, 57. Cited by Weaver, *The Nonviolent Atonement*, 2nd ed. (Grand Rapids: Eerdmans, 2011), 67-8.
9   *Nonviolent Atonement*, 98.
10 Weaver citing Hultgren. Ibid., 67-8.
11 Ibid., 319.
12 "The wrath of God and the love of God represent the two stances from which we view the salvation drama, the two perspectives from which we view the act of God in Christ – as an act of judgment as long as we continue in bondage to the powers of

In these serious engagements with the scriptural salients of atonement the authors are deploying conceptual strategies drawn from Christian thought more widely. The purpose of this article is to identify how Athanasius in *On the Incarnation* (c. 337)[13], understands the relationship of God to the elements of judgment and redemption often indicated in the biblical story by the terms "wrath" and "propitiation", with special attention to the wider strategies within which his treatment sits. Five other classical treatments will then be referred to by way of comparison and extension of Athanasius' approach: Anselm, *Why God Became Man* (c. 1090); John Calvin, *Institutes of the Christian Religion* 2.12-17 (1559); John Owen, *The Death of Death in the Death of* Christ (1647); John McLeod Campbell, *The Nature of the Atonement* (1856); and T. F. Torrance, *Atonement: the Person and Work of Christ* (2009).[14] James Torrance's ministry of reconciliation, and scholarly comment on Athanasius, Calvin, and Campbell also elucidates Athanasius. In that way, we may hopefully identify biblically and conceptually robust resolutions of some, if not all, of the problems that continue to trouble Christian doctrinal construction and proclamation.

Athanasius, *On the Incarnation* (c. 337)[15]

Although Athanasius not infrequently quotes St Anthony's warnings about the wrath of God active against sinners and the coming judgment,

evil that enslave us, and as an act of love that frees us from the powers of evil. These are not consecutive stages in God's attitude toward humankind but differing stages in humankind's perception of God." Ibid., 97-8.

13   Following the dating of Robert W. Thomson, *Athanasius: Contra Gentes and De Incarnatione* (Oxford: Clarendon Press, 1971) (RWT *On Inc.*,), xxi-xxii.

14   This last choice may be proleptic with respect to formative influence on systematic reflection, but its profundity, and the earlier appearance in 1992 of its leading ontological thoughts, suggest that giving it the status of "classical" is more than idiosyncratic. Refer T. F. Torrance, *The Mediation of Christ* (Edinburgh: T&T Clark, 1992 rev. ed.), 109-26; and *The Trinitarian Faith: the Evangelical Theology of the Early Catholic Church* (Edinburgh: T&T Clark, 1993), 154-90.

15   The references here are to the Nicene and Post-Nicene Fathers (*NPNF*) second series volume 2 edition of Athanasius works, cited by the name of the work and the appropriate section or chapter number, and where applicable, subsection number. Capitalisation has been modernised. Unless otherwise stated, the Greek is mainly that of the critical sources used by the *Thesaurus Linguae Graecae* (*TLG*). The critical Greek text and English translation by Thomson of *De Incarnatione* has also been

in his own voice, direct references to the divine wrath are rare.[16] There are none at all in *On the Incarnation*. Neither is there any direct use of the *hilastērion* (propitiation) language to speak of the Son's self-offering to the Father, although he does so in *Against the Arians*.[17] Since Athanasius does not in this work directly draw on the concepts denoted by the terms "wrath" and "propitiation," how does he express God's attitude to sin and the relation to him of its remedy?

Athanasius signals a broad strategy that has two intertwining elements – the scriptural narrative and theological reflection on it against the being and acts of God. The incarnation, death and resurrection of Christ is placed in an atoning movement from creation and fall to new creation, and treated in terms of who this God is and how he acts:

> But to treat this subject it is necessary to recall what has been previously said; in order that you may neither fail to know the cause of the bodily appearing of the Word of the Father, so high and so great, nor think it a consequence of his own nature that the Saviour has worn a body; but that being incorporeal by nature, and Word from the beginning, he has yet of the loving-kindness and goodness of his own Father been manifested to us in a human body for our salvation. It is, then, proper for us to begin the treatment of this subject by speaking of the creation of the universe, and of God its Artificer, that so it may be duly perceived that the renewal of creation has been the work of the

---

consulted – Thomson, *Athanasius*, 134-277. Lexicographic input is from Liddell and Scott, *An Intermediate Greek-English Lexicon* (Oxford: Clarendon Press, 1975), and E. A. Sophocles, *Greek Lexicon of the Roman and Byzantine Periods* (New York: Charles Scribner's Sons, 1910).

16 In his *Apology to the Emperor* 34, it is merely a rhetorical device. But in *De Synodis* 2, in the context of the spiritual devastation caused by the party of Ursacius, Athanasius refers his readers to Romans 2:15 and 24, Isaiah 52:5 and Matthew 18:6, and speaks of the wrath to come as a very real and impending reality.

17 "For when 'the Word became flesh and dwelt among us' and came to minister and to grant salvation to all, then he became to us salvation, and became life, and became propitiation (ἐγένετο ἱλασμός); then his economy in our behalf became much better than the Angels, and he became the Way and became the Resurrection." *Against the Arians*, 1.64.

"Now when became he 'Apostle,' but when he put on our flesh? and when became he 'High Priest of our profession,' but when, after offering himself for us, he raised his Body from the dead, and, as now, himself brings near and offers to the Father those who in faith approach him, redeeming all, and for all propitiating God (ὑπὲρ πάντων ἱλασκόμενος τὰ πρὸς τὸν Θεόν)?" *Against the Arians*, 2.7. Also 2.8, referring to Heb. 2:10-17.

> self-same Word that made it at the beginning. For it will appear not inconsonant for the Father to have wrought its salvation in him by whose means he made it. (*On Inc.*, 1.3-4)

Thus two brackets or outer markers are evident as Athanasius develops the atoning appearance and work of the Word of the Father. Within the first bracket, creation and fall, the curse of God falls on a rebellious humanity that brings with it the related entities of death and corruption. Death is the legally mandated consequence, and corruption the ontological dissolution congruent with having separated ourselves from the source of life, the Word of the Father. Here, Athanasius articulates the divine attitude towards and action against sin using two particular interrelated strategies – the story that unfolds in Genesis chapters 1 to 3, and the nature or character of the God who is the primary actor in the drama of creation and redemption.

Before examining this first bracket more closely, we note that the second bracket concerns the final advent of the Saviour. Although only briefly stated toward the end of his work, this advent is marked by the fulfilment of "the fruit of his own cross, that is, the resurrection and incorruption," and along with it, the final judgment which brings the kingdom of heaven for the faithful and "everlasting fire and outer darkness" for "them that have done evil."[18]

The Curse and its Removal – the Nature and Deployment of Penal Elements

In chapter 25 we find a summary of why atonement through a cross. Athanasius is answering objections concerning the propriety of Jesus public death:

> ... it was well that the Lord suffered this for our sakes. For if he came himself to bear the curse laid upon us, how else could he have "become a curse," unless he received the death set for a curse? and that is the cross. For this is exactly what is written: "Cursed is he that hangeth on a tree. (*On Inc.*, 25.1-2)

Having moved in his explanation from the curse of Genesis 2:16 and 3:1-17 to the lifting of that curse in Galatians 3:13, Athanasius summarises the effects of this death, which is a "ransom for all," by reminding

---

18 *On Inc.*, 56.3.

us that on a cross "a man dies with his hands spread out." Two major consequences are identified: with one outspread hand he might "draw the ancient people, and with the other those from the gentiles, and unite both in himself." And fittingly, also, by those hands outspread into the air, "he cleared the air of the malignity both of the devil and of demons of all kinds." So by suffering death in this way the prince of the air is defeated, and the human race, described in biblical terms of the nation and the nations, is reconciled in the person and work of the Father's Word. More on the nature of this reconciliation at the end.

Athanasius had set this up in chapter 3 where he moved from creation to fall. We have been created, in the sheer goodness of God, by the Word of God out of nothing. Considered from the viewpoint of the rest of (irrational) creation, we are as such innately liable to mortality, to "corruption," which is understood, minimally at least, as dissolution into death and non-being.[19] However, as a gift, an added grace, God makes us, "after his own image." In that way, as "a kind of reflection of the Word," we have a portion of the power of God's own Word, are thus, in contrast to non-human creation, "rational," and are not destined for our native estate of "non-being" but "might be able to abide ever in blessedness." Chapters 4 and 5 elaborate further. By this grace of participation in the Word of the Father, that is, bearing and abiding in the very image of God, we are intended for "a life in correspondence with God." Bound in that fellowship to our creator, we may live a life that is a present abiding in "incorruption" instead of dissolution into non-being (4.4), with an eschatological (heavenly) promise of an eternal "incorruption" (3.4). Here then in outline is Athanasius' theological anthropology. We are created for unmarred fellowship with the Father through the Son, his own Word and Image, a reality that is described with a concept we can identify as both Neoplatonic and Pauline, "incorruption." Neoplatonic in that "incorruption" is the flipside of our natural destiny as creatures out-of-nothing towards non-being, and Pauline in terms of the reversal of physical and spiritual death that the incarnation, death, and especially the resurrection of the Son brings (1 Cor. 15:1-11; 15:20-28; 15:2-49 ARV).[20]

Alongside and related to this notion of "the promise of incorruption" Athanasius now identifies from the narrative another foundational

---

19 Ibid., 4.4-6.

20 American Revised Version.

element supporting this trajectory, the placing of the human race into God's own garden, and giving them a law, the transgression of which would bring death, "that corruption in death which was theirs by nature (3.4)."

> But knowing once more how the will of man could sway to either side, in anticipation he secured the grace given them by a law and by the spot where he placed them. For he brought them into his own garden, and gave them a law: so that, if they kept the grace and remained good, they might still keep the life in paradise without sorrow or pain or care besides having the promise of incorruption in heaven; but that if they transgressed and turned back, and became evil, they might know that they were incurring that corruption in death which was theirs by nature: no longer to live in paradise, but cast out of it from that time forth to die and to abide in death and in corruption. (*On Inc.*, 3.4)

It is evident here from Athanasius' use of the creation narrative, that he views this death, this slide into "corruption," as penal, that is, the penalty (*hupeuthunon*) following transgression of the law.[21] This impression is strengthened in that he further describes this death as the "debt" we owe God and as a "necessary condition" to be met by the death of Christ:

> For the Word, perceiving that no otherwise could the corruption of men be undone save by death as a necessary condition . . . to this end he takes to himself a body capable of death, that it, by partaking of the Word who is above all, might be worthy to die in the stead of all . . Whence, by offering unto death the body he himself had taken, as an offering and sacrifice free from any stain, straightway he put away death from all his peers by the offering of an equivalent. For being over all, the Word of God naturally by offering his own temple and corporeal instrument for the life of all satisfied the debt by his death (*On Inc.*, 9.1-2).[22]

---

21 "[S]eeing, further, the exceeding wickedness of men, and how by little and little they had increased it to an intolerable pitch against themselves: and seeing, lastly, how all men were under penalty of death (ὁρῶν δὲ καὶ τὸ ὑπεύθυνον (liable to, guilty of) πάντων ἀνθρώπων πρὸς τὸν θάνατον): he took pity on our race." "And thus taking from our bodies one of like nature, because all were under penalty of the corruption of death (διὰ τὸ πάντας ὑπευθύνους εἶναι τῇ τοῦ θανάτου φθορᾷ) he gave it over to death in the stead of all, and offered it to the Father – doing this, moreover, of his loving-kindness." *On Inc.*, 8.2,4.

22 "But since it was necessary also that the debt owing from all should be paid again: for, as I have already said, it was owing that all should die, for which especial

With this identification of law, death, debt, and its satisfaction by the death of Christ "instead of all" (*anti pantōn*)[23], and "on behalf of all" (*huper pantōn*)[24] we have here what nowadays may be termed a "penal substitutionary" view of the atonement.[25] But, in the face of not unwarranted criticism that some contemporary presentations of penal substitutionary satisfaction are "abstract" from the ethical life of the believer,[26] several things bear noting in Athanasius' presentation.

1. No Split between the Being of the Believer and the Person and Work of the Incarnate Word

First, there is no split between the being of the believer and the person and work of the incarnate Word. The ontologically inclusivity of all humankind in the incarnation and work of Christ is foundational for Athanasius. Before turning specifically to the incarnation in chapter 8, Athanasius has stressed our racial solidarity from creation through to the Fall. We are "the race of man," "the rational man made in God's Image" (*On Inc.*, 6.1). It is a racial solidarity grounded not in itself, but in God and

---

cause, indeed, he came among us: to this intent, after the proofs of his Godhead from his works, he next offered up his sacrifice also on behalf of all, yielding his Temple to death in the stead of all, in order firstly to make men quit and free of their old trespass, and further to shew himself more powerful even than death, displaying his own body incorruptible, as first-fruits of the resurrection of all." Ibid., 20.2.

23   Ibid., 8.4; 9.1; 20.2,6; 21.3.

24   Ibid., 7.5; 16.4; 20.2,5,6; 21.5; 25.6; 31.4; 37.2.

25   A. J. Doval understands "penal substitution" as Christ dying *for* us, but not *with* us (emphasis his). On that ground, he quite rightly rejects the presence of the idea of penal substitution in *De Incarnatione*. Alexis James Doval, "Multiple Models of Atonement in Athanasius' De Incarnatione," *Studia Patristica vol. 41, Orientalia; Clement, Origen, Athanasius; the Cappadocians; Chrysostom* (Leuven: Peeters, 2006) 153. But there are many who affirm penal substitution in terms of both *for* and *with*, an ontologically grounded substitution and representation. E.g. Robert Letham, *The Work of Christ* (Downers Grove: InterVarsity Press, 1993), 75-79, 84-8. Garry Williams has shown that in two early Fathers, at least, Eusebius of Caesarea and Cyril of Jerusalem, there is a concern to show that a representational Christology is necessary to make the idea of substitution coherent. Garry J. Williams, *A Critical Exposition of Hugo Grotius's Doctrine of the Atonement in De satisfactione Christi* (unpublished PhD thesis, Oxford University, 1999), 79-81. As we will see, this is where Athanasius sits.

26   Green and Baker, *Scandal of the Cross*, 30-1, 33, 91, 132-3. Steve Chalke and Alan Mann, *The Lost Message of Jesus* (Grand Rapids: Zondervan, 2003), 182-3.

the original acts of God that express his being.²⁷ The race is the creation of the One Word of the Father, who has gifted it with "his own image," "a portion even of the power of his own Word" (On Inc 3.3). It is this human race that now suffers dissolution, the disappearance (but not effacement), the staining of God's image.²⁸ So, when Athanasius in chapter 8 states that in the incarnation the Word took "a body of our kind" (but "clean" and "pure"), "one of like nature" to us, "a body of no different sort from ours," he is indicating the Word's ontological solidarity with us, sin excepted. His affirmation of the inclusivity of the whole race in the further work of the incarnate Word follows naturally:

> And thus taking from our bodies one of like nature, because all were under penalty of the corruption of death he gave it over to death in the stead of all (*anti pantōn*), and offered it to the Father (*On Inc.*, 8.4).²⁹

This foundation works in Athanasius' deployment of the concept of "death". Death not only signifies the debt fallen humanity owes due to our transgression of the law in Adam,³⁰ but it also signifies "corruption." "Incorruption" signifies our ontological status, our state of rationality in a life lived in fellowship with the Father through participation in the power of his Word, with the promise of its heavenly fulfilment. Against this original state, Athanasius uses the opposite term, "corruption," to analyse the meaning of both "penalty" and "dissolution," and to relate them.

"Corruption" signifies an ontological state of dissolution. Athanasius mainly deploys the concept of corruption in the context of describing the inveterate "ignorance," "idolatry," "immorality" and the like that mark our flight from God, the good source of all being, and thus into evil, the privation of being.³¹

As indicated in the previous section, "corruption" also describes the outworking of the curse of God against our transgression of his law. That is, although, as Athanasius stresses, it is innate to our flight from God and the Word of the Father who keeps us "rational," it is also a

---

27   *On Inc.*, 54.1.

28   Ibid., 14.1.

29   "The Son, we might say, seizes humanity in the incarnation and in the cross entices it toward the heavenly sanctuary to worship the Father." Peter J. Leithart, *Athanasius* (Grand Rapids: Baker Academic, 2011), 155.

30   Athanasius only refers to Adam by name in 10.5, where he quotes 1 Cor. 15:21-22.

31   Ibid., 4.4-6 cited above.

penalty. Further, even if only lightly portrayed by Athanasius, God is not distant from this corruption that overtakes us,[32] for in it we are receiving the condemnation he has threatened.[33] Further, on the question of the closeness of God to our condemnation, at the last advent in his "glorious and divine appearing to us," the Incarnate Word, the God-man, acts directly both to consummate salvation and render judgment upon those who persist in evil.[34] We will return to the question of the relation of God to the evil that has overcome us at the end of the section.

So, when the cross removes "death" it means not only that a debt has been paid, but also, above all, that corruption is undone. This pattern can be seen in 9.1-2, cited above. Although stated in apologetic mode against the scorn of Greek paganism, chapters 41–55 form a robust statement of realised eschatology, the actual sanctification or deification now of Christian men and women by the appearing and work of the Father's Word. In the Christian community we see that ignorance of God is dispelled, the power of idols vitiated, sexual immorality replaced by the new virtue of continence, courage shown in the face of death, and wars lulled.[35]

As expected from the logic of his exposition in terms of Creator–creation, creation–recreation, Word of the Father–incarnate Word, there is in Athanasius no possible split between the acts and effects of atonement, that is, between the acts of God and the being of the believer.

2. The Legal is not in Antithesis to Actual Standing

Second, we may also note from the same ontological inclusivity, Athanasius exposition undercuts the criticism that the deployment of "penal" notions in the form of "substituted punishment" must inevitably

---

32 Ibid., 4.4-5. 3.4: "καὶ μηκέτι μὲν ἐν παραδείσῳ ζῆν, ἔξω δὲ τούτου λοιπὸν ἀποθνῄσκοντας μένειν ἐν τῷ θανάτῳ καὶ ἐν τῇ φθορᾷ." Thompson's translation is preferable (RWT *On Inc.*, 141-2): "and would no longer live in paradise, but in future dying outside it would remain in death and corruption." The *NPNF* translation by Robertson more directly makes God the actor: "but cast out of it from that time forth to die." This may be justifiable from the surrounding sections, but it is not justified by the Greek text itself.

33 Ibid., 4.4.

34 Ibid., 56.3.

35 See also Gerald Hiestand, "Not 'just forgiven:' how Athanasius overcomes the under-realised eschatology of evangelicalism," *Evangelical Quarterly* 84, no. 1 (2012): 47-66.

only confer a legal standing and not an actual or ontological condition. Amongst others, John McLeod Campbell makes this case against certain penal substitutionary notions of atonement developed in Reformed Orthodoxy that affirmed a limited atonement, and then universalises it to all penal views of substitution. Campbell argues that a legal standing only gives us a title to eternal sonship, at best, not that sonship itself. [36]

In contrast to the Reformed Orthodoxy criticised by Campbell, Athanasius stresses the universal character and scope of the incarnation and the work of the Word of the Father. Everything is made, from nothing, through him (*On Inc.*, 3.1-3), the gift of being in the image of God is given to the whole human race by him (*On Inc.*, 3.4). We are to understand the person and work of the incarnate Word in the context of our origin and our racial transgression (*On Inc.*, 4.2-6; 10.5-6 where he quotes 1 Cor. 15:21-22). In keeping with this, Athanasius stresses that the work of Christ was fully representative and substitutionary, both in payment of the debt and in the restoration to the life of incorruption. "On behalf of all" and "instead of all" are constant refrains:[37]

> thus taking from our bodies one of like nature, because all were under penalty of the corruption of death he gave it over to death in the stead of all, and offered it to the Father – doing this, moreover, of his loving-kindness, to the end that, firstly, all being held to have died in him, the law involving the ruin of men might be undone (inasmuch as its power was fully spent in the Lord's body, and had no longer holding-ground against men, his peers), and that, secondly, whereas men had turned toward corruption, he might turn them again toward incorruption, and quicken them from death. (*On Inc.*, 8.4)

---

36 "[T]he penal infliction is complete in itself as a substituted punishment; the righteousness wrought out is complete in itself as conferring a title to eternal blessedness, *irrespective of results* to be accomplished in those in the covenant of grace" (emphasis mine), John McLeod Campbell, *The Nature of the Atonement* (Edinburgh: Handsel Press, 1996), 127-8. More recently, the lack of ontological or real and good effect is expressed in terms of little or no direct impact on daily discipleship, or even an adverse influence. E.g., Green and Baker, *Recovering the Scandal*, 25-7. Also Weaver, *Nonviolent*, 16-18 and 236-8: it "models submission to abusive authority as a virtue" and "is irrelevant for ethical reflection."

37 *Huper pantōn* – ibid. 7.5; 16.4; 20.2,5,6; 21.5; 25.6; 31.4; 37.2; and *anti pantōn* – ibid., 8.4; 9.1; 20.2,6; 21.3.

He is to come, no more to suffer, but thenceforth to render to all the fruit of his own cross, that is, the resurrection and incorruption (*On Inc.*, 56.3).

Of course, both payment of debt and the renewal of incorruption are also to be understood eschatologically and relationally (*On Inc.*, 56), but the relation of belief and the eschatological denouement in consummation and judgment rest on this fully representative and substitutionary view. The one who "renders to all the fruit of his cross" and judges all with a view to "everlasting fire and outer darkness" is the one who has died "instead of all" and "on behalf of all."

Campbell's criticism also needs to be viewed against the wider historical development in the doctrine of atonement. The problem of a distance or disjunction between the actual end (restoration to sonship, incorruption, theosis) and means that have gained that end – which are understood in forensic terms (payment of debt, satisfaction, penal substitution) – are more acute when the legal is viewed as the first of two movements. This can imply a preliminary state before a final state – removal of the guilt of sin now by baptism and confession before completion of sanctification in heaven. The distance is further accentuated when debt is quantified and God's actions to deal with it are thought of in Aristotelian terms of perfect agent and perfect means that must limit the scope of the divine acts because not all are saved. This John Owen did.[38] But the problem is avoided in Athanasius, not just because the later Augustinian categories of original sin and guilt are absent,[39] nor just because Athanasius does not employ philosophical categories in the way Owen does, but because payment of debt and restoration of life are held together, and universalised, in the person and work of the incarnate Word.

3. His emphasis on "corruption"/"incorruption" does not exclude the idea of punishment from the concept of legal

Third, despite objections to the contrary, "corruption" and "debt-paying death" are not two competing themes in Athanasius, nor does

---

38   In his *Death of Death in the Death of Christ* as he sets up his analysis of the nature and extent of the atonement, book 1, chapters 1–2. Refer *The Works of John Owen*, ed. W. H. Goold (London: Banner of Truth, 1967), vol. 10. pp. 157–63.

39   Cf. Rodolph Yanney, "Salvation in St Athanasius' On the Incarnation of the Word," *Coptic Church Review* 11, no. 2 (1990) 46, 48 regarding western views.

his subordination of the legal to his overarching move from corruption to incorruption (from idolatry to *theopoiesis*) exclude the idea of punishment from the conceptual content of the legal.[40] Rather, they are both conceived of theologically, and are indissolubly interrelated. This can be seen in the way he uses the concept of "death."

"Mortality" or "death" is viewed in two ways. When by our sin we reject the life-giving participation we have with God, we lose the gracious restraint on our innate propensity to mortality. This, of course, is presented by Athanasius in Christian terms of the Father-Son relation and his work in the world, not in the terms of a logico-causal ontology that was available to him through Aristotle,[41] let alone the "inevitable process of cause and effect in a moral universe."[42] As already noted, this death or mortality is marked by dissolution, a flight into non-being, into a deepening corruption and irrationality.[43] In chapters 41-55, his defence against Greek derision of the incarnation is as much an unmasking of the stupidity of idolatry as it is an exposition of the theosis that Christ is bringing about amongst believers. We have been created by the Word of the Father to live in a life- and meaning-giving structure of relationship to him. Athanasius' later writings flesh out the sketch he gives in *On the Incarnation* chapter 3. We are rational (*genomenoi logikoi*), or truly human, because the Father has made us in the image of the One in whom he images and knows himself, his own Son, his own Word (*tou idou Logou*).[44] Thus, as those who image the Image, and have "a portion even

---

40 L. W. Grensted, *A Short History of the Doctrine of the Atonement* (Manchester: Manchester University Press, 1980), 79-80, cf. 72; Derek Flood, "Substitutionary Atonement and the Church Fathers: a reply to the authors of Pierced for our Transgressions," *Evangelical Quarterly* 82, no. 2 (2010) 142-4, 147-50. For an accurate criticism of Flood, refer Garry J. Williams, "Penal Substitutionary Atonement in the Church Fathers," *Evangelical Quarterly* 83, no. 3 (2011) 195-6, 203-10. This combination of the penal and the ontological is also identified by Doval, "Multiple Models of Atonement," 151-54. Moving backward from four widely accepted "models of the atonement" (solidarity, satisfaction, enlightenment, conflict), Doval finds all four groups in Athanasius, and points of integration.

41 In *Metaphysics* Book XII, part 7, Aristotle postulates that behind all substances that move and are moved must be "something which moves without being moved, being eternal, substance, and actuality." Refer *Metaphysics By Aristotle*, trans. by W. D. Ross, http://classics.mit.edu//Aristotle/metaphysics.html.

42 C. H. Dodd, *The Epistle of Paul to the Romans* (London: Hodder, 1932), 23.

43 *On Inc.*, 11.5-7.

44 *Against the Arians*, 1.21: "We understand in like manner that the Son is begotten not from without but from the Father, and while the Father remains whole,

of the power of his own Word," we participate in God's own rationality, and thus, originally at least, live in paradise, "abiding ever in blessedness," and with the promise of heavenly incorruption to come. But having rejected God's law that was given to secure wills otherwise prone to "sway to either side" – a metaphorical description of the temptation to live independently of God, we have departed from the grace of the image of God, and plunged ourselves into irrationality, into corruption. As psycho-somatic entities, we are headlong into death.

"Death" is also the penalty (*to upeuthunon*) for transgressing the law, which was God's kind provision to keep us through the Word in knowledge of him and thus stay us from irrationality. It is Christ who pays the debt of penalty that came from transgressing that law, so that, free from its demands, our ruin may be undone, and we may then be turned towards incorruption. The logic in chapter 8 is inherently Pauline, although there is no direct reference to his writings. Death is both spoken of forensically and hypostasised: our wilful turning from God moves us into corruption, the state of death; the threat of the penalty of death that comes now with breaking God's law gives this corruption even a greater hold, greater mastery; out of pity the Word becomes incarnate, "takes a body of our kind" and gives it over to the penalty of death, our debt, offering it to the Father, "in the stead of all;" thus undoing the law and its hold over us; and that he may turn us toward incorruption.[45]

It is retributive justice that is on view here. The point is not uncontroverted,[46] but Athanasius makes it clear that Christ dissolves the law by meeting the liability (*to upeuthunon*) by meeting its demands, which in this case is death. The law is "concluded" because it was fulfilled. Further, this fulfilment of the penal debt by substitution leads to the bestowal of incorruption. Not only are the notions of death as corruption and penalty interrelated, but also in one passage Athanasius states that fulfilment of the debt brings incorruption as a consequence:

> to this end he takes to himself a body capable of death, that it, by partaking of the Word who is above all, might be worthy

the Expression of his subsistence is ever, and preserves the Father's likeness and unvarying Image, so that he who sees him, sees in him the subsistence too, of which he is the Expression. And from the operation of the Expression we understand the true Godhead of the subsistence." Also, *Against the Arians* 3.6.

45   *On Inc.*, 8.2,4.

46   For example: Grensted, *A Short History*, 7; and Flood, "Substitutionary Atonement and the Church Fathers," 142-4, 147-50.

> to die in the stead of all, and might, because of the Word which was come to dwell in it, remain incorruptible, and that *thenceforth* corruption might be stayed from all by the grace of the resurrection. (*On Inc.*, 9.1 – emphasis mine)

However, although the consequent relationship between the two is clear as the forensic is made to serve the leading idea, restoration of incorruption, Athanasius does not conceptualise them sequentially in time but together, simultaneously, as they are but 2 aspects of the one who himself is our propitiation (Heb. 2:17, 1 John 2:2, 4:10):

> And so it was that two marvels came to pass at once (*amphotera*, simultaneously), that the death of all was accomplished in the Lord's body, and that death and corruption were wholly done away by reason of the Word that was united with it. For there was need of death, and death must needs be suffered on behalf of all, that the debt owing from all might be paid (*On Inc.*, 20.5)

To reiterate, without removing the idea of penalty, Athanasius treats the legal in such a way that it serves the major theme, the restoration of incorruption, knowing and living in participation with God.

4. The Deeper Integration of Penal Justice and Restoration of Incorruption

Further, behind this interrelation stands a deeper integration in the nature and acts of God. Both the gifting of humanity with the image of God, which allows participation through the Son with the Father, and the giving of the law to preserve this state of affairs, are acts of the kindness and love, the grace of the triune God who has made us to participate in himself. Again and again Athanasius speaks of our original creation, our being related to the Father through the image of the Son, and the coming of the Son to redeem us as springing from the "loving kindness of the Father," "the loving kindness of the Word."[47] God's creation of us, bringing us out of nothing to possess being in its created fullness in his image, is the very antithesis of a begrudging niggardliness, it is an expression of his very own being:

> For God is good, or rather is essentially the source of goodness: nor could one that is good be niggardly of anything: whence,

---

47 *On Inc.*, 1.3, 4.2, 4.5, 8.1, 8.4, 12.6, 34.2.

grudging existence to none, he has made all things out of nothing by his own Word, Jesus Christ our Lord. (*On Inc.,* 3.3)

Out of the lavish bounty of his own being,[48] he who is being in itself gave us being who are without being (ek ouk ontōn).

In this way Athanasius paints a picture of God's being as lavishly overflowing generosity, love, kindness and grace. It is against this we are to understand the reference he makes in chapter 6 to the divine rectitude or integrity being at stake in the fall, and lying behind the incarnation. On the one hand, for God not to fulfil his ordination of a penal death for our sins would "be monstrous and unseemly."

> For it were monstrous, firstly, that God, having spoken, should prove false – that, when once he had ordained that man, if he transgressed the commandment, should die the death, after the transgression man should not die, but God's word should be broken." (*On Inc.,* 6.3) On the other, "it were unseemly that creatures once made rational, and having partaken of the Word, should go to ruin, and turn again toward non-existence by the way of corruption. For it were not worthy of God's goodness that the things he had made should waste away, because of the deceit practised on men by the devil (*On Inc.,* 6.4-5).

The placement of the divine rectitude in the context of the divine overspilling of love means that the former is not anterior to the latter, as it is in John Owen's exposition of the atonement, who will insist that God relates himself to all men in justice, but only in love to the elect. Here, justice is the natural attribute of the divine being, whilst love is only an attribute of the divine volition, a movement of the will.[49] Combination of this with thinking of God's saving acts in terms of an Aristotelian conception of perfect agent and perfect means, means that Owen cannot conceive of God's being and his saving acts as an overflowing generosity that can suffer, without detriment to the divine being, even the rejection of that generosity. This is the pathway to his view of limited atonement. But with Athanasius, although he finds conceptual help from a Platonic ontology in articulating the meaning of creation, nevertheless, his major conception of the divine being comes from God's self-revelation in the economy of salvation. Consequently, he configures the divine love and justice otherwise than Owen, for he configures it evangelically. Thus,

---

48 To draw on the *NPNF* editor's perceptive summary of section 3.
49 *Death of Death*, book 4, chapter 2, pp. 319-28.

Athanasius' doctrine of God evident in *On the Incarnation* – his lavish grace seen in the ontological inclusivity of all the human race in Jesus Christ, so that he dies "instead of all" (*anti pantōn*)[50] and "on behalf of all" (*huper pantōn*)[51] – is not made unintelligible by the last judgment, when those, due to their persistent rejection of this generosity, are consigned to "everlasting fire and outer darkness."[52] That is, the perdition of some does not overthrow the nature of the divine being and intentions witnessed to by the fact that on that day the God-Man returns "to render to *all* the fruit of his own cross, that is, the resurrection and incorruption (*On Inc.*, 56.3, emphasis mine)." As Calvin helpfully expresses it, persistent evil and perdition is an accidental shadow thrown by the light of the cross,[53] by the light of lavish generosity.

5. A Trinitarian Integration

It is obvious then that the theological structure of Athanasius exposition of atonement, in the movement from creation to new creation, is trinitarian. It is the Father who creates us, through his own eternal Word, the Son, his very own Image, and recreates us in the sending and incarnation of that Son.[54] This Son of the Father has come to bring us back to the Father. "For he was made man that we might be made God; and he manifested himself by a body that we might receive the idea of the unseen Father (*On Inc.*, 51.4)."

---

50 *On Inc.*, 8.4; 9.1; 20.2,6; 21.3.

51 Ibid., 7.5; 16.4; 20.2,5,6; 21.5; 25.6; 31.4; 37.2

52 Ibid., 56.3.

53 Commentary on 1 Peter 2:8: "This especially deserves to be noticed in case the blame for our fault should be imputed to Christ, for, as he has been given to us as a foundation, it is incidental that he becomes a rock of offence. In short, his proper office is to fit us to be a spiritual temple to God, but it is the fault of men that they stumble at him, because unbelief leads men to contend with God." Cf. his commentary on 2 Peter 2:4: "God has made know what is useful for us to know, that the devils were originally created to obey God, that they fell from grace through their own fault because they did not submit to God's rule: and therefore that the wickedness which cleaves to them was accidental and not organic to their nature, so that it cannot be attributed to God." *Calvin's Commentaries*, trans. W. B. Johnston (Edinburgh: Saint Andrew Press, 1963), 264, 348.

54 *On Inc.*, 3.3, 8.4.

Although *homoousion* is unarticulated, perhaps surprisingly in a document dated 337,[55] nevertheless it accounts for the force of Athanasius argument. If salvation is *theosis* then the Saviour must be *Theos*, not just in part but in himself. Likewise, the Spirit is only directly referred to in the closing benediction. However, it is the assumption throughout of his very person, presence and work as the Spirit of the Father and the Spirit of the Son which gives rational coherence, makes possible, the enlightenment and sanctification, the *theopoiesis* the final chapter highlights. For that is the reason and result of the coming of the Son in the purposes of the Father.

But, Athanasius does bring to the fore the lavish, loving kindness of the Father and the Son in terms of the love between the Father and Son. The common Savior of all is "the beloved Son of the Father (*On Inc.*, 52.1)." The loving kindness of the Word and the Father towards us has a theological anterior. This further consolidates his portrait of the being of God that stands behind and in his saving acts.

The Relation to God of the Curse and its Removal

So, to return to the main question in our investigation, seeing that in *On the Incarnation* Athanasius does not use the terms "wrath" nor "propitiation" in his exposition of the atonement, how does he relate God to the curse and its removal? Are we, as Weaver wants to do in order to overcome several pressing problems in "satisfaction" models of atonement, to conceive of God's relation to curse and removal, especially the penal aspects, only in terms of our stance?[56]

The observation that Athanasius integrates creation, fall, and restoration all the way down into God is important to our question concerning the attitude of God towards the sin of his human creatures and to the relation of the incarnation and the cross to God in himself. Clearly, in the theological structure and underpinning of Athanasius' exposition, God is not distant from his acts.

Within this theological integration, Athanasius expresses the closeness of God to the curse and its removal in three interrelated ways.

---

55 Athanasius' sparing use of the term in his ongoing confrontation with anti-Nicaeans, probably in order to persuade over the Homoeans who are close in mind to Nicaea, is at least a similar reticence, even if not of great explanatory power for *De Incarnatione*.

56 *Nonviolent Atonement*, 98.

He describes God as the author of the threat or curse which will follow transgression of the law given to the "race of men" at creation;[57] the giving of that law and its threat was itself an act of divine kindness, the divine pity, to secure the grace of us being made in his image so that we may not fall into corruption and thus receive incorruption in heaven;[58] and the execution of this curse has created a fundamental problem for the divine rectitude, the divine goodness.[59] Chapter 6 is a sustained exposition on the double dilemma posed to the divine goodness and truthfulness by the necessary exaction of death on the one hand, and on the other, its consequences for God's purpose for his creation. It begins:

> The human race then was wasting, God's image was being effaced, and his work ruined. Either, then, God must forego his spoken word by which man had incurred ruin; or that which had shared in the being of the Word must sink back again into destruction, in which case God's design would be defeated. What then? Was God's goodness to suffer this? But if so, why had man been made? It could have been weakness, not goodness on God's part. (*On Inc.*, 6.1)

That is, the curse and restoration is viewed from the stance of God. Athanasius' wider theological integration of God's acts with his nature will not allow this "stance of God" to be dissolved into a merely human viewpoint or speculation as to the relation of these acts to the mystery of God, for Athanasius insists that the Father sent his very own Image to rescue and restore that image in us. The incarnation means that the curse and its removal are viewed from two stances, sinful humanity seeing itself mirrored in the being and acts of the incarnate Son, and the triune God.

Conclusion: Athanasius' Reserve and Contribution

But, the action of God is not so directly portrayed by Athanasius as it is in the biblical narratives. In the garden, God curses directly (Gen. 3:8-19), and through Moses and the prophets he reiterates both curses and blessings for his people (Deut. 28), and in the historical processes of invasion, pillage, and murder pours out wrath on persistent rejection and mockery of his mercy (Ezek. 7, 33:21-29; Deut. 28:52-7). Part of the

---

57   *On Inc.*, 4.4, 5.2, 8.2, 3.3-4.
58   *On Inc.*, 3.3-4.
59   *On Inc.*, 6.3-5, cf. 8.2.

reason for this reserve lies in the nature of theological exegesis at depth. How are we to understand these harsh realities against who God actually is? Early in his exposition, as did Augustine later, Athanasius adapts and deploys with some skill a conceptual structure from Neoplatonism. Evil is conceived of as privation of being. This serves to both highlight the fact that God, in the overflow of his goodness, is the source and upholder of all being and reason, and at the same time avoids dualism. The outworking of evil may be our and the devil's work, but it is not God's. In our flight from God our being is deprived of its divine centre, its "theosis." In that way, it is not possible to give evil and its arbiters the status of divinity, nor make God the author of it. This construct means, then, that the Christian, or even the not-yet-Christian reader of the biblical narrative, is at the outset turned aside from a polytheistic and even animistic and superstitious reading. Here the Christian doctrine of creation, read in the context the Bible itself gives – re-creation – is doing its evangelical work of cultural transformation.

Further, as we have noted, this deployment of a philosophical concept has not hindered Athanasius from giving a robust theological exposition of "corruption." Viewed both protologically, and most especially against the divine movement of humankind back to incorruption through the incarnate Word, this corruption is never abstractly or moralistically or mechanically conceived. In Athanasius, the relation of God to the world is a real relation, but he does not state it in logico-causal terms, but personal terms, of the triune nature and activity of Father, Son and Holy Spirit. It is that relation that determines both the nature of incorruption as theosis and corruption as deprivation.

Hence, in the giving of the threat and its subsequent unfolding, and by the manner of its remedy in which the Son satisfies the Father by upholding his truthful, good and kind nature and acts, creation and redemption are closely related to who God is in himself. In that way, notions of "moral mechanism" or "stance" are insufficient recognitions of God's working of atonement.

Nor, on the other hand, is this approach patent of the intrusion of foreign or external concepts of retributive justice amongst ourselves, and a piety prone to a merely instrumental view of the work of Christ. With Athanasius, the Father-Son relationship in the economy reflects that of God immanently. Later, building on Athanasius, it is the christological exposition of James Torrance, and the trinitarian exposition of T. F. Torrance, that brings the consequences of this to clearest expression. God deals with us in the person of his Son. Christ's humanity is uniquely and inclusively vicarious humanity. There is a two way mediatorial movement in this. The image of the Father, in whose image we are created as a gift, has assumed the humanity of the whole human race to satisfy *anti pantōn* and *kata pantōn*, the Father's just demands. Further, he has restored us to knowledge of the Father and true rationality, genuine humanity. "Theosis" is how Athanasius expresses our union with Christ, the other side of his union with us, so that we come to participate, in our filial knowledge and worship of God, in the communion of the Son with the Father. This is the Christological underpinning of Athanasius' robust view of the sanctification he observes among believers. On Athanasius' construct, Christ's vicarious work is never reducible to the instrumental cause of faith and the experience of salvation, as in much popular piety nowadays.[60] The "Great Physician" only operates from within and at the very depths of human personhood.[61] "Christ's vicarious humanity" was also the wellspring of James' theological reflection and practice of reconciliation.[62] In the apologetic context of these twin treatises, in addressing Jewish unbelief and pagan idolatry and immorality, Athanasius' evangelical portrait of Christian fidelity "reflects God's concern to give to all their humanity in Christ."[63]

Further, as T. F. Torrance has stressed, the *whole* God is involved in the atonement. Because the incarnation is of the eternal Son of the Father, the incarnation does not at all fall outside of God, but within his very

---

[60] Refer James Torrance, "The Vicarious Humanity of Christ," in *The Incarnation: Ecumenical Studies in the Nicene-Constantinopolitan Creed A.D. 381*, ed. T. F. Torrance (Edinburgh: Handsel Press, 1981), 133-35. It was with John McLeod Campbell as conversation partner that James developed this construct. Refer his "The Contribution of John McLeod Campbell to Scottish Theology," *Scottish Journal of Theology*, 26, no. 3 (1973): 295-311.

[61] *On Inc.* 44.1-6; and refer James' homely exposition, "Vicarious Humanity", p.141.

[62] From the inexhaustible resources of the person and love of Christ, James Torrance sustained a life-long commitment to the practice of reconciliation. Whether in negotiations with Sinn Féin in Northern Ireland, or at theological conferences in Apartheid South Africa, or giving pastoral advice in parish or elsewhere as God put enquiring and needy people in his way, our dear friend and mentor was a faithful witness to Christ who shaped many, myself included. "Blessed are the peacemakers, for they shall be called sons of God." *Soli Deo gloria.*

[63] James Torrance, "Listening to its Challenge," *Journal of Theology for Southern Africa*, 55 (1986), 42. He is responding to the Kairos Document, a theological statement issued in 1985 by black South African theologians, mainly from Soweto.

being and life. Consequently, atonement too must also be conceived of as falling within the life and being of God. It is God as God, in the incarnate Son, and thus the Father and the Spirit, who bears our punishment, who became a curse for us (Gal. 3:13). We do better to leave-off speaking of the "Father punishing the Son," and with James Denney, citing John McLeod Campbell with approbation, speak of our offences and their consequences being absorbed and exhausted in the holy being of Christ.

> This confession, as to its own nature, must have been a perfect Amen in humanity to the judgment of God on the sin of man . . . Let us consider this Amen from the depths of the humanity of Christ to the divine condemnation of sin. What is it in relation to God's wrath against sin? What place has it in Christ's dealings with that wrath? I answer: He who so responds to the divine wrath against sin, saying, "Thou art righteous, O Lord, who judgest us," is necessarily receiving the full apprehension and realisation of that wrath, as well as of that sin against which it comes forth, into his soul and spirit, into the bosom of the divine humanity, and, so receiving it, he responds to it with a perfect response – a response from the depths of that divine humanity – and in that perfect response absorbs it.

And, as Torrance has elucidated, because Christ, so the Father and the Spirit. The whole of God has absorbed and exhausted our transgressions and their dire consequences through and in and with the Beloved Son.

Further, this means that our atonement, understood in the context of the triune relations and the hypostatic union, is of great scope and at great depth.

It may not be possible to find a documentary trail of influence from *On the Incarnation* to Augustine to Anselm to Calvin. All in their own way stress the universal scope of the person and work of Christ that Paul highlights in Colossians 1:15-21. Anselm will uniquely do so by the discussion concerning the question of whether the number of the elect is to make up the number of angels! God has purposed to have a universe that is righteous, that is, is in right order to his majesty and glory. Therefore, to perfectly reflect this, as a heavenly choir so to speak, the number of fallen angels must and will be made up.[64] But Anselm, along

---

64 *Why God Became Man* (*WGBM*), in *A Scholastic Miscellany*, ed. E.R. Fairweather (London: SCM, 1956). 1.16-18. "Whence it may be reasoned that God planned to perfect both at the same time, in order that the inferior nature, which knew not God,

with Augustine and Calvin, also utilises the Athanasian concept of the divine design for creation to account for the nature of the atonement.[65] The concept helps account for the divine mercy, kindness and love in the face of our intractable opposition, as well as to make sense of the scope of this redemptive outpouring. On this point we may hear Athanasius echoed in Calvin's citation of Augustine:

> God's love is incomprehensible and unchangeable. For it was not after we were reconciled to him through the blood of his Son that he began to love us. Rather, he has loved us before the world was created, that we also might be his sons along with his only-begotten Son . . . Therefore, he loved us even when we practiced enmity toward him and committed wickedness. Thus in a marvellous and divine way he loved us even when he hated us. For he hated us for what we were that he had not made; yet because our wickedness had not entirely consumed his handiwork, he knew how, at the same time, to hate in each one of us what we had made, and to love what he had made.[66]

The theologic of Athanasius' treatment also accounts for the depth of the atonement. He expressed this depth in terms of an apologetic stress on the real sanctification evident in the Christian community – their eschewing of idolatry and superstition, their courage, self-control and peaceableness. Both Torrances give the most sustained theological exposition of this. The incarnation means that substitution is at a very great depth. "The whole Christ became a curse for us (Athanasius)."[67]

---

might not be perfected before the superior nature which ought to enjoy God; and that the inferior, being renewed at the same time with the superior, might, as it were, rejoice in its own way; yes, that every creature having so glorious and excellent a consummation, might delight in its Creator and in itself, in turn, rejoicing always after its own manner . . ." *WGBM*, 1.18.

65 Ibid., 1.4.

66 *Institutes of the Christian Religion*, trans. and ed. F.L. Battles (London: SCM, 1960), 2.16.4, quoting Augustine, *Lectures or Tractates on the Gospel According to St. John*, chapter 17:21-23 (Tractate 110.6), *NPNF*, 7.114.

67 T. F. Torrance, *The Trinitarian Faith: the Evangelical Theology of the Early Catholic Church* (Edinburgh: T&T Clark, 1993), 161. *Against the Arians* 2.47: "(W)e do not simply conceive this, that (the) whole Christ has become curse and sin, but that he has taken on him the curse which lay against us (as the Apostle has said, 'Has redeemed us from the curse,' and 'has carried,' as Isaiah has said, 'our sins,' and as Peter has written, 'has borne them in the body on the wood')." In the face of Arian tendencies to use this truth to reduce the full divinity of the Word, Athanasius does not understand the "whole Christ" *simpliciter*. Indeed it is only the unalterableness of the divinity that

All of Christ's life is atoning. Since atonement was *in* Christ himself and not in some external way, therefore the whole man, body and soul, is delivered from penalty, debt, ignorance, law, death and devil. In this way then, the image of God is restored, and we come to know God, to enter into his own inner rationality, to share his life. In the self sanctification of the Son of God, we are sanctified (John 17:17-19).[68] "The benefits of God's free gift of Jesus Christ to mankind are as inexhaustible as his love."[69]

In Athanasius, then, it is the nature of God himself and his actions through the Word of the Father, and thus his personal relation to the world, that are to determine our understanding of the nature of God's aversion to sin and his personal acts to remedy it. Athanasius offers structures of thought that safeguard us, in our engagement with the biblical narrative, from making normative our ordinary and all too human cultural experiences and understandings of "wrath" and "propitiation."[70]

---

facilitates both the full depth of the identification with sinners, and also the reversal of sin – *Against the Arians*, 1.43, 51.

68 *Trinitarian Faith*, 154-90; and *The Mediation of Christ* (Edinburgh: T&T Clark, 1992 rev. ed.), 109-26. Also refer to articles by James Torrance, above.

69 *Trinitarian Faith*, 181.

70 In the end, for all its rich interaction with contemporary Black and Womanist Theologies, insights into Anselm, and posing of important questions about violence, abuse and retributive and substitutionary justice, Weaver's exposition does not allow these starting points and questions to be sovereignly shaped by the biblical narrative. Particularly, Weaver rejects the trinitarian solution offered by W.C. Placher and others to resolve some of these problems – *Nonviolent Atonement*, Kindle version, chapter 7, Conversations: Round One – *Redefinitions, Reemphases, and Rehabilitation* location 2751, 2782 of 5056; and – *Responding to the Defenses of Satisfaction*, 2934-55 of 5056.

Chapter 14

John Calvin and James B. Torrance's Evangelical Vision of Repentance

Andrew B. Torrance, Ph.D.

James B. Torrance was a minister and theologian, devoted to proclaiming the unconditional freeness of the triune God's love and grace for the world. This commitment came not only out of a concern for serious theological teaching but out of a pastoral devotion for those seated on the pews and, indeed, to society in general. In this respect, he followed in the footsteps of John Calvin, who stood as the most critical influence on Torrance's theology.

As Torrance sought to communicate the strengths of Calvin's theology to the church, the academy and society, it was Calvin's covenantal theology of the triune God of grace that stood at the forefront of his teaching. In particular, Torrance set out to follow Calvin by elucidating the way in which the God of the Christian faith is not a "contract God" but a "covenant God." Accordingly, this essay will begin with a brief analysis of Torrance's engagement with this distinction. It was out of his concern to stress the covenantal nature of God's relationship with humanity that Torrance came to emphasise Calvin's distinction between legal and evangelical repentance.

This essay, however, will not primarily engage with Torrance's own discussion of legal and evangelical repentance. One of Torrance's real strengths was his ability to communicate key issues with a precision and clarity that is all too rare in the theological world. This is particularly the case in his discussion of evangelical repentance. Torrance was able to articulate the significance of the distinction between legal and evangelical repentance to a new generation with a clarity and passion that, in many respects, has been unsurpassed. It is for this reason that the relatively few words that Torrance wrote on repentance have had such a major impact on both the church and the theological world. However, due to the brevity of his engagement with the question of repentance, it would be very hard to devote an entire essay to his discussion of this theme. But Torrance did not leave his listeners and readers without anywhere to go for more detail on this subject. He was always very quick to point people towards the primary texts that had informed his thinking, which, in the case of repentance, was Calvin's *Institutes of the Christian Religion*. Accordingly, the majority of this paper will be devoted to engaging in a detailed analysis of Calvin's account of evangelical repentance, with a view to explore the background behind what is unquestionably one of the most central themes in Torrance's theology. We shall then look briefly at Torrance's account of evangelical repentance, as it followed Calvin's trajectory.

1. "Covenant God" or "Contract God"?

To understand the distinction that Torrance draws between "Covenant God" and "Contract God," we first need to be clear about the grammar of covenant and contract. In particular, with respect to God's covenant relationship with his people, we need to recognise that "the *indicatives of grace are always prior to the imperatives* of law and human obligation." For example, "I have loved you, I have redeemed you (indicatives of grace) . . . therefore, keep my commandments (imperatives of grace)."[1] If, however, the order is switched around, making the imperatives prior to the indicatives, we end up with a contractual understanding of the relationship between God and his people: "If you keep the law (imperatives), God will love you (indicatives). If you keep the Sabbath, the Kingdom of God will come."[2] In the case of a contractual relationship, God's gracious activity towards humanity is conditioned by human acts of obedience. Under these circumstances, human persons retain a level of mastery over God, insofar as God's creative purposes are contingent upon a particular form of creaturely activity.

For Torrance, "It is precisely against this inversion of the order of grace (which turns covenant into contract) that Paul protests in Galatians 3:17-22."[3] When God gave the law to his people four hundred and thirty

---

1   James B. Torrance, "Covenant or Contract?: A Study of the Theological Background of Worship in Seventeenth-century Scotland," *Scottish Journal of Theology* 23, no. 1 (1970): 56.
2   Ibid., 56.
3   Ibid., 56.

years after making his covenant with Abraham, God was not making his grace conditional upon the fulfillment of the law. God was not changing his mind and turning the covenant of grace into a contract. Rather, God was revealing to his people what was expected of them if they were to live lives that correspond to God's creative purposes, to his covenant of grace. That is, God spells out the obligations of grace in the form of a law so that the Israelites would not simply *be* God's people by the fact of God's covenant promise but would have a knowledge that would enable them to *live out their lives* as a testimony to the covenant of grace.

If this is the case, how are we supposed to interpret all the instances throughout Scripture where the language about God's relationship to the world does appear contractual? As Torrance contends in his lecture on covenant or contract at his 2001 Warfield Lectures at Princeton (currently unpublished), such appearance is "superficial." Again, for Torrance, God gives the law to his people out of love and grace, so that they might know what it means to live actively as God's people, in *response* to grace. In this way, the law lays unconditional obligations on persons, which, if broken will have consequences. Importantly, however, the reason that such transgressions do not go unpunished – the reason that they have consequences – is precisely because there is a covenant unconditionally in place, on the basis of which our transgressions will (unconditionally) have negative consequences. That is, God does not passively ignore the transgressions of his people.

To put this in context, let us consider the example of a mother's loving relationship to her son. The nature of this relationship will normally be such that she will expect certain activities from her son, which correspond to the nature of this relationship and the order that she seeks to maintain. For example, there might be the expectation that her son will go to bed at a certain time so that he can function properly at school the next day. Under these circumstances, it may well be the case that *if* her son stays up past his bedtime, *then* he will be in trouble. Now, if we were being superficial in our analysis of this relationship, we could jump up and say "look the mother's relationship to her son is clearly contractual; look at the 'if . . . then . . .'" To this, one would retort "of course this instance doesn't imply that this relationship is contractual because the 'if . . . then . . .' that occurs in this instance is not representative of the nature of the relationship as a whole but of the order that is maintained by the mother in this relationship." That is, the "if . . . then . . ." is *descriptive* of what will happen in this order, when certain rules are broken; it is not *prescriptive* of the nature of this (already established) order. The "if . . . then . . ." is indicative of the fact that, out of love, the mother wants to maintain a particular order for her son.

In short, Torrance does not deny a place for "if" language, but he insists that, with respect to our relationship to God, this language needs to be understood descriptively, not prescriptively. In order to understand his position rightly, it is extremely important to grasp this point.

In this way, Torrance recognises that the law is key for instructing persons in what it means to correspond to God's purposes – to live the kind of lives that God seeks for his people within the covenant of grace. Accordingly, Torrance is quite happy to acknowledge that, under God's covenant, *if* the Israelites transgressed the law, *then* they would be punished. However, he firmly denies that the particular nature of the Israelites' response to the law is prescriptive of the nature of God's covenant purposes. So, therefore, God does warn his people that *if* they do not follow his law, and transgress the commandment, *then* disaster will come upon them. However, when God does so, the "if . . . then . . ." is describing what will happen in accordance with the order that God has established and purposed for his people, under the covenant of grace. As such, the transgressions of God's people do not somehow alter or interfere with God's covenant commitment to his people, as if this commitment were conditional upon the Israelite's performing in a particular way.

Because, for Torrance, God's covenant promise to his people is not conditioned by human action, human transgression does not threaten God's covenant purposes for creation. It does not stop God our Father from loving us; it does not take away from the fact that Jesus Christ has redeemed us; and it does not stop the Son from sending his Spirit to draw us into the body of Christ. Why? Because, there is something much greater going on in God's covenant relationship with humanity than could ever be stunted by creaturely failure. This does not mean that Torrance fails to take sin and disobedience seriously; he simply takes them less seriously than the love of the triune God and his eternal purposes of grace. Accordingly, Torrance not only distinguishes the concept of the "contract God" from the "covenant God;" he also distinguishes the "contract God" from the "triune God of love and grace" – the God who *is* love and whose being cannot be separated from his gracious activity.

In light of his theological commitment to the covenant God, Torrance was highly critical of accounts of the Christian existence that were primarily based on religious and moral duty. To interpret the

Christian faith primarily in terms of a religious or moral existence, is to prioritise finite human activity over and above the gracious activity of the covenant God. Consequently, such theologies end up reducing the Christian faith to a human venture that is removed from covenant relationship with the God who actively relates to us in history, in and through the mediation of Jesus Christ. For Torrance, the Christian life flows from the "three great moments" that correspond to the "one work" of the "of the one God, Father, Son and Holy Spirit:"

> . . . the moment of eternity, the eternal love of the Father; the moment of history, when Christ died and rose again nineteen hundred years ago to fulfil for us in time God's eternal purpose, so that (in Calvin's phrase) "all parts of our salvation are complete in Him;" the moment of experience when the Holy Spirit unites us to Christ and brings us to personal faith and repentance.[4]

For Torrance, this refers to "the basic trinitarian structure of the first three books of Calvin's *Institutio*."[5] And Torrance believed that he arrived at his own position by drawing deeply from the theology of Calvin. As we turn to consider Calvin's understanding of repentance, we see the very clear influence that Calvin had on Torrance's covenant theology.

2. Calvin on Repentance

In Calvin's Catechism of the Church of Geneva, written for a minister and a child, the minister asks, "What is repentance?" To which the child responds:

> Dissatisfaction and hatred of sin, and love of righteousness, arising out of the fear of God; for these things lead us to denial of self and mortification of the flesh, so that we yield ourselves to be ruled by the Spirit of God, and bring all the actions of our life into obedience to the divine will.[6]

---

4 Torrance, "The Incarnation and Limited Atonement," *Evangelical Quarterly* 55, (1983): 84.

5 Ibid., 84.

6 John Calvin, "Catechism of the Church of Geneva," in *Calvin: Theological Treatises*, trans. J.K.S. Reid (London: SCM Press, 1954), 107; see also Calvin, *Institutes of the Christian Religion* (two volumes), ed. John T. McNeill, trans. Ford Lewis Battles (Philadelphia: Westminster Press, 1960), III.3.5.

What does this passage tell us about Calvin's understanding of repentance? It gives us the basics. As we can see from this passage, repentance, for Calvin, involves an active and conscious turning away from sin. But it does not only concern a subjective change of mind – a change in the way that a person finds self-fulfilment. It would be mistaken to reduce Calvin's understanding of repentance to a self-conscious effort to turn away from wrongdoing. Why? Because, for Calvin, repentance is not grounded in a person's self-oriented existence. Rather, repentance is an expression of the fact that something world-changing has happened, is happening and will continue to happen from beyond the sphere of person's immanence. As we shall see, it is indicative of the fact that the Christ-event has inaugurated an entirely new way of being human within history. In light of this event, Christian repentance involves the realisation of a person's complete failure to function properly, in and of herself, to the extent that she humbly realises that she has nothing to contribute, not even an act of repentance. It involves the realisation that she is so depraved that a mere reorientation of the flesh is not enough; dying to the flesh is required.

What does this mean? As the passage above tells us, repentance requires us to "yield ourselves to be ruled by the Spirit of God, and bring all the actions of our life into obedience to the divine will."[7] For Calvin, this means that repentance requires God to "extend his hand towards us, and animate us to penitence."[8] Like Irenaeus, however, this is not simply one hand, but the two hands of the Son and the Spirit. At the same time, because God's Word and Spirit are inseparable for Calvin, there is also a complete oneness to these two hands.[9] Indeed, for Calvin, there is a tri-unity in the way that God relates to creation. For the believer, this means that repentance involves a process of becoming reborn in Christ, through his Spirit, "into participation in the Father."[10]

7   Ibid., 107.

8   John Calvin, *Commentaries on the First Twenty Chapters of the Prophet Ezekiel* vol. 2, trans. Thomas Myers (Grand Rapids: Eerdmans, 1948), 245.

9   *Institutes*, I.9.3; see Irenaeus, *Against Heresies*, www.newadvent.org/fathers/0103506.htm (accessed 21/1/2014), V.6.1.

10 *Institutes*, I.8.26. In this way, Calvin goes so far as to affirm that we become "united to God," *Institutes*, I.15.6. For further clarity on this issue, see J. Todd Billings, "United to God through Christ: Assessing Calvin on the Question of Deification," *Harvard Theological Journal* 98, (2005): 315–34. It should be noted here that Calvin's grammar of participation normally emphasizes participation *in Christ*. This quote is

By becoming united into this fellowship with the triune God, the Christian experiences repentance as "a kind of second creation."[11] She experiences it as an activity that is qualitatively new to anything she has experienced before and, as a result, becomes a new creation. Repentance, therefore, is not an act that a person can perform in and of herself, through the working of her imagination or ritualistic practice. It requires the person to be reconciled by a triune activity that cannot be anticipated and certainly cannot be summoned up by the activity of the creature.

As we shall now see, however, repentance itself is not the start of a person's subjective journey with God. The newness of life, which Calvin sees as the goal of repentance is "conferred on us by Christ" and "attained by us through faith."[12] The Christian life begins with the Spirit uniting us with the person of Christ in faith such that Christ takes residence within us, "governing us by the Spirit and directing all our actions."[13] In Christ, we participate in the one who is the objective ground of repentance. More specifically, as we shall see, the central turn to which repentance corresponds, is the turn from death on the cross to life in the resurrection. However, before looking further at how repentance relates to the person and work of Christ in Calvin's thought, it will be helpful to gain some clarity on the way in which Calvin distinguishes repentance from faith.

(a) Faith and Repentance

> ... it ought to be a fact beyond controversy that repentance not only constantly follows faith, but is also born of faith.[14]

Faith, for Calvin, is "the origin of repentance."[15] Over against the Lutheran tradition, he asserts that repentance is not possible without faith.[16] Why does he insist on this? Because unless a person is faithfully participating in fellowship with God, and, therefore, embracing the grace of God, a

---

an exception to this.

11 Calvin, *Commentaries on the First Twenty Chapters of the Prophet Ezekiel* vol. 2, 245.

12 *Institutes*, III.3.1.

13 Calvin, *Commentary on Galatians*, ed. David W. and Thomas F. Torrance, trans. T.H.L. Parker (Edinburgh: Oliver and Boyd, 1965), 43.

14 *Institutes*, III.3.1.

15 Ibid., III.3.2.

16 See Augsburg Confession, Art. xii.

person would have no true reason to turn away from disobedience to follow the commands of God. Moreover, as Randall Zachman points out on Calvin, if a person did not have the faith to know God's forgiveness, it would be impossible for her, as a sinner, "not to flee from God."[17] Accordingly, Calvin thinks that it is "madness" for the Anabaptists and the Jesuits to try to begin with repentance by prescribing "to their new converts certain days during which they must practice penance," which are *only then followed* by their admittance into the "communion of the grace of the gospel."[18] The problem is the suggestion that penance (outward expressions of repentance) can be considered as possible apart from the life of faith and communion that is grounded in and inspired by the grace of the gospel. For Calvin, a person cannot come to know the grace of God by first penitently turning away from the sin which itself cannot be truly known without faith. Also, a person certainly cannot come to know the grace of God by simply practicing penance. Rather, repentance comes from first knowing the grace of God in faith.

So where does faith come from? Faith arises as a person is awakened by the Spirit to hear the gospel message that she has been "freed from the tyranny of Satan, the yoke of sin, and the miserable bondage of vices."[19] For Calvin, a person comes to faith by the Spirit uniting her to Christ, in whom she is adopted as a child of the gracious Father. In unity with Christ, faith is received as "a firm and sure knowledge of the divine favour toward us, founded on the truth of a free promise in Christ, and revealed to our minds, and sealed on our hearts, by the Holy Spirit."[20] As such, faith is not merely a strong conviction about Christianity, nor is it simply an objective gift that God passes on to or implants in a person. Rather, faith arises as an awareness of reality: an awareness that she belongs to God by discovering that she is participating in the Kingdom of God, in which God has graciously claimed her for himself, in Christ. For Calvin, it is only by consciously participating in this fellowship with God that a person starts out on a journey of repentance.

---

17   Randall Zachman, *The Assurance of Faith – Conscience in the Theology of Martin Luther and John Calvin* (Louisville: Westminster John Knox Press, 2005), 155.

18   *Institutes*, III.3.2. Derisively, Calvin then adds, "Obviously that giddy spirit brings forth such fruits that it limits to a paltry few days a repentance that for the Christian man ought to extend throughout his life."

19   Ibid., III.3.1.

20   Ibid., III.2.7.

While Calvin stresses the priority of faith over repentance, he does not suggest that repentance merely presents itself as a possible option to a person once she has come to faith. He insists that repentance flows from faith. As a person is engrafted into the vine of Christ, repentance "is produced by [faith] as a fruit from a tree."[21] "No one," he maintains, "can embrace the grace of the gospel without betaking himself from the errors of his past life into the right way, and applying his whole effort to the practice of repentance."[22]

A challenge that may confront the contemporary reader of Calvin as she tries comes to terms with his ordering of faith before repentance is his interpretation of "repentance" as conversion to God. Is it not strange to consider conversion as subsequent to faith? For Calvin, the Hebrew term for repentance, *shuv*, means "to return," and the Greek term for repentance, *metanoia*, refers to the transformation of the mind. From his analysis of the Hebrew and the Greek, he interprets repentance as a movement in which, "departing from ourselves, we turn to God, and having taken off our former mind, we put on a new."[23] When he does so, he does not interpret a person's conversion as her coming to faith. Rather, conversion refers to the lifelong process of repentance in which a person gradually comes to correspond to the fellowship she has with the Father, in Christ, by the Spirit.[24]

On this journey, the active changes that the Spirit effects in the life of the Christian are grounded in a union with Christ that awakens "the inclination of righteousness, judgment, and mercy."[25] So, while Calvin affirms the importance of self-denial, he does recognise a role for the

---

21 Ibid., III.3.1.

22 Ibid.

23 Ibid., III.3.5.

24 As Alexander Ganoczy writes, Calvin understood conversion "in the biblical sense of 'repentance,' i.e., the fundamental penitential act of the believer." Ganoczy, "Calvin's Life" in *Cambridge Companion to Calvin*, ed. Donald McKim (Cambridge: Cambridge University Press, 2004), 9.

25 *Institutes*, III.3.8. For Calvin, this inclination comes from the grace and promise of salvation. So, when both John the Baptist and Jesus Christ proclaim "Repent, for the kingdom of heaven has come near" (Matt. 3:2, 4:17), Calvin does not see this as a challenge to his ordering of faith before repentance. Rather, he interprets this as suggesting that both John and Jesus "derive the reason for repenting from grace itself and the promise of salvation." For Calvin, the words "Repent, for the kingdom of heaven has come near" would have no impact on the person who did not have a faith to know the grace of God and the promise of salvation. *Institutes*, III.3.2.

conscience, albeit for a renewed conscience. Indeed, he asserts that anyone who "is moderately versed in Scripture will understand by himself, without the admonition of another, that when we have to deal with God nothing is achieved unless we begin with the inner disposition of the heart."[26] Thus, for Calvin, it is a faithful heart and mind that is the beginning of repentance, informed by a Spirit-inspired knowledge of God's love and grace.

Again, however, we need to be clear that Calvin does not view either Jesus Christ or the Holy Spirit as being purely instrumental in the life of the Christian. "Christian" action is not the goal of God's covenant purposes. Rather, in Jesus Christ, God establishes a union with human beings, which is itself the fulfilment of God's covenant purposes (rather than a means to enabling "Christian" action). While it is God alone who brings about this fulfilment, in Christ, this fulfilment is not closed off from the world. Rather, it establishes a new mediation between God and humanity that makes way for a new fellowship (*koinonia*) between God and human beings, which is characterised by adoption into God's family. Within this fellowship, it is not simply a person's inward existence that is transformed. She shares in a new way of being that is *outwardly* defined by fellowship with the person of Jesus Christ, by his Spirit. It is out of and within this fellowship that a person exists Christianly. At the centre of this fellowship, for Calvin, is not interactivity (God's activity seeking responsive human activity) but the Holy Spirit engrafting persons into union with Christ.

Basic to this new way of being in *koinonia*, as I mentioned above, is human self-denial. This self-denial, however, involves much more than a process of the human denying her previous selfhood. It involves God denying the human self to continue in sin, through the life, death and resurrection of Jesus Christ. Accordingly, Christian self-denial involves participation in God's denial of the sinful human self, through indwelling of the Spirit, who delivers the sinner from inwardness of the flesh and clothes her in Christ. Accordingly, as Joel Beeke writes on Calvin, "self-denial is not self-centred, as was often the case in medieval monasticism, but God-centred."[27]

By being outwardly God-centred (living in union with Christ, by his Spirit), the Christian faith distinguishes itself from all merely immanent forms of belief. And, given that Christian repentance is the fruit of

26 Ibid., III.3.16.
27 Joel Beeke, "Calvin on Piety" in *Cambridge Companion to Calvin*, ed. Donald McKim (Cambridge: Cambridge University Press, 2004), 143.

this faith, Christian repentance is qualitatively distinct from all merely "natural" forms of creaturely repentance. Christian repentance refers to the change that a person goes through as she is created anew in fellowship with the triune God, who takes her beyond the self-centred sphere of the flesh. In this respect, as Torrance was clear about, Christian faith and repentance are the fruit of covenant rather then contract. That is, they are an expression of something greater that is going on for humanity, according to the grace of God: something *holy* that God would never leave to be conditioned by the totally depraved dynamics of the fallen world. As we shall see, this theological understanding is at the very heart of the distinction that both Calvin and Torrance draw between legal and evangelical repentance. However, before looking specifically at this distinction, let us look a bit further at what it means to "die to" and "come alive" in Calvin's evangelical vision of repentance.

(b) Mortification and Vivification

As we have seen, Calvin understands that, on the hand, repentance involves a self-denial that is characterised by a dying to the flesh: *mortification*. On the other side, it involves a renewal that is animated by the Spirit, who makes persons alive in Christ: *vivification*. Together, these two movements involve a dying to the self-centred self to make way for a reconciliation into a new way of being-in-*koinonia*, which is the ground of Christian repentance: a way of being in which "believers live outside themselves (*fideles extra se vivere*), that is, in Christ."[28] In these terms, "we do not view him [Christ] as at a distance and without us, but as we have put him on, and been engrafted into his body, he deigns to make us one with himself, and therefore, we glory in having a fellowship of righteousness with him."[29] As Paul Helm clarifies, however, this should not be taken to suggest that Calvin argues for "a gross mixture or transfusion of Christ into us."[30] He explains, quoting Calvin,

> The agent of this union is the Holy Spirit, Christ's Spirit. 'The Holy Spirit is the bond by which Christ effectually binds us to himself', by calling us to Christ and imbuing us with virtues and graces, principally faith. 'For it is by the Spirit alone that he

---

28 Calvin, *Commentary on Galatians*, 42–3.
29 *Institutes*, III.11.10.
30 Helm, *Christ at the Centre* (Oxford: Oxford University Press, 2009), 210.

unites himself to us. By the same grace and energy of the Spirit we become his members, so that he keeps us under him, and we in our turn possess him.'[31]

So how does this relate to Calvin's understanding of repentance as mortification and vivification? Again, for Calvin, mortification and vivification occur in Christ, by his Spirit. On the one hand, this means that mortification requires us to participate in Christ's death, which brings an end to the wickedness of our being: "'our old man is crucified by his power and the body of sins perishes' (Rom. 6:6), that the corruption of original nature may no longer thrive."[32] In this way, "we must acknowledge that in ourselves we are dead."[33] On the other hand, it means that the Spirit needs to vivify us into sharing in Christ's resurrection, in and through which, "we are raised up into newness of life to correspond with the righteousness of God."[34] In these terms, Calvin interprets repentance as an act of regeneration, through which we are "restored in the image of God that has been disfigured and all but obliterated through Adam's transgression."[35]

Repentance, therefore, does not simply involve a process of bettering one's humanity in mind of one's wrongdoing. It involves a process of being made alive into one's true humanity, in the image of God. What is important to understand here, for Calvin, is that human beings are not self-sufficient entities but are dependent upon the life-giving grace of God. The life-givingness of this grace does not just enliven persons by keeping their hearts beating and blood pumping but by drawing them into *conscientious* fellowship with God in Christ, in whom persons long "to live in a holy and devoted manner."[36] With respect to the heart of the believer, this means that *mortification* of the flesh inspires contrition and *vivification* by the Spirit inspires consolation.[37] So "when a man is laid low by the consciousness of sin and stricken by the fear of God, and afterward looks to the goodness of God – to his mercy, grace, salvation,

---

31 Ibid., 210; quoting *Institutes* III.1.1; III.1.3–4; III.1.3.

32 *Institutes*, III.3.9.

33 Calvin, "Treatise on the Lord's Supper" in *Calvin: Theological Treatises*, trans. J.K.S. Reid (London: SCM Press, 1954), 150.

34 *Institutes*, III.3.9.

35 Ibid.

36 Ibid., III.3.3; see also Calvin, "Catechism of the Church of Geneva," 134.

37 Ibid., III.3.8.

which is through Christ – he raises himself up, he takes heart, he recovers courage, and as it were, returns from death to life."[38] This should not be misinterpreted to suggest that Calvin understands mortification and vivification in purely experiential terms – as though "vivification [is] the happiness that the mind receives after its perturbation and fear have been quieted."[39] He writes,

> It is true that for a sinner to beg for forgiveness demands a sorrow of conscience and displeasure at himself. But it is wrong to infer from this that repentance, which is the gift of God, is contributed by men as the movement of their own heart.[40]

For Calvin, the mortifying and vivifying movement of the heart, which characterises repentance, is only made possible when a person is adopted by the Father into union with Christ through his Spirit.

(c) Legal Repentance or Evangelical Repentance?

Prior to Calvin, much of the medieval church, coming out of Rome, had reduced repentance to a legal step that a person is required to make, in advance, in order to be forgiven and restored. To provide guidance as to how a person should go about repenting, the church instituted the sacrament of penance, as an expression of repentance. It was seen to be through a process of penance that a person could find forgiveness and restoration, and thereby enjoy a life of fellowship within the Body of Christ. In response to this situation, Calvin set out to reform how society interpreted repentance by putting forward an account of "evangelical repentance" (*evangelicam poenitentiam*) which would challenge the "legal repentance" (*legalis poenitentiae*) that was being advocated in the church's promotion of penance.

Legal repentance, for Calvin, refers to the repentance that puts the onus on the sinner to try to escape his sin and guilt. It presents itself as an option to the sinner who finds himself so overwhelmed and caught up with a fear and anxiety over God's wrath that he does not know where to turn. He does not know how he can get beyond the consequences of

---

38   Ibid., III.3.3.
39   Ibid.
40   Calvin, *A Harmony of the Gospels: Matthew, Mark & Luke* (Grand Rapids: Eerdmans, 1972), 223 (on Luke 15:20).

his sin because he can only conceive of God "as avenger and judge."[41] As Torrance presents it, the sinner cannot get beyond the interpretation of God as lawgiver, as "contract God." This can be seen, for Calvin, in the torment of Cain (Gen. 4:13), Saul (1 Sam. 15:30), and Judas (Matt. 27:4). In each of these figures, the gravity of their sin is acknowledged with a feeling of utter hopelessness. Accordingly, "their repentance was nothing but a sort of entryway of hell, which they had already entered in this life, and had begun to undergo punishment before the wrath of God's majesty."[42] In each instance, repentance finds the sinner looking to himself and his own inabilities, trying hopelessly to escape his wrongdoing and guilt.

Legal repentance is also evident, for Calvin, in the theology of the scholastic Sophists who "never understood what repentance is."[43] For them, repentance "is sorrow of heart and bitterness of soul for the evil deeds that one has committed, or to which one has consented."[44] Calvin acknowledges that there was a place for this attitude towards sin in the theology of the church fathers. However, he asserts that the fathers merely saw this sorrow and bitterness as a deterrent to discourage believers from "falling again into the same transgressions from which they have been rescued."[45]

It was not, however, just the overbearing anxiety, sorrow and a bitter feeling of hopelessness that bothered Calvin about legal accounts of repentance. This context of misery prompted sinners to find release in a whole manner of different practices.[46] Repentance came to be seen as an activity that could summon the grace of God into one's life – a routine that a person could go through in advance, akin to the penitent speech that the prodigal son prepared for his father. For the Scholastics, this routine was characterised by "contrition of heart (*contritio*), confession

41 Ibid., III.3.4.
42 Ibid.
43 Ibid., III.4.1.
44 Ibid.
45 Ibid.
46 It should be noted, here, that Calvin affirmed a place for ritual symbols of repentance (such as fasting), so long as they were not interpreted legalistically; that is, so long as they were not interpreted as ways of inciting the grace of God. As Randall Zachman points out, "Calvin reinforces his desire to see times of public and communal fasting and weeping [as testimonies of repentance] in the third edition of the *Institutes*." Zachman, *Image and Word in the Theology of John Calvin* (Notre Dame: University of Notre Dame Press, 2007), 370; see 369-72.

of mouth (*confessio*), and satisfaction of works (*satisfactio*)."[47] As Torrance shows throughout his writing, this massively shaped the way people came to interpret worship. Rather than seeing worship as an opportunity for fellowship, rejoicing and gratitude, which participates in the Son's communion with Father, by the Spirit, it came to be seen as a time to appease an angry God; everything became about penance. Consequently, outward exercises became so emphasised that repentance became "a discipline and austerity that serves partly to tame the flesh, partly to chastise and partly to punish faults."[48] With this emphasis, Calvin felt that the Scholastics ended up being "wonderfully silent concerning the inward renewal of the mind, which bears with its true correction of life."[49] The Scholastics, he writes, "torture souls with many misgivings, and immerse them in a sea of trouble and anxiety. But where they seem to have wounded hearts deeply, they heal all the bitterness with a light sprinkling of ceremonies."[50] What bothered Calvin most was not simply that the practice of penance came to define the church's understanding of repentance, but that it came to be seen as "necessary to attain forgiveness of sins."[51] In Calvin's teaching, which was taken up by Torrance, "nothing is more miserable or deplorable" than making the forgiveness of sins conditional upon the sacrament of penance – especially when it is made conditional upon a "due contrition, that is just and full."[52]

For Calvin, the legal accounts of repentance that were being put forward had lost sight of the gospel message of God's forgiveness in Christ. His resistance to this legalism, however, did not incline him to risk asserting that Jesus had come to abolish the law. He acknowledges that "the more earnestly a man measures his life by the standard of God's law, the surer are the signs of repentance that he shows."[53] Under this law, he acknowledges that the sinner would still struggle with the fact that he is a sinner, and he asserted that repentance begins with a sorrow and dread that hates sin (2 Cor. 7:10).[54] Indeed, he affirmed with an almost

---

47 Ibid., III.4.1.
48 Ibid.
49 Ibid.
50 Ibid.
51 Ibid.
52 Ibid.
53 Ibid., III.3.16.
54 Ibid., III.3.20.

Lutheran voice that hatred of sin "first gives us access to the knowledge of Christ, who reveals himself to none but poor and afflicted sinners, who groan, toil, are heavy-laden, hunger, thirst, and pine away with sorrow and misery (Isa. 61:1-3; Matt. 11:5, 28; Luke 4:18)."[55] Also, Calvin was firmly of the view that "repentance proceeds from an earnest fear of God" – that repentance "must be aroused by thinking upon divine judgment."[56] It is this fear that inspires a deep and earnest respect for God, with which a person hands her life over to the grace of God.[57]

So what distinguishes Calvin's account of evangelical repentance? For Calvin, the evangelical believer remembers "to exercise restraint" in his sorrowful and fearful reflection over sin so that his conscience does not cause him to fall into despair.[58] The evangelical does not trap himself in a self-absorbed anxiety over his depravity; he does not continually torture himself with a fear over God's wrath. Instead, he embraces Christ as the one who is "medicine for his wound, comfort for his dread, the haven of misery."[59] For Calvin, evangelical repentance is evident "in all those who, made sore by the sting of sin but aroused and refreshed by trust in God's mercy, have turned to the Lord."[60] It refers to those – such as Hezekiah (2 Kgs. 20:2; Isa. 38:2), the Ninevites (Jonah 3:5, 9), David (2 Sam. 24:10), Peter (Matt. 26:75; Luke 22:62), and, of course, Zacchaeus – who were confronted with the seriousness of their sin and turned toward God for forgiveness.[61]

For Calvin, it is in light of the fact that the triune God has taken away our sin in Christ that we are summoned to faith and repentance. Contra legal repentance, evangelical repentance denies that it is our

---

55 Ibid.
56 Ibid., III.3.7.
57 Accordingly, Calvin quotes the following wonderful passage from Bernard: "Sorrow for sins is necessary if it be not unremitting. I beg you to turn your steps back sometimes from troubled and anxious remembering of your ways, and to go forth to the table end of serene remembrance of God's benefits. Let us mingle honey with wormwood that its wholesome bitterness may bring health when it is drunk tempered with sweetness. If you take thought upon yourselves in your humility, take thought likewise upon the Lord in his goodness." Bernard, *Sermons on the Song of Songs* xi.2 (MPL 183. 824 f.; trans. Samuel J. Eales, *Life and Words of St Bernard* IV. 55); cited in *Institutes*, III.3.12.
58 *Institutes*, III.3.15.
59 Ibid., III.3.4.
60 Ibid.
61 Ibid.

penitent action that summons God to forgive us and restore us. It is only by the Spirit of God reconciling a person into union with Christ, that she participates in forgiveness and restoration: the forgiveness and restoration that has already been accomplished for her in the person and work of Christ.

By becoming united with Christ, the believer starts out on what Calvin describes as a "race of repentance."[62] This is a "firm and constant" race, upon which believers are given to "battle against the evil which is within us, not for a day or a week, but without end or intermission."[63] This race, for Calvin, is the formative process of growing in Christ that constitutes the Christian life. As Brian Gerrish notes, Calvin saw repentance not as "a transient crisis-experience, but the entire life of the Christian."[64] On this race, "the children of God [are] freed through regeneration from bondage to sin," but without obtaining "full possession of freedom so as to feel no more annoyance from their flesh."[65] As such, Calvin follows Augustine in asserting that "there remains in a regenerate man a smoldering cinder [*fomes*] of evil, from which desires continually leap forth to allure and spur him to commit sin."[66] Yet Calvin also distinguishes himself from Augustine by disagreeing with Augustine's interpretation of sin as a weakness rather than a disease. He writes, Augustine "teaches that it becomes sin only when either act of consent follow the conceiving or apprehension of if, that is, when the will yields to the first strong inclination. We, on the other hand, deem it sin when man is tickled by any desire at all against the law of God."[67] For Calvin, sin is the "very depravity which begets in us [inordinate] desires [*concupiscentiis*]." Augustine, however, saw these desires as prompting sin rather than being sinful in and of themselves.[68]

For the evangelical, however, the failures and weaknesses that the Christian experiences on her journey of faith are overshadowed by the knowledge that "Christ became redemption, righteousness, salvation and

---

62 Ibid., III.3.9.
63 John Calvin, "Treatise on the Lord's Supper," 152.
64 Brian Gerrish, *Grace and Gratitude* (Minneapolis: Fortress Press, 1993), 94.
65 *Institutes*, III.3.10.
66 Ibid.
67 Ibid.
68 Ibid.

life (1 Cor. 1:30)."[69] In Christ, the believer "is freely accounted righteous and innocent in God's sight."[70] This means that any attempt on the part of the individual to seek repentance and achieve righteousness by her own effort, will fail completely. Indeed, she will be committing an act of idolatry because she will be turning to a false righteousness that is nothing more than a projection of her own corrupt mind.

A crucial point to note here, which James Torrance was always quick to point out,[71] is that Calvin understood Christ's atonement as being sufficient for all. This meant, as Charles Partee writes, "[a]ssurance of salvation is possible because faith is christologically rather than anthropologically based."[72] Objectively, in Christ, Calvin affirms that "God declares that he wills the conversion of all, and he directs exhortations to all in common."[73] Indeed, he affirms that "God wishes all men to be saved."[74] However, he then adds the critical qualification that this only becomes an actuality for persons *"when they turn themselves from their ways."*[75] In this way, Randall Zachman writes,

> [Repentance] is the necessary condition for our acceptance of God's pardon . . . God makes the offer of reconciliation, forgiveness and pardon contingent upon repentance; for the serious abhorrence of sin, which is the beginning of repentance, opens the door for God's pardoning mercy. The pardon of God in Jesus Christ is not to be understood as yet another way in which hypocrites can escape a serious acknowledgment of their own sin and of God's judgment. Only those who anticipate the eschatological judgment of God by judging and condemning themselves by the testimony of their conscience shall be spared that judgment and receive pardon.[76]

---

69 Ibid., III.3.19.

70 Ibid.

71 See, in particular, James B. Torrance, "The Concept of Federal Theology – Was Calvin a Federal Theologian?" in Wilhelm Neuser (ed.), *Calvinus Sacrae Scripturae Professor* (Grand Rapids, MI: Eerdmans, 1994), 15-40; "The Incarnation and Limited Atonement," 83-94.

72 Charles Partee, *The Theology of John Calvin* (Louisville: Westminster John Knox Press), 208.

73 *Institutes*, III.3.21.

74 Calvin, *Commentary on the First Twenty Chapters of the Book of the Prophet Ezekiel* vol. 2, 247.

75 Ibid. (emphasis original).

76 Zachman, *The Assurance of Faith*, 150.

Importantly, however, this does not mean that Calvin makes the atonement (which is achieved objectively for us, in Jesus Christ) conditional upon subjective human acts of repentance. Rather, it means that a person's subjective participation in Christ's atonement (which involves a sincere acceptance of God's pardon) is conditional upon her being one of the elect who has been chosen by God to be enlivened by the Spirit of regeneration.[77] So, for Calvin, repentance and faith are not, in themselves, meritorious; they are not a condition of God's forgiveness. Rather, true repentance is an expression of the fact that a person has been freely elected by God for salvation in Christ and is thus renewed by the inner workings of the Holy Spirit. In this way, for both Torrance and Calvin, repentance and faith are signs and seals of the covenant of grace. As Dawn De Vries writes, "Faith merely conveys God's adopting grace to those who believe."[78] For this reason, Calvin notes that "the hope of salvation is promised them when they repent."[79] In repentance, a person turns in a way that corresponds to the fact that she has been predestined to participate in the covenant of grace that is fulfilled in Jesus Christ. For Calvin, God renews "those he wills not to perish, shows the sign of his fatherly favor and, so to speak, draws them to himself with the rays of his calm and joyous repentance."[80] However, "he hardens and thunders against the reprobate, whose impiety is unforgivable."[81]

The risk with this position (which Torrance devoted himself to challenging) is that believers end up looking to their own repentance to find assurance of their election, rather than turning to Christ. As Torrance shows repeatedly, this problem was prevalent in the scholastic Calvinism that distorted and misappropriated Calvin's theology (particularly in Scotland). While it was almost inevitable that this problem would arise, Calvin continually insisted, as David Willis-Watkins notes, that "the

---

77   *Institutes*, III.3.21.
78   Dawn DeVries, "Calvin's Preaching," in *Cambridge Companion to Calvin*, ed. Donald McKim (Cambridge: Cambridge University Press, 2004), 117.
79   Calvin, *Commentaries on the First Twenty Chapters of the Prophet Ezekiel* vol. 2, 248.
80   *Institutes*, III.3.21.
81   Ibid. On this point, Calvin drew a dichotomy between the (predestined) elect and the (predestined) reprobate that was rejected by James Torrance, who followed his teacher Karl Barth in affirming a chrisocentric account of humanity that knew no such division.

assurance of faith comes from focussing on Christ and not on ourselves apart from him."[82] As Randall Zachman,

> The object of faith, according to Calvin, is neither justification nor regeneration, but Jesus Christ himself, the image of the invisible Father, in whom the Father has taken away all the evil that afflicts us and has given us every good thing that we lack. The primary object of faith, therefore, is neither forgiveness of sins nor newness of life, but union with Christ. Jesus Christ offers himself to us in the gospel as the fountain of every good sent to sinners by the Father. The Holy Spirit illumines our minds and seals on our hearts the knowledge of Christ, thereby engrafting us into Christ so that we not only participate in all of his benefits but also in himself.[83]

In Calvin's account of evangelical repentance, it is God's mercy that leads a person to repent, not human repentance that leads God to be merciful. Repentance is not "the basis of our deserving pardon."[84] Rather, "because the Lord has determined to have pity on men to the end that they may repent, he indicates in what direction men should proceed if they wish to obtain grace."[85] True repentance, therefore, does not come from our corrupt nature. It is grounded in the outworking of the Spirit in one's life, drawing a person into Jesus Christ. For Calvin, "it is certain that the mind of man is not changed for the better except by God's prevenient grace."[86]

3. Following in the Footsteps of Calvin: Torrance on Evangelical Repentance

The thrust of Torrance's engagement with the question of repentance was directed at challenging the perception that the Gospel message of forgiveness was conditional upon individual repentance: *if* an individual repents of her sin, *then* God will forgive her. In these terms, individual repentance functions as an imperative (pre)condition for receiving the

---

82 David Willis-Watkins, "The Unio Mystica and the Assurance of Faith According to Calvin," *Calvin: Erbe and Auftrag: Festschrift für Wilhelm Heinrich Neuser zum 65. Geburstag*, ed. Willem van't Spijker (Kampen: Kok Pharos, 1991), 77.
83 Zachman, *The Assurance of Faith*, 188.
84 *Institutes*, III.3.20.
85 Ibid.
86 Ibid., III.3.24. Calvin contends that because repentance is clearly "a singular gift of God", "there is no need of a long discourse to explain it." *Institutes*, III.3.21.

gift of grace. To affirm this, the Gospel message ends up being abstracted from God's unconditional and unconditioned covenant commitment to Israel, so that it can be interpreted legally or contractually. That is, the Gospel message of forgiveness is presented as a new deal that replaces God's covenant of grace, allowing God's purposes to become subject to the caprice of creaturely determination and circumstance. For Torrance, the inclination towards this theology is indicative of the fact that "[t]here is something in the human heart which makes men want to bargain with God."[87] As Alan Torrance point out, there are two reasons for this,

> First, it reflects the human desire for control – to be able to condition God's response and earn our deserts, that is, to be in a position to claim credit for the way God treats us . . . Second, there is the desire within the Church, both Catholic and Protestant, to control and motivate its adherents . . . To translate God's covenant relationship into contractual terms in order to manipulate people into either repentance or conversion . . . is to supplant the free, loving and transforming activity of the Holy Spirit, with the worldly manipulation of people's self-interest . . .[88]

This problem, for James Torrance, "emerges most clearly when the Church is most concerned about godly discipline and the relation between forgiveness and repentance," which "was the focal point of the Reformation."[89] While there were many problems with the way that the Reformed tradition engaged with this point (as Torrance shows in his ongoing critique of the so-called "Calvinist" tradition), Calvin's own insistence that our religious experience is not at the centre of the New Testament was invaluable. For Calvin and Torrance, the central theme of the New Testament is the "unique relationship between Jesus and the Father."[90] Torrance continues, following Calvin, "Christ is presented to us as the Son living a life of union and communion with the Father in the Spirit, presenting himself in our humanity through the eternal Spirit to

---

87 Torrance, "Covenant or Contract?" 57.

88 Alan Torrance, "The Bible as Testimony to Our Belonging: The Theological Vision of James B. Torrance," in *An Introduction to Torrance Theology - Discovering the Incarnate Saviour* ed. Gerrit Dawson (London: T&T Clark, 2007), 107.

89 Torrance, "Covenant or Contract?" 57.

90 James B. Torrance, *Worship, Community & the Triune God of Grace* (Downers Grove: InterVarsity Press, 1996), 32.

the Father on behalf of humankind."[91] It is in the person of Christ that God speaks to us "his word of forgiveness, his word of love which is at the same time the word of judgment and condemnation, the word of the cross."[92]

However, Torrance also qualifies, continuing to follow Calvin, "implicit in our receiving the word of grace and forgiveness, the word of the Father's love, there must be on our part, a humble submission to the verdict of guilty."[93] The New Testament informs us that forgiveness is unconditional but "nevertheless demands unconditionally the response of repentance."[94] At the heart of Calvin's account of evangelical repentance is the recognition that "God accepts us, not because of our repentance – we have no worthy penitence to offer – but in the person one who has already said amen for us, in death, to the divine condemnation of our sin – in atonement."[95] This is evident in "the fact that Christ died for us while we were yet sinners" (Rom. 5:8).[96] And, for Torrance, "it is this Word of the Cross that leads a man to repentance."[97] According to the New Testament, "*forgiveness is logically prior to repentance.*"[98] "It is not the case, therefore, as in legal repentance, that 'if you repent, you will be forgiven . . . this do and you will live!'" [99] Rather, as in evangelical repentance, "Christ has borne your sins on the cross, therefore repent!" In this way, Torrance affirmed with Calvin that it is forgiveness that leads to true repentance, not the other way around.

This order has continually been neglected in the history of the church, particularly in Scotland, as Torrance showed throughout his authorship. Exhortation has dominated the proclamation from the pulpit in an attempt by preachers to "produce a conviction of sin and a fear of judgment" that would prompt "the sinner to repent and renounce his sin so that he might receive the word of forgiveness and hear the comforts of

---

91 Ibid., 32.
92 Ibid., 55.
93 Ibid.
94 Torrance, "Covenant or Contract?" 57.
95 Torrance, *Worship, Community & the Triune God of Grace*, 56.
96 Torrance, "Covenant or Contract?" 57.
97 Ibid., 57.
98 James B. Torrance, "The Contribution of McLeod Campbell to Scottish Theology," *Scottish Journal of Theology* 26, no. 3 (1973), 307 (emphasis original).
99 Torrance, "Covenant or Contract?" 57.

the gospel."[100] When legal repentance is preached in this way, it becomes "the false motives of fear of hell and hope of heaven" that drive the Christian life. Consequently, the person of Christ and the person of his Spirit come to be seen as utilities on a person's venture to escape hell and get into heaven. On this road, the Christian is continually haunted by the prospect that she might not be doing enough, undermining any assurance of her salvation. However, when evangelical repentance is preached, the Christian life is encouraged by the "the motives of gratitude and joy," with the Christian finding "assurance of forgiveness in Christ."[101]

4. Conclusion

At the centre of the debate over the meaning of repentance, for both Calvin and Torrance, lies the question of whether the covenant of grace is conditioned by human acts of repentance. That is, is God's covenant commitment to humanity in any way conditional upon persons self-consciously turning away from their wrongdoing, towards God? For both, God's covenant of grace is fulfilled unconditionally in the person of Jesus Christ. It is "made *for* us *in Christ*," such that our faith needs to be interpreted in the "non-contractual terms" of "union with Christ."[102] Therefore, the fulfilment of the covenant of grace is not conditioned by individual acts of faith; rather, faith is our participation in the one in whom the covenant is fulfilled. Faith is our participation in both "who God is for us in Jesus Christ" and "what God has done for us in Jesus Christ." And, for both, repentance is an active expression of our awakening to this faith. Evangelical repentance "is our response to grace not a condition of grace."[103] It is by participating in a life of loving *koinonia* with the triune God of grace – in Christ, by his Spirit, with the Father – that a person starts out on a journey of repentance.[104]

---

100 Ibid., 58.
101 Ibid., 59.
102 Ibid., 63.
103 Torrance, "The Contribution of McLeod Campbell to Scottish Theology," 307.
104 I would like to thank Forrest Buckner for his helpful feedback on an earlier version of this paper.

Chapter 15

The Stuttgart Declaration of 1945: A Case Study of Guilt, Forgiveness and Foreign Policy

Roger Newell

> *The Allied armies are in occupation of the whole of Germany and the German people have begun to atone for the terrible crimes committed under the leadership of those whom in the hour of their success they openly approved and blindly obeyed.*[1]

> *For our own sakes we should not refuse to be the real and sincere friends of the Germans today.*[2]

In the late 1970s I was part of the early stream of postgraduates from around the world to study with J. B. Torrance in Aberdeen. In the years that followed, I discovered that his gift of sharing his skills as a theologian were also matched by his generous pastoral care for his students, for which I remain deeply grateful. From the beginning of my studies with Torrance two themes stood out to me. The first was his integration of the spiritual and the academic life. It is captured in the quotation from P. T. Forsyth which he quoted on more than one occasion: "Prayer is to the theologian what original research is to the scientist."[3] The second was his penetrating theological conversation

---

1 *The Potsdam Declaration*, August 3, 1945. From Henry Morgenthau, Jr., *Germany is Our Problem* (New York: Harper and Brothers, 1945), Appendix C, III. Germany, paragraph one, 216.

2 Karl Barth, *The Only Way. How to Change the German Mind* (New York: Philosophical Library, 1947), 99. Lecture delivered in January, 1945.

3 Forsyth's actual words were "Prayer is for the religious life what original research is for science – by it we get direct contact with reality." P. T. Forsyth, *The Soul of Prayer*. (London: The Epworth Press, 1916), 117.

with international politics. Few theologians have spoken more prophetically to the contemporary church on political issues than Torrance did on his numerous visits to South Africa during the Apartheid years or, closer to his native Scotland, in his lectures and conversations with religious and political leaders in Northern Ireland during the years of 'the troubles.' Moreover, whenever he did address contemporary politics, it was from the center of his theology: the doctrines of incarnation, atonement and justification by grace alone.[4]

Torrance's theological engagement with political realities did not begin in Aberdeen. During his time of study in postwar Basel with Karl Barth, he became well acquainted with Barth's own grappling with the political implications of the Gospel during the tumultuous rise of the Nazis to power in Germany and also in the years of war, devastation and reconstruction in Europe which ensued. As I researched the postwar reconciliation between the Allied and German churches, I began to see how Torrance's unpacking of the meaning of forgiveness casts a clarifying light on how the postwar reconciliation between Germany and her former enemies was accomplished. Moreover, Torrance's reflections offer insight both into the failure of early efforts to rehabilitate Germany (the Morgenthau Plan) and also why later efforts (the Marshall Plan) became a model for international reconstruction.

The Aftermath of War: an Unexpected Visit amidst Chaos

The hurdles for attempting a gathering to restore ecumenical church relations with the Germans were many. How does one re-establish relations between churches whose members have spent the past five years trying to obliterate the other in a total war? The war's end raised perhaps the fundamental challenge of Christian faith, namely how to practice the difficult love of forgiving one's enemy? Moreover, how does forgiveness function within the complexity of international relations? Is it possible for governments to enact policies of a 'victor's justice' or 'collective punishment' when their churches choose the path of forgiveness and reconciliation?

4 Alan Torrance has discussed his father's involvement in further detail in this volume as well as in "The Bible as Testimony to our Belonging: The Theological Vision of James B. Torrance," in *An Introduction to Torrance Theology*, ed. G. S. Dawson (New York: T & T Clark, 2007), 109, 117-118.

Torrance's reflections on forgiveness are especially relevant since recent studies have claimed the gathering at Stuttgart was complicated by a deep disagreement between the Lutheran and Reformed parts of Protestantism, with "acrimonious debates" about preconditions to forgiveness in regard to the question of German guilt.[5] In studying the conversations at Stuttgart, I will suggest that with Torrance's help in clarifying the theological details involved, the notion of acrimonious debates is misleading. Nevertheless a stubborn human reality remains: how do Christians with a shared history of violent estrangement actually practice forgiveness?

The ecumenical gathering was awkwardly aware of the risks should their meeting for reconciliation fail. The memory of the failed peace after the 1919 Versailles treaty hung over everyone. Under the famous Article 231, (known as the War Guilt clause), Germany was forced to be liable, both morally and financially, for total responsibility for the war. The toxic consequences of this policy were many, including futile debates about guilt and blame in which ecumenical relations languished for seven long years after WWI, years of bitter resentment toward Europe which helped Hitler get his start.[6] The representatives at Stuttgart were hoping by God's mercy to shape the trajectory of the second post-war along a different path. It was this hope combined with a sense of urgency that led them to arrange, as soon as humanly possible, a meeting for reconciliation between themselves and representatives of the German Protestant church. For if the church could not practice what they had been called by Jesus to preach to the nations, how could they expect their governments to do anything other than double down on the punitive Versailles policies of World War I?

Willam Visser't Hooft of the Netherlands was the *de facto* leader of what was to become the World Council of Churches.

---

5 Matthew Hockenos, *A Church Divided. German Protestants Confront the Nazi Past* (Bloomington: Indiana University Press, 2004), 74. John Conway asserts that Hans Asmusssen delineated "in true Lutheran fashion" that the acknowledgement of guilt was a necessary prerequisite of merciful forgiveness. John S. Conway, "How Shall the Nations Repent? The Stuttgart Declaration of Guilt, October 1945," *Journal of Ecclesiastical History* 38, no. 4 (October, 1987), 603.

6 Stewart W. Herman, *The Rebirth of the German Church* (New York: Harper, 1946), 21. The economist J. M. Keynes wrote a devastating economic critique of the treaty, which unfortunately was decades ahead of Allied thinking. Cf. J. M. Keynes, *The Economic Consequences of the Peace* (London: MacMillan, 1919).

His autobiography describes the actions which now commenced. Through contacts he discovered that the Council of the Evangelical Church of Germany (renamed and reconstituted after the war) was to meet in Stuttgart in mid October. He knew this council had been chosen for their faithful witness during the church conflict with the Nazis. He wondered: would it be possible to gather a team of church leaders from the Allied nations to visit the council in order to create a presence and a pressure for reconciliation?

Through something of a miracle, just four months after hostilities had ceased, a group of eight ecumenical visitors managed to assemble the various permits from military authorities to travel to Stuttgart, Germany on October 17, 1945. Due to shortness of time and woeful communications, it had not even been possible to let the council know they were coming. "So our arrival caused considerable surprise and also much joy."[7]

Only weeks before the surprise gathering at Stuttgart, Karl Barth had written Martin Niemöller to encourage his old friend that in this dark hour of defeat, Christians of many nations wanted to help Germany. But it was *necessary*, said Barth, for Germans to say frankly and clearly, "We Germans have erred – hence the chaos of today – and we Christians in Germany are also Germans!"[8] Barth knew firsthand that the hands of the Confessing Church were not clean in regards to the German infection. To present herself as untainted by the illness manifest in Nazism was not only "nonsense" but if maintained, would set Germans against one another, the faithful remnant versus the guilty masses, making their lives even more unbearable than they already were.[9] Somehow the church must act in a way that would join in solidarity with the entire people, even though any action would take place amidst chaotic circumstances.

Chaos is not too strong a word to describe Germany at war's end. The word *Zusammenbruch*, disastrous collapse, was frequently used to describe the shambles that was now Germany.[10] Seven million Germans had perished in the war, half of them civilians. One million soldiers languished in POW camps awaiting their fate at the

---

7 W. A. Visser 't Hooft, *Memoirs* (London: SCM Press LTD, 1973), 191.

8 Quoted in James Bentley, *Martin Niemöller, 1892-1984* (New York: The Free Press, 1984), 175.

9 Barth, *The Only Way*, 12,

10 Conway, 603.

hands of their conquerors. At least another million were missing, scattered along the roads stretching East of Berlin as far away as Russia. Throughout the country, food, fuel, housing, and transport were scarce or nonexistent. Industrial machinery that had not been destroyed by bombing was being dismantled and sent away daily by the four Allied nations occupying Germany.[11] Niemöller reported that due to the shocking conditions which prevailed during the first days of Berlin's occupation by the Russian army, over two hundred persons had committed suicide in his former parish of Dahlem, a wealthy Berlin suburb. Such were the conditions in greater Berlin, that twenty pastors had committed suicide.[12] Niemöller related these dark facts not to blame anyone but simply to illustrate how Germany "has reached the brink of the precipice."[13] Daily new reports arrived detailing atrocities perpetrated by the Russians, as they took revenge for Hitler's devastating invasion of their homeland in which more than twenty six million Soviet citizens had perished, including nearly three million Soviet POW's.[14]

How could a nation be reconciled to its neighbors while it is simultaneously being ravaged by chaos? Moreover, with the war over and Hitler dead, who was responsible for the current crisis? One could argue it was all Hitler's fault. But unlike so many things he did, this chaos was now within the power of others to change.[15] Staring at the collapse of all social order, Niemöller saw his fellow Germans both numb and full of self-pity. He wondered: could Germans move from self-pity and blaming others – Nazis, Hitler, Russians, Allies, to begin to take responsibility for their own action and inaction which had enabled this tragedy?[16] He became convinced that a new start was only possible if the church took the lead in self-examination. If he and other pastors led the way on this path, it might help others take a similar responsibility – despite the chaos.

---

11 Hockenos, 90.

12 Bentley, 175.

13 Martin Niemöller, *Of Guilt and Hope* (New York: Philosophical Library, 1947), 22.

14 According to Daniel Goldhagen, *Hitler's Willing Executioners* (New York: Knopf, 1996), 290.

15 Herman, 242, 271.

16 Dietmar Schmidt, *Pastor Niemöller* (New York: Doubleday, 1959), 146.

The gathering at Stuttgart became controversial for many reasons, but one reason rarely noted is that the meeting itself bore witness that the ecumenical church was not content to passively submit to its governments' formulation of postwar policies. To put it bluntly, Allied intentions were ominous. In England, Dietrich Bonhoeffer's friend, George Bell, Bishop of Chichester, was anxious that the tone of public comments thus far, including the Potsdam agreement drafted by Truman, Stalin and Britain's newly elected Clement Atlee, revealed a plan to "humiliate and enslave the German nation."[17] In America it was hardly a secret that President Roosevelt's Secretary of the Treasury, Henry Morgenthau, had prepared a thoroughgoing punitive plan of reparations, partition, and de-industralization; turning Germany back into an agrarian society.[18] This was the grim setting in which the ecumenical church determined not to wait for their governments' intentions to simply play themselves out. Moreover, by taking this initiative, the Stuttgart visitors put a question to the Allied governments: would they pursue a victor's spirit of vengeance or pursue the irenic example of their own churches? Could such contrary approaches co-exist within the same societies or would government and church policies become a house divided?

As early as 1942 Visser't Hooft had received a powerful letter from the Lutheran Pastor Hans Asmussen, stating that he hoped the questions of war guilt would be dealt with spiritually and not politically, in a way that Christians would come together and confess their sins before God and each other. Earlier, with Bishop Bell in Stockholm, Bonhoeffer had spoken plainly that "the only road open to the Christians of Germany was the road of repentance."[19] In July 1945, Visser't Hooft wrote to Otto Dibelius, Bishop of Berlin-Brandenburg, to say that future conversations should include frank discussions about both Nazi crimes as well as the sins of omission of the German people. But there was no wish to be Pharisaic or legalistic![20] Visser't Hooft's wish was to help Germany move in the direction already

---

17 Conway, 610. Conway is especially helpful in setting the political context.

18 Morgenthau, 16, 79-80. Morgenthau, writes Beschloss, was a firm believer in collective guilt for German war crimes. Michael Beschloss, *The Conquerors. Roosevelt, Truman and the Destruction of Hitler's Germany, 1941-1945* (New York: Simon and Schuster, 2002), 52.

19 Visser 't Hooft, 189.

20 Ibid., 190.

spoken by Bonhoeffer as the only way forward for the church's rebirth after the Nazi era had ended.

Visser't Hooft, deeply influenced by Barth's theological witness, writes clearly in his *Memoirs*, that there was no question of seeking to extract a confession of guilt as some kind of precondition; only as a spontaneous gesture would such a confession have any worth.[21] Yet Barth himself had written Niemöller that it was necessary somehow for Germans, *including the German church*, to acknowledge their failure. How could this acknowledgement take place without becoming a kind of necessary precondition?

Let us recall Bonhoeffer's 1937 diagnosis at the height of the Nazi era: the church in Germany had been living within a false dream of cheap grace, that is, grace without discipleship, grace as a presumption due to its privileged Lutheran theological inheritance. There could be only one deliverance from such a distorted vision: repentance. Thus the question arises: in the exigency of the postwar environment, should repentance now be framed as a necessary prerequisite for restoration to fellowship?

Repentance: Evangelical or Legal?

As one of his signal contributions to the study of historical theology, Torrance has described how theology in the West frequently confused the relation between repentance and forgiveness and how this has been profoundly detrimental in the life of the church. Historically, nowhere was this confusion more virulent than during the medieval era, with its penitential scheme by which forgiveness was framed within a schema of meritorious transaction, conditional upon confession, contrition and satisfaction.[22] To understand the representatives who gathered at Stuttgart, it is important to be clear that both Luther and Calvin had broken decisively with the conditionality of the medieval scheme on the grounds that it had turned the personal relation of forgiveness into a legal transaction. Luther himself had written:

---

21 Ibid.

22 J. B. Torrance. "Covenant and Contract, a Study of the Theological Background of Worship in Seventeenth-Century Scotland," *Scottish Journal of Theology* 23 (1970), 51-76.

> Rome maintains that justification and forgiveness depend on the conditions of penance. Therefore we are not justified by faith alone. We maintain that contrition does not merit the forgiveness of sins. *It is indeed necessary but not the cause.* [my italics.] The cause is the Holy Spirit.[23]

Regarding this same topic, John Calvin had left no space between his view and Luther's. He wrote:

> But we added that repentance is not the cause of forgiveness of sins. Moreover we have done away with those torments of souls which they would have us perform as a duty. We have taught that the sinner does not dwell upon his own compunction or tears, but fixes both eyes upon the Lord's mercy alone. . . Over against these lies I put freely given remission of sins…what is forgiveness but a gift of sheer liberality! When can he at length be certain of the measure of that satisfaction? Then he will always doubt whether he has a merciful God; he will always be troubled, and always tremble.[24]

In this moment of crisis when the Protestant churches of Europe sought to model for their nations the way of reconciliation, did they engage in 'acrimonious debates' about the necessity of repentance as a prerequisite to forgiveness? In effect, were the heirs of the Protestant tradition on the verge of repudiating a shared foundation from the heart of the Reformation? If not, how can we understand both Barth and Bonhoeffer's emphasis on the necessity of repentance?

Much of the confusion lies with the word 'necessary' and here is where Torrance is especially helpful. Luther had written four centuries earlier that repentance "is indeed necessary but not the cause." Weeks earlier, Barth had written his friend Niemöller that it was "necessary" for the German church to say "we have erred." But as we have been reminded by the words of Luther and Calvin, both traditions were united in the hope that God's mercy was not the prisoner of preconditions. The kind of necessity Barth and Luther acknowledged was that of response to God's unconditional grace,

---

23 Martin Luther, *Luther's Works*, volume 34, "The Disputation Concerning Justification," 1536 (Philadelphia: Fortress Press, 1967), 171.

24 John Calvin, *Institutes of the Christian Religion* 3.4.3 (Philadelphia: Westminster Press, 1960), 134

not a precondition. That is, repentance was a necessary response to the life-giving power of God's grace. But it is grace alone that releases in the sinner the freedom to confess, to cease making excuses or covering up. It is the same logic of grace which freed Augustine to write his famous *Confessions* – not in order to effect God's pardon, but as a result of having been gripped by God's sheer mercy. As grace had released in Augustine an extraordinary autobiographical honesty, so in Niemöller's mind, grace was the sole grounds upon which the German church could confess its guilt after its long and confusing tale of compromise, collusion and resistance.

Torrance has further noted that to require repentance as a precondition of forgiveness severs repentance from gratitude.[25] For when repentance springs from fear of punishment instead of gratitude, notions of bargaining, merit and cunning rush in to disfigure the true necessity of repentance into what the legal mind of Tertullian unfortunately described as the price of which the Lord awards pardon.[26] Such a framing deforms repentance from the only proper response to grace into a causally necessary act of merit.

Guilt and Hope

On the evening they arrived, the visitors joined in a public service of worship at which Niemöller, Dibelius and chair of the Council, Theophil Wurm, all spoke. Niemöller preached on Jeremiah 14:7-11. "Though our iniquities testify against us, act, O Lord, for thy name's sake." In an unforgettable message Niemöller said it was not enough to blame the Nazis. The church must face its own guilt. "Would the Nazis have been able to do what they had done if church members had been truly faithful Christians?"[27] Hearing such words, Visser't Hooft was hopeful that sterile debates and mutual recriminations concerning guilt (such as those which followed the first world war) would not be repeated.

At their meeting the following day, Visser't Hooft describes their preparations thus:

---

25 From a remembered personal conversation with James Torrance.
26 Tertullian, "On Repentance," *Ante-Nicene Fathers*, 3, 661.
27 Quoted in Visser't Hooft, 191.

> On the one hand, we could not make a confession of guilt the condition for a restoration of fellowship for such a confession could only have value as a spontaneous gesture; on the other hand, the obstacles to fellowship could only be removed if a clear word were spoken. Pierre Maury gave us the right phrase. He suggested that we should say: 'We have come to ask you to help us to help you.'[28]

Again, Visser't Hooft is clear: the conversation that day had nothing to do with negotiations. To begin, Visser't Hooft expressed the delegation's desire to re-establish fraternal relations, and to express gratitude for the Confessing Church's witness. He spoke in particular of the sacrifice rendered by Bonhoeffer. Then he picked up the phrase of Pierre Maury (quoted above). Hans Asmussen spoke decisively in reply. He said he determined years ago that at the first opportunity he would say to brothers from other churches, "I have sinned against you as a member of my nation, because I have not shown more courage." Niemöller as always spoke plainly. As a church, he said, we share in the guilt of our nation and pray that God may forgive that guilt. From the Netherlands, Dr. Hendrik Kraemer responded with deep emotion. These words, said Kraemer, contained within them a call to his own church as well, that it could only live by the forgiveness of sins. "It could not be a matter of bartering."[29] As the session came to a close, Asmussen proposed the Germans meet alone in council to decide about a public declaration in light of their conversation. The following day, Bishop Wurm read aloud the text the Council had agreed upon.[30] Below is the main passage:

> We are all the more grateful for this [ecumenical] visit, as we not only know that we are with our people in a large community of suffering, but also in a solidarity of guilt. With great pain we say: By us infinite wrong was brought over many peoples and countries. That which we often testified to in our communities, we express now in the name of the whole church: We did fight for long years in the name of Jesus Christ against the mentality that found its awful expression in the National Socialist regime of violence; but we accuse ourselves for not standing to our beliefs more courageously, for not praying more faithfully, for not believing more joyously, and for not loving more ardently.

---

28 Visser't Hooft, 191-192.

29 Ibid., 192.

30 See Appendix I: The Stuttgart Declaration of Guilt.

The words were a *personal* confession of guilt offered by the representatives of the Confessing Church, despite the fact that they themselves had shown great courage in resisting the Nazis. And yet, as Niemöller made clear, there was a gnawing personal awareness that their own hands were not clean. In the coming months, Niemöller's many sermons would repeatedly describe a visit he made with his wife, Else, to the concentration camp at Dachau shortly after the war's end. There he read a notice fixed to a tree: "Here between the years 1933 and 1945, 238,756 human beings were incinerated." He sensed God asking him, 'Martin, where were you when these people were being slaughtered?'[31] Of course, imprisonment in a concentration camp was an indisputable alibi from 1937 to 1945. But what about 1933-37? Through the text of Matthew 25, Niemöller sensed God speaking to him personally. To congregations up and down Germany he confessed that when the Communists, and the trade unionists and then the Jews were thrown into concentration camps, he did not recognize Christ in them, suffering and persecuted. He remained silent.

> Here the question of guilt reveals for us Christians in Germany its horrible face. The Lord Jesus Christ asks his disciples, his church, he asks you and me, whether we are really without guilt in regard to the horrors which came to pass in our midst. I cannot reply with a clear conscience: 'Yea, Lord, I am without guilt. Thou wast in prison and I came unto Thee." Indeed I have said: "I do not know this man."[32]

Now amidst the chaos of postwar collapse, wherever one turned, multitudes were sick, underfed, and in real danger of collapse. What was to be done? Niemöller urged every believer not to wait for a pastor to come along, but to go one's self, and not pass by Christ yet again as they had done in 1933. "During these days let us keep our eyes wide open for the misery of our neighbor. If this can happen, then Christianity still has a task to perform in Europe."[33] As expressed in the title of his series of sermons, Niemöller described his postwar preaching as a message both of guilt and of hope, not the one without

---

31 Schmidt, 150-151.

32 Martin Niemöller, "The Need and the Task of the Church in Germany," preached in 1946 and included in *Best Sermons, 1947-48 Edition*, edited by G. P. Butler (New York: Harper and Brothers), 210.

33 *Of Guilt and Hope*, 14.

the other. To meet Christ in one's suffering neighbor and offer mercy was premised upon hope in God's mercy; that in showing mercy to the sufferer, the believer was participating in God's own merciful nature. Torrance's analysis only helps to clarify Niemoller's conviction: the sole premise of offering mercy rests in God's mercy, not as merited by our efforts but as grounded in God's compassionate nature.

The Legacy of Stuttgart

Why did the Stuttgart Declaration become controversial? Why over time did the church come to view it as probably the most important theological document of the Confessing Church following the war? First, we must recall the context of chaos. In October, 1945, Germany's civil and industrial infrastructure was basically destroyed. Germany was an occupied country. It had no self-government. It was unable to take any initiative in its own recovery. Deeply influenced by the Morgenthau Plan, the Allied official orders of occupation (JCS 1067) enforced by the U.S. army, directed that nothing must be done to rehabilitate in any way the German economy.[34] For Germans to grasp Niemöller's astringent message of 'guilt and hope' while living under an occupation based on 'guilt and perpetual collective punishment' was difficult, to say the least. It created strong reactions. Some leaders in the church asked why do we not speak about 'the guilt of the others'?[35] Others felt the clergy had been deviously exploited by the Allies to re-envoke the War Guilt Clause of the hated Versailles treaty in order to justify Germany's perpetual punishment.

In retrospect, Niemöller considered his efforts a failure.[36] His personal acknowledgment of guilt was more than most Germans were willing to imitate. In an interview shortly after Niemöller's escape from his death convoy, an American chaplain asked Niemöller if the world

---

34 Beschloss, 169.

35 For example, Helmut Thielicke, in *Notes from a Wayfarer* (New York: Paragon House, 1995), 231.

36 Sybil Niemöller von Sell, "Who was Martin Niemöller?" in *Remembrance and Recollection*, Volume XII, ed. Hubert G. Locke and Marcia Sachs Littell (Lanham, Maryland: University Press of America, 1996), 21. Conway says for the most part the German people refused to accept the challenge which Stuttgart put before them – to take personal responsibility for their nation's tragic course. "How Shall the Nations Repent?" 619.

should simply say, 'we forgive Germany' and start all over? Niemöller replied that the world would not be able to say: We forgive you, "but the Christians all over the world should say that, and they will start all over again with us. Measures of punishment against the people will not help."[37] Niemöller's words were prophetic. Indeed Christians all over Europe and North America did respond to Stuttgart's message. Many months before any change in Allied policy, food parcels and supplies began arriving from the churches of countries, many of whom had made personal sacrifices in sending them.[38]

Though the reconciling events at Stuttgart evoked no change in Allied policy for many months, evidence from the testimonies shared in churches throughout Europe and America suggests that the Stuttgart Declaration's Confession of Guilt opened the hearts of many people who were tempted to seek perpetual revenge. Visser't Hooft reports that as he relayed the events of Stuttgart to Protestant assemblies in France, Holland, Britain and the U.S., many spoke of how this declaration made it possible for them to acknowledge how their own struggle with the Nazis had not been sufficiently faithful and courageous. Stuttgart was making a more honest Allied response possible. The launching of the World Council of Churches itself in 1948, with the full inclusion of Germany's church would have been impossible without Stuttgart.[39]

Torrance's analysis of legal versus evangelical repentance helps to summarize the conflicted situation between theology and politics in the aftermath of Stuttgart. Gradually the Allied (Morgenthau) policy of collective punishment ('until Germany had learned its lesson') as a kind of precondition before any restoration was possible, was increasingly exposed as simply punitive. Despite the various food and aid parcels from Europe's and America's churches, all duly acknowledged, the sheer scale of Germany's collapsed economy and infrastructure meant it remained stuck in a near starvation state for three long years after the war, unable to sufficiently repent of its misdeeds to satisfy its conquerors, unable to feed itself, unable to repair its economy, unable to escape from self-pity. Moreover, the policy of punishment and de-industrialization was having a toxic effect on the rest of Europe. Germany's economic

37 *Of Guilt and Hope*, 77.
38 Schmidt, 152. The encouragement and hope these parcels gave have been commented on by many pastors during this time, including Dibelius and Thielicke.
39 Visser't Hooft, 193-194.

collapse was threatening to catch up its neighbors in its vortex.[40] But on 17 October of 1945, the ecumenical church had not come to encircle Germany with a list of preconditions. They enacted a parable of taking the initiative to restore communion.

In retrospect, we can see that Stuttgart's message created a crisis for the Allies as well as Germans. None of the Allied governments and their various churches were in any doubt they had rescued Europe and indeed, Germany, from a wicked, anti-Christian regime. But what were the implications of Christ's gospel for how one treats a defeated enemy? Should the triumph of a 'Christian civilization' over its 'pagan' (or apostate) enemies entail policies amounting to the permanent degradation of the defeated, including *de facto* the starvation of the most vulnerable – elderly, women and children?

This was the awkward question facing President Truman when in 1947 he sent former President Herbert Hoover, a committed Quaker, on a fact-finding visit to Germany. In reporting to the White House, Hoover denounced the Morgenthau Plan as "illusory", arguing that it could not work unless the Allies were prepared either to relocate or exterminate twenty-five million Germans. Less than four months later the White House announced Secretary Marshall's plan to reindustrialize Germany, bringing its industrial capacity back to its 1938 levels.[41] It is interesting to note that in preparing this new approach to Germany, Marshall accessed Secretary of War Henry Stimson's private memos to Roosevelt for inspiration. Of all the war cabinet, it was Stimson who had argued most strongly against Morgenthau, insisting that only "through Christianity and kindness" would the problem of German rehabilitation be solved.[42]

In the end, the Marshall Plan was the clearest evidence of an Allied change of heart. The government in effect determined that only by investing in its former enemy rather than continuing to punish, would healthy democracy and economic recovery take place. In our current political climate it is remarkable to consider that the US

---

40 One premise of the Marshall Plan was that the recovery of Europe would not be possible without the restoration of the German economy.

41 Erik S. Reinert, "Increasing Poverty in a Globalized World: Marshall Plans and Morgenthau Plans as Mechanisms of Polarization of World Incomes," in *Rethinking Development Economics,* ed. Ha-Joon Chang (London: Anthem Press, 2003), 455.

42 According to Michael Beschloss, Beschloss, 278. Stimson is quoted in Beschloss, 105.

government decided the way to increase her own security was not to hoard jealously half of world production, but to share it out in order to generate more wealth for all. Between 1948 and 1951 the Marshall Plan channeled $13 billion (equivalent to $130 billion today) to rebuild a war torn Europe. In other words, America devoted "an unheard of" 3% of gross national product and 10 per cent of the federal budget to rebuild Europe, including former enemy, Germany, into a formidable economic rival and partner.[43] The lesson here provides an economic analogue to Torrance's theology of forgiveness: positive change is the fruit of mercy, not its cause.

However, the memoir of Melita Maschmann illustrates Torrance's point at a more personal level. As a committed and unrepentant Nazi activist, Maschmann was sentenced to a prison camp for Nazis after the war. Though she adamantly refused to accept any guilt for her conduct, due to boredom she became drawn to the interesting conversation of the chaplain, and gradually a guarded friendship evolved. Though she avoided Jews carefully even in her internment, one day the chaplain brought along a teacher whose parents had both died in concentration camps. Thus as the chaplain introduced them, the teacher already knew of Maschmann's past role as a Nazi activist. Maschmann describes what happened:

> I will never forget the glow of spontaneous kindness in this person's eyes when she first held out her hand to me. It bridged all the gulfs, without denying them. At that moment I jumped free from the devil's wheel. I was no longer in danger of converting feelings of guilt into fresh hatred. The forgiving love which I had encountered gave me the strength to accept our guilt and my own. Only now did I cease to be a National Socialist.[44]

Only as the teacher graciously grasped her hand did Maschmann experience the inner miracle of acknowledging her guilt. Similarly, only

---

43 Elizabeth Pond, *Beyond the Wall: Germany's Road to Unification* (Washington, D.C.: The Brookings Institution, 1993), 249. Cambridge economist Ha-Joon Chang identifies the abandoning of the Morgenthau Plan in favor of the Marshall Plan as what kickstarted the recovery of post-war Europe. With it, America signaled that it was in everyone's best interest to see that its former enemies prospered. Economically speaking, the result of this strategy was "spectacular." Cf. Ha-Joon Chang, *Bad Samaritans* (New York: Bloomsbury, 2008), 62-64.

44 Melita Maschmann, *Account Rendered: A Dossier on my Former Self* (London: Abelard-Schuman, 1964), 213.

as the Marshall Plan began to be implemented, could German society makes its first steps towards what became known as Germany's economic miracle. The logic of the ecumenical gathering at Stuttgart reflects the same pattern. The Declaration to which it gave birth can be seen as a turning point in truth-telling or better, in encountering the truth that sets us free. Though controversial at the time, the Stuttgart Declaration was not a document acknowledging collective guilt which German pastors were coerced into signing. It was a personal response to the pilgrimage taken by their fellow believers from enemy nations, who took the daring initiative to be reconciled. In response, the Evangelical Church of Germany's Stuttgart Declaration blazed a trail for countless Germans to take unprecedented personal responsibility for their moral failure and in the decades since, many Germans have done so with a vast social consensus. As a result, Germany has proceeded on a trajectory that makes it hard to imagine she will ever again be seduced by the militarism and nationalism that had formerly permeated her institutions and made her so vulnerable to Hitler's message of vengeance masquerading as justice.

Thus we see how Torrance's exposition of the meaning of forgiveness sheds a clarifying light on both the personal and political issues raised by the Stuttgart Declaration of Guilt. When theology erroneously frames the event of reconciliation as conditional upon repentance, much confusion and mischief results. Persons and nations are 'thrown back upon themselves,' (to borrow another phrase from Torrance) to perform or demonstrate that somehow they deserve (merit) a gracious intervention. This approach also misunderstands the motivations of the ecumenical visitors, as if their actions were framed within the medieval penitential *schema* whereby repentance becomes the necessary price of forgiveness. The divine agency in restoring relations is taken for granted and reconciliation becomes essentially a human product, with all the attendant dangers of self-righteousness on one hand and self-loathing and despair on the other. But in life-giving contrast, the extraordinary success of the Marshall Plan confirms Torrance's insistence that truly positive change, which includes taking responsibility for one's moral failure (repentance) is the result of mercy (forgiveness), rather than its cause.

Appendix I

Declaration of the Council of the Evangelical Church in Germany, October 19, 1945

This text of the Evangelische Kirche in Deutschland is frequently referred to as the Stuttgart Declaration of Guilt. [http://www.ccjr.us/dialogika-resources/documents-and-statements/protestant-churches/eur/752-ecg1945]

The Council of the Evangelical [Protestant] Church in Germany welcomes representatives of the World Council of Churches to its meeting on October 18-19, 1945, in Stuttgart.

We are all the more thankful for this visit, as we know ourselves to be with our people in a great community of suffering, but also in a great solidarity of guilt. With great anguish we state: through us has endless suffering been brought to many peoples and countries. What we have often borne witness to before our congregations, we now declare in the name of the whole Church. We have for many years struggled in the name of Jesus Christ against the spirit which found its terrible expression in the National Socialist regime of tyranny, but we accuse ourselves for not witnessing more courageously, for not praying more faithfully, for not believing more joyously, and for not loving more ardently.

Now a new beginning can be made in our churches. Grounded on the Holy Scriptures, directed with all earnestness toward the only Lord of the Church, they are now proceeding to cleanse themselves from influences alien to the faith and to set themselves in order. Our hope is in the God of grace and mercy that he will use our churches as his instruments and will give them authority to proclaim his word and in obedience to his will to work creatively among ourselves and among our people.

That in this new beginning we may become wholeheartedly united with the other churches of the ecumenical fellowship fills us with deep joy.

We hope in God that through the common service of the churches the spirit of violence and revenge which again today is tending to become powerful may be brought under control in the whole world, and that the spirit of peace and love may gain the mastery, wherein alone tortured humanity can find healing.

So in an hour in which the whole world needs a new beginning we pray: "Veni Creator Spiritus."

Bishop Wurm
Bishop Meiser
Superintendent Hahn
Bishop Dibelius
Professor Smend
Pastor Asmussen
Pastor Niemöller
Landesoberkirchenrat Lilje
Superintendent Held
Pastor Niesel
Dr. Heinemann

Representatives of the Allied churches led by W. A. Visser't Hooft included:

George Bell, Bishop of Chichester, England
Gordon Rupp, England
Samuel Cavert, USA
S.C. Michelfelder, USA
Pierre Maury, France
Hendrik Kraemer, Holland
Alphonse Koechlin, Switzerland
Stewart Herman, former pastor of the American Church in Berlin

Chapter 16

Sheep or Persons? What Luke 15 has to Say about Agency and Persons with Intellectual Disabilities

Jeff McSwain

My friend Mark chafes when I talk about Jesus doing everything for us. "Jesus doesn't get me out of bed in the morning; that's something I do," he says.

To which I retort, "You get out of bed by yourself about as much as the branch does anything without the vine!"

"Well, maybe I don't do it all," Mark says, "but what about the word *cooperation*? I cooperate with Jesus in what he's doing. Isn't that a better way of describing things?"

Mark is worried that my kind of comprehensive grace is depersonalizing. In his mind, the word *cooperation* gives more room for human agency, because persons are not so thoroughly dominated by God's activity. One of his favorite parables is that of the prodigal son. The son, he reminds me, turns and comes home. The father goes out to meet the son in the field. The son's repentance and the father's unchanging acceptance and forgiveness meet in the middle; is not that a picture of cooperation? I ask Mark about the earlier parables of Luke 15, which seem to put all of the emphasis on the one who is searching. In those stories, the lost coin and even the lost sheep are unable to make a move to cooperate. And interestingly, it is expressly in the story of the sheep that Jesus says he is teaching about repentance. Yet where is the repentance in that story? Where is the cooperation? What does the sheep do besides get lost? In contrast to the typical evangelical emphasis on our actively doing something to repent, it appears that Jesus is teaching here about that celebratory and humbling *metanoia* that occurs when we have eyes to see ourselves as helpless sheep who have gotten lost and then been found by the Good Shepherd. How *does* the objective emphasis in the sheep story relate to human agency and cooperation? Isn't my friend Mark right – doesn't the prodigal son story send a different message?

When it comes to comparing the apparently different messages of the sheep and son parables in Luke 15 (I'll leave the coin for another day), the popular exegetical answer is something along these lines: The sheep and son parables are meant to complement each other. The one emphasizes God's objective activity, and the other, in the prodigal son's returning home, the activity of the human subject. These are the two poles in a complementary tension. But is there really not any interpretive framework where the two passages can function in a less "complementary" and more congruent way? The exegetically neutral "somehow both poles are true" approach has not in practice worked very well. Unavoidably, Christians through the centuries have chosen sides, taking one of the poles – divine agency or human agency – as the *real* reference point, and giving only a polite nod to the other. Hence the age-old debate, Calvinism versus Arminianism. There is a bit of irony, though, when it comes to evangelism. In this critically important matter, Calvinists and Arminians find themselves on a small patch of "cooperative" common ground. Both would teach converts that they have been found and rescued by the Good Shepherd, but neither is eager to do so until the converts have actually *become* converts by making the appropriate cooperative response.

We should be wary of the notion of cooperation, especially in evangelism. The traditional two-pole approach to Luke 15 is meant to provide balance and to protect humanity from divine domination, but instead it works against us. The cooperative, human agency pole of the two-pole approach in fact depersonalizes us – all of us, but most egregiously the intellectually disabled.

Inadequate Solutions

When it comes to salvation experience, the idea of cooperation appeals to able-minded people. They are able to turn and come home like the prodigal son, to walk the aisle, raise the hand, make an informed decision to give their lives to God, confess their sins, grasp the points of the gospel, and so on. All of these action steps are used to validate salvation experience. But what if a person cannot do any of these things? People with cognitive disabilities often cannot operate within the conventional agency criteria unto salvation. They are simply not able to jump through the hoops.

One solution is simply to ignore the intellectually disabled population when it comes to evangelism. This is an approach not unlike the argument put forth in the missionary world about the "noble savages:" Just leave them alone; ignorance is bliss. But more often, a presumably more inclusive solution is advanced. Instead of ignoring those with special needs, this view accommodates them by ignoring instead the troublesome human agency pole of the "tension" described in Luke 15. One of the parables there – that of the prodigal son – is set aside as non-applicable, because the action steps involved don't fit the existential situation of our special needs friends. Instead, the focus is conveniently fixed on the sheep parable, which doesn't involve any hoop jumping.[1] This is seen as a loving solution – and unfortunately, many who minister in the special needs community have bought into it.[2] But this "inclusive" solution is not really inclusive; there is a kind of reverse segregation at play. It may seem to be making the sheepfold more expansive, but it actually serves only to marginalize those with special needs even more. Consider the reasoning: what is otherwise upheld as exceedingly important, human agency, is somehow deemed expendable when it comes to those with intellectual disabilities. And so those who purport to safeguard the integrity of human response, and who think "cooperation" is good language because it protects us from depersonalizing humanity, are saying in effect that when it comes to people with disabilities, depersonalizing is okay.

This "exception" clause stipulates that while the overwhelming majority of people will be held accountable to the standard of human agency illustrated by the prodigal son returning home, those with disabilities will not. They have been declared free without any human response, carried home on the shoulders of the Shepherd. That may sound loving and kind. But here's the problem: if I have corralled all persons with cognitive disabilities into the sheep story and barred them from the story of the prodigal son, I have called into question their humanity. I may have developed the exception clause as a way of being kind, but by ignoring human agency, I have dehumanized them. In a sense, I have made my friends with disabilities more like sheep than

---

1   Another reason often given for this solution is that the cognitively disabled, no matter how old in years, have not reached the so-called "age of accountability."

2   I do not want to be too hard on the advocates for the intellectually disabled who go with this kind of inclusionary approach. I would like to think that they do so because they do not know of a better alternative.

people. Dismissing human agency in regard to our special needs friends is not the solution to the problem. How can saying that human agency doesn't apply to these friends not relegate them to a status that is less than human? We must stand against any attempt to "include" the intellectually disabled by dismissing the importance of human response. Human response is part and parcel of what it means to be human. What is needed is not a dismissal of human agency but rather a better understanding of what human agency is.

When we make the wrong move to solve the perceived tension between the sheep story and the prodigal son story in Luke 15, a wedge is introduced that splits Scripture from Scripture, divine agency from human agency, humans from humanity, and people from each other. Are we to have two gospels, one for the able-minded and one for those with intellectual disabilities? Surely not. So what is the right move? In the remainder of this article, I will show how we can move forward into a healthy biblical understanding of how human agency (and thus the prodigal son story) *does* apply to those with disabilities, and to all of us, in the area of conversion.

A Christological Basis for Agency

To begin with, we must establish how the sheep story and the son story of Luke 15 are not just complementary but are congruent. The theory of a polar "tension" between divine and human agency does not suffice. Indeed, it can only collapse into an objective-subjective morass, and, I would argue, an accompanying loss of objective truth altogether.[3] As I have suggested, when it comes to evangelism to the able-minded, both

---

3   Objective truth, by its very nature, precedes subjective experience. Anytime we "hold back" objective truth until a subjective decision has been made, we plant in people's minds the mistaken notion that they *created* the objective truth with their personal decision (i.e. "It wasn't true for me until I believed it"). I am convinced that our way of preaching the gospel has gotten twisted over time and has become altogether backward. The only rationale I can imagine for "holding back" objective truth would be if we weren't sure whether it really applied to all people. But then, how could that be objective truth? Philippians 2:10–11 provides all the basis we need for clinging to the unpopular idea that there is one universal, objective truth: "*At the name of Jesus every knee [shall] bow, in heaven and on earth and under the earth, and every tongue acknowledge that Jesus Christ is Lord, to the glory of God the Father.*" Except where otherwise identified, all Scripture quotations are from the NIV (2011).

Calvinists and Arminians might start with the prodigal son story and then move to the sheep story when they see a valid marker of conversion. That is, once a marker of conversion is in evidence, they might tell our new convert the sheep story – that he was actually rescued before he did anything by the pure grace of the Good Shepherd, who pursued and found him. But if we are to achieve an understanding of human agency that applies to our friends with disabilities, we must interpret Scripture in a way that neither five-point Calvinists nor Arminians would do: we must start by making an objective truth claim about the actual redemption of all human beings.

The gospel is a proclamation before it is an invitation: "[Jesus Christ] is the Savior of all people, and especially of those who believe" (1 Tim. 4:10). Whereas we decried using the sheep story to characterize one population (the intellectually disabled) in contrast to another (everyone else), applying it equally to all human beings is another thing entirely. The objective and universal truth is that the Good Shepherd has come looking for the lost – all of us – and though we were thoroughly helpless, he has brought us home on his broad shoulders at great cost to himself. Now, if we use the sheep story as the backdrop to the subsequent prodigal son story, we will get closer to seeing the congruence between the two. Both stories have a going out and a coming back. And the key is to see that Jesus is the primary one who goes out and comes back in *both* stories. It is obvious in the first story that the shepherd is analogous to Jesus. But in the second story, Jesus is hidden. We may theologically posit that he is present because of hints the text gives us (especially the dead-and-alive motif) and through what we find elsewhere in the scriptural witness. Jesus, the only righteous human being, has gathered up in his humanity all of the unrighteous, from the most wicked and rebellious (the younger son) to the most smug and self-righteous (the older son), and every person in between. He has absorbed the consequences of our sinful rebellion and made us right with God, bringing us home to the Father through his death and resurrection.

The so-called tension between divine agency and human agency is resolved once we recognize that the divine agent and the primary human agent are the same person – Jesus! In the sheep story the accent is on Jesus as the rescuer in his divine nature (in solidarity with God, different from us), and in the son story the accent is on him as the rescuer in his human nature (in solidarity with us).

Our Brother and High Priest

Some may be dubious about my theological claim of the unseen Jesus in the story of the prodigal son. Of course, I am confident that Jesus himself knew he was the backdrop! But at times I've wondered whether any of the original hearers understood. Thankfully, we are provided the context of salvation history and holy Scripture to help us along. First, there are hints in the Luke 15 text itself. Some of these hints are by point of contrast. The father's attitude throughout the story is certainly compatible with what we know about the heavenly Father's heart, yet his humble act of running to meet the son is a sort of incarnational move, although it comes a little late in the narrative to do justice to the fullness of Jesus' pursuit of us in the far country. (This is where Jesus as storyteller leaves beautiful space for a later trinitarian interpretation of the story, which of course includes the unseen Jesus we are drawing out.) Similarly, the younger son's return home is to some degree compatible with repentance (and seems even more so when we confuse phrases in the story like "came to his senses" and "going back home" as describing repentance). Yet the son's return home is at bottom because of desperation, and his comments to his father about being a slave betray the fact that he does not understand his father's economy of grace. It is only by conjecture that we can imagine the younger son really "getting it." Playing along with the parable, in my mind's eye I see his moment of repentance and belief occurring somewhere between his father's exclamation to prepare the party and the party itself.

We have been discussing how two stories in Luke 15 encapsulate what James Torrance called the double movement of grace in Christ, the God-humanward movement and the human-Godward movement. The shepherd in the sheep story represents the incarnational direction, or God-humanward movement.[4] And I have asserted that the corresponding human-Godward movement is best evident as the subtext of the following

---

4   Some might say that both movements are represented within the sheep story itself, in that the shepherd became a lamb to lead the other lambs home. While having some theological merit (thinking of the Christ-convergence of the Good Shepherd who laid down his life and the Lamb who was slain), this idea is insufficient because, while the death of the Lamb purchases us a ticket home, it does not really supply the human agency piece in Christ that actually carries us home in his response. It is therefore an interpretation that fits better with non-ontological, penal substitutionary theories of the atonement that do not include our human, personal response as a part of grace or internal to the work of Christ.

story, when Jesus as an unseen third son brings back the other two. The human-Godward movement of grace means that the mediation of Christ for us includes all of the aspects of appropriate response to God, including faith. The book of Hebrews supplies ample substantiation for the premise of Jesus as our true older brother in whose agency all are included. Here we find that Jesus, after tasting death for everyone, has the responsibility of "bringing many sons and daughters to glory." (Heb. 2:9–10) He returns home to the Father as the high priest of our humanity, saying, "Here am I, and the children [you have] given me." (Heb. 2:13) We are also told in Hebrews that Jesus does what no other human can do: he makes a perfect response to the Father. He is the only person who can truly say, "I will be one whose trust reposes in God." (Heb. 2:13 Weymouth) Indeed, Jesus is "the pioneer and perfecter of faith," (Heb. 12:2) apart from whom no one has ever had faith. This is a reality that transcends chronology, for we are told that all the heroes in the "Hall of Faith" (Hebrews 11) were actually participating, whether they knew it or not, in the faith of Jesus on their behalf.

This concept of the high priestly ministry of Jesus gives us an intimate, ontological relationship, a differentiated oneness of being, with our Savior. Just as the high priest, in his person, represented every person before God on the Day of Atonement, so Jesus Christ, in his person, brings every person cleansed before the Father. As our substitute and representative, Jesus acts for us, in our place. In Jesus' ongoing mediation he is sharing his very identity as Son of God with us. In fact, the internal connection is so intimate and complete that whatever Jesus does, we are actually doing it with him.[5]

The subjective dimension of the prodigal son story, then, is not first and foremost related to the lost son's turning and coming home, and it is not first and foremost related to your or my own existential turning or returning; the subjective dimension of the story is Jesus Christ himself. Isn't it strange that in talking about human agency, the one human who is often overlooked is Jesus? My Fuller Theological Seminary mentor, Dr. Gary Deddo, was the first to show me that there is a prominent place

---

5   We *really are* obedient, righteous, pure, and blameless in Christ; there is absolutely no disappointment with us in the Father's eyes. This is important, because all of these attributes, which are given to us in Scripture, would apply to Christ but not genuinely to us if we were not in united to him. (Oftentimes, we instead depict them as an external coating, using *as if* language. In this way of thinking, the Father looks at us *as if* we were righteous, even though we are not.)

for Jesus himself in the prodigal son story if we read between the lines and in the context of the sheep story, which precedes it. It seems that Jesus is trying to get the Pharisees to understand implicitly (and in contradistinction to themselves) that he is the *true* older brother who goes out from the Father to seek and to bring in those who are lost.

I applaud Timothy Keller for drawing our attention to this oft-overlooked aspect of the parable in his book *The Prodigal God*. In exalting Jesus as the true older brother in the story, he gives us a Jesus we can admire and worship, one who has done what we could never do ourselves in filial obedience to the Father. However, in my mind, Keller does not go far enough. His explanation fails to give an ontological connection between Jesus, the true older brother, and every human being. Even if we know that Jesus is the unspoken true and faithful older brother, without a oneness of being – an ontological union – with him, we are still left to connect ourselves into his work for us. Jesus' perfect response doesn't count as *our* personal response until an extra step is made.[6] But by the grace of God it is literally *in* Jesus himself, the Great High Priest in whom all belong and are represented, that all are brought home to the Holy Father. Grace is Jesus' agency for us; his response is our response; his homecoming is our homecoming.

Do you see the import of this for understanding human agency? Instead of saying that some can respond adequately (the able-minded) and some cannot, or instead of saying in a patronizing fashion that human agency doesn't really matter for our friends with intellectual disabilities, we can say that none of us is adequate to respond to God and that Jesus responds to God on behalf of every human being. Grace, then, is not just an offer or opportunity given to us by God; grace even includes our response! Grace is not grace if we are thrown back on ourselves to provide

---

6   At this point people tend to insert the Holy Spirit, but to do so without a prior incarnational and internal connection with Jesus is to give the Holy Spirit the job of finishing a work that Christ himself has not finished. Existentialism creeps in when theologians use the Holy Spirit to make this last step for us and therefore to create an actual truth out of a mere hypothetical one. I have purposely chosen not to spotlight the Holy Spirit in this article, but I hope it goes without saying that everything that happens in Christ happens by the person and power of the Holy Spirit. While I am applying, with biblical support, the phrase *in Christ* to describe humanity's existence in him, Paul uses the phrase especially to describe the body of believers who enjoy the intimacy of the Spirit and the assurance the Spirit gives them that they are indeed embraced by God and included in trinitarian relations. The Holy Spirit lifts us up, as J. B. Torrance never tired of saying, to live in our true selves, freely sharing the Son's relationship with the Father.

the last bit. Jesus not only does the divine part; he does the human part for each of us. Jesus does it all!

Celebrating Human Agency, Rightly Understood

So far we have seen the danger of dismissing human agency for any person, and we are beginning to apprehend the meaning of Jesus Christ as our great high priest in whom all human agency resides. This view of Jesus protects us from depersonalizing those who may not be as cognitively able as we, but it also protects us from the opposite problem. If it is easy to err by not giving enough human agency to the intellectually disabled, it is just as easy to err by giving too much human agency to the intellectually able. By this I mean locating human agency in the wrong place, primarily in ourselves, instead of in our true older brother. If using only the sheep story for our friends with disabilities is depersonalizing, so also is using (or at least starting with) only the prodigal son story, as traditionally understood, for those who are able-minded. It is depersonalizing because it exalts the cooperation model and an individual subject-self that doesn't actually exist. This cannot help but establish a double standard for the intellectually able and disabled; even worse, we end up with a mythological "person" on the one hand and a non-person on the other.

I hope it has been clear that the way to avoid the double standard is *not* by re-instituting the "hoop" version of the gospel when speaking of those with disabilities. No, the idea is to get rid of any hoop version of the gospel altogether; the good news is that the gospel has no hoops! We can celebrate the human agency of all human beings when we know that Jesus Christ is the human agent, the true Subject-self, who acts on behalf of us all. It wouldn't do for us to be rigorously Christ-centered about agency merely up to the point where we finally give humanity its own sliver of ground apart from Christ. We cannot achieve as created persons an ability to stand outside our Creator and to presumptively make detached judgments about him. When we give ourselves a mythological individualism outside of Christ, it is unavoidable that we will fill the intervening space by manufacturing hoops we can jump through, thereby giving ourselves credit for creating the truth of our inclusion in Christ.[7] Against this mind-set, we must insist that the logic

---

7   This sort of semi-Pelagianism is very subtle indeed. It makes religion the most

of our creation and redemption by Jesus Christ dictates that all decisions *about* Christ must begin, literally, *in Christ*! Another way to say it would be that human response-*ability* resides in the one true Human Being who is always sharing his true humanity and faithful response to God with us.

As we have seen, the answer to leveling the playing field for all persons is not to promote human beings to primary subject-self status, nor is it to leave out the subjective dimension altogether; the answer is to make the subjective part of the objective. This leaves us in a place of humble dependence, not with a primary subjectivity for ourselves but with a secondary subjectivity that always acknowledges that it is powerless to create the truth. Keeping agency intact for all people equally can be done by understanding agency primarily *in Christ, for us*, and then secondarily *by us, in Christ*. The latter describes true participation in and with Christ. This participation takes many forms, as we shall see, but at this point a warning is appropriate: even participation can become a hoop. How easy it is for participation to devolve into being the new individualism, where humans get the last say. No, it is always true that "in him we live and move and have our being." (Acts 17:28) This means that even participation is participatory: I believe that Jesus Christ does it all, even my believing, and also my believing that Jesus does it all, even my believing, and also my believing in my believing that Jesus does it all, even my believing, and so on, *ad infinitum*!

This exhaustive Christ provision is enough to drive us Western individualists batty. If human agency is first and foremost about Jesus' agency for each of us, and that he has made and is making a perfect subjective response to the Father for all of us, doesn't that smack of being dominated by Jesus in a way that threatens my own free and personal response to God? This is where my friend Mark is coming from, but as I told him, it is actually just the opposite. This Christ-bracketed way of response is *more* personal, because it takes place inside the dynamic of Christ's humanity, the person in whose image we are made, the person who gives us our personhood and an opportunity to share in his eternal relationship with the trinitarian persons. Inside Jesus' ongoing response

---

insidious form of sin. T. F. Torrance used to say that the chain of our salvation is only as strong as the weakest link, and if that link belongs to us (to whom religion is prone to give it), deep down we know that we are in trouble. To use another analogy, once we allow even the smallest cooperationist, co-redemptive, self-justifying bugs in the sheets, they endlessly plague us with restlessness and a lack of hope and assurance.

for us is where true freedom lies: "If the Son sets you free, you will be free indeed" (John 8:36). The human-Godward direction of grace has already been established: from the Son, to the Father, by the Holy Spirit. We don't get to decide the direction of the wind; we can only ride it or resist it.

Toward Participation: Unlearning Cooperation Language

It is difficult for someone who has long operated by the cooperation model, the idea that I do some and Christ does some, to catch the import of the participation model (where the only "some" we do is in Someone). In order to value the integrity of secondary subjectivity, we must get to the watershed point where we can acknowledge that Jesus' responding and deciding for us is *more personal* than our responding and deciding for ourselves! A proper framework of grace helps us let go of our counterfeit agency as cooperative individuals in order to find our true agency as persons. Jesus said it like this: When you lose your life, you find it. So what do I do, if Jesus does it all? The best answer is still, "Believe!" When asked by the Philippian jailer, "What must I do to be saved?" thankfully, Paul did not say, "Believe in the Lord Jesus, and you will *become* saved." (cf. Acts 16:30–31) One cannot *be* saved unless one *is* saved. Additionally, "What do I do?" is not always a helpful question, because it often reawakens what needs to go away – our deep desire to be in control or to clinch the deal. The Pharisees were quite fond of "what do we do" questions. After Jesus' amazing deed of feeding the five thousand, they asked, "What must we do to do the works God requires?" Jesus' answer: "The work of God is this: to believe in the one he has sent" (John 6:28–29). It seems that Jesus wants us to grow in belief toward the idea that he does it all, to the tipping point where active participation takes care of itself; this can displace the misdirected hustle that often characterizes "godly" activity, not to mention the lethargy that results in license or slothfulness.

Before we further address the experience of salvation, it might help to take a hard look at how we learn and proclaim the gospel in the first place. A lot of our confusion stems from the way we use language. To begin with, we should recognize our misguided efforts to bottle the Holy Spirit or to formulate with words the mystery of Christ. It is obvious that words are inadequate, because every time we say "lose your life," we realize that even surrender must be participatory, just like every other action step in response to the gospel – "repent" or "give your life to God" or "be baptized." Thankfully, Scripture testifies that we don't have to capture the full depth of participation with words before calling others to participate in what Jesus has done and is doing for us. The problem, of course, is that in my sinful nature I am still screaming, "Don't help me; I can do it for myself!" My "abilities" lure me into thinking I am qualified, adequate, and capable. Even when it comes to responding to the gospel, my humanist bent causes me to lapse into a subversive and insidious mode of "fighting" grace by desiring to do something to earn it or to make it happen. Knowing this, we must make meticulous efforts to avoid the use of words in gospel proclamation that feed the wrong tendencies. Yes, let's use words, but let's train ourselves to use them in the right context.

I have found that my growing sensitivity against using action words or metaphors that do not comport with the situations of my friends with disabilities actually provides a helpful "check" when it comes to communicating with all populations. In an effort to make room for personal response, we are often tempted to set human beings apart from Jesus with an invitation to then come to him. This might take the form of a spatial picture, like Jesus being on the water and us being in the boat. But it's helpful for me to recognize that if I am separated from Jesus, I am as deficient in spiritual ability to "step over the side of the boat and walk to Jesus" as my friends in wheelchairs are in physical ability.[8] In the same vein, if I use less-physical phrases, like "give your life to Christ," I should endeavor to do so without investing them with the capital they have been given in the cooperation model (as if the life I would give fundamentally belonged to me). Instead, I might say, "Give your life to Christ, because he has given you his living relationship with the Father," or, "No one loves you more, and you belong to him; talk with God now… 'I love you…I *am* yours…I belong to you…thank you for your forgiveness.' " Again, I am urging the hearer to respond in correlation with reality, not as a means of creating it.

Because of our lamentable propensity to the default mode of self-creation or cooperative doing, I increasingly relish describing our response to the gospel of salvation with what I call non-action action

---

8   It is probably unwise at this point to teach our ontological union with Jesus when telling gospel stories *about* him, but still, against the separation idea, the intimacy between Jesus and sinners in Scripture should always be highlighted. I am thinking here especially of Jesus getting into the boat that belonged to Simon, the "sinful man."

words – expressions of what *not* to do or how *not* to resist God's grace: "don't fight it," "rest," "receive," "welcome," "abide," "repose," "submit," "celebrate," "rejoice." These are things my friends with cognitive disabilities seem to know and do better than I. Finally, having acknowledged that words can't "get me there," I can enjoy a new appreciation of the myriad ways of participatory nonverbal response to the gospel. I can develop an awareness of the nuanced ways the Holy Spirit is moving, especially as I immerse myself in a worshiping community with folks with special needs. Anyone who has experienced this kind of community can tell you that a de-emphasis on words allows for a new revelation of the Word among us. And from the fertile soil of this kind of community often arises the vibrant fruit of nonverbal gospel embodiment: "Dear children, let us not love with words or speech but with actions and in truth." (1 John 3:18)

Community and Self-Isolation

It is possible to participate in Christ when not cognizant of it. But lone individuals who insist that they are participating with Christ in isolation – each "in my own way" – are fooling themselves. Participation is meant to be done corporately. Those anxious to live transformed lives in Christ and to "grow up . . . into [Christ] our head" (Eph. 4:15 NRSV) are called the body of Christ. There is no ontological difference between people in the church and those who are not; it's just that the former are "encourag[ing] one another and build[ing] each other up" (1 Thess. 5:11) through word and sacrament, and "through psalms, hymns, and songs of the Spirit, singing to God with gratitude in [their] hearts" (I hope it is obvious that this outlook on human agency, where Christ is the one who is the primary human agent for all human beings, can only give us an air of anticipation in our worship communities. Grace is happening! If Christ is always and everywhere responding to God for every human being, there is no telling where he is going to "break out" and reveal himself by a validating gust of the Holy Spirit. And as hinted above, our trajectory for evangelism should begin to change dramatically. Instead of taking Christ *to* a community, we begin to understand what it is like to meet Christ *in* the community, whether in the mission field or right under our noses. Instead of a means to an end, evangelism becomes an intrinsic ingredient of worship and communion. Come, taste and see that the Lord is good! (Ps. 34:8) I find Karl Barth's sermons at prison worship services to be wonderful examples of how to preach to both believers and unbelievers. Barth makes a Christ-centered claim of inclusion on his hearers' lives without ignoring or softening the consequences of self-exclusion.[9]

Here we must say a word about the older brother in the prodigal son story. It might be suspected that I have avoided him because he doesn't fit my interpretation. Again, we must go back to the sheep story to get the context. The underlying reality is that Jesus has gone out and gotten the younger brother *and* the older brother to bring them *both* home. But while the younger brother eventually participates in the reality of Christ, the older brother does not. In his pride, he resists the father's economy of grace. If he were to be told the sheep story, he certainly wouldn't see himself as the lost lamb. He's above associating with losers like his younger brother; despite the pleas of his loving father, he will not come in! It is important to note that we are not given any indication that the older brother will eventually participate. To me, this is one of the most graphic portrayals of hell in all of Scripture; it is consistent with the fact that Jesus' warnings about hell are overwhelmingly directed toward religious types. The older son is so close, yet so far. We observed how the father stayed back and waited for the younger son, but the fact that the father "went out" (Luke 15:28) to beseech the older son in his own far country is actually an initiative closer to the extent of the incarnation. Theologically, we are cognizant that Jesus, the true older brother, has not only gone out but has even brought this stiff-necked man home, reconciled, to the Father. The father in the parable goes out in a sense to remind him of that reality: "My son, you are always with me, and everything I have is yours" (Luke 15:31).

In this encounter we see poignantly the rub between cooperation and participation. The son is stuck on cooperation – or, in this case, noncooperation. He doesn't see himself as part of the party but as

---

9 I was going to say "without ignoring the possibility of self-exclusion." But I am sure that Barth would want to unpack that statement in order to do justice to it. For Barth, self-exclusion is in one sense impossible, because it has no ground in reality. At the same time, it is possible, to the extent that we also live in unreality. Upon this basis it should not be difficult to understand how ultimate rejection and the consequence of hell can be described yet not explained. After all, nothing that exists without rooting in reality *is* explainable! These things and evil itself can only be irrational and absurd, albeit deadly and unbearably painful at times. It is unfortunate when pundits project the combination of Barth's thoroughly christological definition of reality and his healthy incomprehension of evil into being a universalism that Barth himself would never allow.

standing on separate turf, with his own independent agency. The father's mentality, however, is incessantly one of participation. The father doesn't give credence to the son's turf outside the house. He doesn't give credence to the son's self-created pity party. Instead, he issues an invitation to join in the only real party that there is (and where the son is in actuality already present, included in the faithful response of the true Son). Yet the father will not force; the son refuses and is left in his bitterness. It is not difficult to imagine the horrible friction of a hell where, while Jesus has responded for you and is continually responding for you, you are rejecting him.

Together at the Center

What if the human agency dynamic we have been describing is what Scripture alludes to as the mystery of Christ? What if the vicarious humanity of Christ and his response on our behalf is not only the background of the prodigal son story but is also the implicit backdrop and context for all of the Epistles and even the Gospels? (Admittedly, in the Gospels, Christ's eternal and spiritual presence as the Subject-self of every person is harder to remember because of Christ's physical presence in the narrative, but it is there nonetheless.) What if, as James Torrance taught us, the whole Bible is fundamentally about the Son's relationship with the Father by the Holy Spirit and only secondarily about Israel's and our participation in that relationship? What if the kingdom of God is shorthand for just this mystery? How does it change our reading of Scripture? How does it fill out our understanding of grace? Some may criticize, "Nobody else I know thinks this way. This sounds like a secret, private knowledge for the elite academic, almost gnostic in character." Again, I would say just the contrary. This is the most public and democratic knowledge possible, because it gives every person the same theological anthropology in Christ, where the ground is level at the foot of the cross. Perhaps the problem is that we are so entrenched in the cooperation paradigm that we cannot enjoy the simplicity of the participation one.

An advantage of this participation approach is that it allows me to embrace my brothers and sisters in the body with a unity-with-diversity mind-set instead of a uniformity one. I can get along with everyone, regardless of denomination, because I know that all of us fall short in our efforts to articulate the gospel perfectly, and that it is the Holy Spirit who moves and draws people into faith through all sorts of verbal and nonverbal means. The manner of speaking doesn't have to be divisive. It's true, some ministers of the gospel may give more "cooperation capital" to their words than I would prefer, while others may not be as overtly Christ-centered as I would like, but knowing the reality under the rhetoric helps me take myself less seriously and increases my chances of finding good connection points for collaboration with others.[10] Another advantage of celebrating the ongoing vicarious humanity of Christ for all people is that I am able to avoid the pitfalls mentioned earlier, where Scripture is split from Scripture, divine agency from human agency, humans from humanity, and people from each other. Without a Christo-centric way to interpret Scripture, human agency, and theological anthropology, artificial categories and double standards are inevitable. Some Christian organizations have even provided different instructions for how to preach the gospel to the able-minded versus those with cognitive disabilities.

One way to move past the patronizing is to stop borrowing the world's descriptions of those with disabilities. Yes, in the world's eyes, they are overlooked and under-served; they are "marginalized." But in the Father's view, they are at the center. Indeed, that is where we all are, in union with Christ the center, the beloved Son of God. We are all there, every human being, all races, all nations, rich and poor, those with cognitive disabilities and those without, those of the more Arminian persuasion (like my friend Mark) and my hyper-Calvinist friends, tax collectors and Pharisees, "younger brothers" and "older brothers," believers and unbelievers, all equally loved as the apple of the Father's eye. Grace is the greatest antidote to my tendency to be condescending. Together with my friends, at the center of the Father's affection in Christ, I am humbled. Jesus' ability exposes my disability. The fact that he has done it all reminds me that I bring nothing to the table. The fact that Jesus has responded faithfully to the Father for me shows me that I did not earn his favor with words. The fact that Jesus has made me whole helps

---

10 It seems unlikely that a time will come on this side of the veil when all parts of the body agree on what the gospel actually is. If we are meant to reach a point where we can all concur on what Paul meant by his definition of the gospel as alluded to in Galatians 1, then I would assert that the foundation of onto-unity with Christ and between brethren is the best place to start. The alternative is to resort to separate claims of doctrine that can only bring hatred and division in the body. If we contend from our splinter groups that we unerringly possess Paul's gospel, then we actually give ourselves biblical permission to damn those who disagree (1:9).

me trust him with my brokenness, and the fact that he has purified me reminds me that I am a sinner in need of him. Yes, we are all sheep and we are all persons. Some of us are called to leadership and shepherding roles, but I am learning the importance of being a sheep before trying to shepherd. I am learning to be carried. I am learning from my friends with disabilities how not to fight God's economy of grace, how to repose in the dependable love of Jesus, and how to be more attuned to his unfailing presence. As I learn to be carried, I will learn as well how to participate as a shepherd in the name of the Shepherd.

Finally, one of the beautiful aspects of the participation/agency model described here is the fact that the judgment of all of us is truly where it belongs, in the Lord's hands. Until that "day," Christ's love compels us to preach, operating out of what we know to be the comprehensive and objective-subjective reality of Jesus Christ: "We implore you on Christ's behalf: Be reconciled to God" (2 Cor. 5:20) – because you *are* reconciled (5:19)! We invite others to join us at the reality party where they belong, worshiping the Lord in Spirit and in truth, giving credit where credit is due. Knowledge of the *ad infinitum* nature of grace is not a prerequisite for participation.

But how much participation is enough? And how long can a person continue to reject reality and live in unreality? Perhaps we have now begun to see that these are the wrong questions.[11] They are laced with cooperationist toxins. Is it not enough to know that a demarcation line does exist, and that no one will be in heaven without repentance and belief in the One who has repented and believed on our behalf? Is it not enough to know that when he comes again he will make all things clear?

---

11 Robert Capon once described Christians as "eschatology junkie[s]." So true. It is difficult for us to stay away from projections. For instance, how many scenarios have been concocted to describe exactly what Phil 2:10–11 will look like on the other side of the veil ("every knee [will] bow . . . and every tongue acknowledge that Jesus Christ is Lord")? It seems that one thing all Christians should agree on is a hope that these words will be said by every person with joy and adoration – even if there are too many warnings about hell in Scripture to warrant any amount of certainty in this regard. Some chide that the ontological route I have taken in this article is unavoidably universalist; this because if "unreality" ends, and our true selves are all that remain, how could we avoid going to heaven since our true selves have no rejection in them but only faithfulness? This kind of Nestorian logic must be resisted. The common denominator of "Joe's" true self and Joe's false self is Joe. It is Joe who knows and loves God, not simply Joe's true self. It is Joe who is a disabled and broken sinner, not simply Joe's false self. And it is Joe who must freely repent and believe. That's as far as we can go; therefore we preach.

In the meantime, we will continue to share the good news that is truly good news for every human being everywhere and that, if embraced, can only give us a greater appreciation for our brothers and sisters as members of the one category of humanity that matters most – *en Christo*.

Chapter 17

Covenant or Contract in the Interpretation of Paul

Douglas A. Campbell

Background

It is both an honor and a delight to acknowledge here the impact that James B. Torrance's work has had on my intellectual life, although I will be concentrating in what follows just on his superb essay "Covenant or Contract," published in 1970. The story of this impact begins with my education as a graduate student in 1980s, which preceded the literally life-changing encounter I had with James Torrance's distinction between covenantal and contractual accounts of salvation in the early 1990s.

Pauline Studies in the 1980s

My graduate education took place at the University of Toronto, and I ended up focusing within it on the apostle Paul, and especially on his letter to the Roman Christians, under the guidance of Richard N. Longenecker. The ostensible thesis paragraph of this letter, Romans 3:21-26, was the subject of my dissertation.[1] I returned in 1989 to a job in Religious Studies at my alma mater in New Zealand, the University of Otago. Like many recent graduate students, my head was bursting with questions and enthusiasms. But I was also confused by the scholarly agenda that I had just absorbed. Moreover, because that agenda extended into critical parts of the Bible, and into its very constructions of salvation, this confusion had a biting existential edge for me, a relatively recent convert to Christianity.

The 1980s was a wonderful time to enter Pauline studies. The field was fomenting as it struggled to respond to questions that in many

---

[1] D. A. Campbell, *The Rhetoric of Righteousness in Romans 3:21-26* (Sheffield: JSOT Press, 1992).

respects are still with us today. Some had been inherited from the tradition of Pauline interpretation in the modern period but had been revitalized by new angles and considerations, while others were freshly arrived. Not all are relevant to this essay,[2] but five need to be articulated briefly here.

1. Since the publication of a landmark essay in 1963 by Krister Stendahl, many Pauline scholars had worried about a particular reading of Paul that he designated "Lutheran."[3] Stendahl's characterization of this construct was powerful and programmatic although not overly precise. He objected to an account of Paul's theology that was obsessive or guilt stricken, and that construed his encounter with the risen Lord on the road to Damascus as a conversion rather than as an apostolic call or commission. Stendahl went on to suggest that the obsessive, "introspective" accounts of both conversion and spirituality in Paul were too heavily informed by later readings of Augustine and Luther.[4] Paul himself possessed a rather more "robust" conscience than his famous later ecclesial interpreters. Hence these challenges reached back behind the modern period to the construal of Paul during the Reformation and earlier, and clearly big questions were at stake. As a result, Stendahl was required reading for students of Paul in the 1980s, and remains so.[5]

2. In 1977 E. P. Sanders published *Paul and Palestinian Judaism*.[6] This powerful book also remains required reading for Pauline interpreters. It summarized definitively a minority tradition from earlier Pauline work of what we might call Jewish protest, namely, the complaint that

2   The sociological and ancient philosophical turns within Pauline interpretation are not so relevant here. These approaches were associated especially with Yale scholars at the time – Wayne Meeks and Abraham Malherbe respectively. Jewish apocalyptic literature was being rediscovered during this period as well. And salvation-history remained a standard topic for discussion.

3   K. Stendahl, "The Apostle Paul and the Introspective Conscience of the West," *Harvard Theological Review* 56 (1963): 199-215. See also his key collected essays, including a reprint of "Introspective Conscience," in *Paul Among Jews and Gentiles, and Other Essays* (Philadelphia: Fortress, 1976).

4   Significantly, Stendahl also emphasized the mission to the pagans in Paul's life; the defense of this activity was the specific context for his "justification" discussions. Unfortunately, I will not have time to develop this critical insight in what follows.

5   I evaluate his work in more detail in my *The Deliverance of God: An Apocalyptic Rereading of Justification in Paul* (Grand Rapids, Mich.: Eerdmans, 2009), 172-76; 247-50; 77-83.

6   E. P. Sanders, *Paul and Palestinian Judaism: A Comparison of Patterns of Religion* (Philadelphia: Fortress, 1977).

the legalistic account Paul seems to provide for Judaism in his day in terms of "justification by works of law" (and so on) is overtly unfair when the Jewish sources themselves are consulted.[7] Sanders' book became one of the most famous New Testament works of the twentieth century, something assisted by its appearance during the 1970s, an especially propitious time for liberational statements.[8] Moreover, the Academy was just beginning to take broader account of post-Holocaust concerns.[9] But Sanders posed the question skillfully and unavoidably: why was Paul's account of Judaism, at least at times, so apparently jaundiced? Students of Paul were wrestling with this challenge in the 1980s, and still are.

3. Another long-running but unresolved debate in the 1980s, which overlapped in certain respects with the foregoing questions, concerned the question of Paul's "center" (something I tend to refer to additionally as his "gospel" and/or his "soteriology"). Scholars understandably debated different principal options. We have already noted Stendahl's hostility to the Lutheran account, along with Sanders' concerns about incipient anti-Jewishness. Drawing on the work of German scholars in the late nineteenth and early twentieth century, some modern scholars advocated a more "participatory" account of Paul's salvation, differing over whether this could be comfortably juxtaposed with Lutheran categories or was in some sort of tension with them.[10] Räisänen argued, somewhat infamously, that this data suggested merely that Paul was confused.[11] Others preferred a more panoramic account of Paul's main concerns in salvation historical terms, usually pointing to Romans 9–11 as Paul's climactic discussion, although this option does not need to be explored so much in what follows. (It can be folded into the participatory approach very effectively.)

---

7   In a typical scholarly irony, many scholars had made this protest earlier but had not been accorded much attention, among them my Doktorvater, Richard Longenecker, who had made much the same point in his *Paul, Apostle of Liberty* (New York: Harper & Row, 1964).

8   I am referring here (i.a.) to Liberation, Feminist, and Black theology.

9   R. Radford Ruether, *Faith and Fratricide: The Theological Roots of Anti-Semitism* (New York: Seabury, 1974).

10   Classic accounts of this view include W. Wrede, *Paul*, tr. E. Lummis (London: Green & Hull, Elsom, 1907 [1904]); A. Schweitzer, *The Mysticism of Paul the Apostle*, trans. W. Montgomery (New York: Seabury, 1968 [1931]); and J. Stewart, *A Man in Christ: The Vital Elements of St. Paul's Religion* (London: Hodder & Stoughton 1935).

11   H. Räisänen, *Paul and the Law* (Tübingen: J. C. B. Mohr [Paul Siebeck], 1987 [1983]).

These principal options were accompanied, however, by various more individual, idiosyncratic suggestions, and many scholars despaired of any solution and pursued different interpretative concerns altogether, generating essentially reductionist accounts of Paul's texts.

Hence, this question was clearly important but its debate was complex and confusing. Somewhat indicatively, most of the leading North American scholars of Paul undertook a collaborative discussion of Paul's theological center at the *Society of Biblical Literature*'s annual meetings through the 1980s, but failed to reach any decisive conclusions.[12]

4. Another localized but significant debate burst into prominence in the 1980s concerning the interpretation of Paul's faith language. Reviving another earlier minority position, Richard B. Hays argued in 1983, in a widely read study,[13] that various phrases in Paul were best understood as references to the "faithfulness of Jesus" as against (Christian) "faith in Jesus."[14] Hays's eloquent advocacy led to the widespread consideration of the former possibility that had previously been more marginalized than debated. But any assessment of Paul's thinking was further complicated by the potential introduction of Jesus's own faithfulness into texts that had previously been read in terms of human faith alone.

5. The final set of debates worth noting here concerned the circumstances surrounding the composition of Paul's letters, and particularly those eliciting Galatians and Romans.

Longenecker's students in the 1980s were very fortunate that he was composing his superb WBC commentary on Galatians at the time.[15] Hence they were intimately familiar with his navigation of the complex debate surrounding the occasion of that letter, Longenecker arguing ultimately

---

12   J. M. Bassler (ed.), *Pauline Theology. Vol. 1: Thessalonians, Philippians, Galatians, Philemon* (Minneapolis: Fortress, 1991); D. M. Hay (ed.), *Pauline Theology. Vol. 2: 1 & 2 Corinthians* (Minneapolis: Fortress, 1993); D. M. Hay and E. E. Johnson (eds.), *Pauline Theology. Vol. 3: Romans* (Minneapolis: Fortress, 1995); D. M. Hay and E. Elizabeth Johnson (eds.), *Pauline Theology. Vol. 4: Looking Back, Pressing On* (Atlanta: Scholars, 1997).

13   R. B. Hays, *The Faith of Jesus Christ: The Narrative Substructure of Galatians 3:1-4:11*, 2nd ed., (Grand Rapids, Mich.: Eerdmans, 2002 [1983]).

14   See esp. Rom. 3:22, 26; Gal. 2:16 (2x), 20; 3:22 (taking 3:26, following the majority manuscript reading, to be a co-ordinate construction and hence "a false positive"); Eph 4:13; and Phil. 3:9a. Various unmodified instances of faith in context are of course immediately affected as well, e.g., Rom. 3:25; Eph. 3:12; and Phil. 3:9b.

15   R. N. Longenecker, *Galatians* (Dallas: Word, 1990).

for the "south Galatian" (and early) hypothesis (see pp. lxi-c). It was clear, moreover, that the results of this debate had important theological as well as historical implications. If Galatians was Paul's first extant letter then the shape of his theological project was rather different from an account that positioned 1 or even 2 Thessalonians first, Galatians rather later on, next to Romans, and most if not all of Paul's other extant letters in between these two points (notably 1 and 2 Corinthians). The language and concerns distinct to Galatians and Romans look rather less programmatic and rather more occasional if the latter biography holds good.[16]

Longenecker's students were also aware at the time, however, of the similar debate surrounding the composition of Romans. The date of this letter, along with its position in the broader sequence of Paul's letters, were not contested, however, as they were for Galatians, as much as the precise circumstances that caused Paul to compose and dispatch this unusually generalized and complex text. A "Romans debate" had been unfolding since the early and mid 1970s over this simple but important question.[17]

In short then we were taught in the 1980s at Toronto that some of the key details in Paul's biography, which affected the interpretation of some of his key letters, were being vigorously contested.[18]

It is probably clear by now that the 1980s was an exciting decade during which to be introduced to Pauline scholarship. Acute, powerful questions were being considered concerning the nature of Paul's gospel. Was Paul's gospel being interpreted overly introspectively? Was it intrinsically anti-Jewish? Indeed, Did Paul have a coherent gospel at all? If so, what was it? What role did faith play in it? And what circumstances gave rise to the key texts in which it was ostensibly being articulated? Did different accounts of those circumstances lead to different understandings of the actual gospel in play?

It is clear then that I was fortunate to be learning my trade during this time – and from such a gifted Pauline interpreter as Longenecker.

---

16   See, e.g., by way of contrast, J. Knox, *Chapters in a Life of Paul* (New York: Abingdon, 1950); and R. Jewett, *A Chronology of Paul's Life* (Philadelphia: Fortress, 1979).

17   K. P. Donfried (ed.), *The Romans Debate* (Peabody, Mass.: Hendrickson, 1991 [1977]).

18   There was a pronounced emphasis at the time in Toronto on Pauline biography, primarily because of the presence there of John Hurd, although seconded by Peter Richardson. See esp. Hurd's marvelous study *The Origin of I Corinthians*, rev. ed. (Macon: Mercer University Press, 1983 [1965]).

But I was also deeply unsettled. There were many complex questions circulating but few apparent answers. Indeed, the situation seemed to be fundamentally confused. And this amounted in certain respects to a crisis, although perhaps more for the church than for the academy. Paul's actual account of gospel had disappeared from view behind a welter of highly complex, entirely legitimate, but deeply difficult questions. Modern scholars could only gesture toward multiple positions and not to coherent agreements on matters as important as Christ's contribution to salvation.

However, when Alan Torrance introduced me to his father's description of covenantal and contractual models of salvation shortly after my return to the University of Otago in 1989, the proverbial light bulb went on. After reading this essay it became apparent in a flash that many of the local debates in Pauline studies were aspects of a broader and deeper collision between covenantal readings of Paul in certain texts and contractual readings of him in others. Torrance's categories consequently both illuminated many of the debates currently taking place for me definitively and pointed the way forward to their possible solution. But in order to appreciate these clarifications it will be necessary to describe briefly just what a covenant is according to James Torrance, what a contract is, and why grasping this fundamental distinction is so essential for healthy Christian theology.

A Covenantal Arrangement

A covenantal relationship for James Torrance is a relationship grounded in love for the other and hence one that is unconditional, permanent, and irrevocable.[19] Because the basis for the relationship is precisely this ground, of love, the covenantal actor reaches out to the other and establishes the relationship independently of any action by that party. It is therefore an unconditional and gracious act, and the relationship with the other is a gifted one. The covenantal actor has "elected" to enter the relationship and so taken the initiative. That actor has also thereby functioned "missiologically" and "incarnationally" – in the case of God literally – in stretching to the other actor's location and, if necessary, meeting them right where s/he is. Once established, moreover, this relationship then extends through time, irrevocably. It lasts as long

---

19 Torrance does not himself use language of "the other" since its widespread use has largely postdated him, but it is useful for explicating some aspects of his thinking.

as the love of the loving covenantal actor lasts, hence, in the case of God, through eternity. And the relationship is consequently characterized by complete loyalty and unswerving fidelity.

Describing a covenantal relationship is in fact relatively easy. The difficulties arise when interpreters introduce qualifications, or even reject covenantalism, because of anxieties about some of its potential implications. However, closer inspection suggests that these implications and their associated anxieties are unnecessary – moments where we can go beyond some of the subtle gestures in James Torrance's original account to respond to any such concerns among his later readers.

Critics of covenantal arrangements effected by God often fear first an erasure of human agency by the initial establishment of the relationship in a moment of initiative and election. If the causality of divine election is understood in mechanistic terms then it seems to eliminate human freedom in any sense, hence those wanting to emphasize human agency understandably resist this entire conception.

But Torrance would immediately suggest that nothing could be further from the truth, as the following qualifications will suggest in still more depth. If divine election is understood in christological terms, and hence as rooted in benevolence, then, on the one hand, no one lies outside its pressure, and, on the other, it results in the establishment and the affirmation of human freedom and not in its converse. But this rejoinder will not be especially intelligible without an appropriate understanding of human agency and its implicit definition of freedom.[20]

James Torrance presupposes the christological account of human agency in terms of correspondence as developed, *inter alia* by Karl Barth, in ultimate dependence on Maximus the Confessor and the struggle by certain patristic thinkers to grasp the relationship between divine and human agency within Christ. The endorser of correspondence here reasons on the basis of Christ's perfect union of divinity and humanity that freedom denotes an aspect of the perfect obedience offered by Jesus's human will to the divine will. Hence this account helpfully specifies that Christ's obedience was *not* mechanical, mechanistic, or coerced in any way – or indeed his human will absent altogether – but was offered without constraint, hence, "freely." It was wholehearted, that is, a loving obedience to the leadings of the divine will offered with all of his heart, soul, mind, and

---

20   Barth's work is definitive here, and is almost certainly generative for James Torrance on these questions; see, regarding election, *Church Dogmatics* (hereafter *CD*) II/2; and, regarding agency, *CD* III/1 and 2, and IV/2.

strength. And in the light of this definition of human agency and freedom a number of critical clarifications to Torrance's account of the divine-human covenant become apparent.

In the first instance it becomes clear that a loving and covenanting God seeks a free partner and will create and establish the conditions that can effect this. Without this sort of freedom no authentic love is possible. Hence a covenantal God will establish and maintain the conditions *for* human freedom rather than override or erase it, provided freedom is properly understood.

Moreover, since freedom denotes an aspect of obedience to the divine will that responds to the divine initiative, it follows that free activity *requires* a prior act of initiative to respond to. Hence, (loving) election and (responding) freedom are now *correlative* and *mutually enhancing conditions*. Far from constituting the basis for a fatal objection to a covenantal arrangement then, human freedom is only intelligible and possible *within* a covenantal arrangement that establishes and maintains it. To be covenantal is to endorse and to protect human freedom precisely by way of divine initiative and election. This set of realizations leads us to a second related, and very important, clarification.

While some fear an erasure of human activity by a divine covenant, presupposing a particular inappropriate, mechanistic notion of election, others fear the opposite, namely, the establishment of an inappropriate ethical situation that is too free. The covenant is unethical because it gives humanity "free rein." That is, it is supposed that a covenant, with its irrevocable benevolence, erases the most important drivers of ethical behavior by humanity so the concern here is in certain respects the opposite of the preceding one; it is feared that covenantalism leads to a dangerous excess of human freedom! There will be no threat of permanent exclusion and no pending judgment within a covenant, it is supposed, hence there is no "accountability" either. Moreover, a covenant creates a somewhat fluid space where the determination *of* ethical behavior is difficult if not impossible. At bottom then it is feared that any activity framed by a covenantal understanding of the divine-human relationship will be shamelessly libertine. If God loves in this way people will indeed sin boldly, while God comes across as "soft on sin."

But Torrance would suggest immediately that these objections rest on further confusions about what is actually the nature of the case in a covenantal relationship. He points out repeatedly that covenantal relationships come with unconditional expectations of behavior (covenantal ones!). The expectations of the loving God who establishes the covenant are that those covenanted with will respond and behave toward one another in the appropriately benevolent and covenantal terms. The very texture of the covenantal relationship is then a source – and really *the* source – of the content of the good. Moreover, Torrance would complement this rejoinder with the observation that a covenantal relationship establishes the highest form of ethical motivation to respond appropriately to these expectations as well.

Ethical pressures generated by different, non-covenantal appeals to future states, and especially to a threatening judgment and future occupancy of an unpleasant or even frightening situation in hell, are driven at bottom by self-interest. (Such accounts can be denoted "extrinsic.") People acting in such terms are not motivated by regard for anyone else; their orientation is entirely selfish. So, for example, in these terms, a husband does not resist committing adultery because he loves his wife dearly and does not wish to shame and to hurt her, but because he does not want to be caught and punished in some way – perhaps suffering practical inconvenience and financial loss. But one result of this ethical situation is then that even when appearing to behave appropriately, such actors fail to act ethically because a particular action is, in its own terms, wicked. Adultery ought to be seen as inherently destructive to the faithfulness and trust appropriate to covenantal relationships, and as harming someone we love and wish to remain faithful to, and not as an activity that can be indulged in harmlessly when there is no possibility of being caught. Even observably righteous behavior when it is motivated in extrinsic terms tends to be deeply sinful.

But ethical activity generated by the pressure of a loving covenantal relationship places the strongest pressures on an actor, as well as the most appropriate. Such actors act out of sheer loving regard for the other, at which moment they are acting – or at least attempting to act – because such actions are inherently constructive and good in interpersonal terms as against destructive and negative. (This ethical situation can be denoted "intrinsic.") And the pressure coming from someone who loves unconditionally creates the strongest desire in its partners to act in a way that respects and affirms that love. So, to return to our earlier example, a husband ought to reason that my wife loves me *so* much, I can't bear to even contemplate behavior that would hurt such a wonderful person. Consequently, there are the highest levels of guidance, pressure, and accountability, present within the intrinsic ethic innate to a covenant, while it is in fact the converse, namely, any countervailing and fundamentally extrinsic account of ethics, that lacks ethical pressure and accountability.

More time would allow me to develop this defense of James Torrance's covenantalism further with an appeal to the intrinsically negative dimension in inappropriate and sinful behavior that should further dissuade people from acting wrongly.[21] But enough has probably been said by this point to suggest that the objections customarily raised against a covenantal account of relationships, whether between the divine and the human or on an entirely human plane, tend to rest on misunderstandings. Covenantalism creates and sustains freedom rather than overriding it – although freedom understood in appropriately counter-cultural terms, in terms of obedience – and it creates and sustains an authentic and powerful ethic. Indeed, deeper considerations of the main objections generally raised initially to covenantalism seem only to strengthen it. But what of a contractual account? Here the opposite dynamics tend to play out.

A Contractual Arrangement

A contractual relationship is conditional, and consequently frequently impermanent. The relationship only exists *if* certain conditions have been met and continue to be met. If they are not then the relationship is dissolved and certain sanctions might even be activated. As a result of this, whenever human actors are involved, expectations of the relationship's longevity should probably be low. Contractual relationships between God and humanity, and within humanity, tend to have their conditions violated frequently – that is, with instances of sin – and the relationships, on this view, are consequently broken and repeatedly so. A critical confusion attending the assessment of contractual relationships should now be noted before we turn to consider some of its key dynamics in a little more detail.

A contractual relationship is conditional in a certain, quite particular sense. It refers to the fulfillment of detailed conditions by personal actors, and the specification of particular results when those conditions are or

---

21 Both he and I would doubtless draw on Barth's discussion of evil in this relation as articulated esp. in *CD* III/3. For a superb and rather briefer articulation of this position in conversation with Augustine, see S. Hauerwas, "Seeing Darkness, Hearing Silence: Augustine's Account of Evil," in *Working With Words: On Learning to Speak Christian* (Eugene: Cascade Books, 2011), 8-32. The implication here is that acting in a non-covenantal and hence evil way is inherently painful and damaging.

are not fulfilled. These specifications are often detailed in written texts that are then enforceable within a broader political framework – the contract. So sanctions have to be carried out in a separate act should the key contractual conditions not be met. Moreover, the specification presupposes that any relationship only holds good when the specified conditions are met. There is no necessary relationship and are no attendant obligations outside of the fulfillment of the requisite conditions.

This conception of human relations has certain quite practical results when it structures society, and they are not necessarily healthy. My green card, or resident alien, status in the U.S.A. is quite a good example of such a contract and of some of its results.

I fulfilled certain rather strenuous requirements – including paying various people and agencies what seemed like a large amount of money at the time – to obtain my current status. I came to a certain, quite specific job, which, strictly speaking, I can only leave with permission. Retaining my status is conditional on keeping a largely unblemished record in relation to most US laws. I must pay my taxes and avoid being arrested. If I am caught in some crime – and this could be quite minor or, alternatively, an act of civil disobedience against injustice – I am at risk of immediate deportation. In short, the US recognizes no obligations to me if I fail to meet the conditions of our relationship as stipulated by the US. If I fail to do so then our relationship is over, despite my past contributions to US society and culture (such as they are). My ongoing life here is consequently somewhat parlous. And I am not the only person in this situation.

It is seldom appreciated that the US constitution provides few protections to its convicted population (which is proportionally very large).[22] People who are convicted are barred from political participation, having no right to vote. Even more strangely, they have no official protection against enslavement. Hence, it is as if the contract with the US state is broken by a criminal violation, even for those born in the country. They cease to become citizens and can in fact be owned by other people and/or the results of their labor expropriated (and this last dynamic is increasingly prominent; prisoners are typically paid wages measured

---

22 The USA makes up around four percent of the world's population but contains around twenty-five percent of the world's incarcerated population. A well-known exposé of the present situation's sinister racial dynamics is Michelle Alexander, *The New Jim Crow: Mass Incarceration in the Age of Colorblindness* (New York: The New Press, 2010).

in cents, not dollars, for an hour's labor, and so usually earn only a few dollars a day).[23]

So the basic political relationship within the USA is contractual. There is no broad underlying covenant (although some "rights" fall into this relationship, for example, the right for those born in the USA to remain). And the results of this can be quite sinister. People classified outside the group of citizens to whom the state and much of wider society recognize obligations, can be treated shamefully and even abusively, and this frequently without compunction. They are *unprotected* and *their dignity as people* per se *is not recognized*.

This essentially personal, conditional situation, along with all its sinister implications, should be carefully distinguished, however, from an impersonal conditional situation, which is spoken of with conditional language as well but must be understood in *consequential* as against contractual terms.

The language of causality is frequently expressed conditionally but these situations are not necessarily contractual. For example, *if* I place my foot in a fire *then* it will get burnt. This situation can be expressed conditionally, but it is clearly not contractual. The fire is not punishing me for a violation of a condition stipulated in a contract! I mention this distinction here because the presence of conditional language in ethical texts can cause confusion.

It is not necessarily clear at first glance if linguistically conditional statements are functioning contractually or consequentially. Because the nature of sin is negating and destructive, any sinful behavior will result, effectively consequentially, in certain unpleasant results. Repeated chronic substance abuse will result in bodily dysfunction, dishonesty, and poverty, not to mention in shattered human relationships. "If you continue to drink then bad things will happen." But, like a foot burning in a fire, these are consequences, not punishments inflicted by alcoholism on an alcoholic, furious that a contract has been violated.

Ethical texts in the Bible often warn in conditional language against the destructive outcomes of sin. But they do not for this reason necessarily denote a contract. Frequently they simply name the appalling consequences

---

23 So this is not technically slavery, but amounts to it; for further background see Daniel Burton-Rose and Paul Wright, *The Celling of America: An Inside Look at the US Prison-Industrial Complex* (Monroe: Common Courage Press, 1998); and James Samuel Logan, *Good Punishment? Christian Moral Practice and U.S. Imprisonment* (Grand Rapids: Eerdmans, 2008).

of sin that humanity, with a recurring predilection for delusional ethical amnesia, tends to overlook. Having said this, however, many ethical appeals do set up or presuppose extrinsic narratives and overarching contracts – although hopefully it will be clear by this point from our earlier discussion of covenantal arrangements that the extrinsic approach to ethics utilized by contractual narratives is both weak and self-defeating. (It can in my view serve a limited temporary role in relation to minors.)

However, when pressed into the service of theology, numerous other problems with contractual approaches besides ethical anemia become apparent as well, and we should now briefly consider some of these because they were the insights that particularly caught my eye, at least at first, in relation to the interpretation of Paul.

Contractual approaches appear to safeguard human agency or freedom, even as covenantal arrangements might seem initially not to. However, they presuppose a fundamentally different account of human freedom from the christological view, and this is itself ultimately problematic. Instead of an emphasis on the uncoerced and voluntary nature of responsiveness to the divine initiative implicit in a covenantal arrangement, contractual accounts tend to emphasize an account of human freedom in terms of *choice*. This activity tends to be associated with the will, which is viewed as a faculty characterized by its capacity to decide between, say, option A and option B. (Numerous subtle variations have of course been developed in this relation.) However, this account of human freedom, in terms of choice, simply builds the capacity to sin into creation, calling the judgment and capacity of the creator into question. Sin is placed on the same ethical plane as righteous or good activity, and its incoherence and unnaturalness thereby excused. An ethic is encouraged that overlooks the critical role that relationships and resourcing play in facilitating free responsive acts. Most important of all, however, is the problematization of the character of God.

The covenantal God is benevolent, elective, and missional, not to mention, enduringly faithful. However, a God whose relationship with humanity is defined by a contract is not fundamentally benevolent at all. A contractual divinity is fundamentally *just*, conceptualizing that dynamic attribute in specifically retributive and penal terms. The integrity of the contract rests on these dispositions. If the contract is broken, sanctions must follow in order to uphold the sanctity of the contract and its broader structuring of human reality, if nothing else.

Hence God will not prove faithful to those who break the stipulated conditions of the contract; indeed, God should not and cannot. And it follows from all this that any benevolent disposition and resulting acts on God's part are circumscribed. Consequently such a God is fundamentally *disengaged*. Benevolent acts can only be conditioned into existence, through the fulfillment of the appropriate contractual conditions. And they can then only be applied to those who fulfill the demands of the requisite contract and continue to do so. So benevolent acts by God under these conditions are inevitably both *exceptional* and *limited*. These are severe qualifications of the Christian understanding of God in covenantal terms that James Torrance never rested from warning against. They are, indeed, actions by a different conception of God altogether. To advocate this God and any associated "gospel" is really to fail to advocate the Christian gospel at all – the gospel in which a God reveals unconditional love for humanity by offering up God's only son while that humanity is still recalcitrant and rebellious.

By this point it should be apparent that a contractual conception of the divine nature conditions its account of Christ rather being conditioned by it; the insights derived from Christology are being subsumed within a more basic contractual narrative. So it is unsurprising to observe that any account of Christ's own contribution to God's saving economy is framed by contractual terms. He will fit in to and *satisfy* the demands of a particular contract, as against defining his saving activity in its own terms – ultimately covenantally.

Much more could be said but hopefully enough has been articulated to suggest that any contractual account of the Christian God is deeply destructive to genuine, healthy, covenantal theology. So at this point someone might ask, "Why then have contractual categories exerted such a pull on so much Christian thinking?" But James Torrance addresses this aspect of the situation masterfully as well.

Contractual accounts of the gospel resonate deeply with modern Liberal culture. They fitted into the emerging narrative of the economy in the seventeenth and eighteenth centuries, and into the parallel development of a political economy, which emphasized rational citizens limiting state coercion through acts of informed consent. (The political agenda here was to limit inherited monarchical power.) Freedom was understood as a space within which choices were made, and any encroachment on that "zone" as a tyranny. (And causality was increasingly understood at the time in mechanistic terms that erased agency.)[24] These assumptions, coupled with an inability to conceive of Christian ethics in the appropriate participatory terms, led to a rejection of covenantal conceptions and an endorsement of contractual categories.

Sadly, this is a repeated story within the Christian tradition. Any Christian thinking that does not guard its reflective starting point in Christ vigilantly is vulnerable to capture by the categories embedded in its surrounding culture – a phenomenon the Bible tends to name "idolatry" – and this history has played out with vengeance as far as the influence of contractualism on appropriate Christian thinking has been concerned. Moreover, the penetration of Christian discourse by these essentially alien but profoundly intelligible categories seems to have been especially deep in the North America, where it now persists, buttressed by anti-intellectualism (which discourages the reading and learning necessary to recognize these categories), and a simplistic biblicizing exegesis (which claims to read this schema straight off of the pages of the Bible, ignorant of the role that prior interpretative commitments are playing in that act of reading).[25] Perhaps it is no surprise then that having been taught how to recognize the difference between a covenant and a contract, I suddenly discerned their operation in all sorts of different ways within the modern interpretation of Paul as I had been taught that in North America in the 1980s.

Illuminations

In the first instance I realized that several of the most intractable difficulties facing Paul's modern interpreters were arising out of a fundamentally contractual reading of some of the apostle's texts. But in order to grasp this common causality it is important to appreciate that contractualism within Pauline interpretation runs in its own particular variation that we must pause to quickly introduce.

A useful text for illustrating the contractual reading of Paul is Galatians 2:16a, rendered in the NRSV ". . . we know that a person is justified not by the works of the law but through faith in Jesus Christ . . ."

---

24 See now esp. J. Begbie, "Room of One's Own? Music, Space, and Freedom," in *Music, Modernity and God: Essays in Listening* (Oxford: Oxford University Press, 2013), 141-75.

25 *Deliverance*, ch. 9, 284-309; see also, in more general terms, S. Hauerwas, *After Christendom: How the Church is to Behave if Freedom, Justice, and a Christian Nation are Bad Ideas* (Nashville: Abingdon, 1991).

This text lays out two situations that most interpreters connect together as two stages within one single progression to salvation. The first stage is characterized by "works of law," and seems as a result to be bound up tightly with Judaism. People become Christians, most interpreters suppose, by acting first within this stage. Their attempted activity there leads to several important realizations, most notably, that "all have sinned and fallen short of the glory of God" (cp. Rom. 3:23) and are therefore liable to God's punitive judgment (cp. Rom. 2:6-10). That is, attempted "justification" by performing "works informed by the law" clearly fails to overcome sin and only elicits God's anger. Hence, when presented with the gospel, rational individuals eagerly seize it by faith, and enter the second, saved state. The act of faith grasps on to Christ's atonement for sin, which satisfies the demands of God's judgment (cp. Rom. 3:25). Individuals exercising such faith are fortunate then to be justified by faith *alone* (cp. somewhat curiously Jas. 2:24, which objects to this view, or to something like it).

This interpretation of Paul's gospel is of course well known. Its popularity is doubtless due in part to the fact that it possesses certain strengths. It is clear. It is also relatively simple. It is readily comprehensible to any inhabitants of modern, fundamentally liberal, societies. It provides a simple formula for evangelism. And it apparently addresses sin and judgment seriously. God has an appropriately "hard" side,[26] although this is balanced by the apparent generosity of the second offer, made in the gospel. Moreover, a clear account is supplied of Christ. He comes to do the work of atonement, which is achieved by his death.

But it is critical to grasp that this account of salvation in Paul, often spoken of in terms of "justification," is clearly a *contractual* account of salvation that has generated certain important rhetorical and textual advantages by arguing for a progression to Christianity in terms of *two* contracts. The first contract fails, and is really designed to do so. But the pressure generated by this failure should lead to the eager embrace by all of Christian salvation by faith, while the comparative easiness of the second contract suggests that God is fundamentally kind and generous. The collapse of the first also handily explains the abandonment of the law and of Judaism by the early church. The entire salvific progression is then very much "a tale of two contracts." And with these realizations we

---

26 He is what George Lakoff would call "a strict authoritarian" parent; see his *Moral Politics: How Liberals and Conservatives Think* (London & Chicago: University of Chicago, 2002 [1996]).

are finally in a position to see how various supposedly distinguishable local debates within Pauline scholarship are being generated by a single underlying reading, debates including many of those I had been struggling with since graduate school in the 1980s.

The first contractual stage, with its strenuous attempts but ultimate failure to achieve salvation through "works of law," generates Stendahl's concern with an overly guilt-ridden, obsessive, and anxious theology. This initial journey is both tortured and introverted. But the model consequently also thereby generates at least the principal dimensions of the legalistic, crassly mercantile, description of Judaism in Paul that so concerned Sanders – a Judaism characterized contractually by attempted justification through perfect law observance, along with an ongoing failure to recognize the futility of this exercise. The second contract's all-important offer of faith explains the widespread expectation among Pauline scholars that when Paul speaks of faith he is always speaking of a human activity, and hence the equally widespread resistance to the suggestion that subtle signals in some of Paul's texts indicate Jesus's fidelity. The latter reading is not only unexpected but is largely unintelligible. What role does *Jesus's* faith actually *play* in the contractual account of Paul's gospel?! And the need to read Paul's justification texts essentially systematically, as universal accounts of the generic journey to salvation, generates some of the biographical problems apparent in the field as well.

The key contractual texts occur mainly in Galatians and Romans (see esp. Gal. 2:15–3:26, and Rom. 1:16–5:1 and 9:30–10:17). It is helpful then if Galatians occurs early in Paul's career as his first extant letter, and, furthermore, if Acts can be introduced into Paul's biography strongly as well since Paul seems to "convert" there so emphatically and dramatically (see Acts 9:1-22; 22:4-16; 26:9-18). An early placement of Galatians facilitates an immediate and comprehensive use of Acts. Similarly, it is helpful if Romans is a systematic treatise rather than a letter written to deal with particular circumstances at Rome; this critical text would then seem to start its body with a systematic account of salvation in terms of justification. These helpful biographical moves generate much of the tortured complexity that characterizes modern attempts to account for Paul's life – confusion over *when* Galatians was composed and *why* Romans was written. And they lead to a widespread resistance to alternative biographies.

In sum, a contractual reading of Paul, in two characteristic stages, seems to explain several of the localized debates concerning various aspects of his interpretation within the modern academy. Contractual dynamics *specifically generate these questions and/or their key dynamics.* But its presence explains a further, broader debate as well.

We have already seen that contractual and covenantal accounts of salvation are fundamentally different. Their underlying depictions of God prioritize different dispositions and activities along with, ultimately, different understandings of Christ and his saving activity. A contractual reading privileges retributive justice in the divine character and focuses on Christ's propitiating death, whereas a covenantal reading privileges divine benevolence and emphasizes a broader story about Christ running from his incarnation through his ascension. It seems obvious *a priori*, moreover, that large swathes of Paul's texts are covenantal – although this is best appreciated when the participatory dimension implicit in the covenantal account is understood, something I have not had time to emphasise here. But, if this is the case, then the reading of Paul in certain texts in contractual terms and in other texts in covenantal and participatory terms must generate a fundamental collision within his thinking as a whole. At bottom, Paul must endorse completely different understandings of salvation at different times – and frequently *within the same letters.*

It is no wonder then that scholars have struggled to identify Paul's center conclusively – a question that has been particularly overt since the work of German scholars on Paul's "comparative religious" thinking in the late nineteenth and early twentieth centuries, who identified and emphasized his participatory categories that can be explicated fairly ultimately in covenantal terms. Paul clearly has more than one center once these alternatives have been discovered. However, in view of their tension, one is justified in asking whether Paul lacks a principal center altogether and is merely confused, as Räisänen suggested more controversially but perhaps also more honestly. Hence the presence of contractualism within Pauline interpretation helps to explain one of the most important modern debates in modern Pauline scholarship – concerning the center of his theological thought and much of its currently confused discussion.

In sum, a clear-sighted appreciation of James Torrance's work on covenantal and contractual conceptions of salvation allows the Pauline scholar to explain much of the modern academic discussion of Paul in terms that are both simple and powerful. A degree of order can be brought to a complex and even confused field. Moreover, the key issues come to light. But these distinctions do not just correlate various pressing questions together helpfully. In doing so they point the way forward to their solution.

Most of the acute problems just noted will be resolved if any contractual commitments are eliminated from Paul's thinking and he is construed more consistently in covenantal terms. Morbid introspection, legalistic Judaism, monolithically anthropocentric faith, and circumstantial opacity in relation to Galatians and Romans, will be erased, along with the massive conceptual tension between contractual and covenantal categories in Paul's account of God's saving work in Christ. But the Pauline scholar will probably immediately respond that this is all somewhat obvious but that the interpretative task, "on the ground," amongst Paul's texts, looks next to impossible; the exegetical challenge looks insurmountable. Can his contractual, which is to say, his justification, texts really be interpreted in an unconditional fashion, thereby resolving these problems?

However, the very existence of all the localized interpretative debates that we noted earlier on – concerning introspection, Judaism, faith, and provenance – suggests that the answer to this question could well be "yes"; these questions are, precisely, debated. There are alternatives. And James Torrance's work provides still further assistance at this critical juncture.

As we have already noted, one of the key dimensions in his discussion of contractual thinking in "Covenant or Contract" was his perceptive delineation of the way in which its Christian variations were informed by modern Liberal culture. He focused, understandably, on the infiltration of Scottish Presbyterianism through the eighteenth and nineteenth centuries by conditional categories in the form especially of Federal Calvinism. But Torrance's analysis is clearly transferable to other modern locations, denominations, and centuries – for example, to Protestant interpretative discourses in the USA in the late twentieth and early twenty-first centuries (and I have made some beginnings extending his work here).[27] And this set of cultural correlations raises an interesting possibility for Pauline exegetes.

They can now ask if Paul is being read contractually at certain points under the impress of these broader cultural assumptions, which have presumably often penetrated church discourses, to the point that subtle countervailing signals in the relevant texts are being overridden. Such interpreters might be reading Paul anachronistically, rather than strictly exegetically. Putting things bluntly, James Torrance opens up the

---

27 See my *Deliverance of God*, ch. 9, 284-309.

question acutely whether modern Pauline interpreters have constructed Paul at certain critical textual loci in their own contractual image? At the least, his demonstration of the compatibility between contractual thinking and the modern reader's context gives grounds for suspicion.

Unfortunately, it has proved strangely difficult to have a constructive conversation about these presuppositions with modern readers of Paul, presumably largely because a putative construal of the gospel, however inadvisedly, is at stake. But suffice it to say that when the hermeneutic of generosity supporting the contractual reading of Paul is stripped away, and an appropriate degree of suspicion is directed against its textual claims, it is surprisingly easy to detect textual problems that it has failed to treat, and then to generate a close reading of the key texts in different, unconditional terms. A more circumstantial account of Paul's arguments in his celebrated justification texts does indeed reorient them in a direction that is ultimately compatible with a covenantal account of his thinking as whole (and Stendahl reenters the conversation at this point)[28] – a reading that is also decidedly less anachronistic in cultural and political terms.[29]

These are important breakthroughs in Pauline interpretation for all sorts of reasons, although their communication remains a challenge. Pauline scholars have tended to drag their feet to date. However, such scholars will, I suggest, only benefit from a clear understanding of the nature of, and the differences between, covenantal and contractual accounts of salvation, notions articulated with matchless insight and clarity by James Torrance. Grasping these dynamics will allow Paul's modern interpreters to grasp an entire range of difficult localized interpretative questions in their discipline with precision, to focus on the real issues and texts at stake, and to detect unhelpful anachronistic biases in the apostle's interpretation that are distorting the construal of some of his most famous texts. And perhaps some of them will even thereby push on by way of more sensitive readings to a consistently covenantal and hence ultimately constructive construal of the Pauline gospel.[30] We have indeed then much to be grateful to James Torrance for – provided we continue to listen to him.

---

28 See n. 3 above.

29 See esp. my *Deliverance of God*, chs. 14-21, 519-930.

30 I cannot recommend the work of J. Louis (Lou) Martyn too highly in this relation: see esp. his *Galatians: A New Translation with Introduction and Commentary* (London & New York: Doubleday, 1997); and *Theological Issues in the Letters of Paul* (Edinburgh & Nashville: T & T Clark & Abingdon, 1997).

Chapter 18

"The One for the Many" Theme in James Torrance's Theology

Jeannine Michele Graham

On the occasion of James Torrance's retirement from the theology faculty at the University of Aberdeen in the late 1980s, his B.D. students presented him with a huge and most ambitiously frosted sheet cake. Reproduced in colored icing with painstaking detail on the surface of the cake was what any theology student of Torrance would quickly recognize and refer to affectionately as "the diagram."[1] Such a diagram, ubiquitously present throughout his teaching, was Torrance's attempt to depict God's redemptive plan in terms of its triune outworking of relationship with Israel, Jesus and the Church. Inasmuch as postgraduate students were also included in this celebration, I found myself gravitating to the table where the cake had been cut and was now being distributed. Happily ensconced in devouring my allotted piece, I turned to my esteemed mentor and asked him this question: "Professor, how are we to understand Paul's statement in Romans 9: 'Jacob have I loved, but Esau have I hated'?" I will never forget his response. Looking somewhat quizzically at me, he said simply, "You're *eating* it!" Apparently, my piece of cake was taken from the part of the diagram which dealt with Israel's elective role toward God and toward the world, expressed in lines indicating an all-important link from the one to the many.

    Such an endearing memory has over the years seared home in my mind how replete this theme of the one for the many is throughout Torrance's thought. Richly embedded within it are hermeneutical clues which shed light on some of the most pivotal aspects of his theology. I would venture to say that it permeates the entire dogmatic landscape, figuring into Torrance's understanding of virtually every core doctrine of the Christian faith.

1 See page 282.

Rooted in the Outgoing Love of the Trinity

One could say with ample justification that this one for the many theme gives expression to the biblical notion of election. For Torrance, as for Barth, election is grounded in God's self-determination as the one who freely moves lovingly toward the other.[2] In this sense one can discern elective elements of the one for the many even within the triune being of God. For Torrance the doctrine of God has nothing to do with alien concepts of a static, impassible, unmoved mover, which owes more to ancient Greek thought than to the biblical witness. Rather, a trinitarian portrait of God is saturated with notions of eternally dynamic, self-giving, outgoing loving interchange among Father, Son and Spirit. Reminiscent of John Zizioulas' book *Being As Communion*, which was the subject of a postgraduate seminar of which I was a part under the tutelage of Torrance, God's being is not triune merely as a tangential expression of how God relates externally to the world though God could be something else within his eternal being; rather, Torrance is strongly insistent, along with his brother T. F. Torrance, that what God shows himself to be in relating to the world is utterly consonant with who God is in God's uttermost being. The relations of Father, Son and Spirit are not add-ons to God's being; rather, they *constitute* the oneness of nature shared among them. In the most intimate sense each triune member mutually indwells the others in perichoretic oneness-amidst-diversity. God exists in no other way than as this onto-relational triune reality, as God's self-revelation in Jesus reveals.[3]

This fundamental triune vantage point colors all of God's redemptive activity. The intratriune dynamic of Father, Son and Spirit being for the

---

2   I have elaborated on Barth's view of this under the heading "The Grace of Election: God's Self-determination to Be For Us," in my book *Representation and Substitution in the Atonement Theologies of Dorothee Sölle, John Macquarrie and Karl Barth* (New York: Peter Lang, 2005), 198–200.

3   Though we might speak of the Trinity as the ontological "signature" of God's Being from all eternity, it is abundantly clear throughout the writings of both J. B. and T. F. Torrance that our *noetic* grasp of this reality is unmistakeably incarnationally accessed. That is to say, it is grounded and anchored in God's self-revelation in Jesus Christ. The term *homoousios* (i.e. of the same substance or nature) is frequently employed to undergird the premise that since "only God knows God," our knowledge of who God is must derive solely from Jesus whose being is unequivocally *homoousios* with God and therefore fully divine. That he is at the same time and without compromise fully human (*homoousios* with us) creates our accessibility to real knowledge of God as mediated by the Spirit who unites us to him by faith.

other, moving toward each other in an eternal, euphoric embrace (or, to capture the dynamism even more strongly, an eternally vibrant "dance" of love and joy, as some have termed it),[4] is a suitable prelude to how Torrance construes election. To speak of election, or predestination, as Torrance sees it, is not to invoke a principle God wields by which to dispense grace to some and not to others. It neither precedes grace (i.e., as a pre-selection of who will be saved, which Christ is then assigned to execute in rescuing those elected individuals – as 5-point Calvinists might contend) nor follows grace (i.e., as a consequence of a prior human choice for God, which God foreknows and rewards with the gift of salvation – as Arminians might contend). Election *is* grace, God's gracious will in moving toward the world to reclaim us from our self-destructive ways and realize his unfathomably good purposes to set all things right that we might share in the overflow of his triune love. It is God's relentless self-determination to be *for* us, despite our mutinous defection from God.

Israel's Mission: The Particular for the Sake of the Universal

Once election is seen first and foremost as the heart and will of the one electing God reaching out to redeem and restore the many in the sense of the *entire creation*, not merely a pre-selected subset, then we are in a position to appreciate the stratagem that underlies the various biblical expressions of the one for the many concept. God chose Israel among all nations not because God was playing favorites and did not care about any other people but so that Israel might become the particular vessel through whose relationship with God played out on the stage of history all nations might ultimately come to know God's heart and their desperate need to be reconciled with him. Understood from this context, the statement previously mentioned – "Jacob have I loved but Esau have I hated" – is not an expression of prejudicial preference but a condensed way of referring to God's decision to work in and through the particularity of Israel's history (the one) with the eventual goal of blessing all nations (the many). Paul's vigorous argument in the book of Galatians for the legitimacy of preaching the gospel of grace to the Gentiles attests to the

---

4   C. S. Lewis, *Mere Christianity* (New York: Macmillan Publishing Co., 1943), 152-153.; cf. also Baxter Kruger, *The Great Dance* (Jackson, MI: Perichoresis Press, 2000).

universal scope of God's mercy, embedded at the outset in the covenant promises established with Abraham.[5]

Seen in this light, God's will is not driven by two competing purposes – to extend mercy to some but withhold it from others. Rather, God's heart is singularly pitched toward rescuing, saving, restoring and renewing his entire damaged creation. It is through this lens that we come to appreciate the various manifestations of election in the history of Israel. Israel's status of being chosen by God carries with it both privilege and responsibility, summoning them to a life of holiness and witness to the world. Their calling to be God's people both conveys blessing and calls them to the mission of being the conduit of blessing to others, a light to the Gentiles – one nation charged with responsibility for witnessing to and benefiting the many.

Within Israel's history we see further expressions of election. Following the exodus event of liberation from oppression in Egypt the firstborn male offspring of every womb were set apart as belonging to the Lord. Every firstborn son was to be redeemed with a sacrificial animal as a sign of remembrance to commemorate God's mighty act of delivering his people from their distress – the one (firstborn sons) representing the redemption of the many (the people of Israel).[6] The role of the Levites is yet another example of God's elective tactics at work. The tribe of Levi was designated as those charged with special priestly functions to facilitate the worship life of the community, anticipating the day when the true Priest, God's Son, would come. As such they did not receive the same kind of allotment of land territory in the Promised Land as the other eleven tribes of Israel, though they were granted 48 cities interspersed throughout Israel, precisely because their mission was to assist the many in their devotional response to God.[7]

Torrance sees the preeminent depiction of the one for the many concept within the life of Israel as focused on the role of the high priest on the Day of Atonement.[8] Once a year the people of God would

---

5   Gen. 12:3; Gal. 3:8: "The Scripture foresaw that God would justify the Gentiles by faith, and announced the gospel in advance to Abraham: 'All nations will be blessed through you.'"

6   Ex. 13:11–16.

7   J. B. Torrance, "The Vicarious Humanity of Christ," in T. F. Torrance, *The Incarnation*, (Edinburgh: The Handsel Press), 137.

8   James Torrance, *Worship, Community and the Triune God of Grace* (Downers Grove: InterVarsity Press, 1996), 56. Cf. also "The Vicarious Humanity and Priesthood

gather before the high priest, their divinely appointed representative, symbolically bringing their collective guilt and sins accumulated over the year to him in anticipation of his mediation on their behalf before God. The names of each of the twelve tribes inscribed on onyx stones inlaid on his breastplate symbolized the fact that he was acting on their behalf as their representative. The high priest would then engage in ceremonial washings, don special linen garments, and sprinkle himself with the blood of a sacrificed animal to atone for his own sins prior to discharging his ministry on behalf of the people. Two goats were brought before the priest, one to be sacrificed in atonement for the sins of the people and the other to be designated the scapegoat who would be driven into the wilderness symbolically carrying away the guilt of the people. In this ritual the high priest would lay his hands upon the animals vicariously confessing both the people's transgressions and affirming God's righteous judgment upon them. Then the priest would collect the spilled blood of the slain animal and enter the Holy of Holies, once again acting vicariously to intercede on behalf of the people, pleading with God to remember his covenant promises and petitioning for his mercy. Torrance cites Calvin's commentary on Hebrews 6:19 to underscore the notion that the high priest was not acting merely as an individual but in his representative capacity on behalf of the many. Even though it was only the high priest who appeared before the altar, the people saw the high priest's mediatory acts as *including* them: "All Israel entered in his person."[9]

Eve and "Pre-redeemed" Mary

In turning to the New Testament Torrance offers an interesting application of the one for the many theme in relation to Mary, the mother of Jesus. In striking similarity to the parallelism of Adam with Jesus in Romans 5:12–21, Torrance perceives a correlation between Eve and Mary.[10] Through the disobedience of the first woman (Eve) death intruded; through the obedience of the second woman (Mary), who said yes to God in freely offering up her body to God for his purposes, life came through the birth of the Savior. Careful not to suggest that Mary's obedience rendered her in any way a co-redemptrix along with Jesus, Torrance nevertheless refers to Mary

---

of Christ in the Theology of John Calvin," unpublished paper, pp. 7–8.
9   James Torrance, *Worship, Community and the Triune God of Grace*, 49.
10 J. B. Torrance, Systematic Theology II unpublished course notes – 7/17/87.

as the one through whom God's promises on behalf of the human race (the many) were fulfilled. God's gracious choice of her to be the mother of Jesus is met on her part with the perfect response to her election. In that response grace is conceived. She becomes the symbol of grace, the perfect paradigm of sovereign electing grace and free will comingling without diminution of divinity or compromise of human freedom. God's election of her evokes and enables the perfect response of faith. Torrance goes so far as to say that through her faithful response to God, she becomes an appropriate symbol of the Church participating in Christ predicated on the fact that she herself participates as one "pre-redeemed"[11] by the blood of the Son she will birth. The contemporary song "Mary, Did You Know?"[12] captures this sense well. As the song imaginatively depicts Mary contemplating the wonder and magnitude of the angelic announcement that God has chosen her to bring the Savior into the world, we hear this thought-provoking lyric: "This Child that you delivered will soon deliver you."

Incarnation and the Double Movement of Grace

Of course, central to the biblical drama is God's redemptive grace manifested in the incarnate Son of God, the supreme expression of the triune God's search-and-rescue mission for human beings seemingly bent on self-destruction. For both Torrance brothers, the historical outworking of God's relationship with the people of Israel is not mere window-dressing, a sort of Plan A that didn't work out and therefore necessitated Plan B implemented by Jesus. As T. F. Torrance put it, it was through Israel's tumultuous relationship with God – increasingly uncomfortable as they were over time brought ever nearer to a holy God – the vital categories were forged by which the character of God, the depth of human alienation and the provisions for overcoming that alienation could be meaningfully related to the atoning mission of Jesus.[13]

Once again, Torrance resonates with Barth in seeing election not as a mysterious decree determined on some basis apart from Christ but rather as God coming in human form as the person of Jesus to a desperately

---

11 J. B. Torrance, "The Contribution of John Duns Scotus (c. 1265–1308) to the Theology of the Christian Church," pp.4–5. Unpublished paper.

12 Words and music by Mark Lowry and Buddy Greene.

13 T. F. Torrance, *The Mediation of Christ* (Exeter: The Paternoster Press, 1983), 16-19.

needy world. The incarnation is neither God choosing an already existing human being in whom to dwell and adopt as his intermediary nor God changing into a human being so that he is no longer God. To safeguard the undiminished divinity and uncompromised humanity of Jesus, the early Church Fathers' gravitated to the words *anhypostasia* and *enhypostasia*, a distinction Torrance finds most helpful. *Anhypostasia* affirms the notion that the Son of God, without ceasing to be divine, also became human, assuming the human nature of all humanity. If there were no Son of God who became incarnate, there would be no Jesus, for he is the sole Subject of Jesus' personhood. *Enhypostasia* affirms the concrete reality of Jesus' existence as a genuine human person; he is not an ideal abstraction or a docetic charade of merely appearing to be human. No, he is bone of our bones and flesh of our flesh, truly in solidarity with us.

One of the great contributions of the Torrance brothers to an understanding of Jesus' atoning mission is their solid grasp of the Nicene-Chalcedonian categories of Christ's identity as fully human and fully God not as static descriptions of Jesus' incarnate makeup but as functioning *dynamically* throughout Jesus' whole ministry. One can no more interpret Jesus' ministry as mostly divine actions and only incidentally human than one can construe Jesus' actions as primarily human – a man like us, though ahead of his time, yet one through whom God worked in powerful ways. On the contrary, from Bethlehem to Calvary to the empty tomb to his ultimate ascension into heaven, Jesus must be viewed at every stage of his existence through the dual lens of divine and human actions inseparably interwoven, as if looking through binoculars with both eyes wide open. This is where the category of representation is so useful. As fully divine, Jesus represents God to us. His words and acts are God's words and deeds addressing and engaging with us. At the same time, Jesus as fully human represents us to God – the faithful human counterpart and covenant partner of God whose entire life of faithful, trusting obedience to God perfectly fulfills that role in a way that neither Israel nor we can do.

In my teaching I find that this latter sense of Jesus' representative role – representing us to the Father – becomes difficult for many of my students to grasp. By and large, they have little problem envisioning Jesus as God-with-us, coming to exert his divine powers to extricate us from our entanglements in sin and thus fulfill the covenant promise from the side of God toward humankind: "I will be your God..." They might even acknowledge Jesus' humanness, largely in terms of such mundane acts as experiencing fatigue, feelings hunger pangs such as during his 40 days in the wilderness while being tested. But what poses the real obstacle for them is grappling with the idea that Jesus' entire life of faithful, trusting obedience to the Father constitutes the covenantal response which fulfills the covenant relationship from the human side as well. The idea that Jesus' entire life, not just his death, could constitute the acceptable human response to the Father in our place and on our behalf seems utterly foreign to most of these students. Their sense of the significance of Jesus' obedient life either fixates on qualifying him for his atoning death as the sinless sacrifice for us on the Cross or defaults to some notion of Jesus serving as a moral or spiritual exemplar which we then are called to imitate. He trusts, prays, obeys, and shows loving compassion to show us how we can and ought to follow suit. His consistent lifelong self-offering to God of utter faithfulness shows us how to offer our response to God. But to speak of Jesus as doing those things *in our stead* in a way that *includes* us leaves them characteristically befuddled. Such a thought flips into a different paradigm entirely.

For Torrance, this inability to grasp what he calls the "double movement of grace"[14] – Jesus' doubly representative actions on behalf of God toward humankind as well as on behalf of humankind toward God in fulfillment of the covenant from both sides – illustrates the glaring need to recover the continuing priesthood of Jesus which lies at the heart of the theme of one for the many.[15] As we have seen earlier, this is no importation of an alien concept onto the biblical witness but arises from within the history of Israel, most clearly as it revolves around the role of the high priest in relation to the worship life of the community. On the contrary, it is far more likely that contemporary Western culture with its tendency toward hyper-individualism has contributed greatly toward skewing our grasp of corporate inclusion in biblical priestly mediation.

Jesus as the Focal Point of Electing Grace

We have seen previously that for Torrance the gospel is anchored in the triune being of God, whose very being is outgoing love that reaches out to draw in. To speak of Jesus as the self-revelation of God is to affirm that what we see throughout Jesus' ministry is who God actually is in

---

14   James Torrance, *Worship, Community and the Triune God of Grace*, 32.
15   Ibid., 17.

his innermost Being, a God eminently and relentlessly self-determined to be *for* us, a God whose compassionate grace is not at loggerheads with holiness (as if to be holy requires holding sinners at bay) but rather is exemplified by Jesus sidling up to them to rescue them from sin's suffocating stranglehold. As both Torrance brothers frequently have said in their writings and teaching, "there is no God behind the back of Jesus" who will turn out to be something contrary to what we see in the face of Jesus.[16] Consonant with his fully divine identity, Jesus in all his words and deeds represents the heart of the Father toward us in loving pursuit to reclaim lost sinners as his own.

At the same time Jesus is the focal point of election, the Elect One in whom God's redemptive purposes at the most cosmic level find ultimate fulfillment.[17] The entire book of Ephesians directs our attention squarely to the person of Jesus, repeatedly affirming that it is "*in Him* we were chosen . . . *in him* we have redemption through his blood . . . *in Christ* . . . under the *one head, even Christ*" that all things are brought to their fulfillment "which God purposed *in Christ*."[18] "*In him* we may approach God with freedom and confidence."[19] "*He himself* is our peace . . . God's purpose was to create *in him* one new man out of the two [Jew and Gentile]."[20] "*In him* the whole building [God's people] is joined together"[21] to become God's holy dwelling place. Colossians sounds similar notes, adding that we were made *through him and for him*.[22] Jesus did not merely come to show the way but to *be*

16 The following biblical texts are frequently cited by the Torrance brothers to underscore the need to ground our knowledge of God squarely in the self-revelation of Jesus and not in some other source. Matt. 11:27: "No one knows the Son except the Father, and no one knows the Father except the Son and those to whom the Son chooses to reveal him." See also John 14:9–11: "Anyone who has seen me has seen the Father . . . I am in the Father, and the Father is in me." Also John 17:25–26: "Righteous Father, though the world does not know you, I know you, and they know that you have sent me. I have made you known to them, and will continue to make you known in order that the love you have for me may be in them and that I myself may be in them."

17 Here again we find echoes of Barth's extended portrayal of Jesus as simultaneously the Electing God and the Elect Man, both the subject and the object of election, which reflects his similar understanding of the dynamic outworking of Jesus' fully divine, fully human identity.

18 Eph. 1:3–11.
19 Eph. 3:12.
20 Eph. 2:15.
21 Eph. 2:19–22.
22 Col. 1:16.

the way itself, the Head of humanity, the very venue in whose humanity God would bring his restorative purposes to fruition. As Torrance, citing Calvin, never tires of reminding us, " . . . salvation is not simply through the work of Christ (*per Christum*) but is primarily given to us in his person (*in Christo*)."[23]

In probing further into Torrance's understanding of God's redemptive activity within the humanity of Jesus we can hardly miss two indispensable concepts: representation and substitution. How are we to understand the nature of Jesus as Head of humanity, the Elect One in whom God's saving grace transforms the many? Let me offer four observations.

Exclusive: The One for the Many.[24]

Torrance is unequivocal on this point. Jesus Christ, the incarnate Son of God, is not merely one in a long line of prophets sent by God to get his wayward people back in line. He is not merely one more moral teacher whisked in to impart illuminating insights and prod us to aspire to pursue new heights of moral rectitude. He is not merely one more priestly guru whose exceptionally well-developed God-consciousness aimed at sparking a following of like-minded spiritual devotees. Nor is his significance exhausted by the uncommon compassion he so routinely demonstrated in championing the cause of the underdog in order to inspire similar humanitarian gestures from us. He is *the* prophet, *the* teacher, *the* priest, *the* Man-for-others because he is uniquely the one in whom God in all his divinity is at the same time fully and inextricably enfleshed in our humanity. Here we behold the mystery of mysteries: *God in Person as one of us!*

By way of illustration, let me offer a brief anecdote. During a ski holiday as I was riding the chairlift to the top of a run, something happened to which I was totally oblivious at the time. It was only as I dismounted and prepared to ski down the run that a man riding in the

---

23   James Torrance, *Worship, Community and the Triune God of Grace*, 28.

24   I originally formulated this fourfold interpretation in relation to Barth's theology under the heading of "The Nature of Elective Headship," in my book *Representation and Substitution in the Atonement Theologies of Dorothee Sölle, John Macquarrie and Karl Barth* (New York: Peter Lang, 2005), 203–220. I think it applies to Torrance's understanding of Jesus' vicarious humanity as well, which is hardly surprising in view of his having studied under Barth and been heavily impacted by Barth's thought.

chair behind me caught up with me and told me that he had seen a wad of money fall out of my pocket on the way up. I could have responded any number of ways to that report. I could have chosen not to believe him and gone about my business of skiing down the mountain. Or I could have thanked him for his observation but chosen to search for my lost money in a different spot than where the man had described seeing it fall because I preferred to search in a place where the light would be better. I could even have concluded that it would be silly to limit my search to just one spot when there were innumerable places where money might be found. Or I could trust the testimony of the witness to where the event actually occurred and let the revelation unfold there. For Torrance, God's self-revelation has earthed itself in an utterly unprecedented way in human flesh and blood as this One Person Jesus of Nazareth. The event of the incarnation of the Son of God is the singular place where not only God's self-revelation touches down into our sphere but where God's reconciling grace can begin to reach and transform us at the ontological roots of human existence.

While some contemporary ears might wince at any mention of exclusivity in regards to a Savior, Torrance is unyielding simply because he sees Jesus as not merely a man in whom God works (as a sort of divine hand inserted into the "glove" of Jesus' humanity in order to accomplish a task) but God *becoming* truly human without ceasing to be God. Jesus as *homoousios* (i.e., of the same identical nature) with the Father means that he is not just one more vessel through whom God works but God coming in Person as Jesus. The writer of the Book of Hebrews drives home the point in no uncertain terms: Jesus is better, greater, surpassing all others because nothing trumps the incarnate God.[25] To what higher court could one possibly appeal that would surpass the words and deeds of God himself? Jesus alone as the Elect One is the focal point of God's elective will.[26] For Torrance, everything hinges on who Jesus is. If he is anything less than fully enfleshed divinity, then all bets are on for one's

---

25 Hebrews portrays Jesus as superior to the angels, Moses, the Levitical priesthood, animal sacrifices, and the old covenant. Cf. also Paul's strong affirmation in Col. 2:9: "for in him the whole fullness of deity dwells bodily. . ." In no sense can this be understood as God choosing to inhabit the independently existing man Jesus. As stated previously, the concept of *anhypostasia* ensures that there is no Jesus apart from the Son of God taking upon himself human nature.

26 A point stressed continually by Karl Barth, *Church Dogmatics IV.2, The Doctrine of Reconciliation,* ed. G. W. Bromiley and T. F. Torrance, trans. G. W. Bromiley. Edinburgh: T. & T. Clark, 1958, p. 33.

preferred Savior-figure du jour. No, Jesus is no mere mask portraying the impression of divine presence, fine for his day and age but relativized by other divine-like manifestations appearing in different ages or cultural contexts. He is not a divine knock-off but rather the genuine article.

In addition, Jesus' ministry correlates with the representative role of the Old Testament high priest. As mentioned earlier, every act of the high priest on the Day of Atonement had vicarious overtones. Similarly, Jesus as the incarnate Word-made-flesh shared genuine solidarity with humankind – bone of our bones, flesh of our flesh – and could therefore represent us with utter integrity as one of us. His high priestly prayer in John 17 voiced his intentional act of sanctifying himself for his imminent sacrifice on our behalf. His baptism at the hands of John the Baptist signified his further solidarity with his people and represented his identification with and confession of the corporate sin of Israel, even while he himself did not commit sin.[27] In voluntarily submitting his life to death on the Cross he was taking upon himself the mantle of the Suffering Servant who bore the sins of others, not his own.[28] As both priest and sacrificial victim, Jesus both interceded for the people and presented himself as the sacrificial offering, at every point attesting to the rightness of God's judgment of sin. And finally, the risen Christ returned to his disciples with the assurance of forgiveness and the blessings of peace through a healed, restored relationship with God. All this Jesus accomplished as the

---

27 Torrance extends this notion of Jesus' high priestly representation to include the notion of vicarious penitence, a concept he finds in John McLeod Campbell's classic *The Nature of the Atonement*. To those who would find it incomprehensible, to say nothing of morally unpalatable, to speak of innocent, sinless Jesus confessing the sins and guilt of others, Torrance would echo Campbell in asking who else could know the grievousness of sin but one who shares the heart of the Father and therefore, who else could offer a more worthy confession of it that corresponds to the gravity of the offense to holiness?

28 Barth refers to this as the Elect One willingly becoming "the Rejected of God." I describe his view thusly: "It is Jesus' perfect obedience in a life of utter filial faithfulness to God that qualifies him to fulfill the Father's will. As the One who corroborates the Yes of God's righteous will by sharing God's opposition to sin, Jesus repudiates sin by shouldering it in place of all others and defeating it by submitting himself to divine rejection for that vicariously borne disobedience . . . It is as One who, in the affirmation of God's positive will, undertakes to act as 'Pledge and Substitute,' [Barth's words] assuming the posture of rebellious humankind in order to come to our aid." Jeannine Graham, *Representation and Substitution in the Atonement Theologies of Dorothee Sölle, John Macquarrie and Karl Barth* (New York: Peter Lang, 2005), 204-205.

one high priestly representative whose actions were rendered on behalf of the many.[29]

Inclusive: The Many in the One

Having stressed Jesus as the exclusive one for the many, the Elect One, we must qualify this by saying it is precisely this exclusivity which permits Jesus' election to be "all-inclusive."[30]

God's election for incarnation was not merely the choice to inhabit a singular body as a private individual but to be the Head of humanity, through which the covenant relationship between humankind and God could be effected ... The Head is meaningless without the body it implies, just as the body is lifeless without its Head.[31]

The Adam-Christ parallelism in Romans 5:11–21 is one such text in which inclusive representation is very apparent. Whereas Adam's disobedience represents the downward trajectory of the human race as it replicates similar defiance of God, Jesus (the second Adam) reverses Adam's disastrous legacy through his life of obedience, issuing in life and justification. The contextual cues are clear: this is not merely describing the acts and consequences of two individuals but rather of two representatives, each of whose actions (the one) include repercussions for the whole human race (the many). Paul's point is hard to miss here:

> For if the many died through the one man's trespass, much more surely have the grace of God and the free gift in the grace of the one man, Jesus Christ, abounded for the many ... If, because of the one man's trespass, death exercised dominion through that one, much more surely will those who receive the abundance of grace and the free gift of righteousness exercise dominion in life through the one man, Jesus Christ. Therefore just as one's trespass led to condemnation for all, so one man's act of righteousness led to justification and life for all. For just as by the one man's disobedience the many were made sinners, so by the one man's obedience the many will be made righteous.

Note how this passage highlights the atoning value of Jesus' *life* rather than just restricting it to his death. Torrance cites Irenaeus appreciatively

---

29 James Torrance, *Worship, Community and the Triune God of Grace*, 56.
30 Cf. Barth, *CD II.2*, 117.
31 Jeannine Graham, *Representation and Substitution . . .*, 208.

for his concept of recapitulation, which would seem to draw support from this Romans 5 text.[32] Jesus' atoning mission began not at Calvary but at Bethlehem. Jesus entered this world in order to inhabit our flesh and reconstruct it from the inside out, bending our rebellious wills back to God at every stage of existence and substituting his righteousness for our folly.

Another way to understand Jesus' humanity as inclusively representative of all is once again to return to the Who question, as Torrance is so fond of reminding his students. The composite witness of John 1, Colossians 1 and Hebrews 1 attests Jesus' identity as the eternal Creator Word through whom all things were created who became flesh and dwelt with us. Thus, he does not have to create a relation *de novo* with the rest of creation because he is already ontologically linked with every creature. John 1:11 tells us that he came *to his own*, those whose being derives from him as the Creator-become-also-creature.[33] Paraphrasing Barth, this Creator Word-made-flesh does not encounter us as a stranger, or even a semi-stranger, but as the Creator who, by virtue of having created human existence, has the power and right mercifully to *re-create* it as well.[34]

Quite frankly, these very issues propelled me across the ocean to study with James Torrance. Though I did not doubt that Jesus' atonement somehow mediated salvation and was willing to embrace it by faith, I nonetheless wondered how what happened with one man two thousand years ago could actually alter my human nature. Hearing Torrance speak often of the ontological link between Jesus' vicarious humanity and ours by virtue of who he is as the Creator Word was enormously illuminating to me. It was as if I could begin to fathom how God could, in effect, do

---

32   James Torrance, *Worship . . .*, 52.

33   Cf. T. F. Torrance, ed. and trans. *The School of Faith. Catechisms of the Reformed Church* (London: James Clark & Co., 1959), p. cxii–cxiii, who discerns a vital ontological relation between Christ on the twin fronts of his identity as the Creator Word and his status as Head of all creation: "There is thus an ontological relation between the creature and the Creator reposing upon His sheer grace . . . because He is the Creator Word who became Man, even as the incarnate Word He still holds all men in an ontological relation to himself. That relation was not broken off with the Incarnation . . . He is not only the Head of believers but the Head of all creation and that all things visible and invisible are gathered up and cohere in Him – from which we cannot exclude a relation in being between all men and Christ." No doubt James Torrance would readily endorse his brother's insight here.

34   Jeannine Graham, *Representation and Substitution . . .*, 211.

surgery on the human nature of all persons through Jesus' vicarious humanity because it includes our own.

Preclusive: the Many Displaced by the One[35]

At first glance this assertion might seem scandalous. It breathes substitution, which is currently taking much fire from critics. When construed in strictly penal terms, it can invite charges of "divine child abuse" – God the Father beating up on Jesus, who nobly agreed to be the "whipping boy" so that sin can be properly punished and holiness satisfied. In another sense it can be seen as dehumanizing. To paraphrase Dorothee Sölle, a prime critic of substitution, a substitute permanently replaces persons, obliterating them by treating them either as dead, useless or unavailable. It is total removal of that person by the substitute, who remains totally detached from any personal connection with the one replaced.[36] But once the Torrancean categories of "one for the many, many in the one" are brought to bear on the subject, it becomes possible to speak of *inclusive* substitution/representation.[37] In reminding us that *Christus pro nobis* must precede *Christus in nobis*,[38] Torrance sounds a strong note of substitution by acknowledging that God has graciously come to do for us in Christ what we cannot do for ourselves. Who of us can render a perfect response of utter fidelity, love and obedience to God as is befitting our role as covenant partners of God? If Galatians 3:22 gives an accurate read on human nature as imprisoned in sin, who can escape those shackles by their own efforts? If the human condition

---

35 I am well aware of Elmer Colyer's insistence that T. F. Torrance disavows the idea that the "*total substitutionary* character of Jesus Christ's vicarious humanity might seem to undermine or displace *our* humanity and *our* human response..." I wholeheartedly concur with his observation. It is decidedly not a displacement of all notions of human response but only a displacing of any posturing of the human self claiming ontological status apart from the Creator Word. See Elmer Colyer, *How To Read T. F. Torrance* (Downers Grove: InterVarsity Press, 2001), 117.

36 Jeannine Graham, *Representation and Substitution . . .*, 39–40, citing Dorothee Sölle, *Christ the Representative* (London: SCM Press Ltd., 1967), 19–23.

37 T. F. Torrance affirms the necessity of affirming the themes of both representation and substitution, using the term "total substitution" to designate this combination of the two. Cf. *The Mediation of Christ*, pp. 80–81.

38 James Torrance, *Worship, Community and the Triune God of Grace*, 28, 75; cf. T. F. Torrance, *Mediation of Christ*, p. 75.

apart from Christ is as dire as being "dead in our transgressions and sins" (Ephesians 2:1), who can enliven herself?

Yet Christ takes our place to act in our stead not to obliterate us but rather to displace our pseudo-self, the attempt to ground our lives in some independent source other than the true source of our being. What is precluded is the attempt to live our life as if we are not ontologically linked with the Creator Word, as if we aren't bound to the head of humanity. To believe that Jesus has not acted in his vicarious humanity on our behalf and in our place is to embrace the lie.

Conclusive: The Many Re-placed by the One

In speaking of Jesus in substitutionary terms as the One who acts in our place, offering the perfect response to the Father in our name, it might seem to lend credence to the objection that our human response has been crowded out. But Torrance is clear that Jesus' vicarious acts do not eliminate the need for our response; rather, in doing for us what we cannot do for ourselves – i.e., making the perfect response of love and penitent submission to the verdict of guilty – we are freed from the treadmill of trying (and failing) to measure up. Jesus' response for us doesn't eliminate but rather enables and summons our response.[39] Both Torrance brothers allude to the paradox of Galatians 2:20: "we live, yet not we but Christ in us."[40] "All of grace" does not mean "nothing of humanity." Elmer Colyer captures this idea aptly:

> Just as there is not simply grudging space, but a full and glorious place, for the *human* being and *human* response of Jesus in the incarnation (no one is as fully human and personal in response to God as Jesus was), so also there is an analogous full and complete place for *our* human response within Christ's vicarious human response for us . . . [quoting T. F. Torrance] *"all of grace means all of man,* for the fullness of grace creatively includes the fullness and completeness of our human response in the equation.[41]

---

39   James Torrance, *Worship, Community and the Triune God of Grace*, 53–54.
40   Ibid., 91. Cf. also T. F. Torrance, *The Mediation of Christ*, p. 98.
41   Elmer Colyer, *How To Read T. F. Torrance* (Downers Grove: InterVarsity Press, 2001), 119.

Resounding throughout Torrance's theology is the notion that we were made for communion with others and with the Triune God who has his being-in-communion. His words reverberate in my memory: "We are never more truly human, never more truly persons, than when we find our true being-in-communion."[42] The spotlight James Torrance shines on Jesus as the one who acts on our behalf in our place – taking upon himself our fallen flesh in order to heal, restore and give it back to us – illumines God's earnest desire that we be delivered from all that dehumanizes us so that we may be *repersonalized* in him.

Torrance makes a helpful distinction between a biblical notion of the one for the many and a Platonic construal of the one and the many. In Plato's worldview, which finds expression in some Eastern ideologies today, it is not the particulars which have supreme value but only their participation (*methexis*) as imperfect, partial expressions of the One, the Ideal or Form. It is timeless, eternal, abstract universals which are all-important, not the fluctuating, temporally limited manifestations of the empirical world. This stands in stark contrast to the biblical sense of personhood, which upholds the sanctity and integrity of human beings with whom God deals in eminently personal ways. We are not simply like drops of water whose distinct identity dissipates as we merge into the ocean of Being. Jesus is not simply an "ideal embodiment of humanity," the messenger and expression of a principle; rather, his unique personhood as a particular person is absolutely germane to his mission. Torrance verges on overkill to make his point about the personalizing Person and work of God in Christ:

> The New Testament is thoroughly non-dualistic about Jesus being not only a man, but the One Man, the one person in whom God has given himself personally to the world and for the world, that his purposes for all humanity might be brought to fulfillment. There is an absolute uniqueness to the person of Jesus Christ, deeply concerned for every single one of the many to bring every single one into personal union with himself, to share his personal union with the Father. Thus in Jesus Christ 'the one and the many' means at once the one for the many, the one who stands in for the many, the many represented personally in the one, the one who comes by the Spirit to each one of the many whom he loves and knows by name to say: "It is for you, John, and for you, Mary, and for you, Peter." Whereas

---

42 James Torrance, *Worship, Community and the Triune God of Grace*, 72–73.

the Platonic 'one and the many' is impersonal and disinterested in the particular, the biblical 'one and the many' is intensely personal.[43]

God is not out to squelch or squash human personhood but quite the contrary, to call forth and celebrate the beauty and creativity of each person, summoning each one to discover and grow into their identity as the unique persons God has designed them to be in Christ.

Church's Mission: Called to Participate in Christ's Ministry to the World

It is clear throughout Torrance's thought that the gospel of gracious inclusion in the vicarious humanity of Christ our representative and substitute, who acts on our behalf and in our place to lift us into a life of union and communion with the triune God, is not construed merely as pertaining to the salvation of the individual believer.[44] Just as Israel's identity as the people of God was inextricably wrapped up in her calling to be the unique vehicle through whom God's redemptive plan would unfold as the means of drawing in all nations, so also the Church also finds its identity as the redeemed people of God called to participate in Christ's ongoing ministry to the world. Corresponding to the twofold ministry of Christ for us in representing God to humankind and humankind to God, there is a twofold ministry of the Spirit in us: a God-humanward movement of creating, revealing, renewing and gifting as well as a human-Godward movement of leading us to the Father through interceding for us and lifting us into a life of communion with God. The "vicarious priestly work of the Spirit" in us is an indispensable dimension of Christ's ongoing priestly work for us through his vicarious humanity and of our understanding of worship.[45]

Called to belong to Christ necessarily involves belonging to his people as the Body of Christ; it is not an optional extra but fundamental to what it means to participate in Christ. Likewise, participating in Christ's mission of bearing witness to, serving and loving the world

---

43 James Torrance, *Worship, Community and the Triune God of Grace*, 51-52.

44 James Torrance, "From a trinitarian standpoint, God is in the business of creating community." *Worship, Community and the Triune God of Grace*, 40:

45 J. B. Torrance, "The Vicarious Humanity of Christ," in T. F. Torrance, *The Incarnation*, 145.

Jesus loved and served is also not optional but organically mandated. "As Christ was anointed by the Spirit in our humanity to fulfil his ministry for us, so we are united by the same Spirit to share his ministry."[46] Belonging to Christ and being summoned to mission on behalf of others are two sides of the same coin. Said differently, participating in Christ and participating with him as "'co-lovers' . . . participating together in the very life of God and in his love for the world"[47] are inseparately bound. Thus Israel's commission to be a royal priesthood on behalf of all nations is replicated in the Church's commission as the Body of Christ, the new Israel whose royal priesthood reaches out to all nations. Paul's designation of Christians as ambassadors for Christ through whom God is making his appeal to the world to be reconciled in light of the reconciliation that has already taken place in Christ conveys a similar sense of identity and mission as an outgrowth of what has first been done for us in Christ.[48]

Torrance sees the term "participation" as ideally suited to express the "for us" and "in us" dimension of the Gospel of grace.[49] Our identity as Christians is formed both by participating in what Christ has done for us in his inclusive humanity and by our active participation in his mission to the world. As Jürgen Moltmann so eloquently puts it,

> It is not the church that has a mission of salvation to fulfil to the world; it is the mission of the Son and the Spirit through the Father that includes the church, creating a church as it goes on its way . . . The church participates in Christ's messianic mission and in the creative mission of the Spirit . . . The church participates in the uniting of men with one another, in the uniting of society with nature and in the uniting of creation with God . . . Thus the whole being of the church is marked by participation in the history of God's dealings with the world.[50]

---

46 Ibid.

47 James Torrance, *Worship, Community and the Triune God of Grace*, 94.

48 2 Cor. 5:18-20.

49 J. B. Torrance, "The Vicarious Humanity of Christ," in T. F. Torrance, *The Incarnation*, 145: "'Participation' is thus an important word. It holds together what WE do, and that in which we are given to participate – the Son's communion with the Father, and the Son's mission from the Father to the world."

50 Jürgen Moltmann, *The Church in the Power of the Spirit* (Minneapolis: Fortress Press, 1993), 64-65.

Seen in this light, the identity and commission of the Church is not something she must invent *de novo* in imitation of Christ's life of selfless service to the world. Rather, it is a natural outgrowth of God's gracious embrace of us in Christ. The Church is called to join with the ongoing ministry of the triune God in the world; it is a summons to join the moving train of God's redemptive mission to all nations – the one for the many theme reappearing this time in ecclesiological garb.

A Christological Postlude . . . True to Form

To conclude on a personal note, I well remember one rather dismal day during my postgraduate years in Aberdeen when I felt so overwhelmed and discouraged that I found myself staring blankly out the window for at least an hour. The next day I related that incident to Prof. Torrance. Whether or not we talked at length or just in passing, I do not recall. But what is seared into my memory was this simple exhortation, "Look away from yourself to Christ."[51] It was so telling . . . and it was enough.

---

51 James Torrance, *Worship, Community and the Triune God of Grace*, 93-94: "When we focus on the question of who, we can rejoice together *as we look away from ourselves to him* [my emphasis], that he may sanctify us and lead us together into the presence of the Holy Father." Also cf. p. 107: ". . . the Spirit lifts us out of any narcissistic preoccupation with ourselves to find our true humanity and dignity in Jesus Christ, in a life centered in others, in communion with Jesus Christ and one another, in a loving concern for the humanity of all." And still further, p. 117: "Jesus Christ is the true leader of our worship, and if we take our eyes off him we fall back on ourselves . . ."

Chapter 19

"Thrown Back on Ourselves": James Torrance's Critique of Pelagianism in Christian Life and Worship

Stephen May

"Thrown back on ourselves" is a phrase which is repeated in James Torrance's pithy and concise (yet sadly small) number of writings: it refers to a pattern of human activity occasioned by our encounter with what we perceive as our religious duty, whether in worship or in Christian life.[1] Faced with what we think we ought to do, we think we have no alternative but to try to dredge up the capacity from within ourselves. As James puts it right at the beginning of his presentation of two ways of worship, this leads to weariness rather than joy;[2] we try to find from somewhere within

---

1   J. B. Torrance, "The Vicarious Humanity of Christ," in *The Incarnation*, ed. T. F. Torrance (Edinburgh: Handsel, 1981), 134, 144; and *Worship, Community and the Triune God of Grace* (Carlisle: Paternoster, 1996), 18. "It seems to me that in a pastoral situation, our first task is not to throw people back on themselves with exhortations and instructions as to what to do and how to do it, but to direct us to the gospel of grace . . ." (*ibid.*, 34). It is also used by T. F. Torrance with regard to both ontological and epistemological issues, notably against Bultmann: thus, "Cheap and Costly Grace," in *God and Rationality* (London: OUP, 1971): 58, 61 respectively. In "The Eclipse of God" (ibid., 50), he discusses how a false view of God and so-called human maturity might lead to people wanting to be "flung upon (their) own resources" – not entirely unlike Pelagius.

In this essay, I will use the terminology of Jock Stein in his editing of *Gospel, Church and Ministry* (Eugene: Pickwick, 2012) by using "TF" for T. F. Torrance in the footnotes – and either "JB" (as he was familiarly known by students) or "James" for J. B. Torrance. There are as many references to TF as to JB's works in these footnotes simply because he wrote far more in total – but JB *talked* about it more, and it was a key part of what he did write. It was his understanding of his own central calling, as the relationship between theology and science perhaps was for TF.

2   Ibid. 128, 130; also J. B. Torrance, *Worship, Community and the Triune God of Grace*, 7; also, "Covenant or Contract? A Study of the Theological Background of Worship in Seventeenth-Century Scotland," *Scottish Journal of Theology* 23, no.1 (Feb. 1970): 60, where he says it "can become 'a yoke grievous to be borne.'"

ourselves what we know we ought to be like – enthusiastic, peaceful, filled with love for God and our neighbour. However, this is a fruitless activity, for we simply lack the capacity we need.[3] And so we are faced with the classic dilemma of trying to do that which, deep down, we know we cannot. It is in fact what Paul wrote about: "For I have the desire to do what is good, but I cannot carry it out. For what I do is not the good I want to do; no, the evil I do not want to do – this I keep on doing" (Rom. 7:18-19, NIV).[4]

3   As I argue below, this is an *a posteriori* rather than *a priori* judgement, based on encounter with God rather than self-analytic anthropology. Pelagianism of course asserted that we can! Pelagius was a British monk who, arriving in Rome in 410 A.D., was appalled by its moral laxity; he saw a prayer of Augustine in his *Confessions,* Book 10: *da quod iubes et iube quod vis* ("give what you command, and order what you will") as implicit justification for this depravity because it suggested that we needed God's aid. For him, God provided for humanity in creation the *posse* (ability), and we should provide the *esse* (being) and *velle* (willing) in response; it was an insult to God to suggest he asked us to do what was beyond us. Pelagius asserted that Scripture told us that Adam, Eve and Cain had sinned, but it did not tell us that Abel had - so he had not! For Pelagius, as in the usual attribution to Kant, "ought implies can." By contrast, Augustine asserted we were unable *not* to sin: *non posse non peccare*. An extensive debate involving many over an extended period of time ended in official condemnation at the Council of Ephesus in 431. For the debate, cf. Peter Brown, *Augustine of Hippo* (London: Faber and Faber, 1967); John Ferguson, *Pelagius* (Cambridge: Heffer, 1951); Robert F. Evans *Pelagius: Inquiries and Reappraisals* (London: Adam and Charles Black, 1968); Theodore de Bruyn, *Pelagius' Commentary on St. Paul's Epistle* (Oxford: Clarendon, 1993), and – of course – Augustine's own voluminous anti-Pelagian writings. A repeated theme for Augustine was that Pelagius' theology "rendered the Cross of none effect" (*On Nature and Grace,* 7) and showed base ingratitude (*Ep.* 176.2; 175.1). Pelagianism then and now has had many voluble supporters, particularly in the mediating form known as semi-Pelagianism which speaks of human co-operation with God. It has a considerable subsequent life in various medieval and subsequent theological disputes, including those surrounding Luther's debate with Erasmus over the bondage of the will, Jansenism, and (perhaps) Arminianism. The use of the term is in the manner of J. B. Torrance – as theological shorthand – without unwrapping further the various issues arising in these controversies, except implicitly, for example, in remarks about "free will" ("Vicarious Humanity," 128; *Worship*, 7). The concentration of this essay is on content rather than form (insofar as they can be separated), though another approach would be to analyse the way in which James' theology is oriented around issues of order – repentance before forgiveness, indicatives before imperatives, incarnation before atonement, Christology before soteriology, etc. – and oppositions – covenant rather than contract, evangelical repentance rather than legal repentance, worship as Christ's work rather than ours, and so forth.

4   This is also the passage identified by Krister Stendahl as significant in what he regards as a fundamental misreading of Paul, "The Apostle Paul and the Introspective Conscience of the West," *Harvard Theological Review* 56, no.3 (Jul., 1963): 199-215. I attempt to deal with what I suspect would be his criticisms of my argument below!

Now, this of course is also the insight of Martin Luther, which delivered him from personal agony as he sought repeatedly as a monk to live without sin. Yet he found that this did not work because the moment he had finished confessing one round of sins, he thought of some others he had not thought of and so had to return to the confessional.[5] We can well believe his confessors found this somewhat irritating, and might encourage him to be less scrupulous. Any less conscientious man might well have followed that advice.[6] But for Luther there were no half measures. One could not simply elide over difficulties. Luther found from his own experience and scrupulous self-examination that he could never attain to the holiness he believed essential to his existence as a monk. Thankfully, Staupitz (the Vicar General of his Augustinian order, and his personal confessor) directed him to the New Testament,[7] and it is from that attention to Scripture that the Reformation ensued. He discovered in Romans that the righteous shall live by faith, not by works. This was his moment of liberation.

It is with the same degree of logic that James Torrance examines the rationale of Christian worship. Like Luther, he tells us that Christ has done it right, unlike us. Like Luther, he accepts no half-measures, no blurring of the question, no "there's always truth in different points of view." Rather he drives the logic on inexorably to a truth that is simultaneously rigorous and liberating. Like a poet who has found the precise verbal expression for his insights, James tends to use the same formulations, sometimes the same words over and over again.

People encountering James Torrance's writing on this subject frequently find it astonishingly liberating, as I know both from students and strangers I have encountered. A Pentecostal minister I met once in Australia (and have never seen again) told me how James' lectures on worship had revolutionised his life. James put his finger, he said, on exactly what was the problem with the worship in the church he led. And once he had seen it, he could never un-see it.[8]

---

5   W.A. 40.ii.15.15, quoted in G. Rupp, *The Righteousness of God* (London: Hodder and Stoughton, 1953), 116.

6   Ibid., 115-17. Rupp argues, "there is a world of difference between the scrupulosity of the saints and a self-centred scrupulosity which denotes moral obtuseness," 117.

7   Ibid., 117. For other treatments of Luther, cf. Graham Tomlin's concise and pithy *Luther and His World* (Oxford: Lion Hudson, 2012); Heiko A. Oberman, *Luther: Man between God and the Devil* (Yale: Yale U. P., 2006, orig. 1989); Bernhard Lohse, *Martin Luther's Theology* (Edinburgh: T&T Clark, 1999); and the lively classic Roland Bainton account, *Here I Stand* (Nashville: Abingdon, 1991, orig. 1950).

8   I sometimes wonder if this is the same man whom James says told him that

It is one thing to see something and another to see and communicate it in its vitality and importance. There is thus both an irenic *and* polemical aspect to James' writings, which seeks to persuade by illumination and a reduction to strikingly expressed essentials. It is necessary not just to indicate that something is right but that something else is *wrong*.[9] T. F. Torrance could have been speaking of his brother when he wrote that the Gospel should be proclaimed, "with all the clarity and simplicity that is possible, otherwise it will never reach its target, that is, not even begin to offend."[10] Thus James' comments on worship were for some life, but for others death. However, one has to say that, given his own charming and benign personality, when there was offence (which seemed to be rare), it was only that of the gospel![11]

for ten years he had been "whipping up" himself and his congregation, and that his encounter with James led to his "conversion" (*Worship, Community and the Triune God of Grace*, 22-23). How often we meet ministers (or worship leaders!) who tell us that we have not been enthusiastic enough in our singing!

9   D. Bonhoeffer argues that critical or negative christology is as necessary as positive christology, and that the abandonment of the category of heresy is a terrible loss: "There can be no credal confession without saying, 'In the light of Christ, this is true and this is false!'" Bonhoeffer, *Christ the Centre* (San Francisco: Harper and Row, 1978, E.T. by Edwin H. Robertson, 1968), 75. This was, of course, in the context of the growth of the false religion of messianic Nazism. As Helmut Thielicke points out, to declare at a 1930s German Berlin Sports Palace assembly (in which the suffering Christ was being mocked) that Christ was the Messiah was theologically correct but safe (because not understood); to cry out that, "Christ is our Leader in time and eternity; those who reject him are seducers" was to formulate his statement in terms of the leader-cult of Nazism, be immediately understood and thus invite martyrdom. It is pointed, and brings about a response. Thielicke, *Modern Faith and Thought*, E.T. by G. Bromiley (Grand Rapids: Eerdmans, 1990), 44.

10   T. F. Torrance writes: "Luther was surely right when he declared that no matter how clearly and simply you preach justification, the common people react to it like a cow staring at a new gate. But in the teaching of university students I find that the reaction may also be one of anger and resentment when they understand more than they can accept" ("Cheap and Costly Grace", 71). "Blessed is the one who is not offended in me," Matt. 11:6, quoted in Bonhoeffer, *Christ the Centre*, 109, 111. Cf. also S. Kierkegaard, "The Paradox and the Offended Consciousness" in *Philosophical Fragments* (Princeton: Princeton UP, 1967, E.T. by David F. Swenson, 1936), 61-68.

11   I personally experienced great kindness from T. F. Torrance, but it has to be said that not everyone saw it that way; Jock Stein acknowledges in *Gospel, Church and Ministry* (18, n27) that this towering intellectual figure did not suffer fools gladly. It was a joke at New College in the early 1970s that the Dogmatics Department had its own Trinity: TF (utterly incomprehensible and ineffable), JB (who ministered the things of TF to common mortals) and Alasdair Heron (who transmitted the Torrantian vision at a practical level to students with regard to issues like essays)! Whilst largely unfair, it has

James' method is often by the presentation of differing models, between which the reader is invited to choose. It is Socratic in the sense that the approved direction of thought is wholly clear, yet honest in that the different models are described fairly, in their strongest form (for example, regarding Harnack).[12] Thus the reader can tell that she is not being manipulated deceitfully and has room to argue. Yet the explanatory power of such models is that for the most part they are utterly convincing; they are described without any fudging and with ruthless attention to the key points, being reduced to the most cogent form possible. In fact, they (along with their attendant diagrams) bear the hallmark of scientific modelling.[13]

It makes perfect sense to see Jesus as the mediator of our worship. However, is it not astonishing that so few have made this connection before the Torrances? Not just our default human viewpoint but theology also has assumed that worship is "our work," our response to what God has done. Even when the alternative position has been refuted, the alternative has rarely been thought through for Christian life and worship.[14] This is

---

to be admitted that there were elements of truth in this caricature. On one occasion, an Honours Calvin class with Alasdair Heron was interrupted by an unexpected visit by TF, of whom we all stood in awe. We had been discussing a knotty problem (about why science had not developed under Eastern Orthodoxy if its theology was so much better than the West's!). Alasdair said, "You can now ask the horse's mouth!" I think TF *was* approachable, but JB always *felt* approachable.

12   Graduates were treated at Aberdeen to a series of detailed lectures on 19th Century theology, which sadly remain unpublished but some of it had a clear parallel in his Edinburgh colleague Alasdair Heron's *Protestant Theology in the 20th Century* (London: Lutterworth, 1980), 32-36. James regaled us with the tale of Harnack delivering the lectures that became *Das Wesen des Christentums* (trans. as *What is Christianity?*) to a huge adoring crowd in Berlin at what some of us would regard as a most ungodly hour!

13   It is therefore ironic that, according to members of the family, James' brother, Thomas – the great pioneer of the relation of theology and science – looked rather disparagingly at such diagrams, surely misconstruing here the meaning of "imageless thinking" (e.g. *The Mediation of Christ*, Exeter: Paternoster, 1983, 30).

14   As James explains, this has much to do with the Arian struggle in which the divinity of Christ was affirmed with such difficulty, distracting attention from the equal necessity to affirm the true humanity of Christ and his vicarious worship on our behalf: thus J. Jungmann, *The Place of Christ in Liturgical Prayer* (London: Chapman, 1965); J. B. Torrance, *Worship, Community and the Triune God of Grace*, 54-55; T. F. Torrance, "The Mind of Christ in Worship: the Problem of Apollinarianism in the Liturgy," in *Theology in Reconciliation* (London: Chapman, 1975), 142. A "golden thread" of recognition of Jesus' vicarious humanity runs through the history of theology. The acknowledgement of his assumption of our *fallen* humanity is less common (T. F. Torrance, *Mediation*,

one of the great achievements we are honouring, something so essential, so simple, so easy to grasp once it has been grasped, it is a way of seeing as radical a change as Einstein's theory of Relativity is in the scientific sphere.[15] What we had previously thought unalterable, like Newton's absolute reference of the space-time container within which everything happens, is utterly relativized by this new insight. As TF argues, if it is the speed of created light which is absolute in our world, it is Uncreated Light to which everything is relative spiritually.[16]

This also has a parallel in the Copernican revolution, for the centre of the universe changes: it is Christ, rather than the individual self, around whom all revolves. I wrote above that it makes perfect sense for many to see Jesus as the one who stands in our place to do for us what we cannot do for ourselves, but it also requires *metanoia*, a change of mind to see that the centre of gravity has changed, that Jesus is the centre.[17] *Christ the Centre* is indeed the title of the English translation of Bonhoeffer's christology lectures. He replaces our multiplicity of individual selves, all caught up in ourselves and our own importance. Christ both dethrones us from our hubristic illusion, and re-enthrones us in himself, replacing our alienation, competition and anxious self-seeking with his love and self-giving. We find ourselves in him. Our warring individualistic pursuit of our own goals is replaced by harmony in him. It is here too that the gospel calls us to look beyond the conflict of capitalism and communism to an economic system that is not predicated on "To the devil with the hindmost!"[18] There is a

---

49-50; J. B. Torrance, *Worship*, 43), and was even denied – to my shock – by George Dragas, a friend of the Torrances, in a public lecture at Aberdeen in the early 1980s.

15 "As in every great scientific advance we have to engage in a desperate struggle with ourselves in order to make the radical change in meaning that it involves ... By its very nature (the Gospel) cannot be apprehended without a profound change in our natural habits of mind, without a desperate struggle with ourselves and our aversion for change," T. F. Torrance, "Cheap and Costly Grace", 72.

16 *Christian Theology and Scientific Culture* (Belfast: Christian Journals, 1980), 73-104, especially 74-5.

17 Thus T. F. Torrance refers to justification as "at once the most easy thing and yet the most difficult thing to understand, for it is the most easy and yet the most difficult to accept ... Justification by grace alone is equally difficult for the man in the parish and the man in the university," "Cheap and Costly Grace," 70-71. It, "calls for a radical self-renunciation, a displacement of the self by Jesus Christ... in which you do not think out of your own self-centredness but out of a centre in the Incarnate Word who summons you to leave all and follow Him," 70.

18 It is to be noted that James Torrance was politically more left-wing than T. F. Torrance, though both regarded apartheid as an abomination (personal conversations

vast difference between "to be is to be in relationship" and "to be is to be in competition."[19]

This application too is an example of the way in which theological apprehension is akin to genuine scientific discovery in being both fruitful and challenging; as time goes on one perceives the implications piercing further and further.[20]

With James' third theological model, Christ is at the centre; we are at the periphery. Our life is a sharing in the life of Christ, of the new Adam who has fulfilled both sides of the covenant ('the God-humanward' and 'the human-Godward' movements).

The whole comparison is extraordinarily illuminating in revealing exactly what is at stake. It becomes clear that even in the evangelical-seeming 'existential' second model God is on the periphery, acting as the solution to our self-diagnosed problems. It is for this same reason that Karl Barth refused the Tillichian analysis of the human predicament: that humanity works out what the questions are and the gospel provides the answers! As Barth argues, the gospel reveals the questions as well. (This statement also makes a fundamental methodological point to which we will return.) Just so, James spoke with scorn of the 1960s dictum that "the world sets the agenda!" The issue of the proper starting point in theology is crucial, and so often resolves into the question: are we dealing with theology or anthropology?

Anthropology and Subjectivism

I have drawn an analogy with Luther, but Luther's (or Lutheran*isms!*) understanding of justification has been interpreted by some as purely forensic: God, by virtue of Christ's death, looks at us not as we are but as we are in Christ. *Simul iustus et peccator*, unless interpreted as a continuous and dynamic relationship, can make our justification "an

---

with members of the family).

19 Cf., for example, the clash of communities between the diabolic N.I.C.E. and the heavenly St. Anne's in C.S. Lewis' *That Hideous Strength* (London: Pan, 1956). One chapter uses George MacDonald's saying, "Real Life is Meeting," 181.

20 Cf. the implications of a perception of what it means to be a human person grounded on the doctrine of the Trinity: J. B. Torrance, *Worship, Community and the Triune God of Grace*, and – among many other works – Colin Gunton, *The One, the Three and the Many: God, Creation and the Culture of Modernity* (Cambridge: CUP, 1993).

empty legal fiction."[21] Whilst concurring that what we have is an *aliena iustitia* – salvation achieved *extra nos* – for James Torrance this comes by participation in the person of Christ. We are not simply viewers of a transaction enacted over our heads. Everything we have is not just *per Christum* or *proper Christum* but *in Christo*.[22] Luther's emphasis on faith, even though it is really grace perceived by faith (Ephesians 2:8), can lead to the subjectivist concentration on the act of faith and the required need then for a "personal decision for Christ" which is decisive for the salvation of the individual.[23] This can turn faith itself into a "work", an act of co-redemption.[24] James spoke of how this is putting the emphasis in the wrong place: rather faith arises as we perceive that Christ has done everything for us.[25] Thus Paul writes, "But of him are ye in Christ Jesus, who of God is made unto us wisdom, and righteousness, and sanctification, and redemption." (1 Corinthians 1:30, KJV)

---

21   T. F. Torrance, "Cheap and Costly Grace," 83-84; also 59-60. Cf. also "Justification in Doctrine and Life," in *Theology in Reconstruction* (London: SCM, 1965), 156, 160; "The Roman Doctrine of Grace from the Point of View of Reformed Theology" (ibid.), 186; *Mediation*, 50. A thorough treatment of the doctrine of justification is needed to respond to Douglas Campbell's criticisms in *The Deliverance of God* (Grand Rapids: Eerdmans, 2013), which argues that the whole notion is contractual and opposed to an emphasis on participation. McLeod Campbell viewed justification as, "not just a non-imputation of sin in which we believe; that would be some kind of justification by *our* faith. On the contrary, justification is bound up with a feeding upon Christ, a participation in his human righteousness." T. F. Torrance, "The Mind of Christ in Worship: the Problem of Apollinarianism in the Liturgy," 141. Gal. 2:20 – translated as "the life I now live I live by the faith *of* the Son of God" (rather than "faith *in*") was as much a favourite of that Campbell as it is of the newer version! Cf. also T. F. Torrance, *Mediation*, 107-8.

22   Similarly, our worship is not just *dia Christon*, because of the work and merits of Christ, but *dia Christou*, through Christ. J. B. Torrance, "The Vicarious Humanity of Christ," 136.

23   T.F. Torrance, *Mediation*, 102-4; "Cheap and Costly Grace," 58.

24   T. F. Torrance, "Cheap and Costly Grace," 57, 58.

25   He told the story of a man who once told him of his conversion in a South Wales coal mine in great detail, but who was taken aback when James responded by telling him of *his* conversion two thousand years ago when Christ was born, lived, died and rose again! T. F. Torrance tells a similar tale (*Mediation*, 95-6). Both seem to have drawn from Barth's story about Kohlbrügge who, when asked about when he was converted, replied, "On Golgotha!" Arthur C. Cochrane in *How Karl Barth Changed My Mind*, ed. Donald McKim (Grand Rapids: Eerdmans, 1986), 16. The story is told slightly differently by J. B. Torrance, *Worship, Community and the Triune God of Grace*, 64.

When one perceives this, one is having faith, not something one tries to whip up oneself from within one's own resources, but as the subjective correlate of an objective concentration on what God has done on our behalf in Christ.[26] As Karl Barth puts it,

> ... the fact that we believe can only be, *a priori*, a secondary matter, becoming small and unimportant in face of the outstanding and real thing involved in the Christian proclamation – *what* the Christian believes . . . It is noteworthy that, apart from this first expression, "I believe," the Confession is silent upon the subjective fact of faith. Nor was it a good time when this relationship was reversed, when Christians grew eloquent over their action, over the uplift and emotion of the experience of this thing, which took place in man – and when they became speechless as to *what* they may believe.[27]

In other words, if one tries to have the subjective (faith) without the objective (what God has done in Christ), then one has neither; if one concentrates on the objective, one has the subjective as well.[28]

It is noteworthy that the modern age finds itself unable to think except in subjectivist categories that emphasise the voluntarist character of faith: thus the pivotal song "When you believe" in the (otherwise quite good) animated biblical epic, *Prince of Egypt* (1998),[29] or the typical debate between Pastor Book and Malcolm Reynolds in the film *Serenity* (2005): "When I talk about belief, why do you always assume I'm talking about God?" The repeated notion of "the leap of faith" into the void (*Indiana Jones and the Last Crusade*, 1989, and just about *passim*) lays the basis

---

26 Although the subjective reality and possibility of revelation is the Holy Spirit for Karl Barth (*Church Dogmatics*, chapter 16).

27 Barth, *Dogmatics in Outline*, trans. by G. T. Thomson (London: SCM, 1966, orig. 1949), 15-16.

28 To adapt Christ's saying, one has to die to one's faith in order to have it. "Here too it is true that whoso would keep his life shall lose it; but whoso shall lose it for My sake shall gain his life" (ibid., 16). It is only by concentrating on something greater that we have the lesser. This is a frequently repeated theme in the writings of C.S. Lewis which we might call it the "law of inattention." Thus Lewis argues that it is only by putting our minds on heavenly things that we have earthly things; it is only by wanting something other than friends that we do have friends. "First and Second Things," in *First and Second Things: Essays on Theology and Ethics*, ed. W. Hooper, (London: Fount, 1971), 22.

29 The words, "Who knows what miracle you can achieve when you believe?" subsume faith under the category of the American dream; perhaps it is no surprise this song won an Oscar!

for accusations of irrationality. Denuded of its cognitive content, faith is repeatedly contrasted with a science construed in a positivist manner with supposed factual certainties and a bogus value – and hypothesis-free "scientific method" (thus Dawkins *et al*).[30]

James Torrance, as a good reformed theologian, is of course in debt more to Calvin than Luther. Luther, for all his profound insights into the nature of Christian life has a distinctly anthropological emphasis, as James would point out. That is to say, he approached the question of God from the viewpoint of humanity, from the issue of "What can God do for us?" The central question becomes, "Where do I find a gracious God?"[31] This, James argued, is the anthropological thrust of Western Christianity, proceeding from before Augustine, and contrasting with the Eastern emphasis on the being of God. It finds its climax in the theology of Albrecht Ritschl in the 19th Century, as James showed in his detailed lectures in the topic.[32] For Ritschl, this was the core of Christianity, to follow the clue in Luther's colleague and successor, Philip Melanchthon: "To know Christ means to know his benefits and not to reflect on his natures and modes of incarnation." This is fundamentally an instrumental approach to Christ, not who he is *in himself* but rather *what he can do for me*.[33]

---

30 *Contra*: M. Polanyi, *Personal Knowledge* (London: RKP, 1958), and T. F. Torrance, *passim*.

31 Thus T. F. Torrance, "Justification," 160.

32 As James pointed out in his lectures on Albrecht Ritschl, his model of Christian existence as a series of ellipses with two foci – Jesus as one focus and the Church as the other – gives the whole game away. Christ ceases to be the sole focus and centre, and ultimately it is the self who truly becomes the centre. Jesus is only a means to an end, effectively a tool for human self-realisation. Herbert Butterfield believed that Christianity had betrayed its mission when drawn into various power systems and concluded his *Christianity and History* with the words, "Hold to Christ, and for the rest be totally uncommitted" (London: Collins Fontana, 1957, orig. 1949), 189. The notion that "Christianity And" was a betrayal was echoed by C. S. Lewis, *The Screwtape Letters* (London: Fount, 1982, orig. 1942), 35-7, 101, 106. "And," remarks Karl Barth, always turns into the other focus becoming the *only* focus. *Church Dogmatics, Vol. II. 1*, ed. G. Bromiley and T. F. Torrance, trans. T. H. L. Parker and others (E.T. Edinburgh: T&T Clark, 1957), 175. For Barth, the copulative particle "and" was "a trojan horse within which the superior enemy was already drawn into the city" (ibid., 173). In a similar manner, James Torrance identified the phenomenon of "civil religion" in Northern Ireland, South Africa and the United States, a blend of nationalism, political or economic identity and religious affiliation.

33 Torrance, *Worship, Community and the Triune God of Grace*, 17; "Vicarious Humanity," 134-35; also T.F. Torrance, "Cheap and Costly Grace," 63-4.

Yet, as James Torrance showed in his lectures, the "turn to the subject" that was so obvious in Ritschl had also taken place in the theology of Schleiermacher and Hegel. All manifested aspects of the human subject as the new centre for theology whether it be the cognitive (Hegel, the intellect), volitional (Ritschl, the will) or affective (Schleiermacher, the emotions). Barth too identified the same problem in Schleiermacher, of whom he writes that "he made the Christianly pious person into the criterion and content of his theology."[34]

However, this turn was scarcely restricted to the 19th century. Perhaps ever since the Renaissance and certainly with Descartes and the Enlightenment, attention had been subtly shifting from "our apprehension of *God*" to "*our apprehension* of God." Barth concurred with Feuerbach's criticism of religion as projected self-concern, thus clearing the ground for a thunderous concentration on revelation "vertically from above" by the "wholly other," a rediscovery of the "Godness of God."[35]

As much as Luther, Calvin thought our Christian existence depended on what Jesus had done for us, but was more concerned with ontological issues. To use scholastic terminology also employed by James, he moved on from the *ordo cognoscendi* (order of knowing) to think more about the *ordo essendi* (order of being). James identified that it was essential to make the latter the true theological and methodological starting point.[36] Otherwise (as with Tillich above) the starting point determines the ending. The answer will be shaped by the question in a restrictive manner so that you never learn more than you began with.

James' son, Alan has made much use of the analogy of the Procrustean bed.[37] It is a powerful metaphor which ably describes how questions have to be "open" to the reality they seek to investigate. James himself frequently used the "Have you stopped beating your wife?"

---

34 *Concluding Unscientific Postscript on Schleiermacher* 1968, in Clifford Green, *Karl Barth, Theologian of Freedom* (London: Collins, 1989), 66-90, here 80. With all these, theology had become anthropology (89).

35 Heron, 76-77; K. Barth, *The Humanity of God*, trans. C. T. Deans (London: Collins, 1967), 41.

36 Or, as he called it, the dogmatic starting point (*Worship*, 58). It was critical for the distinction between the "who" and "how" questions which he saw key to Bonhoeffer's Christology (17), and the dangers of pragmatism (59).

37 Procrustes in Greek myth was a brigand who preyed on travellers and tied his victims to a bed. However, any who were too small were stretched till they "fitted" whilst those too large had the relevant parts of their bodies removed.

question to illustrate how questions can be closed and unjustly determine the possible answers in advance.[38]

The point here is not just that questions must be open (though they must) but that whilst we inevitably start "from where we are," we should not stay there.[39]

Soteriology and Pastoral Issues

At this point, it is necessary to return to our opening discussion, but with an altered perspective. Our sin or incapacity cannot be known introspectively (as part of the Western *ordo salutis*) but only in relationship to God and above all to Christ. As Bonhoeffer pointed out, it is only thus that we know who we are.[40] Similarly, Calvin links self-knowledge together with knowledge of God.[41]

However, this would only be an aching burden – creating a cloud of guilt over us, whether rejected or accepted by us – did we not also know that it was forgiven. Thus we can only properly know sin in the light of forgiveness.[42] As Ezekiel puts it, when God will restore Israel:

> Then you shall remember your evil ways, and your dealings that were not good; and you shall loathe yourselves for your iniquities, and your abominable deeds. (Ezekiel 36:31)

38 T. F. Torrance showed how Christ frequently responded to questions by "questioning the questioners" – right up to the roots of their being, revealing how their questions showed who they really were. "Questioning in Christ," in *Theology in Reconstruction*, 117-27.

39 In John 2:35-51, the disciples follow Jesus not because they fully know who he is but because (selfishly, if you like) they see him as the answer to a "felt need." He is "Lamb of God," "Rabbi," "Messiah" and so forth to them as they first encounter him. That is inevitable – the epistemological starting point (the *ordo cognoscendi*) – but the important point is that they need to go beyond that, to go beyond Jesus as existing on the periphery of their being to his being instead at their centre and thus illuminating them and their being – the ontological starting point (the *ordo essendi*). Jesus as they come to know him is much greater than what they originally looked for in him, and so their vision changes.

40 Bonhoeffer, *Christ the Centre*, 31.

41 Calvin, *Institutes*, I.1.

42 E. Jüngel, "Living Out of Righteousness: God's Action – Human Agency," in *Theological Essays II*, trans. A. Neussfeld-Fast and J. B. Webster (Edinburgh: T & T Clark, 1995), 242: "The whole weight of human sin and guilt is first known where sin and guilt are moved into the light of forgiveness. By making us whole, God shows us what destroys."

I have already discussed the dangers of a self-diagnosed anthropology setting the criteria for theology: does this then mean that a pastoral or soteriological approach is wrong? Certainly Bonhoeffer and others assert that a discussion of the person of Christ should not start with soteriology!⁴³ However, the witness of the church is that soteriological concerns are nonetheless vital. Thus, quite apart from Luther's experience in the cloisters, there is the fact that the formation of christological dogma was grounded soteriologically.⁴⁴

That this is true is supported by the fact that the key debates on christology resolved down to two fundamental statements:

Jesus had to be fully divine so that we were *saved*.⁴⁵

Jesus had to be fully human so that *we* were saved.⁴⁶ (The unassumed is the unredeemed!)⁴⁷

---

43 Bonheoffer, *Christ the Centre*, 37-39. Bonhoeffer acknowledges, once he has established the priority of the christological question over the soteriological, that this is to establish a theological method; it would be wrong to conclude that this means the person and work can be separated, and the christological question must be addressed to the one complete Christ, who can never be separated from his work (39).

44 Archibald Robertson writes in his introduction to Newman's translation of Athanasius' works that Athanasius' "theological greatness lies in his firm grasp of *soteriological* principles, in his resolute subordination of everything else, even the formula *homoousios*, to the central fact of Redemption, and to what that fact implied as to the person of the Redeemer." *The Nicene and Post-Nicene Fathers, Vol. IV* (Grand Rapids: Eerdmans, 1980, orig. 1891), lxix.

45 T. F. Torrance's powerful argument in his introduction to *The Incarnation*, xi-xxii, esp. xiv-xvii: "What would it mean for mankind if in the last resort ... there is no real bridge in being or nature between (Jesus) and God?" (xvi).

46 T. F. Torrance, "Apollinarianism in the Liturgy," 139-214, esp. 147-55. It is important to see that *both* the Orthodox and Apollinaris (143-47, 152) were motivated by soteriological concerns, but the Orthodox response was more profound in its realisation of what we need to be saved *from*. It is necessary for salvation not only that the Son of God becomes who we truly are, that is, subject to the same weaknesses and temptations, but that he also *changes* this from within, from the old to the new, sanctifying it. Rather than his taking on of our humanity polluting him – as Apollinaris thought – it is necessary so we can be, sharers through the Holy Spirit in Jesus' new humanity. "For we do not have a high priest who is unable to sympathise with us in our weaknesses, but we have one who in every respect has been tested as we are, yet without sin" (Heb. 4:15). Cf. also Heb. 2:14-18 and the whole thrust of the Epistle. Contrast Millard Erickson: "For the humanity of Jesus was not the humanity of sinful human beings, but the humanity possessed by Adam and Eve before their fall." *Systematic Theology* (Grand Rapids: Baker, 1983), 736. Cf. also n14.

47 Gregory of Nazianzus, *Epistle* 101; Cyril of Alexandria, *In Ioannis Evangelium*, MPG, LXXIV, 89 CD.

In other words, soteriology rules! Yet it is soteriology informed by christology. As James Torrance argues, the incarnation must interpret the atonement and not the other way round.[48] Then we are dealing not merely with a forensic act which deals with our sin and guilt, but with an ontological one which deals with our sinful nature, one that changes our being.[49] This changes the nature of repentance too: the problem is not merely bad things we might do that grieve us, but our whole nature, inclined to evil – in C. S. Lewis' word, "bent."[50]

Jesus' assumption of our humanity is twofold for James: first he carves out a new humanity from within our flesh,[51] performing the righteous

---

48 "The Doctrine of the Trinity in our Contemporary Situation," in *The Forgotten Trinity 3*, ed. A. Heron (London: BCC, 1991), 13-14; "Introduction" to J. McLeod Campbell, *The Nature of the Atonement* (Edinburgh: Handsel, 1996, orig. 1856), 1-16.

49 The problem then is guilt rather than the defect in our natures. This is exemplified by the picture in John Bunyan's *Pilgrim's Progress* (1678) of the great burden on Christian's back rolling off when he looks at Golgotha, and disappearing into the sepulchre. (To be fair to Bunyan, this takes place very early in the story.) If the problem is merely one of guilt, then our nature remains unchanged, for sin is external to us. Moreover, those feeling an injustice often concentrate on trying to make others feel guilty, but – if they are successful – the others' main motivation may be therapeutic, in order to feel better rather than because they are full of compassion. By contrast, the gospel – by announcing the forgiveness of sins – enables action for the right outward-looking reasons. This is James' distinction between legal and evangelical repentance.

50 "Repentance gives no exemption from the consequences of nature, but merely looses sin." Athanasius, *De Inc. Verbi*, 7.11-12, trans. R. Thomson (Oxford: Clarendon: 1971).

51 James' nephew, James B. Walker was fond of suggesting that Luke: 2.52 means that Jesus "boxed his way forward" as he sanctified our nature. The Greek word *prokope* is usually translated as "advanced" (cf. also Phil. 1:12, 25), but literally means a pioneer cutting a way forward. Cf. also T. F. Torrance, "The Logic and Analogic of Biblical and Theological Statements in the Greek Fathers," in *Theology in Reconstruction* (London: SCM, 1965), 38-39. Roland Walls – James Torrance's friend and colleague at New College, Edinburgh – gave a memorable illustration of this in his pneumatology lectures. First he held his hand flat and said, "this is how we are"; then he held it vertical and asked, "so what use is it to us if Jesus comes like this?"; finally he held it flat and, shudderingly and with great struggle, brought it slowly upright till he triumphantly attained the vertical; "this is what it means for the Son of God to become human and save us," he ended. Luke clearly indicates that Jesus is recapitulating the history of Israel, but *doing it right where they did it wrong*. Thus after his (Red Sea) baptism, he goes out into the wilderness to be tempted like the Israelites – in his case for 40 days rather than 40 years – but resisting temptation whereas they succumbed to it. Eventually he accomplishes his own "exodus" in Jerusalem (Luke 9:31). In Jamesian fashion (though, to the best of my knowledge,

demands of the Law (the *dikaiomata*) and sanctifying it as he goes along the lines of Irenaeus' *anakephalaiosis* "'recapitulation'").[52] Secondly, he surrenders the old humanity to the righteous verdict of God, the *katakrimata*.[53] This means that both resurrection *and* crucifixion are necessary. Jesus is the "Judge judged in our place" (Barth), the one who – unlike us – accepts the verdict of God's "No" on sin; therefore he bears our suffering as the one who once more stands in our place. There is here no notion of "satisfaction" nor of "penal atonement" (in the commonly accepted use of the term). Nor do we have an angry God needing to be appeased or a contractual theology in which God requires something done before he can forgive us. It is all about human transformation, a change from the old Adam to the new. God acts, as James repeated constantly, because of the covenant, because of his unconditional commitment to humanity which leads him to bear all suffering for our sake simply through love. Here God's holiness cannot be opposed to his love, as if atonement theology was a matter of "squaring the circle," of somehow reconciling the two opposing aspects of God's being, his love and his justice.[54]

---

this is not one of his), I have myself repeatedly used the diagram of an extended x, with true Israel being narrowed down eventually to the solitary figure of Jesus on the Cross, abandoned and betrayed even by his friends, before expanding after the resurrection with the new people of God sharing in Christ's humanity through the Spirit.

52   *Adversus Haereses,* II.xxii.4; also III.xvi.6; V.xx.2-xxi.2; III.xviii.1; III.xviii.7; III.xxi.10; III.xxii.3. Irenaeus' insights on this topic are scattered hither and thither rather than being gathered together, showing how unsystematic theology is at this point.

53   Torrance, *Worship, Community and the Triune God of Grace,* 46-47.

54   E. Jüngel, "Living Out of Righteousness," 250-56. This is an excellent exposition of the best aspects of Luther, emphasising his understanding that God's righteousness is his making of us righteous, that God is righteous in his grace (251). Anselm's theological method may well be exemplary in the *Proslogion*, but he also operated with a feudal notion of divine honour that makes God into a prickly sovereign, jealous of his dignity (*Cur Deus Homo*). Some modern "evangelical" hymns still adopt a pre-Lutheran understanding of justice: thus, "My sinful soul is counted free/ For God the just is satisfied" ("Before the throne of God above", Charitie Lees Bancroft and Vikki Cook, 1997) and, quite notoriously in the UK, "till on that cross when Jesus died/ the wrath of God was satisfied" (the otherwise beautiful "In Christ alone", Keith Getty and Stuart Townend, 2001). This line has also been rewritten variously, including, "the love of God was magnified," and "the arms of God were opened wide."

Forgiveness and Repentance

James' close analysis of Scottish church history since the Reformation revealed several insightful (and relatively lonely) prophetic theologians disputing legalistic, contractual and forensic accounts of the work of Christ and dualistic accounts of God, whose remorseless and (un-Lutheran!) justice was his primary characteristic.[55] Among these were the Marrowmen and John McLeod Campbell. James' introduction to Campbell is invaluable, as he reveals Campbell's (and his own) pastoral heart:

> I came to see that, in reality, whatever I preached, they were only hearing a *demand on them to be* – not hearing the Divine Secret of the Gospel as to how to be – *that which they were called to be.* Of this they themselves had no suspicions; they said, and honestly, that they did not question Christ's power to save, neither did they doubt the freeness of the Gospel or Christ's willingness to save them: *all their doubts were as to themselves.*[56]

In any case, who is able to repent? To be able to do so implies that we are not really sin*ful*, but only occasionally sin and are capable of turning back to God from our own resources. Yet Scripture tells us that what we need is a real change of heart – a heart transplant:

> A new heart I will give you, and a new spirit I will put within you; and I will remove from your body the heart of stone and give you a heart of flesh. I will put my spirit within you, and make you follow my statutes and be careful to observe my ordinances. Then . . . you shall be my people, and I will be your God (Ezekiel 36: 26-28 NRSV).[57]

This is associated with radical cleansing (Ezekiel 36:25), and in Jeremiah with a new covenant in a passage much quoted in the New Testament:

> The days are surely coming, says the Lord, when I will make a new covenant with the house of Israel and the house of Judah. It will not be like the covenant that I made with their ancestors when I took them by the hand to bring them out of the land of

---

55   J. B. Torrance, "Introduction" to McLeod Campbell, 8-9.
56   J. McLeod Campbell, *Reminiscences and Reflections*, 32, quoted ibid., 3.
57   Cf. also 11.19-20. This is part of a prophecy of returning to the land of Israel. Note the Pneumatology which reminds us of the vision of the valley of dry bones (Ezek. 37).

> Egypt – a covenant that they broke, though I was their husband, says the Lord. But this is the covenant that I will make with the house of Israel after those days, says the Lord: I will put my law within them, and I will write it on their hearts; and I will be their God, and they shall be my people. No longer shall they teach one another, or say to each other, "Know the Lord," for they shall all know me, from the least of them to the greatest, says the Lord; for I will forgive their iniquity, and remember their sin no more. (Jeremiah 31: 31-34)

What we see here prophesied is the new covenant, in which God comes himself to fulfil our side of the covenant, and to enable us to fulfil the *dikaiomata* of God by sharing in the new humanity of Christ through the Spirit. This means that we will know God *internally*, in the depths of our being and we will live with transformed hearts and minds. This will be by participation in what he has done for us.

As James argued constantly, then, there is no need for that particular impossibility – our own independent repentance – for Christ, as McLeod Campbell argued, has repented for us. There is nothing we can add to what Christ has done in order to make it ours; nor is there any way we can separate ourselves from it. There is no distance between Christ's work and ourselves.[58] Indeed, as Jüngel argues, it is closer to us than we are to ourselves.[59] We are invited to share in it.

For James it was pivotal that forgiveness was logically prior to repentance.[60] He picked up a distinction he attributed to Calvin between legal and evangelical repentance, and built on it considerably.[61] Along

---

58 However, for T. F. Torrance, this does not exclude the possibility of Hell (*Mediation*, 104). When TF was asked about this by students, he said it was like two millstones going in opposite directions and thus grinding upon one another: the top one says, "I love you; I love you: I love you," but the bottom repeats constantly "I don't want you: I want myself. I don't want you: I want myself." Surely this is the dreadful "impossible possibility" for the elder brother in the parable of the Prodigal Son. Cf. also C. S. Lewis – e.g. the fate of the dwarves in *The Last Battle* (Harmondsworth: Penguin, 1964, orig. 1956), and those living in hell and refusing heaven in *The Great Divorce* (London: Fontana, 1983, orig. 1946).

59 E. Jüngel, "Living Out of Righteousness", 245-46. "Faith is in the strongest sense an exclusion of every kind of human self-realization. For the believer trusts in the work of God" (254). We might also say that Jesus, through the Spirit, is closer to us than our own breath (*pneuma*).

60 Torrance, "Vicarious Humanity," 142-44; *Worship*, 44-46; "Introduction" to *The Nature of Atonement*, 12-13.

61 Ibid., 11-12. Calvin does not *exactly* affirm this. In *Institutes* III.3.4 Calvin

with these fundamental distinctions was one repeated continuously between covenant and contract, and the relationships between indicatives and imperatives[62] and incarnation and atonement.[63] In all these, alongside McLeod Campbell, pastoral considerations were vital, though always theologically grounded. This clarification of issues is one of our primary debts to him. They provide key resources for ministry.[64]

Of course, we can always refuse to be forgiven and cling to our own sense of self-righteousness. Barth is unimpressed by those who speak of being "unable to forgive themselves."

> By this we shall be judged, about this the Judge will one day put the question, Did you live by grace, or did you set up gods for yourself and possibly want to be one yourself? Have you been a faithful servant, who has nothing to boast of?[65]

Thus Kierkegaard remarks of some supposedly mighty-souled person: "He can never forgive himself for it – but now in case God would forgive him for it?"[66] These are the ethics of gratitude.

---

indeed explains the distinction between legal and evangelical repentance, but attributes it to "others." He begins the following section (III.3.5) with the words, "Although all these things are true, yet the word 'repentance' itself, as far as I can learn from Scripture, is to be understood otherwise." This is because Calvin distinguishes between faith and repentance. Therefore the order becomes: proclamation of the Gospel, to faith in what God has done, to repentance (turning to the merciful God). Calvin as a true humanist quotes both the Hebrew and Greek senses of the word "repent." It is clear, however, that James and Calvin are at one on the heart of the matter, the unconditionality of grace. Thus *Institutes* III.4.3 reads: "We have said in some place that forgiveness of sins can never come to anyone without repentance . . . but we added, at the same time, that repentance is not the cause of the forgiveness of sins . . . We have taught that the sinner does not dwell upon his own compunction or tears, but fixes both eyes on the Lord's mercy alone" (ed. J. T. McNeill, trans. F. Battles, Philadelphia: Westminster, 1960).

62 Torrance, *Worship, Community and the Triune God of Grace*, 59.

63 Heron (ed.), *The Forgotten Trinity*, 13-14.

64 For example, in the preaching of wedding sermons (covenant, not contract)!

65 *Dogmatics in Outline*, 152. "I can testify that they have a zeal for God, but it is not enlightened. For, being ignorant of the righteousness that comes from God, and seeking to establish their own, they have not submitted to God's righteousness" (Rom. 10:2-3). Quoted by Augustine, *On Nature and Grace*, 1. The trouble is that some people are *not* "ignorant of the righteousness that comes from God" and still prefer their own!

66 *The Sickness unto Death* (Princeton: Princeton U. P., 1968, orig. trans. by W. Lowrie, 1941), 242.

An outstanding biblical scholar who has come to the same conclusion on the order of repentance and forgiveness is Kenneth Bailey. In a series of books beginning with *Poet and Peasant*,[67] he has returned repeatedly to the parable of the Prodigal Son, showing from his deep knowledge of Palestinian village culture not only the way in which the father repeatedly and publically humiliates himself, but also that the son's repentance does not occur (as is too often assumed) when he "comes to himself" in hunger but when he is met by the running, self-humiliating father. The first, as Bailey ably shows, is simply a moment of prudential and contractual calculation by an unrepentant man who still does not see what it means to be the father's son and simply seeks to worm himself back into some sort of position as a better alternative to starvation.[68] Whether the elder brother repents from his hardhearted and no less contractual attitude (in which he is no true son either) the parable leaves us to imagine. What is key is the father going out after each of them and not leaving them to stew, or sulk, in their own juice. This is the mystery and wonder of God and which should arouse in us simply gratitude and wonder too.[69]

If we are thrown back on ourselves for repentance, there are two possible responses: pride (I have adequately repented), or despair (I have not, and cannot). We are liberated from both by the news that Christ has done it for us, and invites us to share in his repentance.

Here we come to the nub of the problem which brings us back to Luther's dilemma, with which I began. Calvin indeed proclaims the same:

> If there is anything in the whole of religion which we should
> most certainly know, we ought most closely to grasp by what

---

[67] Kenneth E. Bailey, *Poet and Peasant* (Grand Rapids: Eerdmans, 1976), 158-206; *Finding the Lost: Cultural Keys to Luke 15* (St. Louis: Concordia, 1992); *The Cross and the Prodigal: Luke 15 through the eyes of Middle Eastern Peasants* (Wheaton: IVP, 2005); *Jacob and the Prodigal: How Jesus retold Israel's Story* (Wheaton: IVP, 2011).

[68] Thus, J. B. Torrance sees, he is trying to "buy" himself back into favour (*Worship*, 57). As he says, there is something in us which always wants to bargain with God, whereas all we can do is throw ourselves on his mercy ("Covenant or Contract," 57).

[69] During a mission in the early 1970s, I was part of a team in a school re-enacting this parable. It was with horror that I heard one of the mission leaders, playing the part of the father, say to the prodigal (in front of schoolchildren), "Now, are you really sorry for what you have done? Because I can't forgive you if you haven't!" Cf. "The Vicarious Humanity of Christ", 147, n20. This replacement of the Gospel with moralism (and/or sentimentality) is common, as in the treatment of Edmund in the disappointing 2005 film version of C. S. Lewis' psychologically profound *The Lion, the Witch and the Wardrobe* (1950). Because the approach to sin is so condemnatory and thus damning, the only alternative seems to be to find excuses.

> reason, with what law, under what condition, with what ease or difficulty, forgiveness of sins may be obtained![70]

What does one do if one is faced with the demand for the three things in repentance required for the forgiveness of sins – namely contrition, confession and satisfaction (*contritio, confessio, satisfactio*)?[71]

Unless this knowledge remains clear and sure, the conscience can have no rest at all, no peace with God, no assurance or security; but it continuously trembles, wavers, tosses, is tormented and vexed, shakes, hates, and flees the sight of God. But if forgiveness of sins depends upon these conditions which they attach to it, nothing is more miserable or deplorable for us.

> Yet if we look only at contrition, what *is* sufficient? . . . when such bitterness of sorrow is demanded as may correspond to the magnitude of the offence, and be weighed in the balance with confidence of pardon, miserable consciences are sadly perplexed and tormented when they see that the contrition due for sin is laid upon them . . . If they say we are to do what in us lies,[72] we are always brought back to the same point; for when will any man venture to promise himself that he has done his utmost in bewailing sin? . . . If they say that this is a calumny on my part, let them come forward and point out a single individual who, by this doctrine of contrition, has not either been driven to despair, or has not, instead of true, opposed pretended fear to the justice of God.[73]

What is true of repentance is equally true of conversion, of becoming a Christian. T. F. Torrance shows how unevangelical so-called evangelical preaching often is,[74] adding "a subtle element of co-redemption."[75] If people are saved "only if they make the work of Christ real for themselves by their own personal decision . . . this is to make the effectiveness of the work of Christ conditional upon what the sinner does, and so at the

---

70 Calvin, *Institutes*, III.4.2.
71 J. B. Torrance, "Introduction" to *The Nature of Atonement*, 12.
72 This is a reference to the theology of Gabriel Biel, one of Luther's major influences, shaken off by him with vigour. Tomlin, *Luther*, 28-29.
73 Calvin, *Institutes*, III.4.2-3 (Florida: Macdonald, translator and date not known: the translation here is more eloquent than McNeill's edition). He proceeds to deal in detail with confession and satisfaction.
74 T.F. Torrance, *The Mediation of Christ*, 102-3.
75 Torrance, "Cheap and Costly Grace," 58.

crucial point it throws the ultimate responsibility for a man's salvation back upon himself."

To preach the gospel in that conditional or legalist way has the effect of telling poor sinners that in the last resort the responsibility for their salvation is taken off the shoulders of the Lamb of God and placed upon them – but in that case they feel that they will never be saved. They know perfectly well in their own hearts that if the chain that binds them to God in Jesus Christ has as even one of its links, their own feeble act of decision then the whole chain is as weak as that, its weakest link.[76]

As he shows, such a gospel is not really good news.[77] By contrast, a declaration of forgiveness both calls and simultaneously enables us to repent and believe.[78] His faithfulness undergirds our own stumbling faith.[79]

The Mind of Christ in Worship: the Problem of Pelagianism in the Liturgy

According to the Church of England *Common Worship* (2000), God's forgiveness on us is conditional on our repentance.

In Order One – the more modern one – the priest begins the absolution with the words: "Almighty God, who forgives all who truly repent." This informs us then that he does *not* forgive those who do not truly repent.

---

76 T.F. Torrance, *The Mediation of Christ*, 103.

77 That TF is not exaggerating, I know from my own experience insofar as I once refused to say the Lord's Prayer in church on the grounds that I did not really mean it. My life at that time (in a hothouse university Christian Union environment) was an oscillation between thinking I had sufficiently given my life to Christ and dark periods of near-despair when I doubted it. It was only a mediated Torrancian emphasis on Christ's faith on my behalf that delivered me from drowning in sand to standing on a rock, from the "swing to and fro between pride and anxiety" that Barth says is human life without (real) faith – that is faith in what God has done for us, rather than faith in faith (*Dogmatics in Outline*, 20.)

78 Whilst a curate I had an encounter with an attention-seeking lady in our parish who succeeded, as was her intention, in disrupting a home communion. After some time, when my anger had inevitably abated, she approached me and said, "It's so good to know I'm forgiven." I am afraid I sighed heavily (she was a repeat offender) when what I should have said was, "Of course you're forgiven! So stop doing it!"

79 T. F. Torrance, *The Mediation of Christ*, 108.

Previously we worshippers have declared that we, "are heartily sorry and repent of all our sins," before going on to ask that God forgives us "all that is past" – "for the sake of thy Son Jesus Christ, who died for us."

This follows the pattern of the Book of Common Prayer (1549, 1552 and 1662) which is the basis for Order Two "in contemporary language." There is no difference here:

> Almighty God, our heavenly Father,
> who in his great mercy
> has promised forgiveness of sins
> to all those who with heartfelt repentance and true faith
>   turn to him:
> have mercy on you,
> pardon and deliver you from all your sins,
> confirm and strengthen you in all goodness,
> and bring you to everlasting life,
> through Jesus Christ our Lord. Amen.

There are many beautiful words here, and the assuring words are reinforced by the Comfortable Words (with four quotations from Scripture) that follow, but they help to obscure the conditionality of the forgiveness that is being offered. In all cases, it depends on our prior repentance, and not just any old repentance either, but one which is "true," "hearty" or "heartfelt." Forgiveness is declared by the priest (acting on God's behalf) on the basis of what God has done: "for the sake of thy Son Jesus Christ, who died for us."[80]

Now, in psychological terms, of course, this can "work."[81] A person, suddenly convicted of sin, may come to church full of contrition. In the absolution he hears God's forgiveness of what he has done wrong and he is enormously comforted. There is no doubt that the words of forgiveness are very powerful, yet here they embody a completely false theology.

One cannot justify these words on the basis of "pastoral" practise (a cover for too many faults and too often used to excuse poor theology)[82] nor

---

80 It is on the basis of what Christ has done, not in and through him, i.e. *per* and *propter* rather than *in*.

81 James used to say that the fact that something "works" does not mean it is necessarily true.

82 James often spoke of how irritated he was by the ministers who stood up in the General Assembly of the Church of Scotland and began their remarks with the words: "I am not a theologian but . . ." As he pointed out, the question is not whether one is a theologian or not (for everyone is), but whether one is a good or poor one! For a similar reaction, cf. Karl Barth, *Evangelical Theology: an Introduction*, trans. Grover

on the basis that people do not realise, or are not really paying attention to, what they are saying – a pretty feeble approach on any terms. Words creep into our way of thinking; they condition our attitudes, assumptions and beliefs.

What the words of the confession and absolution do is to make us think, subliminally maybe, that God's forgiveness of us is conditional, that the bottom line is how much we have repented and how genuine that is: in other words, it comes down to us. In the end, it is what we do, think and feel that matters in relation to our salvation. We are "thrown back on ourselves."

As a priest of the Church of England, I am required to say these words whenever I celebrate the eucharist, and I hate it every single time. I think it enshrines a bad theology at the heart of our worship, in a way that may be more influential than a sermon that follows, one that explicitly declares that God has unconditionally forgiven us our sins. To my mind, it is the latter that declares the gospel, the good news of God. The words of confession and absolution are in fact "bad news": they tell us that our ultimate salvation depends on us. Thus a contradiction is enshrined at the very heart of the communion service, for the Anglican order goes on to the reception of the body and blood of Christ, reminding us ("anamnesis") that Christ died for us "while we were yet sinners" (Romans 5.8), that God did not wait before sending his Son for us to repent! Anglicans are repeatedly reminded that we come to communion "with empty hands."[83]

Yet this means that we do not even bring our repentance with us to the foot of the Cross. As TF used to emphasise, we come with nothing – not our good deeds, not our devotion, not our piety. We come with nothing to receive what the Lord has so generously given to us, not because of any merits on our part, but solely dependent on his grace.

Unfortunately my experience is that many (most?) other denominations are as bad, something that other denominational members I have discussed this with have confirmed. It is not just an Anglican problem; it is a universal problem.[84] The fact that this is not

---

Foley (London: Collins, 1965, orig. 1963), 42.

83 As in the hymn "Rock of Ages," quoted by T. F. Torrance, *Mediation*, 98.

84 However, Anglicans can seem particularly complacent. Thus Samuel Wells writes blithely: "Huge controversies have raged over the correct sequence of repentance, forgiveness, and penance. And yet surely what matters is that they all be treasured and practiced as gifts of God to the church." *God's Companions* (Oxford: Blackwell, 2006), 119. No!

a burning issue with liturgists seems to suggest that they need to talk to systematic theologians – or good ones anyway like James Torrance!

What are the implications of saying that forgiveness is dependent on our adequately repenting? Clearly the human race (or, at least that part of it which goes to church) is divided into those who sufficiently repent ("truly," "heartily," "heartfeltly") and those who do not. Some are forgiven and some are not on the basis of the adequacy of their repentance.

This means that the human race tends to be divided into churchgoers ("adequate repenters") and non-churchgoers ("sinners"). But then we are back with the division between righteous Pharisees and sinful tax-collectors, which Jesus so radically and repeatedly exposed as profoundly false.[85] Jesus came to save sinners, not the (self-)righteous. I cannot be the only minister who was ever tempted to think that the people who should be in church are the very ones it tends to repel (and vice-versa)!

A second liturgical point is surely also vital. The present setting of the act of confession and absolution is separated by large tracts of the service from the act of communion (participation); yet that is the place where we actually feed on the one who gives us life – where the act of forgiveness (and transformation) is presented symbolically. This separates a *supposed* place of forgiveness from the actual place of forgiveness, and fails to comprehend that in God forgiveness is not just a word, but an action, an action in which we are reconciled with the Father through the mediator Christ.[86] At the present, the liturgy embodies a terrible theology of forgiveness and repentance, bad news rather than good news. Who knows how many people have been alienated from the Church? Radical action is needed so that our worship embodies explicitly and implicitly the mediatorship of Christ, his vicarious humanity.

An old joke (yes, with many variations) asks, "What is the difference between a terrorist and a liturgist?" The answer, of course, is, "You

---

85 Cf. Francis Spufford, *Unapologetic* (London: Faber and Faber, 2012), 47: "Of all things, Christianity *isn't* supposed to be about gathering up all the good people (shiny! happy! squeaky clean!) and excluding the bad people (frightening! alien! repulsive!) for the very simple reason that there aren't any good people . . . What it's supposed to be is a league of the guilty."

86 Because, of course, the word that goes out from God's mouth does not return empty without accomplishing that for which it was sent forth (Isa. 55:11). In fact, the word of God cannot be separated from act in Scripture, for it refers to the person of Christ.

can negotiate with a terrorist." It is long past time that liturgists and theologians – of the kind like James Torrance – did some negotiating.[87]

Conclusion

This essay began with the statement that "being thrown back on ourselves" was the epitome of a humanity ignoring "the fact that God has already provided for us that response which alone is acceptable to him."[88] James Torrance offered an alternative – a life of "being lifted up" instead, into that activity of Christ on our behalf, "the gift of participating through the Spirit in the incarnate Son's communion with the Father."[89] It is a summary of the gospel that he embodied in his life as well as throughout his teaching. For him theology was in consequence, in Barth's phrase, a joyful science.[90]

---

87 This joke was told to me by a liturgist. I am neither giving a superior position to theologians who – as we know all too well – need constant correction, nor am I implying that all liturgists are theologically-incompetent villains!: just that a debate needs to take place, in which James Torrance's theological perceptions are given full weight. As he pointed out, the sacraments are the ways in which the truth of the Gospel is embodied day after day. It has been suggested that Anglicans will be saved by their liturgy; i.e. even when the sermon is terrible, the Eucharistic liturgy is declaring the truth of the Gospel time after time. If so, it certainly needs improvement here. I am not here prescribing exactly what should be done; just that the work needs to start.

88 Torrance, "Vicarious Humanity," 134.

89 *Worship*, 24. Thus too T.F. Torrance talks of Jesus Christ as, "the one point in our human and historical existence where we may be lifted out of ourselves and escape the self-incarcerating processes of human subjectivism." "The Eclipse of God," 55.

90 *Church Dogmatics IV.3/2*, ed. G. W. Bromiley and T. F. Torrance (Edinburgh: T & T Clark, 1992), 881.

Chapter 20

James B. Torrance on the All-Inclusive Humanity of Jesus Christ

Gary W. Deddo

James B. Torrance is well-known, especially among his former students like myself, for pointing out and demonstrating the theological significance of the incarnation. The meaning of the incarnation of the eternal Son of God was, in his view, crucial not only in its own right but as a central reality that oriented every other aspect of faithful Christian understanding. Much of JB's teaching showed that an explication of any other theological point that failed to orient itself to the reality of the incarnation would prove to be inadequate if not misleading to Christian faith and worship.

The doctrine of the incarnation, as all Christian doctrines, was not itself to serve as an ultimate object of faith. This doctrine is meant to point beyond itself to the real object of our faith, Jesus Christ himself. More particularly this doctrine is meant to identify who the Jesus of biblical revelation was and is. Accordingly, Jesus Christ is to be identified as the incarnate eternal Son of God. It follows then, that all that he did and said in his earthly ministry are to be understood as the words and deeds of the incarnate one.[1]

---

1 This means that the object of our faith is actually a subject. The reality, the subject of our faith, exceeds what any doctrine can specify. But doctrinal statements can be faithful to their object/subject if they are formulated *a posteriori* upon an apprehension of the subject. And we can only apprehend the subject of our faith first because of God's own gracious action to give himself to us in revelation, a revelation that culminated in the self-revelation enacted and embodied in Jesus Christ. And second, we may apprehend the actual subject of our faith because the complex of revelation has been handed-down and preserved for us in the apostolic witness and is made actually accessible to us by the continuing gracious work of the Holy Spirit. In this process of faith seeking understanding we do then, by grace, come to know more fully Jesus Christ himself and so respond more fully in faith to him. We also can achieve then faithful articulations regarding who we have come to know him to be.

Any theological formulation aiming to be true to its subject must be informed and regulated, even determined, by the given revelation itself. In large measure all of Christian theology amounts to just that: finding words, concepts, ideas, illustrations, analogies, narratives that identify clearly and accurately today the subject matter of biblical revelation so that it contributes to a real knowing of the subject. Thus the meaning of the incarnation can only be gained by apprehending again and again the Jesus of biblical revelation in a way that corresponds to the nature of the revelation itself. This means that he himself is the object/subject of our study and the norm for any theological conclusion. A faithful christology then would direct us to the exact same Jesus referred to in the biblical revelation and worshipped in the Christian church, beginning with his appointed apostles. And JB never tired of reminding us that we do this by maintaining that the central theological question to be addressed was the "who?" question, directed towards God's self-revelation in Jesus Christ.[2]

J. B. Torrance's Particular Concern

The particular concern of JB was to give fresh articulation to the meaning and significance of the humanity of Jesus in a way that at least matched in breadth and depth those creedal and theological affirmations founded upon the biblical revelation that had been formulated down through the ages of the Christian church. A special concentration was needed, he believed, because much contemporary Protestant theology, liberal or conservative, had neglected or misappropriated its meaning. Corrective was needed. However, I believe that while providing just such a corrective by making considerable use of faithful theological reflection throughout church history, JB actually made his own contribution to the church's ability to bear a more intensive and extensive witness to the truth and reality of the identity of Jesus Christ, the incarnate Son of God.

The theological gift JB bequeathed to the church is well captured in a simple phrase he coined. More than simply re-affirming an orthodox proclamation of the complete and real humanity that Jesus assumed in the miracle of the incarnation, JB wanted to highlight and more clearly

---

2   See James B. Torrance, *Worship, Community, and the Triune God of Grace: The Didsbury Lectures 1994* (Carlisle, UK: Paternoster Press, 1996 and Downers Grove, IL: InterVarsity Press, 1997), 83.

specify the particular nature or character of his humanity. Jesus' humanity was, in his poignant phrasing, an "all-inclusive humanity."[3]

What did JB mean by this theologically rich phrase? It turns out that the reality to which it points stands at the crossroads where so much of Christian theology as a whole intersects. JB demonstrated how the all-inclusive and vicarious nature of Jesus' humanity[4] (or human nature) is essential to any faithful apprehension of his particular humanity, which in turn is requisite for Christian faith in him and a life lived in joyful worship and service to him. This theological phrase represents, I believe, a fruitful development in Christian theological articulation since it serves as a means of disclosure, extending illumination into a wide area of Christian theology and theological ethics.[5]

---

3 JB could also speak of the "all-inclusive vicarious humanity" of Christ. Given the limits of this essay, we will not be commenting much on the very important aspect of vicariousness. The primary references to this phrase can be found in *Worship, Community*, 40–42; and in James B. Torrance, "The Vicarious Humanity of Christ", in *The Incarnation: Ecumenical Studies in the Nicene-Constantinopolitan Creed, A.D. 381*, ed. Thomas F. Torrance (Edinburgh: The Handsel Press, 1981), 137, 140.

4 It can easily be assumed that "humanity" means all of what individual human beings are. But this would be in error. Natures are to be distinguished (although not separated) from persons, whether in christology or anthropology. The term "humanity," stands for, more properly, human nature. As in all orthodox christology the Son of God assumed "human nature." Two things are being assumed in speaking and thinking this way. First, the Person of the Son is distinguished but not separated from the natures he has. The person of the Son has the natures but is not simply the natures. So the Son of God remains the same person before and after assuming to himself human nature. Second, this means that the Son of God did not assume individual human persons, that is, human subjects to himself. While no human persons exist apart from human nature, the person or subject can be distinguished from the nature (analogously to christology). Human beings have in common human nature, but they do not have in common their persons. So the Son of God assumed what all human persons have in common, namely, their human natures. While neither JB (nor Thomas F. Torrance) explicitly asserted the non-assumption of human persons, it is entailed by what they did claim and is consistent with the many other affirmations made regarding christology and anthropology. Assuming that persons and natures are ontologically identical is at odds with JB's (and TF's) meaning. This must be kept in mind, for if not, then christology becomes incoherent. So while JB most often spoke of Christ's humanity, I will use interchangeably with it, "human nature."

5 The idea that true theological development is identified by its serving as a kind of heuristic that discloses aspects of revealed biblical truth heretofore ambiguous, hidden, or obscure was discussed by T. F. Torrance, JB's older brother, in a number of his books and essays, including *The Ground and Grammar of Theology* (Belfast: Christian Journals Limited, 1980), 125.

An Ontological Connection

By identifying Jesus' human nature as being "all-inclusive" JB was pointing out that Jesus' humanity was vitally and really, that is ontologically, linked to all humanity, to every single human being. The human nature that Jesus assumed was not simply his own individual or autonomous humanity, one relatively independent of all other human beings. No, the human nature he possessed was shared by all humanity. The human nature he assumed he held in common with every human person.

This understanding of Jesus' humanity sums up for JB what is captured throughout biblical revelation. The Apostle Paul's designation of Jesus as the last Adam (1 Cor. 15:45) and also his identification of him by direct inference as the archetype or original Adam (Rom. 5:14) reveal his unique relationship to all humanity. The effect that Jesus is said to have upon all humanity throughout the New Testament also comports with Jesus' unique place. Jesus' ontic solidarity with all humanity as well as the purpose (*telos*) of his incarnation being "for the sake of" or "on behalf" of all humanity, for instance as its great High Priest and worship leader, conveys the same meaning.[6] It is likely that Jesus' primary self-designation as the Son of Man also points to his unique location in relation to all humanity. This means that his self-identification as Lord does not simply note his deity over all humanity, but rather that his lordship is established, from the inside, as one of all humanity by his sharing their human nature.

JB was not pointing out simply that Jesus' humanity was revealed to be like ours, another instance of a generically classified aggregate of a certain kind of living beings. In the light of the humanity of Jesus, we cannot think of humankind as nothing more than a conventional way to name the collocation of similar characteristics exhibited by certain relatively autonomous individuals – a theological nominalism. Rather Jesus' incarnation and ministry reveals that humanity or human nature is a feature of created reality that is shared among certain creatures, namely persons, so that persons are actually linked to one another at the most fundamental level of their being, that is, ontically. As some theologians have put it, referring all the way back to Irenaeus, humanity is like a tree,

---

6   The entire letter to the Hebrews promulgates these elements but of course the explication of his death being for the sake of salvation and being the basis for the reconciliation of all humanity to God has the same import (2 Cor. 5:14-19).

with individuals being the branches or leaves of it. Being a human person means being linked to all other human persons by sharing in one and the same nature. In theological perspective, human nature is actually a shared reality that makes human beings what they are at the most fundamental level. Jesus was human in that his human nature was ontically linked to all other human beings. JB liked to speak of Jesus as the one for the many, the one in the many and the many in the one, reflecting particularly the thought of Paul in Romans 5 and Ephesians 1.[7]

More than Simply Shared Humanity

But what JB meant by "all-inclusive" meant more than simply "shared." In his view biblical revelation indicated that there is a structure to our shared human nature. Human nature has a source or origin represented by the first Adam, off from whom branches every human being. So all human beings are related to and share in created Adam's human nature. We cannot understand our being apart from the origin of our human nature. But humanity cannot simply be grasped in terms of its created origin. For the humanity of Jesus has included all human beings in a way that both subsumes and supercedes our link to the created and fallen Adam of our origin. This Jesus is, first of all the archetype of the first Adam, the created root of all humanity. He is the original source and origin of human nature at its very foundation. But more than this, by his incarnate life, including his death and resurrection, he has overtaken the deadly effects insinuated at the root of humanity by the first Adam so that in and through the one man, Jesus Christ, now come acquittal, righteousness, and life.[8]

Biblical revelation indicates that Jesus' humanity incorporates all humanity, re-connects every human being, and reorients human nature

---

7   See Torrance, *Worship, Community and the Triune God of Grace*, 39, 40, 56, and "Vicarious Humanity," 137-41.

8   Torrance is here following the exposition of Paul in Rom. 5:12-21 and the recapitulation/re-heading up (*anakephalaiosis*) in Eph. 1:10. We will have more to say later on the biblical foundations upon which JB's views are built. Karl Barth's line of thought on Romans 5 goes in the same direction. See Barth's "Christ and Adam: Man and Humanity in Romans 5," *Scottish Journal of Theology* Occasional Papers, no. 5, trans. T. A. Smail (Edinburgh: Oliver and Boyd, 1956, reprint, 1963). An overlapping account can be found in a rather surprising source, Philip Edgcumbe Hughes, *The True Image: The Origin and Destiny of Man in Christ* (Grand Rapids: Wm. B. Eerdmans Publishing Company, 1989).

itself. The incarnate Son of God, Jesus, is ontically related to every human being but uniquely so in such a way that the destiny of all humanity, the trajectory of human nature through history, is affected by who he is. Humanity itself, its very nature, has been redirected, reoriented, placed on a new basis through the assumption of it into the life of the incarnate One. The regeneration and renewal spoken of in Titus 3:5 first occurred to human nature in Jesus. His human nature alone includes, in this definitively ontological way, all humanity.

Corrective to Modern Anthropology

This understanding of not only Jesus' humanity, but of all humanity and every human being, may come as quite a shock to modern hearers. First of all, in modern western culture we largely think of human beings as relatively independent and even leaning towards autonomy. We consider ourselves relatively unaffected by others, especially at the level of our natures. In some quarters the very idea of a shared human nature is actually denied. The idea of a human nature is regarded simply as a social construction. The all-inclusive humanity of Jesus, if regarded as actual and true, will have profound implications for our anthropology and all the related social sciences.

Second, in our contemporary western context Jesus Christ is more and more viewed as being a source of division among people, not a source of unity. This perspective is increasingly found even among those who want to continue to identify themselves in some way as Christian and despite its leading to a form of prescriptive religious pluralism.[9] But many who otherwise hold to an orthodox faith, even within evangelicalism, have long assumed that common ground with those outside the Christian faith can only be found and established on some basis other than Jesus Christ – since his identity is what people are in disagreement over. This has been especially the case in the area of Christian apologetics, a discipline which seems perpetually to be in search of more adequate common ground than the last tried and largely failed candidate proved to be.[10]

---

9   This is in contrast to a descriptive and/or pragmatic pluralism.
10 This issue brings to recollection the sharp debate between Barth and Brunner over the "point-of-contact" (*Anknüpfungspunkt*).

The all-inclusive humanity of Jesus, if regarded as actual and true, would have profound implications for not only our apprehension of who Jesus is, but for the proclamation of the Gospel itself, not to mention its defense. If the exclusive claim of Jesus Christ is that only in him can all humanity, in truth and reality, be united, then the church's message formulated on that basis could, in turn, perhaps have a significant impact upon our wider culture's perception of Christian faith and worship. The false dichotomy of Christianity being either inclusive or exclusive would be undermined. However, this approach would require that the ultimate foundation for such a claim would not be our beliefs, our doctrines, but the reality of who Jesus Christ really is. He himself is God's appointed point of contact among all humanity at its origin and its destiny. He exclusively is the inclusive one.

Christ's Humanity in Biblical Revelation

The grounds for JB's emphasis on the all-inclusive humanity of the incarnate Son of God is not found simply in the fact that Jesus, as accounted for in the New Testament revelation, has all the characteristics of being a human being in the same way we are. The foundation is laid in the meaning and significance given by the biblical revelation to his humanity in relation to all others. This reaches a high point in Paul's designation of Jesus as the prototypical Adam (the created Adam being the type, Rom. 5:14) and as the last (*eschatos*) or second (*deuteros*) man/Adam (1Cor. 15:45-47). This Jesus is presented in biblical revelation as the actual new life-giving head of humanity, not just in name, but in being and so in actual effect. He is in fact the Lord of all humanity – as one of humanity. Witness to this fact can be found not only in Romans 5 but also in Ephesians 1 where, as Irenaeus saw, the place where all humanity was re-gathered, reunited, re-headed up (*anakephalaiosis*, v. 10) was in the very person of Jesus.[11]

The epistle to the Hebrews also points to just this same reality. All that Jesus does in his earthly ministry is "on our behalf" and "once for all." And his ministry has the absolute and definitive effect it does because he alone, the Son of God, has "taken on"[12] our identical human nature,

---

11   See "Vicarious Humanity," 140-41 and *Worship, Community*, 41, 42.
12   The word in Greek is *epilambanetai* and means "to seize" or "take hold of." English translations such as "concerned" or "helps" are very wide of the meaning.

not an angelic nature or that of any other sort of creature (Heb. 2:16). He "partook of the same nature" (Heb. 2:14) and "was made like his brethren in every respect" (Heb. 2:17). And this ontic connection is something that other priests, not to mention sheep and goats, could not accomplish (Heb. 7:20-28). His saving work essentially involves sharing in our human nature in order to transform it from the inside out. His ministry of sanctification is effected by his own self-sanctification in and through his assumption of our human nature. "The one who sanctifies and those who are sanctified [are] all of one." (Heb. 2:11).[13] The effect of his saving work flows through the ontological channel of our shared human nature.

Likewise, Jesus' prayer in John 17 seems also to point in exactly the same direction. Our sanctification is the product of his self-consecration on our behalf (v. 19). We do not have our own sanctification, but by the Spirit actually receive his and so benefit from it as ours. Salvation involves an exchange at the ontological level so that what was ours became his and what was his becomes ours by the Spirit. This seems to be what Paul was thinking when he spoke of Jesus taking on our poverty so that we could share in his riches (2 Cor. 8:9). Salvation, then, involves a regeneration of our very human natures not just a change in God's mind or in our legal standing or relational status, much less in our spatial location, either in heaven or in hell. And that regeneration of our humanity was an event, the achievement of the incarnate Son that we can benefit from only by being united to him, to Jesus' sanctified humanity. Salvation, then, involves a transformation of our human being, that is, the restoration, reconciliation and perfection or glorification of our human nature.

So JB often summarizes this point by echoing Calvin and saying that our salvation is not just accomplished "by means of Christ" or "on account of Christ," but "in Christ." And of course behind this understanding lies the pervasive language found throughout the New Testament that conveys just that: our salvation is the product of being "in Christ" (εν Χριστω, εισ Χριστον or δια Χριστου) not simply "by means of Christ" (κατα Χριστον or δια Χριστον).[14]

---

13 The words "of one Father," "of the same Father," "of the same family," "of one source," or "one origin" found in various English translations are all absent from the original Greek. Sanctifier and sanctified are simply "all of one" (εξ ενος παντες, *ex henos pantes*). The idea of Jesus and his people being united in some third thing is entirely unwarranted. That they are united one to another via the shared human nature is the clearest meaning supported by the context.

14 See Torrance, "Vicarious Humanity," 136; and *Worship, Community, and the Triune God of Grace*, 40. See Calvin's *Institutes*, III.11-14.

Another closely related point JB regularly brought out in lectures was that the regeneration (*palingenesias*) of our humanity, spoken of in Titus 3:5-6, does not refer to the moment of our response to grace, as important as that is, but rather to what was accomplished "when the goodness and loving kindness of God our Savior appeared" to "save us ... by the washing of regeneration and renewal in the Holy Spirit" which was subsequently "poured out upon us ... through Jesus Christ." Regeneration first took place in Jesus, upon his human nature. We then receive that from him. Jesus does not make the renewal of our humanity possible, only becoming actual and real in the moment of our receptivity. It was accomplished first in Jesus Christ himself in our place and on our behalf as our great high priest. He shares with us what is first his. JB would at this point refer to Athanasius' way of explaining Jesus as the great physician of our humanity. He writes:

> Christ does not heal us by standing over against us, diagnosing our sickness, prescribing medicine for us to take, and then going away, to leave us to get better by obeying his instruction – as an ordinary doctor might. No, he becomes the patient! He assumes that very humanity which is in need of redemption, and by being anointed by the Spirit in our humanity, by a life of perfect obedience, by dying and rising again, for us, our humanity is healed *in him*.[15]

For many the profound depth of the need, the extent of the transformation required for us to have God's life in us, may be shocking and offensive. The default assumption, perhaps especially in the modern West, is to have a rather superficial notion of what is called for if we are to realize the best of human potential, much less have an eternal fellowship and communion with the living God. We wonder: Can anything more be needed than simply having new information, a better technique, a higher ideal or an improved idea, attitude or will? It is beyond modern imagination that humanity might need to be entirely remade, regenerated in its very nature.

Moreover the means needed to accomplish this radical end may also astound. That the assumption of our human nature was essential to Christ's work, and that we need to be united in our very natures to him in death so that we might have life, can also press us to the edge of our modern imagination. However, such a means and end also can be apprehended as being absolutely glorious since they show not only

---

15 Torrance, "Vicarious Humanity," 141. Emphasis in original. Cf. *Worship, Community and the Triune God of Grace*, 42-43.

the depth of our need but the extent of God's gracious love toward us. Contemplating such glory and grace, however, will call for the death of human pride. The biblical witness is clear on that count as well.

Early Church Teaching

Of course JB is by no means alone in bringing out the profound meaning of the incarnation for our salvation. He explicitly brought forward the teaching of the early church found especially in Irenaeus, Athanasius, the Cappadocian fathers, and in Cyril of Alexandria, to name just a few of the most prominent ones. The saying circulating throughout the early church that captured this reality was "the unassumed was unredeemed."[16] This concern was pointedly preserved in the deliberations of the Council of Constantinople (381) and brought forward at Chalcedon (451) to counter the teaching of the Apollinarians by affirming the perfect or complete (*telion*) humanity of Jesus.[17] John Calvin, JB notes, also was concerned to make prominent our union with Christ in relation to his sole priesthood.[18] If Jesus' human nature is essential to our salvation and not just instrumental or extrinsic to it, then how we understand salvation and the very nature of our relationship to Jesus Christ is profoundly impacted. We can no longer regard Christ as external to ourselves nor his gifts, for example his righteousness, as separable from him. The gift is the giver as JB liked to put it.

Creation and Redemption

The all-inclusive humanity of Jesus has, for JB, further soteriological significance. He consistently gave significant weight to the biblical insight

16 See the discussion in Torrance, "Vicarious Humanity," 141; and *Worship Community and the Triune God of Grace*, 42.
17 See Torrance, *Worship, Community and the Triune God of Grace*, 42.
18 See Torrance, "Vicarious Humanity," 137. To avoid misunderstanding it must be emphasized that consistent with orthodox and evangelical theology, union assumes a continuing distinction between what (or who) is united. JB did not mean by union with Christ that we become entirely one in being with him. We remain distinct persons. But, by the Spirit, we can share in all of what is Christ's, including his responses to the Father on the basis of the human nature he assumed into his person and regenerated. We respond by the gift of the Spirit with our persons on the basis of the assumption of our regenerated human nature in Christ. Of course, how exactly this takes place is beyond human explanation. There is only one instance of it.

that all human beings were created through the eternal Son of God and for his inheritance (John 1, Colossians 1, Hebrews 1) and that, in his assumption of human nature itself, he became the new head of humanity, the new Adam. By way of both creation and incarnation all humanity is related to the Son of God. Any grasp of the nature of his atoning work, then, must take both these connections into account. The eternal creator Son of God is the incarnate, atoning, and redeeming one. This Jesus does what he does and can accomplish what he does because of who he is – one in nature with God and one in nature with the whole of humanity that was created through him and for him. The Council of Chalcedon (451), JB reminded us, brought out both these connections by including double statements of the *homoousion* (of identical nature). Jesus Christ is there declared to be *homoousion* "with the Father in Godhead" and also *homoousion* "with us in humanity."[19] These ontic links to his person identify who he is and substantiate his absolutely unique place in relation to all humanity and its destiny.

The Theological Cost of Overlooking the All-Inclusive Humanity of Jesus Christ

While it is more often recognized, especially in evangelical circles, that Jesus' absolutely unique place in the economy of salvation is based upon his unique relationship to God, his divinity, it is often overlooked that his unique relation to humanity as its source and as its new head is just as essential. Failure to give full weight and scope to all of who Jesus is in relation to God *and* humanity, as its ultimate source and as its new head, disengages his work from his person and undermines any claim that Jesus alone stands in relation to humanity as its Savior and Lord. Discounting Jesus' ontic connection to all humanity just as much misrepresents who Jesus is and the nature of his saving work as does a denial of his deity.

If Jesus' humanity stands in no unique relation to all other human beings, but is just one among many individuals, then his humanity serves no essential part in his saving work – any one else's humanity would have served just as well. But this would mean that his saving work would not involve the displacement of Adam as the first head of humanity. Further, without this connection Jesus could not serve as the new link that creates the one new humanity, between all human beings, Paul speaks of in

---

19   See Torrance, "Vicarious Humanity," 132, 135.

Ephesians 2:14-15. The result of such a truncated christology, despite its preservation of Jesus' divinity, is the evisceration of this profound aspect of his saving work and the concealment of his full identity as the Lord and Savior of humanity as one of us.

The significance of his human life, in both earthly and heavenly states, is thereby limited to his example and his teachings, just those things that any other human being potentially could have offered by means of their human agency. JB's persistent teaching on the sole priesthood of Christ, grounded in the entire message of the book of Hebrews, was aimed to show that Jesus' mediatorial ministry required his acting in our place and on our behalf as one of us. For his atoning work involved not simply a substitutionary death, but a substitutionary life. Jesus not only mediated the things of God to man but the right responses of humanity to God. Christ's priesthood, in order to complete his mediatorial work, had to involve both a God-manward movement and a man-Godward movement. This double movement of mediation was clearly prefigured in the Aaronic priesthood where the high priest represented not only God to all Israel, but all Israel to God, wearing all the symbols of all the tribes on his ephod as he entered the holy of holies once a year on the Day of Atonement. A one-sided, single movement priesthood would have been incomplete and ineffective. For we need not only to have God brought near to us, but we being brought near to God. This is the message of the book of Hebrews. The entire vicarious nature of Christ's work can be fully appreciated only by highlighting the man-Godward action of his ministry, as one of us, sharing our human nature, in our place and on our behalf.[20]

The Nature of Salvation Misconstrued

Of course without reference to all of who Jesus is the very nature of his salvation then must necessarily have a different configuration. A salvation that comes from one who is also the source and rightful heir of humanity is very different from a salvation that does not. A salvation delivered by one who is the head of humanity is not the same as one that is not. A salvation that is not accomplished by one who has grasped on

---

20 This topic is the burden of his entire article, "The Vicarious Humanity of Christ." See especially 141-144. The chapter "The Sole Priesthood of Christ, the Mediator of Worship" in *Worship, Community and the Triune God of Grace* also details the same argument, 32-57.

to human nature itself so as to regenerate it in himself and gives it back to us offers us a very different kind of salvation than what was given. A salvation in which Jesus' entire life is substitutionary and not just his death, results in a very different depiction of the relationship between the Savior and his people.

The Scope of Christ's Atoning Ministry

Given Jesus' absolutely unique relationship with God and with all humanity, JB saw every reason to let stand without qualification those biblical passages that indicate that the work of Christ was accomplished on behalf of all humanity. He died for all, just as Paul says in 2 Cor. 5:14,15. God's intention was to be "merciful to all" (Rom. 11:32). Jesus was "the Lamb of God who took away the sins of the world" (κοσμος, Jn. 1: 29) and "He is the propitiation for ours but also the sins of the whole world" (κοσμος, 1 John 2:2). If what God did in Christ did not apply to all humanity then the atoning and reconciling work he accomplished would be torn asunder from and incongruent with who he was as the creator and new head of humanity. Such a dislocation requires interpreting his work on some basis other than his person. His person would then be irrelevant to his work and belief/faith in his work would be disconnected from belief in his person. His work would be regarded as external to and independent of his person. In effect then, there would be no essential reason other persons could not be savior. Although in that case the salvation such a one would be able to supply would be of a very different sort because consisting of very different kinds of relationships between God and humanity.

Moreover, an interest in his work and all its benefits could, then, be taken up without any regard for his person or an ongoing relationship with him. A focus on his work and benefits apart from his person means regarding Jesus simply as a means to an end, as an instrument or a tool. And once the job is over, the result achieved, a tool can be dispensed with. Such a view severs the gift from the giver as if salvation consisted of the creation of some kind of stuff (e.g. righteousness) that could be amassed and then distributed to others in separate packets for safekeeping. Martin Luther sternly warned against looking to Christ for his blessings, but taking no interest in Christ himself. Such, he said, are no better than those soldiers who cast lots for the robe of Jesus, leaving him standing there naked and abandoned to crucifixion. There are no blessings, he said, apart from Christ himself. We receive Christ "clothed with his blessings" or nothing at all. Christ cannot be divided into parts. JB regularly noted that Paul's view was that Jesus himself was our wisdom, righteousness and sanctification (1 Cor. 1:30). He does not distribute packets of these things and then walk away from us. We cannot have the gifts without being united to the giver.

Torrance also notes from time to time that John Calvin had no problem in his commentaries attributing a universal scope to Christ's atoning work.[21] In particular Calvin declared in no uncertain terms that, in passages such as John 1:29; 3:15, 16, 17; Romans 5:18, and Colossians 1:14, the biblical writers meant Christ's work applied to "all men." In connection with Matthew 26:28 and the parallel in Mark 14:24, "my blood . . . shed for many for the remission of sins," Calvin says, "By the word many He means not a part of the world only, but the whole human race."

JB's view can be summed up as upholding unlimited atonement but rejecting universalism. Jesus Christ, as the new Adam through whom every human being was created, is indeed the universal (cosmic) Lord and Savior. He is everyone's Savior, he is Lord of all. But not all are necessarily saved (universalism). The full effects of his work do not work mechanically or automatically, impersonally or causally. In this Torrance follows closely the coordinated thoughts found in Hebrews: Jesus "tasted death for everyone" (2:9), "but the message they heard [the good news regarding Christ's rest] did not benefit them, because it did not meet with faith in the hearers" (4:2). The reality of who Jesus is and what he has done for all in our human nature calls for a response, a receptivity, to that which is unconditionally provided. That response comes from our individual persons by the gift of the Holy Spirit operating on the basis of the regeneration of our human natures in Christ.

Why JB Rejects Universalism

Universalism does not follow because neither faithful theological understanding nor valid logical arguments are made by simple logical inferences. When it comes to relating facts no simple logical inference

---

21   See James B. Torrance, "The Incarnation and 'Limited Atonement,'" *Evangelical Quarterly* LV, (1983): 83-94, for his fullest discussion. Cf. Thomas F. Torrance, "Universalism or Election?" *Scottish Journal of Theology* 2 (1949): 310-18.

from them is ever necessarily true. Charging that unlimited atonement necessarily means (implies) universalism is logically fallacious. Denying universalism does not necessarily logically require denying that Jesus is in deed the Lord and Savior of all. One may be logically consistent in denying universalism while affirming the unlimited scope and intention of Christ's work as the new head of humanity.

Furthermore arguing that universal salvation *necessarily* follows from affirming that Jesus is in truth and reality the Savior of all involves also grave theological error. First, it must assume that we are one in being with Jesus Christ, denying the distinction of his person from human persons. Or assume, what amounts to the same thing, that God's will effectively (casually, mechanically, automatically) displaces (directly or indirectly) human subjects with their wills.

Second, arguing the necessity of universalism must assume that God works effectively in the same way humanity or nature works, namely by causal chains of action. The claim imagines God interacting with creation as if God were a creature and so as if limited to created causal and mechanical means and ways to bring about ends. Such theological reasoning violates the very first principle of any Christian theology: God is not a creature and to think of God as if God were one is to commit mythology, to engage in idolatry and to participate in ungodly and inaccurate speculation – making the same error as did the early church heretic Arius, as Athanasius clearly pointed out.

The truth and reality of who Jesus is as the Son of God incarnate for us and our salvation calls for a response of repentance and faith which, by the gift of the Spirit we receive into ourselves all the benefits of who Christ is. And essential to those benefits is being given a share in Christ's own faithful responses as our great high priest, our representative and substitute, our living mediator. By our response we either affirm and receive the truth and reality of who Christ is and what he has done or we deny it. But our response, our choice, has no possibility to change the truth and reality of who Christ is and what he has done for us.[22]

---

22   In my view, the alternative to JB's understanding represents the most radical form of theological relativism imaginable. If Jesus does not remain consistently who he is in relation to all humanity, then his essential identity turns out to depend upon the nature of his relationship to different human beings. Whether he is or is not Lord and Savior becomes relative to others. In the case of those who reject him (or whom he rejects) he is not Savior. In the case of those who accept or receive or put their faith in him (or he accepts/elects them) he is Savior. In either case Jesus is construed as having at the root of his being a dual identity. He both is and is not Savior. And what determines which

ALL-INCLUSIVE HUMANITY OF JESUS CHRIST   273

The choice we are given is to affirm and live by reality or to live in denial of reality. We have no possibility of creating *ex nihilo* an alternative reality counter to that established and upheld by God through Christ. "God has made him Lord and Christ" (Acts 2:36). While there are serious and potentially eternal consequences for individuals who persistently deny the reality, one of the consequences is not undoing or nullifying the reality of who God is in Christ.[23]

Ethical Implications and Obligations

Let me explore one final area in which the all-inclusive humanity of Christ has special significance. That is the sphere of ethics.[24] James Torrance was well known for introducing certain topics by saying, "Have

---

identity he assumes in each case is the divergent nature of his relationship with differing human beings.

A further irony is that within that theological relativist framework those who deny that Jesus is their Lord and Savior end up telling the truth. In their case he isn't Lord or Savior – because either God (the Father?) has made it so (some forms of Calvinism, by divine decree) or individual persons have made it so (Arminianism, by way of foreknowledge). It should also be noted then that his name, Jesus, only faithfully tells us who he is in relationship to some, that is, Savior, Deliverer. His name actually entirely misrepresents who he is in relationship to those he rejects (Calvinism?) or who have rejected him (Arminianism?). We have then no stable and non-relative way to identify who this Jesus is. Who he is remains, then, essentially unknown or unknowable.

Torrance's position cannot be rightly or accurately described as either (high federal) Calvinism nor Arminianism. JB regarded both views to be mistaken. Both operate with *the same* mistaken theological or philosophical assumptions that do not allow for a full account of the relationship of the person and work of Christ. Those who think his view sides with one or the other have yet to benefit from what he actually taught! See his rejection of both in *Incarnation and Limited*, 87.

23 To eliminate speculation, it needs to be said that James Torrance did not think there could be any meaningful answer as to why or how one could reject "the Savior who bought them." There is no biblical revelation in answer to that question. He, like Calvin, regarded all attempts to fill in that gap in our understanding as pure theological speculation that calls in to question what biblical revelation does clearly affirm about the person and work of Christ and his relationship in act and being with the Father and the Spirit. We could say that JB affirmed irresistible grace but not absolutely irresistible salvation.

24 The following is taken from personal notes and reminiscences of mine from the many lectures I heard JB give at two extension courses for Fuller Theological Seminary in So. California (1986) and in the series of BD courses delivered during my three years at Kings College, Aberdeen, 1987-1990.

I told you about the time I was in . . .?" He would often then relate to us a particularly poignant interaction he had when in Northern Ireland, South Africa, or in the South of the United States, all places that at the time were experiencing social upheaval involving tremendous violence. JB felt a special calling to go to these hotspots of desperate conditions bringing the gospel of Jesus Christ not only to the greater society but to the churches in them. He traveled to each of these locales more than once during the 1960s and 70s, taking part himself in the ongoing struggles and on some occasions exposing himself to potential physical harm. But although the situations of apartheid, civil rights, and the Nationalist-Unionist unrest were different in many ways, the upshot of his message remained constant and it was profoundly grounded in the all-inclusive humanity of Jesus Christ.

Who was Jesus Christ and what did he come to accomplish? He was the eternal Son of God, who out of his love and mercy assumed our humanity to make it his own, recreated it in himself, reconciled it to God in order to give us back a healed humanity in right relationship with God and others. Taking on a broken and alienated humanity, he has "made both one" creating "in himself one new humanity" (Eph. 2:14, 15). Salvation, as sharing in the Son's communion with the Father in the Spirit, meant God's purpose for humanity was brought to its *telos*, its final purpose in him, humanity fully alive, as Irenaeus had expressed it. In receiving the gift of sharing in the Son's communion with the Father we receive our healed, forgiven, and reconciled humanity. In receiving our human nature sanctified in Christ, we become fully human as God intended it from the beginning of creation.

JB would then relate to us how on that basis he would challenge the church to take up her proper ministry, one that consists in participating in Christ's own ongoing ministry. He would say that the proclamation of the gospel could not possibly be reduced to giving people a *message* about Christ, about the potential blessings of heaven if they would repent. No, Christ came to give us a healed restored and reconciled humanity. That was what he held out to us; his own humanity in right relationship to God and in right relationship to all others. He would ask: How could we in the church attempt to offer anyone the gospel and still withhold from them their humanity? – if we treated them socially, politically, or individually as less human than we are? – as if we did not share with them the same human nature Christ assumed for the sake of their salvation? Such duplicity constituted a denial of the gospel not its affirmation. Suffering under the violation of their very personhood, these people were crying out for the healing of their very human being. Faithful to Jesus Christ, whose humanity includes the humanity of all, we must not offer people a message of eternal hope yet deny them their humanity here and now. For the only gospel there is, is one that offers people Christ, clothed with his all-inclusive humanity. The proclamation of the gospel must include the offer and effort to participate with Christ in giving them a restored and healed humanity. Only in that way does the church witness to the fact that there is "one new humanity" in Christ.

It was during these extraordinary moments that so many in JB's courses discovered the deep interconnection between theology and life, between faith and obedience, between personal piety and social justice. The all-inclusive humanity of Jesus holds together what so often falls apart: the person and work of Christ, doctrine and practice, worship and witness. We saw and heard in James Torrance's life and teaching that a profound christology does not lead to abstract ontological speculations but to a concrete grasp of who my neighbor is in relationship to Christ and in relationship to me at the deepest conceivable level. It calls me, and even sets me free to act towards my neighbor on the basis of our shared true identity forged and revealed in Jesus Christ, who as Lord and Savior offers us a share in his judged, healed, reconciled, and renewed all-inclusive humanity.

PART III

Primary Source Essay

The Unconditional Freeness of Grace[1]
James B. Torrance

James Denney, the beloved Scottish theologian and New Testament scholar, used to say that, in the ideal church, all our theologians would be evangelists and our evangelists theologians. He was echoing the language of Plato's *Republic* when Plato said that, in the ideal state, all our politicians would be philosophers and our philosophers politicians.

Scotland has certainly been blessed in the past by a great tradition of men who were both preachers of the gospel and scholars who sought to use their minds to understand the meaning and implications of grace and to be ready to give an answer to those who ask a reason for the faith that is in them. One thinks of the names of John Knox, Samuel Rutherford, Thomas Boston, Ralph and Ebenezer Erskine, Edward Irving, John McLeod Campbell, Thomas Erskine of Linlathen, James Denney, and a host of others.

In all ages, issues have emerged which have tended to obscure the meaning of grace, but God has raised up men like the apostle Paul, Irenaeus, Athanasius, Augustine, Luther, Calvin, the Wesleys, George Whitfield, Kierkegaard, and Karl Barth to call the Church back to her foundations in Christ. When one thinks of the Protestant Reformers, one thinks at once of their avowed concern to recover the gospel of grace, and who knows how many lives have been enriched by Luther's *Commentary*

---

[1] The Editor acknowledges Alan and Andrew Torrance's permission to use this essay. Other primary sources include James Torrance's *Worship, Community & the Triune God of Grace* (Downers Grove, IL: IVP, 1996) and *A Passion for Christ: The Vision that Ignites Ministry*, co-authored with James' brothers Thomas and David (Eugene, OR: Wipf & Stock, 2010). Finally, an interview with JB Torrance is available: https://www.youtube.com/watch?v=dT3sjlaqGcU.

on Galatians, Bunyan's *Pilgrim's Progress* or Henry Scougal's *Life of God in the Soul of Man* which Susannah Wesley gave to her two young sons, and which Charles Wesley gave to George Whitfield when he came as a young enquirer to Oxford, and which he tells us led to his conversion.

In our own day, within Protestantism, both liberal and evangelical, as well as in mediaeval Roman thought, there are attitudes and emphases and ways of preaching which can obscure the unconditional freeness of grace, undermine peace and assurance, and lead to sectarian divisions. Sometimes even the very Churches which have taken their avowed stand on "the doctrines of grace" are the very ones which then make their acceptance of others *conditional* upon their subscribing to their particular formulations of the meaning of grace, and have forgotten the New Testament injunction to love and accept and forgive others as freely and unconditionally as God in Christ has loved and accepted and forgiven us (Rom. 15:7; Eph. 4:32; Col. 3:13ff.; 1 John 4:19ff.; etc.).

What are some of the issues for which we should contend together if we are to comprehend with all saints something of the wonder of the love of Christ, that we might be filled with all the fullness of God – that we might enter more and more by faith into that fullness which we already have in Christ? What is the nature of the love shed abroad in our hearts by the Holy Spirit?

Covenant or Contract?

One of the most significant words of the Bible is the word "covenant." We read about God making a covenant with Abraham, and renewing that covenant at Sinai; about David making a covenant with Jonathan, and again with the elders at Hebron when he became king. Jeremiah speaks of a day when God will make a new covenant with the house of Israel, and in the New Testament Jesus is presented to us as the mediator of the new covenant. "This cup is the new covenant in my blood."

On the one hand God binds himself to men like Abraham and David with solemn promises. On the other hand he binds Israel to himself under solemn obligations, proleptic of the day in which he will bind himself to mankind and mankind to himself in Jesus Christ in covenant love. Again we read about men like Joshua, Hezekiah, and Josiah binding themselves and the nation in loyalty to God in covenant. A great deal of research has been done in recent years by scholars like Mendenhall, Hillers, McCarthy, and others on Ancient Hittite suzerainty treaties, whose pattern bears a striking similarity to the covenants of old Israel.

Likewise, in post-Reformation – especially Scottish – history, in the upheavals of the sixteenth, seventeenth and eighteenth centuries, with the break-up of feudalism and the emergence of the late post renaissance doctrine of the divine right of kings and the resultant struggles for liberty, we read about men making "bands," "pacts," "covenants," "contracts," and "political leagues" to defend their freedom, to preserve the rights of a people *vis a vis* his subjects.

For example, when Charles I sought to impose uniformity of worship on the Scottish church by the introduction of Laud's Liturgy, the response was the National Covenant signed in the Kirk of the Greyfriars in Edinburgh in 1638. Five years later came the Solemn League and Covenant in 1643, with the opening of the Westminster Assembly, as a parliamentary commission to achieve a "covenanted uniformity in religion" . . . "in doctrine, worship and government" . . . "betwixt the Churches of Christ in the kingdoms of Scotland, England and Ireland." The key word throughout was *foedus* – "covenant" (the word from which our word "federal" comes) – a word which was rich in theological significance as well as a revolutionary symbol in a nation struggling for freedom.

It was precisely this period, the late 16th-17th centuries, which marks the rise of the so-called "federal theology" or covenant theology – the federal Calvinism which was to become the criterion of Protestant orthodoxy for the next 250 years. The Westminster Confession of Faith, with the Larger and Shorter Catechisms, was the first Reformed confession to enshrine the scheme of federal theology, though in a mild way. But it was certain features of this which were to bring the protest, first of the so-called "Marrowmen" (Thomas Boston, the Erskine brothers, etc.) in Scotland in the early eighteenth century, and the more vigorous protest of Edward Irving, John McLeod Campbell,[2] and Thomas Erskine of Linlathen in the nineteenth century, in their concern – in their different ways – to recover the universality of grace and the unconditional freeness of grace. Edward Irving's sermons on the Incarnation, preached in London in the 1820s – that Jesus Christ, as creator and redeemer of mankind, was

---

[2] See the article on Irving and McLeod Campbell by Gordon Strachan, "Theological and Cultural Origins of the Nineteenth Century Pentecostal Movement," in *Theological Renewal* 1 (Oct/Nov 1975).

anointed by the Holy Spirit in our humanity to heal our fallen humanity, and that we might participate free and unconditionally in his anointing by the same Spirit – echoed the theology of the great Greek Fathers of the Church like Irenaeus, Athanasius, and the Cappadocian divines, in the passionate conviction that "the unassumed is the unredeemed" and that Jesus Christ is the head of the whole human race, and that in and through Christ, God our Father has given himself in love, by the Spirit of adoption to the world.

What were the features of "federal theology" which led to the protest of these theologians and which led Irving to republish the older Scots Confession of 1560? Primarily it was the view that Jesus Christ is only the mediator for some men, the elect (the doctrine of limited atonement); that law is prior to grace, that God is related to all men by a law as contrasting sovereign and judge, but only to some in grace; the resulting loss of joy and assurance as men and women looked inward to see if they could see "evidences" of election rather than outward to Jesus Christ the head of all things and the saviour of mankind. None of these men were universalists but they passionately believed in the universality and unconditional freeness of grace. They believed in the love of God, and they knew that there is no such thing as conditional love – though men might sin against the Holy Spirit and deny the Lord who bought them.

To understand the issue, it is fruitful to look at the meaning of the word "covenant." The background of seventeenth century "federal Calvinism" was the emerging socio-political philosophy of "social contract," "contract of government," with its doctrine of the "rights of man" based on "natural laws," illuminated by the light of reason and given divine sanction by revelation. This was the political philosophy of the many Puritans who left these shores to get away from the "tyranny" of British kings and feudal overlords for the "free world" where they would be free to worship God as they pleased, and with whom they pleased, with liberty of conscience, and where no one would "tell them." If on the one hand this was to prove so influential in the rise of modern democracy (and the so-called "American way of life"), on the other hand it was to have a profound influence on the preaching of the gospel throughout the Puritan world. Just as people today understand the language of trade unions, civil rights, protest marches, etc., so the people of the 17th century understood the language of bands, pacts, covenants, contracts, natural law, the rights of man, and the rights of the people. To make a protest in the defence of liberty, people banded together, drew up a covenant, stated the conditions of their allegiance, and fixed their signatures. Here was a conceptual framework within which Reformed theology was to be recast as "federal theology Calvinism," and her preachers found a language of communication, a kind of "theology of politics" which could be readily grasped by the man in the street in a land struggling for freedom.

What then do we mean by the word "covenant" – *foedus*? Clearly there are different meanings of this word, not only in law and politics, but also in the Bible, and a flood of light has been thrown on this by recent studies. Let me suggest one fundamental meaning. Theologically speaking, *a covenant is a promise binding two people or two parties to love one another unconditionally*. Think for example of the marriage service. During the Reformation, the word "covenant" was used in the English Service Book of 1549 and has been retained in the Scottish marriage service. The bride and bridegroom "promise and covenant" to love one another "for better, for worse, for richer, for poorer, in sickness and in health, to love and to cherish, till death you do part."

What does all that mean? In a word they promise to love one another *unconditionally*. To use a different illustration, let us suppose here are two people who have a quarrel, and things become so bad that they decide to call in the minister to help them effect a reconciliation. He listens to one side of the unhappy story and then to the other, and no doubt there are faults on both sides. But there comes the point when he says, "Listen, you must forgive and forget!" But so often, back comes the reply, "Well, I'll forgive him IF …" The moment the minister hears the big word "IF" he knows the person is not going to forgive. Forgiveness is love in action, and *there is no such thing as conditional love*. Only when they are prepared to forgive one another unconditionally, and where there is mutual acceptance of forgiveness, can there be true reconciliation. If someone says "I'll forgive you IF . . . ," that person does not know the meaning of love. There is no such thing as conditional love in God or in man, and that fact is enshrined in the theological concept of a "covenant of love".

It is precisely this which makes a covenant so different from a *contract*! *A contract, in common parlance, is a legal relationship in which two people or two parties bind themselves together on mutual conditions* to effect some future result. The business world and political world are full of such contracts. They take the form "If you do this, then I will do that." Society at large is built on a network of such contractual arrangements.

No doubt in Scots (and Roman) law, a covenant and a contract mean the same thing, though lawyers distinguish different kinds of contract – they are not always bi-lateral. Traditionally we have talked about the marriage contract. Samuel Rutherford in his Catechism could speak about the covenant of grace as "a contract of marriage" between Christ and the believer, and then go on to speak of the conditions of the contract. The Latin word *foedus* perhaps obscured the difference, for it means both a covenant and a contract. But theologically it seems to me they must be carefully distinguished.

In the Bible there were many kinds of covenant. For example, there were (a) bilateral covenants, as in the classical example of David and Jonathan, covenants between equals. Marriage is a bilateral covenant. On the other hand, in the Bible, there were (b) *unilateral* covenants, as when in old Israel, at the time of his coronation, a king made a covenant *for* his people, rather in the manner of the suzerainty covenants of the Hittite kings. "This is the kind of king I am going to be and this is the kind of people you are going to be," as when Solomon's son Rehoboam came to the throne. But the fact that it was a unilateral covenant did not eliminate the need for response on the part of the people. Indeed the people either said "Amen" to it, "God save the king!", or "to your tents, O Israel, we shall not have this man to reign over us!" In that instance, you remember, Rehoboam's high-handed measures split the kingdom in two. The ten northern tribes went off and made Jeroboam the son of Nebat king.

The important thing is that in the Bible, God's dealings with men in creation and in redemption – in grace – are those of a covenant and not of a contract. This was the heart of the Pauline theology of grace, expounded in *Romans* and *Galatians*, and this was the central affirmation of the Reformation. *The God of the Bible is a covenant-God and not a contract-God.* God's covenant dealings with men have their source in the loving heart of God, and the form of the covenant is the indicative statement, "I will be your God and you shall be my people." The God and Father of our Lord Jesus Christ is the God who has made a covenant *for us* in Christ, binding himself to man and man to himself in Christ, and who summons us to respond in faith and love to what he has done so freely for us in Christ. Through the Holy Spirit, we are awakened to that love and lifted up out of ourselves to participate in the (incarnate) Son's communion with the Father.

Two things are therefore together in a biblical understanding of grace, the covenant of love made for man in Christ, between the Father and the incarnate Son. (a) On the one hand, it is *unconditioned* by any considerations of worth or merit or prior claim. God's grace is "free grace". (b) On the other hand, it is *unconditional* in the costly claims it makes upon us. God's grace is "costly grace". It summons us unconditionally to a life of holy love – of love for God and love for all men. The one mistake is so to stress free grace that we turn it into "cheap grace" by taking grace for granted – the danger of the "antinomianism" against which Wesley protested. The other mistake is so to stress the costly claims of grace that we turn grace into conditional grace, in a legalism which loses the meaning of grace.

The fallacy of *legalism* in all ages – perhaps this is the tendency of the human heart in all ages – is to *turn God's covenant of grace into a contract* – to say God will only love you and forgive you or give you the gift of the Holy Spirit IF ... you fulfill prior conditions. But this is to invert "the comely order of grace" as the old Scottish divines put it. In the Bible, the form of the covenant is such that the indicatives of grace are prior to the obligations of law and human obedience. "I am the God of Abraham, Isaac, and Jacob, I have loved you and redeemed you and brought you out of the land of Egypt, out of the house of bondage, therefore keep my commandments." But legalism puts it the other way round. "If you keep the law, God will love you!" The imperatives are made prior to the indicatives. The covenant has been turned into a contract, and God's grace – or the gift of the Spirit – made conditional on man's obedience.

Grace prior to law or law prior to grace?

It was precisely against this inversion of the order of grace that Paul protested in Galatians chapter 3. You remember his argument. God gave his promises to Abraham, and only 430 years later came the law at Sinai, not to annul the promise, not to impose conditions of grace, but to spell out the obligations of grace, to be the schoolmaster to lead us to Christ. Against the Judaizers, Paul is arguing that in authentic Judaism, grace is prior to law. As Martin Buber argued so powerfully in his book on *Moses*, the Book of the Covenant in *Exodus* is a covenant, not a contract. Judaism is NOT synonymous with legalism, whatever may have happened at times within Judaism.

To put it in other words, love, like marriage love, always brings its obligations – its unconditional obligations – but the obligations of love are not conditions of love. To turn a covenant into a contract is to turn categorical imperatives into hypothetical imperatives (to use Kantian language), and hence to weaken the imperatives. Legalism always weakens the character of love. "Do I weaken the law" says the Apostles – by seeing it in the context of grace? "No, I strengthen it!" (Rom. 3:31) This question of the relation of law to grace is of paramount importance, because much evangelical preaching can go wrong at this point. It is possible to do two things which can lead to a misunderstanding of Paul. (a) The first is to take the text, "the law was our schoolmaster to bring us to Christ," (Gal. 3:24) out of its context in the chapter and build a theology, or a complete preaching technique on it. Then our pattern becomes: man – law – sin – repentance – grace. This is what theologians call the Western *ordo salutis*, which grew up in the Latin Middle Ages, and was too often absorbed in later Puritan and Calvinist preaching. It not only inverts the biblical order but led to a form of "legal preaching" (as the older Scots divines called it) and to regarding repentance as a condition of grace.

Paul's exposition in Galatians and Romans makes it abundantly plain that this order was a different one: promise – law – fulfilment for us in Christ – therefore faith and repentance. For Paul faith and repentance are not conditions of grace but our response to Christ. (b) A second mistake is to generalise from Luther's very wonderful conversion experience and then read it back into Paul's own experience or make it a paradigm for all authentic conversion experiences, as though there must first be a deep sense of sin and a struggling for justification by the law and good works, before there can be the experience of grace. This is to read back into Paul what has been called by K Stendahl "the introspective conscience of the West." Sometimes it is the discovery of grace – of the love of Christ and the meaning of Calvary – which first discovers to us our sin and our condemnation under the law. When John Calvin wrote the first edition of his *Institutes* in 1536, he followed the order of law – grace, the order of Luther's Catechism. But in all subsequent editions he abandoned it, and argued very powerfully for the opposite as in Book Two of the 1559 definitive edition. In spite of this however, later scholastic Calvinism, by its distinction between a covenant of works (law) and a covenant of grace – a distinction unknown to Calvin, but which first grew up among the Puritans in England after 1583 and became foundational in federal Calvinism in Scotland – reverted to the order of law-grace, reading it right back into the doctrine of God, and interpreting creation and redemption in terms of this order. So Jonathan Edwards in New England taught that justice is the essential attribute of God, by which he is related to all men as law giver, but his love is arbitrary, by which he is related to the elect alone in grace.

It was against this inversion of "the comely order of grace" that McLeod Campbell maintained that in the Bible, "the filial is prior to the judicial," and Edward Irving preached his sermons on the Incarnation. God is love in his innermost being, as Father, Son, and Holy Ghost, and it is this triune God who is active in creation and redemption and who gives us the law to lead us to Christ, that we might receive the adoption of sons. Jesus Christ as the head of the race has received from the Father the gifts of the Spirit in our humanity, that out of his own fullness he might give the Spirit to us to fulfil in us the filial purpose of creation. "That Man," McLeod Campbell used to tell his congregation, "has the Holy Spirit for you."

Evangelical repentance or legal repentance?

Few distinctions in theology are more important than Calvin's distinction (*Institutes* III.3) between "legal repentance" and "evangelical repentance," drawn in his critique of the mediaeval sacrament of penance. "Legal repentance" says, "Repent! and IF you repent, you will be forgiven!" It makes love and grace and forgiveness conditional upon our repentance, our "conversion." So the mediaeval world said that if the sinner is truly contrite, if he confesses his sins and makes amends (*contritio, confessio, satisfactio*) then he may be forgiven and receive absolution. This was the root of the mediaeval doctrine of merit. Calvin argued that this inverted the evangelical order of grace, and made repentance prior to forgiveness, whereas in the New Testament *forgiveness is logically prior to repentance* (conversion). Repentance is our response to the word of the Cross which through the Spirit converts and heals and reconciles. The Christ who died for us and rose again for us to wipe out our sins and present us in himself as righteous to the Father, through the eternal Spirit, now unites us with himself through the Spirit in a life of daily *mortificatio* and *vivificatio* of dying and rising with Christ (Rom. 6). Repentance is the work of the Spirit in bringing home to us the meaning of Calvary – a response to grace, not a condition of grace. Nothing is more needed today than a recovery of a proper theology of conversion (both individual and social) which enshrines this Reformation insight. Much contemporary evangelism and many calls for social action are what our forefathers would have called "legal preaching." But the law never converts. The Holy Spirit is given to us in Christ, not through the law. We think again of Paul's words in Galatians chapter 3. "Did you receive the Spirit by the works of the law (by fulfilling conditions) or by the hearing of faith?" The clear answer is that they received the Spirit by faith alone – by faith in Christ and him crucified.

The same argument is elaborated in his First Epistle to the Corinthians (chapters one and two) to a Church divided on the subject of the gifts of the Spirit. When Paul preached Christ and the Cross, then the Spirit came in power, and made them one body, freely giving them all their gifts, nourishing them at the one Lord's table. "Legal repentance" is not only the fallacy of the mediaeval sacrament of penance, but also of much Protestantism, both liberal and evangelical. It obscures the gospel of grace. It is a failure to understand the meaning of the Cross and, as in Paul's day, it is divisive.

Descriptive and prescriptive "ifs"

Calvin found that he had to defend the doctrine of evangelical repentance against the Anabaptist left as well as the Roman right. Doesn't the New Testament say, "If we confess our sins, he is faithful and just to forgive us our sins," and "If thou shalt confess with thy mouth that Jesus is Lord and believe in thine heart that God has raised him from the dead thou shalt be saved?" Does this not imply that faith and confession and repentance are conditions of grace? By a careful and thorough examination of all relevant passages, Calvin showed that this interpretation is due to shallow and faulty exegesis. It is beyond our scope here to follow his conclusive arguments. What are we to make of this "if" language?

In the Old Covenant and in the New Covenant, there is a clear pattern: – (1) *grace*, covenant, election of Israel, the New Covenant; (2) *unconditional obligations*, e.g. the ten commandments, repent! believe! obey! etc.; (3) *consequences* of obedience and disobedience, the promises and warnings, blessings and curses of Gerizim and Ebal, which follow IF Israel keeps covenant, IF we repent and believe. That is, the "if" language belongs to column (3) not to column (2). They are "descriptive IFs," ways of describing the consequences of fidelity and infidelity not "prescriptive IFs" – not prescriptions for grace. So in the New Testament, it is because

(1) Christ died to take away our sins on the Cross and seal the New Covenant with his blood, that we are summoned, (2) *unconditionally* to repent and believe and be baptized (Acts 2) and that therefore (3) we are given wonderful promises that "If we confess our sins ..." etc. we shall find the joys of forgiveness, peace, assurance, fellowship in the Spirit, life in Christ, as a wonderful consequence.

Indeed, this threefold pattern is the grammar of *all* loving relationships, between husband and wife, father and son, brother and sister. My covenant of love with my wife, lays me under unconditional obligations to be faithful, loyal, not to commit adultery. But I can go on to say that "If I am faithful, I shall grow more and more into the joys of a happy marriage." Because my marriage is basically a covenant and not just a contract, the "ifs" are descriptions of the consequences of our love, not prescriptions for love. I do not say to my wife, "If you are faithful, I will love you!"

There are also of course prescriptive "IFs" in the Bible. But they come, for example, in the context of case law in the civil code of Exodus 20:22-23:33. Because we live in a world where people do transgress God's unconditional commandments, and do commit murder and adultery, the civil law has to prescribe penalties: "IF murder, then ...," "IF adultery, then ...," "IF injury, then ... eye for eye." It was the mistake of the Pharisees to read these prescriptive IFs back into the heart of the Torah – to confuse apodictic law with casuistic law. But when they brought certain cases to Jesus, (e.g. the woman taken in adultery), Jesus showed that the real inner prescription of the law was to love and forgive unconditionally! Love is the fulfilling of the law, and there is no such thing as conditional love in God or in man.

God's love, so understood, should find focal expression at the Lord's table, for such love is creative of community, for there Christ gathers his people and gives himself to them freely and unconditionally by the Spirit and lifts us up out of ourselves and our introspectiveness and social lethargy, and frees us to love him and to love all men in his name – where he converts us into being a loving, caring, and believing community, members of his missionary body in the world.

In the language of the older Scottish divines, sacraments are signs and seals of the covenant of grace – converting ordinances, not badges of our conversion. We are called by the word of the Cross daily to evangelical repentance through life in the Spirit, and we receive the Spirit by faith alone.

Part IV

Poems and Memorabilia

Two Poems
Jock Stein

In January 2017 the Scottish Church Theology Society, which James Torrance's elder brother T. F. Torrance co-founded, will have as its theme "Theology and Poetry." The relationship between the arts and the church in Scotland has not always been an easy one, even though the Church of Scotland set up the Gateway Theatre after the Second World War, and has continued to own the Scottish Story Telling Centre (now an integral part of John Knox House in Edinburgh's High St.).

JB encouraged people to understand their humanity as a gift from God, wonderfully redeemed in Christ. If our Lord Jesus came to give people back their humanity, we should embrace the arts, as Calvin taught and Knox practised in earlier times.[1]

Because of fear of deterioration through people touching the ancient stones, in Spain the Granada Authorities have designated certain places in the Alhambra as "touching points."

At New College, JB lectured on how different theologians approached Christology. Both he (and of course TF) emphasised that in the incarnation, the divine and the human really intersected, met ("touched" in the poem) so that God was not pretending to be human; and for God the incarnation was a real voyage of discovery, as in the person of Christ he was picked on by the authorities and eventually crucified.

JB would explain how a Jesus who really made atonement in his own person had been watered down by liberal theology to a Jesus who makes us "feel good" by the story of his life and death as merely an

---

1   Cf Calvin's *Institutes*, 1.11.12.

example of love. But while that "touchy-feely stuff" is moving, something deeper is required if human hearts of stone are to be really touched and transformed.

Touching Point

They decided it for me;
I became a 'touching point',
with my own arrow sign,
my location minuted
in Alhambra documents.
The few who noticed me
presented fingers, thumbs:
clean, stained, smelly,
delicate, hoary, cracked,
bored, pushy, hesitant . . .
I was really moved by
all this touchy-feely stuff.

What a pity I am stone.
If I were human flesh, I would
not keep my feelings to myself;
and if I were divine, I should
discover what it's like when people
put the finger on me, and conclude
their accusations with my death . . .
I would become a touching point for good.

Granada, Spain, June 2014

The Director's Cut

> She knew its hidden presence,
> reached for it in her mind,
> put her hands and heart there,
> got down to it, to find
> our image, as yet uncut
> from that great lump of stone.
> How could she learn to hammer
> with a skill home grown
> and, come to that, a chisel?
> It came to this: the sculptress
> had to occupy that rocky
> place herself, and learn to dress
> the stone as she herself
> now dressed – in mineral wear,
> plain as only God could be,
> love in hardened clay laid bare.

Beech Hill, Haddington, Scotland, June 2014

The ambiguity of the title reflects the double aspect of incarnation, *enhypostasia* and *anhypostasia*, as well as the link between incarnation and atonement. The feminine is used, not because God is feminine (or masculine) – as JB would often point out in the context of the "reimagining God" controversy – but because the subject of the poem is "wisdom," which in the Old Testament is a feminine word. English (of course) has only "he" or "she" for personal pronouns; and whereas today in many circles it is appropriate simply to use the word "God" instead of a pronoun, here we are referring to a "personalised idea" from the book of Proverbs who is only later identified with the *logos* who became incarnate in the person of Jesus of Nazareth, the eternal Son of God.

Hymn

I know not how to pray, O Lord,
A learner, just, am I –
Lord Jesus, in your wondrous love
You hear, you hear my anxious cry
And ever pray for me.

Although I know not how to pray,
Your Spirit intercedes,
Convincing me of pardoned sin:
For me, for me in love he pleads
And teaches me to pray.

O draw me to your Father's heart,
Lord Jesus, when I pray
And whisper in my troubled ear
'Your sins, your sins are washed away:
Come home with me today'.

At home within our Father's house,
Your Father, Lord, and mine,
I'm lifted up by your embrace
To share, to share in love divine,
Which floods my soul with joy.

I'll love you, O my Father God,
Through Jesus Christ, your Son,
I'll love you in the Spirit, Lord,
In whom, in whom we all are one,
Made holy by your love.

James B. Torrance

This hymn has been put to music by Christine Dieckmann and published in *A Passion For Christ* (Edinburgh: The Handsel Press, 1999), 53. It can also be sung easily to Repton if the last line is repeated.

A PERSONAL NOTE FROM KARL BARTH TO JB AFTER HE BROKE HIS LEGS SKIING WITH MARKUS BARTH... KB EXPRESSES THE HOPE THAT HE WILL SOON BE BACK WALKING *PER PEDES INCOLUMES APOSTOLORUM* (IN THE SURE/SAFE STEPS OF THE APOSTLES)... KB USED TO HAVE JB SITTING AT HIS SIDE IN SEMINARS READY, AT HIS REQUEST, TO TRANSLATE LATIN TEXTS INTO ENGLISH.

J. B. TORRANCE

JAMES AND MARY TORRANCE, ON THE WEST COAST OF SCOTLAND

JAMES B. TORRANCE WITH HIS OLDER BROTHER TOM. JAMES IS HOLDING A COPY OF HIS FESTSCHRIFT VOLUME, *CHRIST IN OUR PLACE*.

J.B.'s Teaching Diagram
Trinitarian, Incarnational Model
(Nicaea, McLeod Campbell, Barth)

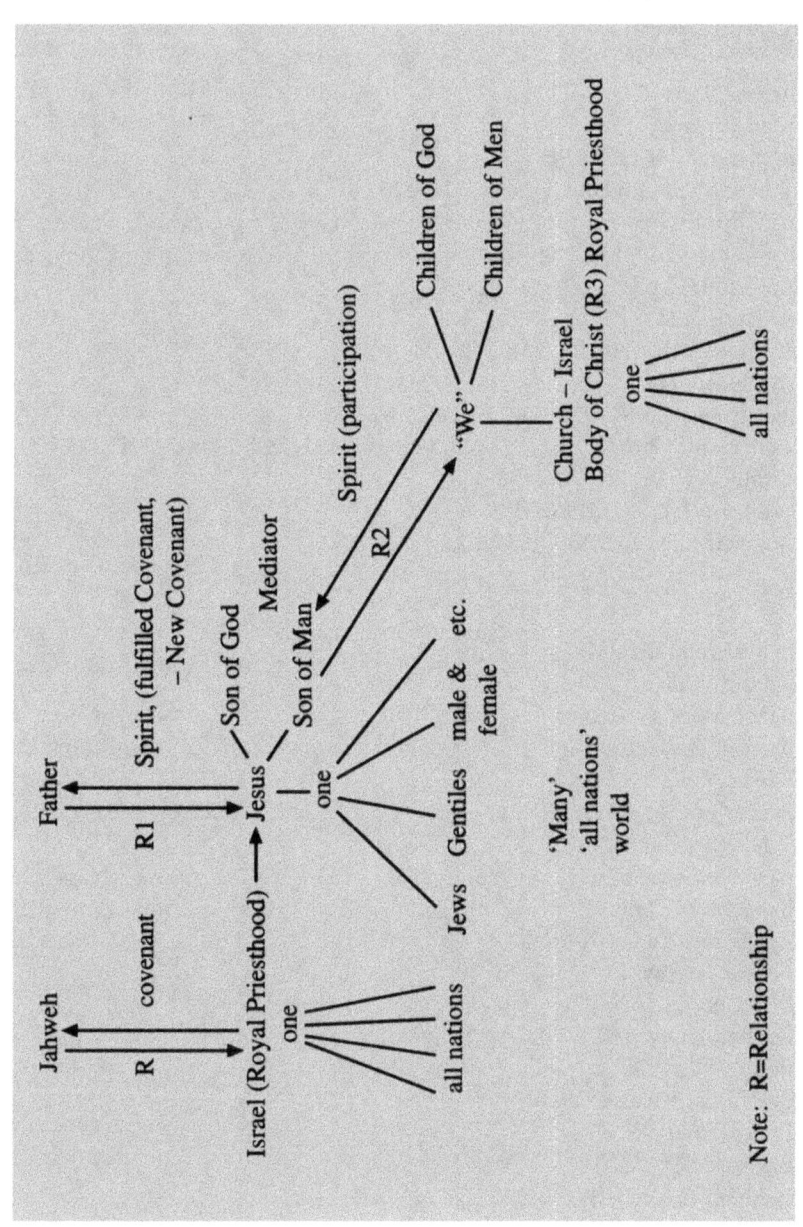

Index of People and Subjects

A

Adams, Jerry 8
Alan Torrance 154
Alexander, Michelle 203
anhypostasia and enhypostasia 219, 278
Anselm 131
apartheid 7, 19, 130, 274
Appleton, George 75
Aristotle 121–122
Arminianism 176, 215, 234, 273
Asmussen, Hans 166
Athanasius 20, 94, 97, 109–133, 245, 246, 272
atonement 57, 80–81, 86, 92–108, 109–133, 151, 247, 270–271, 271, 287
   limited 6, 14, 120, 125, 138, 151
   universal 2, 9, 131, 216
Augustine 59, 132, 150, 165, 202, 234

B

Bailey, Kenneth 251
Bainton, Roland 235
Baker, Mark D. 109
Barmen Declaration 8
Barrett, C.K. 110
Barth, Karl 14, 20, 33, 104, 152, 157, 160, 199, 214, 223, 250, 254, 257, 262, 291
Basil the Great 57
Bassler, J.M. 196
Beeke, Joel 143
Begbie, Jeremy 17–22, 43–52, 207
Bell, George 162
Bentley, James 160
Berlin, Isaiah 35
Beschloss, Michael 162
Best, Harold 73
Biel, Gabriel 252
Bonhoeffer, Dietrich 59, 162, 166, 236, 238, 244
Boston, Thomas 278

Bowden, John 36
British Council of Churches 31
Brown, Colin 110
Brown, Peter 234
Brunner, Emil 63, 263
Buckner, Forrest 156
Bultmann, Rudolf 233
Bunyan, John 246, 277
Burns, Robert 26
Burton-Rose, Daniel 204
Butterfield, Herbert 242

C

Cairns, David 29
Calvinism 8, 19, 27, 31, 41, 152, 176, 211, 215, 273
Calvin, John 6, 19, 20, 71, 95, 112, 132, 134–156, 164, 217, 244, 249, 251, 267, 271, 284, 287
Campbell, Douglas A. 193–212
Campbell, John McLeod 20, 31, 34, 41, 91, 102, 112, 120, 224, 240, 248
Canlis, Julie 95
Capon, Robert 191
Chalke, Steve 117
Chang, Ha-Joon 171
China 4
Christ
  ascension 88, 102, 104
  cross 64, 71, 92–108, 99, 100, 104, 109–133
  high priest 58, 68–76, 81, 87, 180, 224
  resurrection 86, 102, 104, 106
  vicarious humanity 10, 48, 85–91, 86, 90, 130, 184, 216, 227, 233, 258–275, 279
Christ's College (Aberdeen). *See* King's College (Aberdeen)
Cochrane, Arthur 240
Colyer, Elmer 227, 228
communion 57–60, 83–4, 88, 92, 214, 229
conversion 142, 236, 240, 284-5
Conway, John 159
covenant and contract 11, 135–136, 154, 193–212, 251, 277ff.
Cozens, Brian 36
Cranfield, C.E.B. 110
creation 7, 58, 59, 79–80, 88
crucifixion 47
curse 109–133. *See also* judgment

D

Daly, Cahal 8
Dawson, Gerrit 74, 86, 154, 158
Dearborn, Kerry 53–61
Dearborn, Tim 53, 62–67
de Bruyn, Theodore 234
Deddo, Gary 181, 258–275
De Klerk, F.W. 7
Denny, James 276
DeVries, Dawn 152
Dibelius, Otto 162, 165
Dilthey, Wilhelm 33
disabled people. *See* special needs
Dodd, C.H. 110, 122
Donfried, K.P. 197
Doval, A.J. 117
Doyle, Robert C. 109–133
Dragas, George 237
dualism 129

E

ecumenism 3, 19, 31, 159–174
education 45–46. *See also* theological education
Edwards, Jonathan 98, 283-4
Einstein, Albert 238
election 213–232, 285
epistemology 37, 77–84
Erskine of Linlathen 278
ethics 11, 58, 65, 137–138, 158–174, 198–212, 275
Evangelical Quarterly 138, 271
evangelism and social action 284-5

F

Fairweather, E.R. 131
faith 37, 140, 153, 208
fall 80, 81
federal theology 278ff.
Ferguson, John 234
Feuerbach, Ludwig 243
forgiveness 66, 153, 157–174
Forsyth, P.T. 67, 157
freedom 16, 27, 60, 82–84, 85, 107, 200, 275
Fuller Theological Seminary 273

G

Gaza 66
gender 278
Germany 157–174
Gerrish, Brian 150
Goldhagen, Daniel 161
gospel and law. *See* grace and law
grace and law 28, 86, 89–90, 134–156, 163, 200, 252, 276ff.
Graham, Jeannine M. 213–232
Green, Joel B. 109
Gregory of Nazianzus 81, 97, 106
Grensted, L.W. 122, 123
Grenz, Stanley J. 109
Gunton, Colin 36, 95, 239

H

Hahn, H.C. 110
Hamann, J.G. 35
Hartley, E.P. 35
Hart, Trevor 25, 63, 90
Harvard Theological Review 234
Hauerwas, Stanley 46, 202, 207
Hay, D.M. 196
Hays, Richard 196
Hegel, Georg 33
Hein, Rolland 93, 97
Helm, Paul 144
Herbert, George 51
Herder, J.G. 35
Herman, Stewart 159
hermeneutics 34, 37, 39
Heron, Alasdair 25–31, 90, 236
Hiestand, Gerald 119
Hilary of Poitiers 94, 99
Hockenos, Matthew 159
Holy Spirit 49, 53, 79, 87, 88, 91, 92, 98, 102, 104, 107, 182, 271, 277
Hoover, Herbert 170
Hultgren, Arland J. 111
humanity 4, 35, 98, 103, 145, 258–275, 279. *See also* Christ, vicarious humanity
Hurd, John 197

I

incarnation 10, 88, 94, 96, 96–97, 109–133, 218, 258–275
indicative and imperative 28, 89, 135, 283ff.
intercession 23, 54. *See also* Christ, high priest
inter-Faith relations 65–67
Invergowrie 20
Irenaeus 93, 97, 105, 139, 247
Irving, Edward 284
Islam 65
Israel 213–232, 246
IVF 5

J

Jeffery, Steve 92
Jewett, R. 197
Jinkins, Michael 32–42
Journal of Theology for Southern Africa 91, 130
judgment 92–108, 109–133, 151, 249
Jüngel, Eberhard 244, 247
Jungmann, Josef 237

K

Kant, Immanuel 40
Keller, Timothy 182
Kemp Smith, Norman 5
Keynes, J.M. 159
Kierkegaard, Søren 35, 45, 236
kingdom of God 67, 82, 83, 114, 189
King's College (Aberdeen) 18, 26, 32, 55, 273
Knox, John (N.T. scholar) 197
Knox, John (Reformer) 276
Kohlbrügge, Hermann 240
Kraybill, Donald 66
Kruger, C. Baxter 92–108

L

Lakoff, George 208
language 39
Lectio Divina 73
legalism 282ff.
Leithart, Peter J. 118
Letham, Robert 117
Lewis, Alan 1

Lewis, C.S. 75, 215, 241, 246, 249, 251
liberal theology 5, 45
limited atonement. *See* atonement, limited
Lloyd Jones, Martin 6
Longenecker, Richard 193, 196
Lord's Supper 9, 71–2
  and children 9
love 12, 42, 79–80, 107–108
Luther, Martin 164, 234, 276

M

MacDonald, George 93, 97, 101, 239
Mackintosh, H.R. 29, 33
Macmurray, John 5, 20, 44
Macquarrie, John 214, 224
Malherbe, Abraham 194
Mann, Alan 117
Manuel, Abuna 66
marriage 11, 250
Marshall Plan 158, 170
Martyn, Louis 212
Mary (mother of Jesus) 69, 217–218
Maschmann, Melita 171
Maury, Pierre 166
Maximus the Confessor 199
May, Stephen 233–257
McDiarmid, Hugh 26
McKim, Donald 143
Meeks, Wayne 194
Melanchthon, Philip 242
Merton, Thomas 70, 95
missiology 62–67
mission 62, 67, 175–192, 230–232
Moltmann, Jürgen 92, 104–105, 231
Morgenthau, Henry 157, 162
Murray, Andrew 20

N

New College (Edinburgh) 17, 28, 287
Newell, Roger 157–174
Newton, Isaac 238
Nicene Creed 94, 293
Niemöller, Martin 160, 164
Northern Ireland 7, 54

O

Oberman, Heiko 235
ordo salutis 48
Ovey, Michael 92
Owen, John 64, 125

P

Packer, James 6
Parker, T.H.L. 86
Partee, Charles 151
pastoral care 89, 244–245
Pelagius 2, 234, 253
perichoresis 60, 63, 65, 99, 214–215
Placher, W.C. 133
Plato 45, 125–126, 229, 276
Polanyi, Michael 242
political engagement 158–174. *See also* under Torrance, J.B.
Pond, Elizabeth 171
Potsdam Declaration 157
prayer 27, 61, 68, 68–76, 72, 88, 108, 157, 254, 279
  family 73
  the Lord's Prayer 72, 253
prisoners 203
propitiation. *See* atonement

R

Radcliff, Alexandra 85–91
Rae, Murray 23–24, 45
Räisänen, Hekki 195
rationality 123
reconciliation 104, 109–133, 158–174
Redding, Graham 68–76
Regent College 6
Reinert, Erik S. 170
repentance 13, 134–156, 163, 248–249, 256, 284
Ritschl, Albrecht 242
Robertson, Archibald 245
Rodin, R. Scott 77–84
Roslin 15
Ruether, R.R. 195
Rupp, Gordon 235

S

Sach, Andrew 92
Salmond, Alex 19
sanctification 60, 85–91, 119
Sanders, E.P. 194
Schleiermacher, Friedrich 33–42
Schmidt, Dietmar 161
Schweitzer, Albert 33, 195
Scots Confession 279
Scottish Church Theology Society 287
Scottish Journal of Theology 35, 89, 163, 271
Scotus, Duns 20
Scougall, Henry 277
silence 70–71. *See also* prayer
Smedes, Lewis 60
Smith, Bryson 109
Sölle, Dorothee 214, 227
South Africa 158. *See also* apartheid
special needs 175–192
Spufford, Francis 256
Stein, Jock 86, 233, 287-9
Stendahl, Krister 194, 212, 234, 283
stewardship 77–84
Stimson, Henry 170
Stuttgart Declaration 157–174

T

Taizé Community 73
Tedrick, Jim 25
Tertullian 165
theological education 29, 43–52, 55, 193. *See also* Torrance, J.B., teacher
theological renewal 278
theology
  Scottish Reformed 27, 31, 233, 278
Thielicke, Helmut 168, 236
Thimell, Daniel 25, 63
Thiselton, Anthony 42, 52, 213
Thomson, Robert W. 112
Tillich, Paul 243
Tomlin, Graham 235
Torrance, Alan 1–16, 90, 198, 243
Torrance, Andrew 134–156

Torrance, J.B. 1, 213
  diagram 28, 43, 77, 213, 237, 293
  evangelical experience 3
  family 21, 22, 74
  hospitality 18
  inspirer 21, 25, 49
  love of scripture 9
  pastor 2, 21, 134, 157
  political engagement 2, 158, 274
  qualifications 20, 26
  teacher 14, 17, 21, 25–31, 29, 32–42, 37, 43–52, 62, 77, 157, 237
Torrance, T.F. 64, 95, 105, 112, 129, 132, 218, 233, 240, 252, 260
Trinity 9, 54, 60, 74, 90, 93, 98–102, 107, 131, 138, 189, 214

U V

universalism 188, 191, 271. *See also* atonement
Vico, Giambattista 35
Visser't Hooft, W.A. 159, 163
von Sell, S.N. 168

W

Walls, Roland 246
Weaver, J. Denny 111, 127
Webster, John 90
Wells, Samuel 255
Wesley, Charles and Susannah 277
Westminster Confession 278
Williams, Garry 117, 122
Williams, Rowan 48
Willis-Watkins, David 153
Wittgenstein, Ludwig 52
World Alliance of Reformed Churches 31
World Vision 65
worship 11, 57, 70, 75, 76, 82, 83–84, 233–257
  trinitarian 55–56
  unitarian 55–56
wrath. *See* judgment
Wrede, William 195
Wright, Paul 204
Wurm, Theophil 165

Z

Zachman, Randall 151
Zizioulas, John 214

Index of Scripture References

Genesis
2:16 114
3:1-17 114
3:8-19 128
4:13 147
12:3 216

Exodus
13:11–16 216
20:22 – 23:33 286

Deuteronomy
28 128
28:52-7 128

1 Samuel
15:30 147

2 Samuel
24:10 149

1 Kings
19:12 69

2 Kings
20:2 149

Psalms
22:1 101
34:8 187–192
46:10 69

Isaiah
38:2 149
53:3 100
53:6 100
55:11 256
61:1 103
61:1-3 149

Jeremiah
14:7-11 165
31: 31-34 249

Ezekiel
7 128
11.19-20 248
33:21-29 128
36:25 248
36: 26-28 248
36:31 244
37 248

Joel
2:28 106

Jonah
3:5,9 149

Matthew

6.7 69
11:5 149
11:6 236
11:27 221
11:28 149
16:21 100
20:18-19 100
26:28 271
26:75 149
27:4 147
27:46 101

Mark

10:33-34 100
14:24 271
15:34 101

Luke

1:38 69
4:18 103, 149
9:31 246
11:1 69
15 175, 178, 180
15:28 188
15:31 188
19:10 101
22:62 149
23:46 102
24 72
24:7 100

John

1:1 97, 107
1:1-4 94, 95
1.1-14 268
1:11 100, 226
1:14 96, 106
1:18 97
1:29 271
1:29, 33 99
2:35-51 244
3:15-17 271
3:16 64
6:28-29 185
6:51 71
8:36 185
14:9-11 221
14:20 107
15:1-17 60
16:32 102
17 265
17:3 98, 105
17:17-18 86
17:17-19 133
17:24 50, 97, 102
17:26 98, 103
18:35 100
19:15 100
19:16, 18 100
19:30 102

Acts

2 286
2:17 106
2:36 273
2:42 71
9:1-22 209
16:30-31 185
17:28 184
22:4-16 209
26:9-18 209

Romans

1:16–5:1 209
2:6-10 208
3:22 196
3:23 208
3:25 196, 208
5 262
5.8 255
5:11–21 225
5:12–21 217
5:14 261, 264
5:18 271

6:6 145–156
7:18-19 234
8 23–24
8:3 103, 104
8:15 107
8:17 94
8:21 107
8:26 54, 70
8:34 87
9:13 213
9:30–10:17 209
10:2-3 250
11:32 270
14:17 67
15:7 277
15:13 67

1 Corinthians

1:30 240, 271
2:16 107
8:6 94
15:1-11 115
15:20-28 115
15:21-22 118, 120
15:42-49 115
15:45 261

2 Corinthians

3:1-2 21
5:14 106
5:14-19 261
5:18-20 231
5:19 102, 104
5:20 191
5:21 99
7:10 148

Galatians

1:9 190
1:16 107
2:1 196
2:15–3:26 209
2:16 207
3:8 216
3:13 100, 114, 131
3:17-22 135
3:22 227
4:6 107

Ephesians

1 262
1:3–11 221
1:10 262
2:1 228
2:4-6 106
2:13ff 87
2:14-15 269, 274
2:15 221
2:19–22 221
3:12 196, 221
4:8 106
4:13 196
4:15 187
4:18 107
4:32 277
5:27 88

Philippians

1:12, 25 246
2:5 70
3:9 196

Colossians

1 268
1:13-19 63
1:14 271
1:15-21 131
1:16 221
1:16-17 94
1:20 59
1:21 107
1:27 107
2:9 223–232

3:1-4 106
3:3 60
3:13ff. 277
3:16 187

1 Thessalonians

1:9-10 109
5:11 187

1 Timothy

2:1-6 87
2:5 103
4:10 179

Titus

3:5 263
3:5-6 266

Hebrews

1 268
1:1-3 94
2:9 271
2:9–10 181
2:10 101
2:11 265
2:13 181
2:14 106
2:14-18 245
2:16 265
2:17 124, 265
4:2 271
4:12 103, 107
4:14 87
4:15 245
6:19 217
7:20-28 265
7:25 54, 87
9:9-14 107
9:14 102
9:24 87

9:28 100
10:10 87
11 181
12:2 181
12:3 100

James

2:24 208

1 Peter

1:3 106
2:8 126
2:24 100
3:18 101

2 Peter

1:4 66
2:4 126

1 John

1:5 97
2:2 124, 270
3:18 187
4:10 124
4:19ff. 277

Revelation

3:14 96
21:3-6 103

www.ingramcontent.com/pod-product-compliance
Lightning Source LLC
Chambersburg PA
CBHW061429300426
44114CB00014B/1598